JUST
PRACTICE

Related books of interest

The Practice of Social in North America:
Culture, Context, and Competency Development
Kip Coggins

Essential Skills of Social Work Practice:
Assessment, Intervention, and Evaluation, Second Edition
Thomas O'Hare

Advocacy Practice for Social Justice, Third Edition
Richard Hoefer

Social Welfare Policy: Responding to a Changing World
John G. McNutt and Richard Hoefer

Clinical Assessment for Social Workers:
Quantitative and Qualitative Methods, Fourth Edition
Catheleen Jordan and Cynthia Franklin

An Experiential Approach to Group Work, Second Edition
Rich Furman, Kimberly Bender, and Diana Rowan

Modern Social Work Theory, Fourth Edition
Malcolm Payne

The Helping Professional's Guide to Ethics: A New Perspective
Valerie Bryan, Scott Sanders, and Laura Kaplan

Why Are They Angry with Us? Essays on Race
Larry E. Davis

JUST

A SOCIAL JUSTICE APPROACH TO SOCIAL WORK

PRACTICE

JANET L. FINN
UNIVERSITY OF MONTANA

OXFORD
UNIVERSITY PRESS

OXFORD
UNIVERSITY PRESS

Oxford University Press is a department of the University of Oxford.
It furthers the University's objective of excellence in research, scholarship,
and education by publishing worldwide. Oxford is a registered trade mark of
Oxford University Press in the UK and certain other countries.

Published in the United States of America by Oxford University Press
198 Madison Avenue, New York, NY 10016, United States of America.

Library of Congress Cataloging-in-Publication Data
CIP is available online.

ISBN 978-0-19-065707-9

7 9 8

Printed in Canada

*This book is dedicated to the University of Montana MSW students
who continue to teach me about the meaning
and power of social justice work.*

CONTENTS

FIGURES

TABLES

PREFACE

The challenge of social justice is to evoke a sense of community that we need to make our nation a better place, just as we make it a safer place.

Marian Wright Edelman (2001)

AN INVITATION AND CHALLENGE TO OUR READERS

Welcome to the complex and dynamic terrain of social work. Some of you will be reading this book because you are planning to pursue a career in social work. Perhaps your image of the field is still fuzzy, waiting to be developed in the coming weeks and months. Others may encounter this book after years of experience in the social work profession. Perhaps your own life and work experiences, political commitments, or concerns about people's everyday struggles for survival, rights, and dignity have brought you to these pages. You may have a clear image of social work practice in mind. Depending on your experience, you may wish to emulate this image or you may wish to change it.

We invite you to accompany us on this journey into social work and social justice. This is not a guided tour in which the reader is the passive recipient of the guides' wisdom. Rather, this is a journey that we take together—teaching, learning, and creating knowledge as we go. *Just Practice* is a different kind of book. It is not a collection of facts about the practice of social work. It does not offer *cookbook solutions* to various human problems. *Just Practice* poses more questions than it offers answers, and it encourages question posing as a key component of practice. It is a foundation and starting point for ongoing dialogue and critical inquiry, which, in turn, can serve as a base for your own critical and creative practice of social work.

Just Practice tells a story of both the complexities and possibilities of social work. It is in part a reclamation project, recovering the histories, stories, and sense of urgency and possibility that have sparked the imagination and fueled the commitment of those engaged in social-justice-oriented work over time. *Just Practice* tells a story of the meanings, contexts, histories, power, and possibilities of social work and its relationship to social justice. It offers insights grounded in people's everyday practice of social work and everyday struggles for social justice. It provides a framework for diverse voices to be heard. It informs a new way of imagining and practicing what we call social justice work.

We invite you to be more than a reader of the text. We challenge you to be an active participant in crafting the possibilities for bridging social work and social justice. We challenge you to walk the talk of social justice in the daily practice of social work. We encourage teachers and students alike to take risks; to move from safe, familiar pedagogical spaces and practices; to challenge assumptions; to sit with ambiguity; and to embrace uncertainty. We hope you find the journey into social justice work both informing and inspiring.

WHY *JUST PRACTICE?*

Many textbooks have been written about the practice of social work. Why do we need another one? What does *Just Practice* offer that is different from books that have come before it? *Just Practice* puts social work's expressed commitment to social justice at center stage. We offer a framework for thinking about and practicing social work that engages with the visions, hopes, and challenges of building and living in a just world. It is one thing to say that social workers are *against* injustice or *for* social justice. It is another to translate that claim into an integrated model for practice. In brief, *Just Practice* offers a critical approach to social work. Michael Reisch (2005, p. 157) argues that critical social work can "serve as a conceptual framework or vehicle that will contribute to efforts to resist contemporary political-economic developments such as globlisation." The *Just Practice* framework provides a guide to critical social work that integrates politics, ethics, and rights; translates the concept of social justice into concrete practice; and responds to the complex terrain of twenty-first century social work.

Social work in the twenty-first century faces profound challenges. While advances in information and communication technologies have shrunk distances of time and space, the expansion of the global market has contributed to a widening gap between rich and poor (Oxfam America, 2014). The effects of the global recession of 2008 continue to reverberate, with particularly harsh consequences for the poor and disenfranchised. Access to safe affordable housing, food, and water has grown ever more precarious in the United States and abroad. We are experiencing increasing rates of both global aging and child poverty. The displacement and migration of human populations in response to war, economic dislocation, and environmental disasters pose challenges to states and nations and notions of social welfare. Nearly sixty-eight years have passed since the signing of the Universal Declaration of Human Rights, yet violations of those rights continue in the United States and worldwide.

When we first introduced the Just Practice framework in 2003, the United States had not yet declared war on Iraq. Our country has now been engaged in wars for fifteen years, with a tremendous toll at home and abroad. We have militarized our borders and expanded our prison systems in the name of security.

We have criminalized immigrants and turned back those desperately seeking to escape political, economic, and social violence. We have repeatedly witnessed acts of racism and violence claiming the lives of black people from Sanford, Florida, to Cleveland, New York City, and Ferguson, Missouri, that speak not only to racism in law enforcement and justice systems, but to its persistence in U.S. society. These realities speak to the urgent need for alternatives to *us* and *them* thinking, for dialogue, and for policies and practices that honor human dignity and rights.

We have also witnessed powerful social movements for immigrant rights and social, racial, economic, and environmental justice across the United States. We have seen the power of organized civil resistance around the globe—often led by young people—claiming the streets and social media in demands for rights, voice, and participation in the decisions that affect their lives. We have seen the redoubling of oppression in some parts of the world and the opening of spaces of possibility in others. The challenges we face are daunting. Social work in the twenty-first century calls for new ways of thinking and acting in order to address these challenges and realize our professional commitment to social justice. It demands that social workers think and act critically, creatively, and courageously. *Just Practice* seeks to respond in an integrated way to these challenges and offers new possibilities for theory and practice.

THE JUST PRACTICE FRAMEWORK

Just Practice introduces a new framework for social work that builds upon five key themes: *meaning, context, power, history,* and *possibility*. How do we give meaning to the experiences and conditions that shape our lives? What are the contexts in which those experiences and conditions occur? How do structures and relations of power shape people's lives and the practice of social work? How might a historical perspective help us to grasp the ways in which struggles over meaning and power have played out and to better appreciate the human consequences of those struggles? We argue here that meaning, power, and history are key components to critical understanding of the *person-in-context*. It is from that culturally, politically, and historically located vantage point that we appreciate constraints and imagine possibilities for justice-oriented practice.

Just Practice is based on a pedagogy of popular education that envisions knowledge development as a mutual teaching-learning process. We argue that a participatory process, grounded in dialogue and critically attuned to questions of power and inequality, is fundamental to social justice work. This book is designed to facilitate participatory learning in the classroom and to prepare students for participatory approaches to *engagement, teaching/learning, action, accompaniment, evaluation, reflection,* and *celebration,* the seven core processes of the Just Practice framework. Linkages among practice, research, and policy are integrated throughout the text. We pay particular attention to the diversity of social work practice and to the possibilities of transforming spaces of inequality, oppression, and marginality into spaces of hope, places of connection, and bases for action.

We draw knowledge and inspiration from many committed social work practitioners, scholars, and activists who have come before us. We explore the contradictions in the field of social work in which the rhetoric of social justice has often been inconsistent with practices of containment and control (Dlamini & Sewpaul, 2015; Margolin, 1997; Reisch, 2014). We seek insight from those who have lived the consequences of unjust social arrangements and from those who have posed challenges to injustice only to find their voices silenced and their contributions neglected in the history of social work practice (see Reisch & Andrews, 2001). We draw inspiration from social workers actively engaged with the personal and political dilemmas of linking a commitment to social, economic, and environmental justice to their everyday practices in their organizations and communities. They have pushed us to challenge our own certainties about the world and to open ourselves to transformative possibilities.

Just Practice is written with an audience of students in U.S. schools of social work in mind. However, we believe that meaningful engagement with questions of social justice demands a global perspective. We draw on the history of social justice in U.S. social work and beyond U.S. borders to expand our thinking. In this age of transnational movements of people, power, and information, social work practice needs to embrace a commitment to social justice that crosses national, geographic, cultural, and disciplinary boundaries. *Just Practice* provides possibilities and tools for thinking globally even when we are engaged in the most micro and local levels of practice.

Just Practice is the product of a long-term process of collaboration, dialogue, and reflection. The original framework and text were developed by Janet Finn and Maxine Jacobson through a process of critical reflection regarding the challenges of social work practice and education, the tensions and contradictions of the profession, and our places therein (Finn & Jacobson, 2003). Our varied histories of employment in human services (child welfare, juvenile justice, chemical dependency treatment, domestic violence, sexual abuse investigation and treatment, and foster care) and the challenges of social justice we faced became a starting point for reflection and dialogue. The dialogue was expanded through engagement with critical theory and through learning about the innovative work of colleagues both in and beyond the United States. The *Just Practice* perspective has been informed, enriched, and expanded through twelve years of engagement with students, colleagues, practitioners, and service users. *Just Practice* is an ongoing work in progress as it is absorbed, challenged, and reinvented over time.

Just Practice is informed by contemporary directions in critical social and cultural theory (e.g., feminist, social constructionist, narrative, practice, and critical race theories) that attend to questions of meaning, context, power, history, and possibility in understanding and shaping processes of individual and social change. We address the power of current neoliberal ideologies regarding social welfare, market-based approaches to social work, and their consequences in the everyday lives of poor and vulnerable populations. We encourage readers to examine the social construction of human problems and their solutions and the ways in which the language and labels of helping professions map onto practices of caring, containment, and control.

Questions of gender and gender expression, race, class, age, sexual identity, ability, and citizenship are explored not as issues of populations at risk but as key axes around which practices of and beliefs about inequality and difference are structured, reinforced, and contested. We challenge readers to examine the classism, heterosexism, and racism embedded in social life, in the social work profession, and in our own experience before turning attention to *target populations*. We argue that ongoing critical questioning of our own certainties and critical reflection on our location in complex webs of privilege and oppression are central components of social justice work.

PLAN OF THE TEXT AND OVERVIEW OF THE CHAPTERS

Just Practice presents an innovative intervention in theory and skills for social work practice. Its central theme—a social-justice-oriented approach to social work—reflects the mandates of the Council on Social Work Education to better integrate themes of social, economic, and environmental justice, difference and diversity, human rights, social science knowledge, ethics, and research into the theory and practice of social work. *Just Practice* responds in a critical and integrated way to each of these concerns. It provides a new framework for social work that articulates the linkage of epistemology, theory, values, and skills of practice.

Just Practice is divided into eight chapters in which the five key concepts of meaning, context, power, history, and possibility and the seven core processes of engagement, teaching-learning, action, accompaniment, evaluation, critical reflection, and celebration are developed. The text itself is designed to be inter-active and to provide a model for integrating theory and practice. Each chap-ter contains action and reflection exercises in which substantive material is accompanied by practical opportunities for individual or group action, skill development, and reflection. The chapters contain a variety of examples and resources that exemplify the integration of social work and social justice or provide an opportunity for synthesizing material presented in the chapter. These are designed to engage readers as partners in dialogue in the teaching-learning process, to develop critical thinking skills, and to promote practice competence. Discussion questions, suggested readings, and short essays on practice are included at the end of each chapter to stimulate further critical inquiry.

Chapter 1 begins the process of imagining social work within a social jus-tice context and examining the challenges and possibilities this poses for the social work profession. Readers are introduced to ways of conceptualizing social work and social justice, the linkage between them, and the implications for practice. International meanings of social work are presented that further explore the cultural, historical, and political context of practice. Readers are introduced to the concept of positionality, which refers to their location in the social world and the intersections of privilege and oppression that shape the social work experience. The five key concepts of the Just Practice framework—meaning, context, power, history, and possibility—are introduced, developed, and illustrated through exercises and examples.

Chapter 2 tells a story of the emergence and development of social work as a profession, with primary emphasis on U.S. social work. The chapter exam-ines the significance of history and a historical perspective on social work prac-tice. Both development of social work theories and practice models and the grounded actions of key figures in the profession are addressed. Readers are invited to explore the tensions and contradictions as well as achievements in the history of social work and to consider the implications for contemporary social work. Special attention is paid to the contributions of advocates and activists whose stories often go untold. The chapter foregrounds the economic and political contexts that shaped the profession and practice of social work from its beginnings in the late nineteenth century to the present.

Chapter 3 examines the concept of values, the practice of valuing, and the relationship of values to social work practice. Readers are introduced to the core values of the profession as articulated by the Code of Ethics of the National Association of Social Workers. We explore values and ethics in context, look at the historical evolution of the code of ethics, and examine alternative conceptualizations of social work ethics and frameworks for ethical decision making. The discussion moves from a broad perspective on values and valuing to the personal level and engages the reader in the work of self-assessment regarding personal and professional values. The chapter presents the Universal Declaration of Human Rights as a foundation for ethical practice and introduces the concept of an *ethics of participation* as a starting point for social justice work.

Chapter 4 addresses the concept of theory and the practice of theorizing. We explore theorizing as part of our human capacity for making sense of the world and our experience in it. The relationship of theory to the standpoint and values of the theorist is examined. The chapter reviews the dominant theories shaping contemporary social work practice and critiques each approach in terms of its strengths and limitations. We introduce a range of critical social theories, including post-structural, feminist, critical race, and practice theories, and consider their implications for social justice work. The core processes of the Just Practice framework—engagement, teaching-learning, action, accompaniment, critical reflection, evaluation, and celebration—are presented and defined.

Chapter 5 develops the skills, activities, and issues involved in the process of engagement. Readers are encouraged to explore the meaning of engagement as both a process and a commitment. Engagement provides the entrée to social justice work in community, organizational, group, and interpersonal contexts. We examine the centrality of relationship to social justice work. We develop the concept of anticipatory empathy as a time for self-reflection and preparation for engagement with participants in the change process. We explore a range of listening and communication skills central to the process of engagement. We pay particular attention to engaging groups, given their importance in social justice work.

Chapter 6 introduces and defines the core process of teaching-learning and reframes assessment as a process of co-learning. We problematize conventional approaches to assessment and examine issues of power and positionality in the assessment process. Readers are introduced to the processes of mutual aid that contribute to effective teamwork. The chapter provides guides and tools for systematic inquiry into multiple contexts of practice. We present both traditional and alternative methods for teaching and learning about people in interpersonal, organizational, and community contexts.

Chapter 7 introduces and defines the core processes of action and accompaniment. Action involves the varied activities of planning, decision making, resource mobilization, support, and advocacy involved in creating change. Accompaniment refers to the people-to-people partnerships central to action. Readers explore the thinking and skills of action and accompaniment and are introduced to the roles of social justice work. We develop strategies for participatory planning, decision making, and activating the change process. Skills and strategies for social justice action in interpersonal, organizational, community, and policy contexts are introduced. We consider the possibilities of popular education for engaging people in the daily issues that affect their lives.

Chapter 8 presents the final three core processes of evaluation, critical reflection, and celebration. The chapter looks at why evaluation is important, what should be evaluated, and how to go about conducting evaluations. We define and discuss the possibilities of participatory approaches to evaluation that include in the process those affected by our policies, programs, and services. We address the process of critical reflection, explore its linkage to social justice work, and consider ways to develop reflective capacity. We claim celebration as an integral component of justice-oriented practice and consider ways to celebrate the joy and beauty of the work. We conclude by offering principles of social justice work synthesized from the Just Practice approach.

Just Practice concludes with a brief epilogue that speaks to social justice work as a practice of resistance and a practice of hope. Readers are invited to consider the place and power of love in the quest for justice.

JUST PRACTICE AND THE 2015 CSWE EPAS COMPETENCIES

The Council on Social Work Education (CSWE) has adopted a competency-based framework to guide educational policies and practice standards. It has put forth nine competencies as essential for entering into professional social work practice (CSWE, 2015a). *Just Practice* both addresses and problematizes the concept of competency. Each of the nine core areas of practice competency outlined by the CSWE is addressed in the text. At the same time, we caution against the allure of a notion of competency that makes social work practice appear clear and precise, thereby masking its complexity and ambiguity (Todd, 2012). We encourage social workers to practice from a place of humility and commit to a lifelong search for competence (Moch, 2009). We caution against competency models that privilege a single, unitary approach to practice over the richness and diversity of multiple *social works* (Campbell, 2011, p. 313). We encourage a process of ongoing question posing that recognizes the partiality and limits of our knowledge and skills and invites the possibility of discovering new ways of knowing and approaches to practice. The Just Practice approach to each of the CSWE competencies is outlined in the following paragraphs.

COMPETENCY 1: DEMONSTRATE ETHICAL AND PROFESSIONAL BEHAVIOR

Just Practice provides a comprehensive overview of the concept of values and practice of valuing and explores the relationship between values and ethics in chapter 3. Readers are introduced to the NASW Codes of Ethics, IFSW Statement of Ethical Principles, and alternative perspectives on practice ethics from both U.S. and other national contexts. Frameworks for ethical decision making are examined and the case is made for a dialogical approach to ethical decision making. Readers are encouraged to engage in critical reflection on their own positionality as it relates to ethical decision making and to come to know themselves ethically. They are invited to explore the ethical complexities of contemporary practice as it intersects with new forms of communication and technology. Finally, readers are challenged to critically examine the meanings of professionalism, the political nature of social work, and the ethical and professional responsibilities involved in the practice of social justice work.

COMPETENCY 2: ENGAGE DIVERSITY AND DIFFERENCE IN PRACTICE

Just Practice places questions of difference and diversity center stage, starting with differing conceptualizations of social work itself. It provides a conceptual framework to guide thinking about difference, diversity, and the relations of power therein. Chapter 1 introduced readers to the concept of *positionality*, and opportunities for exploring positionality in relationship to social work practice are developed in subsequent chapters. Throughout the text readers are challenged to explore the workings of discrimination and domination that affect the lives and life chances of service users. Critical self-reflection and reflexive practice, key aspects of engaging difference and diversity, are addressed throughout the text. In chapters 5 through 8, social workers and clients are recognized as both teachers and learners; the meaning and power of clients' voices, stories, and worldviews are valued; and participants in the change process engage in the co-construction of knowledge, strategies, action plans, and evaluation processes.

COMPETENCY 3: ADVANCE HUMAN RIGHTS AND SOCIAL, ECONOMIC, AND ENVIRONMENTAL JUSTICE

Just Practice provides a framework and rationale for envisioning and practicing *social justice work*, a holistic approach that addresses the dynamic interplay among structural arrangements, social contexts, and people's everyday struggles and strengths. Chapter 1 introduces readers to key structural issues of social, economic, and environmental injustice that contribute to personal struggles and social problems. The Just Practice framework, introduced in chapter 1 and developed throughout the book, provides an integrated approach for analysis that attends to the ways in which social, economic, and environmental injustices are manifest in the intimate spaces of people's everyday experience and guides possibilities for justice-oriented action. In chapter 3 readers are asked to consider human rights as a foundation for ethical decision making. Chapter 6 explores the connections between human rights and social work through the teaching-learning process. Concrete examples of human-rights-based practice with individuals, families, and communities are presented in chapters 6 and 7.

COMPETENCY 4: ENGAGE IN PRACTICE-INFORMED RESEARCH AND RESEARCH-INFORMED PRACTICE

Just Practice offers a multifaceted approach to bridging research and practice. Chapter 2 provides readers with an overview of the historical development of social work and encourages critical inquiry into ways of knowing and sources of knowledge that shaped the development of the profession and the tensions therein. Chapter 3 provides a critical foundation in values and ethics through which the research-practice nexus can be examined. Chapter 4 prepares readers to be critical consumers of theory and to query the theoretical premises that inform research and practice. Chapter 6 provides tools for problematizing approaches to practice and asking critical questions that disrupt certainties and offer open spaces for new ways of knowing. Chapter 7 brings research-informed examples to bear that illustrate justice-oriented practice possibilities. Chapter 8 focuses on evaluation of practice.

COMPETENCY 5: ENGAGE IN POLICY PRACTICE

Just Practice provides a framework for exploring the dynamic interplay of policy and practice. Chapter 1 introduces the core concepts of Just Practice—meaning, power, context, history, and possibility. In chapter 2, readers are introduced to the complex and contested interplay of policy and practice over the course of social work's development as a profession in the late nineteenth and the twentieth century. The chapter offers diverse examples of grounded action by social workers for policy change. This historical perspective is key to understanding the political, social, and cultural influences shaping policy and practice today. The critical thinking skills required to analyze, formulate, and advocate for just social policies are addressed throughout the book. Chapter 4 provides a concrete example of participatory community engagement in policy change in the practice of public housing redevelopment. Chapter 7 introduces specific skills for policy practice and advocacy for social justice.

COMPETENCY 6: ENGAGE WITH INDIVIDUALS, FAMILIES, GROUPS, ORGANIZATIONS, AND COMMUNITIES

The Just Practice framework provides an integrated approach to engagement in multiple contexts of practice. Chapter 1 introduces the concept of positionality and practice of critical self-reflection needed for effective engagement. Chapter 4 prepares readers to critically engage with theory to guide practice. Chapter 5 explores the concept, processes, and skills of engagement. Readers are introduced to engagement in cultural-political, community, organizational, group, and interpersonal contexts. Skills and practices of anticipatory empathy, observation, bearing witness, body consciousness, active listening, and dialogue are addressed. Particular attention is paid to issues of power, difference, and resistance in the engagement process. Readers are introduced to the concept of cultural humility as a basis for engaging and honoring difference and diversity. Chapter 5 also addresses the power of popular education and possibility of engaging groups as contexts for mutual aid and collective action.

COMPETENCY 7: ASSESS INDIVIDUALS, FAMILIES, GROUPS, ORGANIZATIONS, AND COMMUNITIES

Chapter 6 frames assessment as a mutual, dialogical, ongoing process of teaching-learning. Top-down and one-way approaches to assessment are problematized and questions of power and positionality are addressed. Readers are introduced to specific skills and practices of teaching-learning in the context of communities, groups, organizations, families, and individuals. At the community level, readers are introduced to basic guides for community assessment, listening surveys, and strategies for community mapping. At the organizational level, readers are offered a basic guide for getting to know your organization, force field analysis, and strategies of appreciative inquiry. At the individual and family level, biopsychosocial assessment processes are critically examined and possibilities for strengths-based assessment are explored. Readers are introduced to classic social work assessment tools, such as ecomaps and genograms, and to variations on these approaches.

COMPETENCY 8: INTERVENE WITH INDIVIDUALS, FAMILIES, GROUPS, ORGANIZATIONS, AND COMMUNITIES

Chapter 7 reframes *intervention* in terms of the interrelated processes of action and accompaniment. The language of action draws attention to possibilities beyond "person-changing" interventions, and accompaniment speaks to the significance of joining with others on their journeys of change. Issues of risk, rights, and responsibilities in the change process are explored. Emphasis is placed on participatory possibilities for justice-oriented action from the level of individual therapy to community and organizational change, policy advocacy, and system transformation. Readers are introduced to skills and practices of action and accompaniment and possibilities for participatory planning, decision making, and practice. Chapter 7 offers an enhanced perspective on the roles of social work and on the skills and practices needed to support socially just organizations. Particular attention is paid to transformative practice possibilities in the criminal justice system. Chapter 7 also provides concrete examples of social justice work through photovoice, popular theater, and the linkage between social and environmental justice and human rights.

COMPETENCY 9: EVALUATE PRACTICE WITH INDIVIDUALS, FAMILIES, GROUPS, ORGANIZATIONS, AND COMMUNITIES

Just Practice introduces critical reflection on self and practice as a core aspect of social justice work and develops the concept, process, and skills of critical reflection throughout the text. Chapter 8 links critical reflection and evaluation, provides a rationale for the importance of evaluating practice, and offers a multifaceted perspective on what social workers should evaluate and how. Readers are introduced to participatory evaluation, which values service users as partners in the evaluation process. Chapter 8 presents key principles of participatory evaluation and illustrates diverse methods used to conduct participatory research. Grounded examples of youth as evaluators in participatory action research illustrate transformative possibilities. Readers are also provided concrete tools and resources to carry out basic program evaluation informed by participatory principles. Finally, *Just Practice* contends that evaluation and critical reflection are enhanced through celebration of successes large and small as an integral part of practice.

ACKNOWLEDGMENTS

Just Practice has been shaped by many people and experiences. The initial framework took shape through many conversations with Maxine Jacobson, who co-authored earlier editions of the book and whose thinking about social justice work resonates throughout these pages as well. I am grateful to social work colleagues Jennifer Stucker, Sadye Logan, Lynn Nybell, Ann Rall, Jeff Shook, Linwood Cousins, and Scott Nicholson, who continue to challenge and inspire me regarding the possibilities of social justice work. Special thanks to University of Montana social work colleagues Keith Anderson, Jim Caringi, and Laurie Walker, whose research has provided concrete examples of bringing social justice to bear in the everyday practice of social work at the individual, organizational, and community level.

I also thank Anya Jabour, professor of history at the University of Montana, for her contributions to my course on the History of Social Welfare, Justice, and Change that have deepened my thinking about chapter 2, "Looking Back." Jabour's current work on Sophonisba Breckinridge will make a significant contribution to social work history.

Special thanks to Bonnie Buckingham, Katherine Deuel, Debby Florence, Robin Graham, Alex Kulick, Sadye Logan, Scott Nicholson, Seth Quackenbush, Ann Rall, Cynthia Tobias, Laurie Walker, Laura Wernick, and Marilyn Bruguier Zimmerman for offering their critical reflections and personal accounts of social justice work in action that are included in the book. Finally, I thank David Follmer, Tom Meenaghan, and reviewers Samuel Copeland (Stephen F. Austin University), May Friedman (Ryerson University), Carolyn Campbell (Dalhousie University), and Nina Koen (Southern Illinois University) for their insightful feedback that pushed me to think more critically and carefully about Just Practice; Tom LaMarre for his long-term commitment to the publication of *Just Practice;* and Brent Jacocks and Sarah Butcher for their dedicated work in the final editing and production.

Chapter 1

Imagining Social Work and Social Justice

Social justice is the end that social work seeks, and social justice is the chance for peace.

Former Attorney General Ramsey Clark, 1988

OVERVIEW

In chapter 1 we locate social work within a social justice context. We examine broadly accepted contemporary definitions of social work in the United States and in an international context, and we consider the implications of these diverse meanings for social work practice. Likewise, we probe the challenges of defining social justice, even though it is embraced as a core value of social work. We ask readers to consider the following questions:

- What is the relationship between social work and social justice?
- What are the common goals?
- How do the definitions of social work and social justice shape social work practice?
- How are both social work and social justice tied to questions of difference, inequality, and oppression?
- How do we engage social justice in our everyday practice of social work?

We will explore concepts of social work as a critical, political, and transformational practice; consider the social work profession itself as a site of struggle; and highlight challenges and possibilities of that struggle. We will offer the concept of *social justice work* as a way of linking social work and social justice in both theory and practice. We will introduce the Just Practice *framework* and its five key concepts—meaning, context, power, history, and possibility. The Just Practice framework will provide the foundation for integrating theory and practice of social justice work. The framework will push us to explore

1

common assumptions about reality—those ideas, principles, and patterns of perception, behavior, and social relating that we accept without question. As learners, this will move us beyond the bounds of familiar and comfortable contexts and encourage us to critically examine commonly held beliefs and ways of thinking.

MEANING OF SOCIAL WORK

The Idea of Social Work

Each of us has an idea or an image of social work that we carry in our head. For some of us this image comes from experiences as paid or volunteer workers in a state-based agency or community service organization. Others may have known social work from the other side as a recipient of services—perhaps as a child in the foster care system, a resident of a women's shelter, a client in a community mental health center, or a single parent trying to survive on Temporary Assistance to Needy Families (TANF), the time-limited public assistance program that replaced Aid to Families with Dependent Children (AFDC) as a result of the 1996 welfare reform in the United States.

Some of us may have little or no experience with the practicalities of social work. Perhaps we have taken a course or two or we have known social work mainly through its representations in the media, with social workers stereotyped as villains or heroes who take children from their families. Nonetheless, we have a mental image of social work and what we envision ourselves doing as social workers. Each of us too has an idea or an image of social justice. For some, social justice relates to notions of fairness, equality, tolerance, and human rights. Others know social justice through its absence, for example, through personal experiences of discrimination, exploitation, exclusion, and violence.

> **Class Learning Activity:**
> **Meanings of Social Work and Social Justice**
> Take a few minutes to consider what social work and social justice mean to you. What image or words come to mind when you think of social work? What context do you imagine? What is the social worker doing? Who else is involved? Do you see yourself as the social worker? What meanings might you attach to this image of social work? Briefly note your responses. Now consider what image comes to mind when you think of social justice. What context do you imagine? Who is involved? Do you see yourself in this

image? What are some of the meanings you might attach to this image of social justice? Briefly note your responses.

Now share your reflections on social work and social justice with another class member. Where do you and your partner find similarities and differences in thinking about social work? About social justice? What do your images suggest about the relationship between social work and social justice? Come together as a group and share some of your images and impressions of social work and social justice. Generate a list of examples on a white board or newsprint; then consider your collective impressions of social work and social justice. What are the similarities and differences in your impressions of the two concepts? What insights do you take from this exercise? What questions does it raise?

Struggles over Definition

Perhaps there are as many meanings of social work as there are social workers. As we will discuss further in chapter 2, there have been struggles for control of social work's definition and direction since its inception. Forces both within and outside social work have influenced its dominant definition. To some extent, this struggle is attributable to what some believe is social work's dualistic nature and location, wedged between addressing individual need and engaging in broad-scale societal change (Abramovitz, 1998; Withorn, 1984). A justice-oriented definition of social work challenges the boundaries between the individual and the social. It considers how society and the individual are mutually constituting: We individually and collectively make our social world and, in turn, through our participation in society and its institutions, systems, beliefs, and patterns of practice, we both shape ourselves and are shaped as social beings (Berger & Luckman, 1966). Progressive U.S. social worker, educator, and activist Bertha Capen Reynolds (1942) called this "seeing it whole" (p. 3).

Let's take a look at some commonly held contemporary definitions of social work in the United States and then move to alternative and international definitions. We ask you to consider this question: How is it that a profession that calls itself by one name—social work—can have such diverse meanings and interpretations? Also, think about the different contexts that shape these meanings and how these translate into different ways of conceptualizing and engaging in social work practice. How might practitioners in other national and political contexts interpret social work differently from practitioners in the United States? How might definitions vary among practitioners in the United States? What might be reasons for these differences?

Official Meanings

Professions have formal organizations that oversee their functioning, determine standards, and monitor practice. The Council of Social Work Education (CSWE), for example, is the accrediting body for schools of social work education in the United States. Its primary roles are to ensure the quality and consistency of social work education and to ensure that students earning BSW and MSW degrees possess the knowledge, skills, and values needed to be effective practitioners. According to CSWE,

> The purpose of the social work profession is to promote human and community well-being. Guided by a person and environment framework, a global perspective, respect for human diversity, and knowledge based on scientific inquiry, the purpose of social work is actualized through its quest for social and economic justice, the prevention of conditions that limit human rights, the elimination of poverty, and the enhancement of the quality of life for all persons, locally and globally. (CSWE, 2015a, p. 5)

The National Association of Social Workers (NASW) is the largest organization of professional social workers in the United States. It works to enhance the professional growth and development of its members, both BSW and MSW practitioners. It also helps to create and maintain professional standards and to advance social policies. The Preamble to the NASW Code of Ethics contains the following definition of social work:

> The primary mission of the social work profession is to enhance human well-being and help meet the basic human needs of all people, with particular attention to the needs and empowerment of people who are vulnerable, oppressed, and living in poverty. A historic and defining feature of social work is the profession's focus on individual well-being in a social context and the well-being of society. Fundamental to social work is attention to the environmental forces that create, contribute to, and address problems in living.
>
> Social workers promote social justice and social change with and on behalf of clients. "Clients" is used inclusively to refer to individuals, families, groups, organizations, and communities. Social workers are sensitive to cultural and ethnic diversity and strive to end discrimination, oppression, poverty, and other forms of social injustice. These activities may be in the form of direct practice, community organizing, supervision, consultation, administration, advocacy, social and political action, policy development and implementation, education, and research and evaluation. Social workers seek to enhance

the capacity of people to address their own needs. Social workers also seek to promote the responsiveness of organizations, communities, and other social institutions to individuals' needs and social problems. (NASW, 2008, p. 1)

These definitions may seem both global and somewhat idealistic. They do not tell us much about what social workers actually do. Interestingly, NASW has a definition for social work practice that differs from that of social work:

Social work practice consists of the professional application of social work values, principles, and techniques to one or more of the following ends: helping people obtain tangible services; counseling and psychotherapy with individuals, families, and groups; helping communities or groups provide or improve social and health services; and participating in legislative processes. The practice of social work requires knowledge of human development and behavior; of social and economic, and cultural institutions; and of the interaction of all these factors. (NASW, 2015b)

This depiction of practice makes no mention of social injustice, oppression, or discrimination. Why might that be?

The *Social Work Dictionary*, published by NASW (Barker, 2003), provides another variation on the definition of social work:

The applied science of helping people achieve an effective level of psychosocial functioning and effecting societal changes to enhance the well-being of people.

According to NASW, "social work is the professional activity of helping individuals, groups, or communities enhance or restore their capacity for social functioning and creating conditions favorable to this goal" (p. 408).

Let's pause for a moment and think about these definitions. What do these definitions of social work mean to you? Where do you see common ground and differences? Do they align with your own definition of social work? Why is there a difference between definitions of social work and social work practice? Might this suggest differences between the vision and ideals of the profession and how social workers are socialized to actually engage in practice?

Like other definitions of a profession, these embody the value systems of their creators. The CSWE and NASW have the power to officially sanction not only how we define social work but also how we outline the parameters of its practice and articulate the values believed to be central to the work. This official sanction refers not only to words and to the language we use to describe what we do, but also to the actions we take that exemplify our practice. These definitions are also evolving, responding to pressures from constituents and social conditions. For example, prior to its 2008 revision of its *Educational Policy and Accreditation Standards* (2015a), the CSWE did not specifically charge social workers with the responsibility to respond to conditions that limit human rights or to embrace a global perspective. In addition, the policy document provides little guidance regarding *how* to bring social, economic, and environmental justice, human rights, and a global perspective to bear in social work education and practice.

Reflection Moment:
Shifting Meanings

What meanings are communicated by the CSWE and the NASW in their definitions of social work? How might these meanings guide practice? Envision yourself working with children and families or in a health care or community center. Given these definitions, how might you relate to the people, the neighborhoods, and the communities with which you work? Would your relationships be top-down, bottom-up, or side-by-side? How would you work to promote, restore, maintain, and enhance human functioning? What actions would you take to correct conditions that limit human rights and quality of life? Where would you turn to gain an understanding of human rights? How would you employ a global perspective?

Now let's shift our vision from inside the profession and look at meanings of social work from the outside, through the eyes of those whom social work is meant to serve. For example, imagine yourself to be:

- a person experiencing homelessness who is turned away from a full shelter for the third night in a row
- a nine-year-old child in a receiving home awaiting temporary placement in a foster home
- an undocumented resident of the United States whose young child, born in the United States, is in need of emergency health care
- a person seeking the services of your practicum agency

How would you define social work through these eyes? As you look at the meanings of social work from an outsider's point of view, do your conceptions of social work change? What concrete actions and results would demonstrate to you that the social work profession is realizing its stated purposes?

The CSWE and NASW are powerful meaning makers in defining the nature of social work in the United States. More often than not, social work texts include these definitions of social work in their introductory chapters (for example, see Miley, O'Melia, & DuBois, 2013; Sheafor & Horejsi, 2012). Although these are certainly the dominant definitions, they are not the only ones. Next, we will look at some alternative meanings, those that challenge and go beyond the dominant definitions. These meanings of social work speak directly to its inescapable *political* nature and ask us to consider issues of power as they concern social workers' relationships to those with whom they work.

Other Meanings to Consider

Social Work as a Transformative Process

Paulo Freire argues that social work is a transformative process in which both social conditions and participants, including the social worker, are changed in the pursuit of a just world (Moch, 2009). Freire, a Brazilian educator and critical theorist, is noted for his contributions to popular education, a social change strategy whereby people affected by oppressive social conditions come together to reflect on their circumstances, become critically conscious of the root causes of their suffering, and take liberating action (Checkoway, 1995; Freire, 1974). (Popular education will be discussed further in chapters 5 and 6.) Freire taught literacy to Brazilian farm workers through group discussion that prompted critical reflection on their life conditions. Kathleen Weiler (1988) writes,

> [Freire] is committed to a belief in the power of individuals to come to a critical consciousness of their own being in the world. Central to his pedagogical work is the understanding that both teachers and students are agents, both engaged in the process of constructing and reconstructing meaning. (p. 17)

Freire has also articulated his critical understanding of social work (Moch, 2009). In his view, social work involves critical curiosity and a life-long committed search for one's own competence; congruence between words and actions; tolerance; the ability to exercise "impatient patience"; and a grasp of what is historically possible. Similarly, Stanley Witkin (1998, p. 197) asks us to consider social work as contextually relevant inquiry and activity focused on individual and social transformation that promotes human rights, social justice, and human dignity. Robert Adams, Lena Dominelli, and Malcolm Payne (2005) frame social work as a transformational, reflexive, and critical practice with individuals, communities, families, and groups that enhances social solidarity, deepens social interaction, and reduces inequality. They argue that transformation does not mean revolution. It is about continuity as well as change. It is a creative process that moves beyond technique, procedures, and managerialism—the neoliberal notion that social problems can be resolved through management (Fitzsimons, 1999)—it engages with the structures of people's lives (pp. 12–14). They state,

> Ultimately, we may achieve transformation of the service user's situation, the setting for practice, the policy context, and, not least, ourselves. In transforming ourselves, we enhance our capacities for self-awareness, self-evaluation, and self-actualization or personal and professional fulfillment. (p. 14)

Social Work as a Political Process

A number of writers have argued that social work practice is fundamentally a political activity, both in the process of theory development and in the ways in which social workers envision and engage in practice (Dominelli, 2008; Gray & Webb, 2013; Payne, 2014; Sheedy, 2013). Donna Baines (2011, pp. 5–6) contends that social work is not a neutral caring profession but an active, contested, political process. David Gil (2013) makes the case for radical social work, which rejects notions of political neutrality and confronts the root causes of social problems by transcending technical approaches to practice and embracing the liberatory possibilities of social work as a political practice.

Like Freire, Gil asserts that social work must promote critical consciousness, that is, an acute awareness of the interconnected nature of individuals, families, and communities and a society's political, economic, and social arrangements. To achieve these ends, Gil contends that social workers must strive to understand their own and others' oppression (and privilege) and consider alternative possibilities for human relations. He too argues that there is need for fundamental social change. Dennis Saleebey concurs, stating that "practice that is guided by social and economic justice requires methods that explicitly deal with power and power relationships" (2006, p. 95). Similarly, Adams and colleagues (2005) contend that our behavior as practitioners "is a social and political statement about how we think social relationships should move forward" and how we confront barriers to social justice (p. 3).

Social Work as Critical Practice

In a similar vein, advocates of *critical social work* argue that the central purpose of social work is social change to redress social inequality. They examine notions such as class, race, gender, sexuality, and age not as neutral or *natural* categories to describe human difference. Critical social workers see these as socially constructed concepts around which ideas of difference and relations of power and inequality are produced and contested, with material consequences for individuals and groups. They too pay particular attention to the structural arrangements of society that contribute to individual pain (Allan, Pease, & Briskman, 2009; Fook, 2012; Mullaly, 2010; Payne, 2014). According to Michael Reisch (2005), who has documented the history of critical social work in the United States,

> Critical social work challenges conventional assumptions about poverty, race, and gender, and the basic functions of a market-driven political-economic system. In addition, critical social work heightens awareness of the historical and contemporary relationship between social justice and social struggle. (p. 157)

As Jan Fook (2012) describes, Western social work is partly rooted in a critical tradition whereby early social workers involved in the Settlement House Movement critiqued the conditions of everyday life for urban immigrant working classes wrought by the political and economic arrangements and labor demands of industrial capitalism. She points to a revitalization of critical social work in the 1960s and 1970s as articulated through models of structural and radical social work, which were informed by Marxist critiques of political economy (Bailey and Brake, 1975; Galper, 1975; Moreau, 1979; Mullaly, 2006). Similarly, early feminist, empowerment, and anti-oppressive models of social work emerging in the 1970s and 1980s critically examined the relationship between personal struggles and political issues, critiqued existing social arrangements and mainstream social work's complicity therein, and called for emancipatory social work practice (Baines, 2011; Dominelli & McLeod, 1989; Solomon, 1976). We will explore this history further in chapter 2.

These overlapping conceptualizations of social work as a critical, political, and transformational process are central to our understanding of social justice work. Throughout the text we will draw on the insights of critical thinkers and practitioners who have contributed to these conceptualizations as we challenge the bounds and expand the possibilities of practice.

International Meanings of Social Work

International Federation of Social Workers' Definition

Much can be learned about social work when we broaden our view beyond the U.S. context. For example, the International Federation of Social Workers (IFSW) is a global organization whose stated purpose is to "promote social work to achieve social development; advocate for social justice globally; and facilitate international cooperation" (IFSW, 2016). In 2014, replacing a definition adopted in 2008, the IFSW developed a "global definition of social work":

> Social work is a practice-based profession and an academic discipline that promotes social change and development, social cohesion, and the empowerment and liberation of people. Principles of social justice, human rights, collective responsibility and respect for diversities are central to social work. Underpinned by theories of social work, social sciences, humanities and indigenous knowledge, social work engages people and structures to address life challenges and enhance wellbeing. (IFSW, 2014)

How does this compare with the definitions put forth by the NASW and CSWE? Where do you see similarities and differences? The IFSW definition is also a work in progress. For example, the concept of indigenous knowledge was not part of the previous definition, adopted in 2001. Indigenous knowledge refers to a respect for diverse, local, and culturally grounded ways of knowing and specifically knowledge grounded in the epistemologies (ways of knowing), theories, and histories of indigenous people (Gray, Coates, & Yellow Bird, 2008).

Critique of IFSW Definition

The IFSW definition has been subject to criticism by groups such as the Latin American Association of Social Work Education and Research (Asociación Latinoamericana de Enseñanza e Investigación en Trabajo Social [ALAEITS]). Coming from a critical social work perspective, ALAEITS contends that the definition takes a functional rather than critical approach, focusing on how people are functioning within given societal structures rather than questioning structural arrangements. According to ALAEITS, the IFSW definition addresses human rights as a principle but does not locate social work in the struggle for their universal fulfillment. It puts forth social justice as a value, but does not associate it with the fulfillment of economic, social, or environmental rights or with achievement of people's autonomy. Further, it puts forth the idea of social development but does not consider how that plays out in the context of global capitalist development. Finally, ALAEITS contends, the IFSW definition speaks to cultural diversity but makes no mention of social and economic inequality (ALAEITS, 2013).

Alternatively, ALAEITS defines social work as a transformative *praxis*—the ongoing process of critical reflection and action—based on democratic principles and committed to confronting social inequalities and strengthening people's autonomy, participation, and exercise of citizenship in the defense and achievement of human rights and social justice (ALAEITS, 2013).

What might be at stake in these differing definitions of social work? How do the ways in which we frame social work as a profession shape the ways we think about how and where change should occur, the approaches we take, and the constraints we might place on our assumptions about *professionalism*?

Reflecting on Social Work in Diverse National and Cultural Contexts

Although the IFSW definition seeks a unifying global vision of social work, critics point to the challenges of defining social work outside of the particular historical, cultural, social, and political contexts in which it has developed as a profession. For example, culture-bound ideas about the self and individualist biopsychological notions of personhood that have a prominent place in much of Western social work practice may have little resonance in more collectivist cultural contexts where personhood is fundamentally a social concept. Likewise, social work as a profession has been defined from the ground up within diverse national contexts, at times in resistance to imported models.

Let's consider two examples of the national context of social work beyond the United States. The emergence of social work in Canada paralleled that in the United States. It was influenced by both U.S. and British traditions and practices of organized charity work and the more community-based Settlement House Movement. The first Canadian school of social work was established in 1914 at the University of Toronto. In 1926, the Canadian Association of Social Workers was founded. As in the United States, there were tensions within the profession regarding the political nature and role of social work. Given that the U.S.-based CSWE served as the accrediting body for Canadian schools of social work until 1970, U.S. influence on social work education remained strong. Canadian social workers were also developing their own identity and direction through conferences, journals, and political action (Jennissen & Lundy, 2011). By the 1970s Canadian social work educators, through the leadership of Maurice Moreau at Carleton University, were leading the way in development of a structural approach to social work. This shift came about, in part, through student action that challenged a clinically driven model of social work and called for greater emphasis on advocacy, political action, and systems change (Moreau, 1989). Canadian social workers and educators have continued to play a leading role in the development of structural and anti-oppressive social work practice grounded in a commitment to human rights (Baines, 2011; Jennissen & Lundy, 2011; Lundy, 2011; Moreau, 1989).

Now let's consider the example of Chile. Social work emerged in Chile in the 1920s, initially adopting European models of professional practice. The profession underwent a profound change in the 1960s as peoples' movements around the country pressed for rights, voice, and participation in the decisions affecting their lives. The theories of Paulo Freire, the noted popular educator mentioned earlier, who was living in exile in Chile at that time, had a transformational impact on social work education and practice. Social workers engaged in consciousness raising; critiqued the power dynamics inherent in the social-worker-client relationship; contested imported, individualistic, and apolitical models of social work; and joined with broader social movements in demands for human rights and social justice. During the years of military dictatorship in Chile (1973–1990), many social workers suffered from direct repression and the silencing of political voice. Some schools of social work were closed and others were reconfigured as sites of technical training for *social assistants*, not advocates engaged in social change. Quite literally, there was a political struggle over the very definition of social work. Because and in spite of repression, many social workers in Chile continued to embrace a critical approach to practice, in line with the understanding of social work outlined by ALAEITS (Finn, 2005, Jimenez & Aylwin, 1992; van Wormer, 2007).

> **Individual Learning Activity:**
> **Social Work in Different National Contexts**
>
> Use online and print sources to search for a definition of social work and description of the profession's development in a national context outside the United States. For example, what can you find about the meaning and history of social work in India, Japan, Nicaragua, or South Africa? Was social work imported? If so, how was it developed, contested, or reinvented? How is the history of social work located in a larger national history? Write a brief summary and share your findings with class members. Reflect on your collective findings. Where do you see important similarities and differences? What have you learned about the shifting meanings of social work across national and cultural contexts?

Considering Indigenous Social Work

Mel Gray, John Coates, and Michael Yellow Bird (2008) have brought together a diverse group of scholars and practitioners to examine social work from indigenous perspectives. They assert that indigenous peoples have intimate knowledge of the destructive side of social work and are well positioned to critically consider the meaning of social work. They critique the problematic export of Western models of social work and address ways in which Western assumptions so deeply embedded in social work may be in conflict with local knowledge and practices.

Yellow Bird and Gray frame indigenous social work as a deliberately political process that challenges individualist interpretations of human behaviors and human rights and recognizes the effects of globalizing and colonizing processes on people's lives and livelihoods. Indigenous social work recognizes the importance of history, the "ever present memory of unjust treatment of indigenous peoples," and the fact that indigenous history does not begin with colonization (Gray, Coates, & Yellow Bird, 2008, p. 50). They offer a view of what social work with indigenous people might look like it if held true to its values and claims:

> Wanted: Social Workers to assist with Indigenous Peoples: Indigenous Peoples are seeking highly motivated social workers to serve their communities' drive for self-determination, empowerment, and complete return of their lands and other resources illegally stolen by colonial societies. The social workers will be required to develop aggressive programmes of decolonization that can be used to enlighten and reform members of mainstream society. (p. 59)

Yellow Bird and Gray call for a decolonizing approach to social work in which we reexamine the Eurocentric nature of social work theory and practice and the ways in which colonial knowledge and power structures are embedded in professional standards, language, and basic assumptions. We draw inspiration from a decolonizing approach as we continually encourage readers to question certainties and remain open to transformative possibilities of practice. As the above discussion suggests, defining social work is a contested and political process, as is the practice of social work. Now let's turn to the subject of social justice.

MEANINGS OF SOCIAL JUSTICE

Perspectives on Social Justice

Like social work, the meaning of social justice is complex and contested. The ideas we have about social justice in U.S. social work are largely derived from Western philosophy and political theory and Judeo-Christian religious traditions. Our conceptions of justice are generally abstract ideals that overlap with our beliefs about what is right, good, desirable, and moral (Blackburn, 2001). Notions of social justice generally embrace values such as the equal worth of all citizens, their equal right to meet their basic needs, the need to spread opportunity and life chances as widely as possible, and finally the requirement that we reduce and, where possible, eliminate unjustified inequalities.

Some students of social justice consider its meaning in terms of the tensions between individual liberty and common social good, arguing that social justice is promoted to the degree that we can promote positive individual freedom. Some argue that social justice reflects a concept of fairness in the assignment of fundamental rights and duties, economic opportunities, and social conditions (Miller, 1976; Reisch, 1998a, 2002). Others frame the concept in terms of three components: (1) legal justice, which is concerned with what people owe society; (2) commutative justice, which addresses what people owe each other; and (3) distributive justice, or what society owes the person (Reichert, 2011; Van Soest, 1994, p. 711). The U.S. Catholic Bishops' Conference, in its 1986 Pastoral Letter, outlined three interlocking aspects of justice. *Commutative justice* calls for fundamental fairness in all agreements and exchanges between individuals and social groups. *Distributive justice* requires that the allocation of income, wealth, and power in society be evaluated in light of its effect on people whose basic material needs are unmet. *Social justice* implies that people have an obligation to be active and productive participants in the life of society and that society has a duty to enable them to participate in this way. Social justice also includes a duty to organize economic and social institutions so that people can contribute to society in ways that respect the freedom and dignity of their labor (U.S. Catholic Bishops, 1986). This understanding suggests that social justice is concerned not only with societal choices regarding the distribution of goods and resources, but also with the structuring of societal institutions to guarantee human rights and dignity and ensure opportunities for free and meaningful social participation. How does this understanding of social justice fit with your view?

Discussions of social justice often address three differing philosophical approaches used to inform societal decisions about the distribution or allocation of resources: utilitarian, libertarian, and egalitarian. *Utilitarian* theories emphasize actions that bring about the greatest good and least harm for the greatest number. From this perspective, individual rights can be infringed upon if so doing helps meet the interests and needs of the majority (McCormick, 2003; Van Soest, 1994). *Libertarian* theories reject obligations for equal or equitable distribution of resources, contending instead that each individual is entitled to any and all resources that he or she has legally acquired (Nozick, 1974).

They emphasize protection of individual freedom and the fundamental right to choose (McCormick, 2003). *Egalitarian* theories contend that every member of society should be guaranteed the same rights, opportunities, and access to goods and resources. From this perspective the redistribution of societal resources should be to the advantage of the most vulnerable members of society. However, as noted by Elisabeth Reichert (2011) and Karen Morgaine (2014), the idea of social justice as expressed in these theories remains elusive when it comes to translation into social work practice.

Social Workers Conceptualize Social Justice

Within social work, social justice is variably defined as an ideal condition, a goal, a perspective, and a process. The *Social Work Dictionary* defines social justice as

> an ideal condition in which all members of a society have the same rights, protection, opportunities, obligations, and social benefits. Implicit in this concept is the notion that historical inequalities should be acknowledged and remedied through specific measures. A key social work value, social justice entails advocacy to confront discrimination, oppression, and institutional inequities. (Barker, 2003, p. 405).

Too often, social workers take the meaning of social justice to be self-evident rather than probing how it is addressed in practice (Gil, 2013). Michael Reisch (2011) argues that a lack of consensus regarding a definition has impeded social justice action in social work. Reisch states that a social justice framework for social work and social welfare policy would "hold the most vulnerable populations harmless in the distribution of societal resources, particularly when those resources are finite. Unequal distribution of resources would be justified only if it served to advance the least advantaged groups in the community" (1998a, p. 20). This, he contends, would require broad structural change that would challenge the profession to engage beyond the level of direct practice with individuals and families.

John Rawls and Social Justice

A number of social workers and social theorists concerned about questions of social justice have turned to the work of philosopher John Rawls (1971/1995) and his theory of justice. Rawls asks what would be the characteristics of a just society in which basic human needs are met, unnecessary stress is reduced, the competence of each person is maximized, and threats to well-being are minimized. For Rawls, distributive justice denotes "the value of each person getting a fair share of the benefits and burdens resulting from social cooperation," in terms of both material goods and services and nonmaterial social goods, such as opportunity and power (Wakefield, 1988, p. 193). Rawls tries to imagine whether a small group of people, unmotivated by selfish interests, could reach consensus regarding the characteristics of a just society. In his book *A Theory of Justice* (1971/1995), he imagines such a small group, selected at random, sitting around a table. He places an important limit on this vision: None at the table know their economic status or racial identity. Rawls assumes that, without knowledge of their own immediate identities, they will not be motivated by selfish considerations. He concludes that the group will arrive at two basic principles:

1. *Justice as fairness*: "According to this principle, each person has an equal right to the most extensive basic liberty compatible with a similar liberty for others" (Albee, 1986, p. 897).

2. *Just arrangements*: "Social and economic inequalities are arranged so that they are both to the greatest benefit of the least advantaged and attached to offices and positions open to all under conditions of fair and equal opportunity" (Albee, 1986, p. 897).

From this perspective, society must make every attempt to redress all those social and economic inequalities that have led to disadvantage in order to provide real equality of opportunity. This demands a redistribution of power; the rejection of racism, sexism, gender oppression, colonialism, and exploitation; and the search for ways to redistribute social power toward the end of social justice (Albee, 1986, p. 897).

Social Work Perspectives on Distributive Justice

The concept of distributive justice has become central to a number of discussions of social justice and social work. Dorothy Van Soest and Betty Garcia (2003, p. 44) write, "Our conception of social justice is premised on the concept of distributive justice, which emphasizes society's accountability to the individual. What principles guide the distribution of goods and resources?" Van Soest and Garcia address five perspectives on distributive justice that help us grasp the complexity of the concept and critically examine our own thinking. Three of these perspectives—utilitarian, libertarian, and egalitarian, addressed above—

are prescriptive, speaking to a view of what social justice should be. The fourth view, the racial contract perspective, offers a description of the current state of society and its unequal system of privilege and racism. This view recognizes the entrenched racism in U.S. society and contends that a meaningful conceptualization of distributive justice must confront these historically deep and structurally broad inequalities. A fifth view, the human rights perspective, makes human rights central to the discussion of social justice. Proponents argue that the Universal Declaration of Human Rights could serve as a conceptually clear framework for distributive justice and for the integration of social justice into social work (Ife, 2012; MacDonald, 2006; Reichert, 2011; United Nations, 1948). Van Soest and Garcia's overview of these five perspectives is summarized in table 1.1.

Table 1.1
Five perspectives on distributive justice

Utilitarian	Justice is arrived at by weighing relative harms and benefits and determining what maximizes the greatest good for the greatest number.
Libertarian	Distribution of goods and resources occurs by natural and social lottery and is inherently uneven. Justice entails ensuring the widest possible latitude of freedom from coercion regarding what people accumulate and how they dispose of it.
Egalitarian	Every member of society should be guaranteed the same rights, opportunities, and access to goods and resources. Redistribution of resources is a moral obligation to ensure that unmet needs are redressed.
Racial contract	The focus is the current state of society rather than the way things should be. The notion of the social contract as the basis of Western democratic society is a myth. The contract did not extend beyond white society. Thus, white privilege was a constitutive part of the social contract and must be dismantled in the struggle for social justice.
Human rights	Social justice encompasses meeting basic human needs, equitable distribution of resources, and recognition of the inalienable rights of all persons.

Based on Van Soest and Garcia's discussion in *Diversity Education for Social Justice* (2003, pp. 44–50).

Class Learning Activity:
Applying Perspectives on Distributive Justice

This activity provides an opportunity to apply and reflect on these five approaches to distributive justice. Your instructor will assign the class a short, one-page reading on a contemporary subject related to social work and social justice, such as a brief news article on the criminalization of homelessness in the United States or a brief report and fact sheet on child poverty at a state, national, or global level. Divide your class into five groups, with each group representing one of the perspectives on distributive justice. The groups will have twenty to thirty minutes to develop a five-point plan for addressing the social justice issue described in the reading from their assigned perspective. Each group will write its five-point plan on a sheet of newsprint, post it for the class to see, and offer a two-minute presentation describing its plan and how it fits with its assigned perspective on social justice. Regroup as a class and then take time to debrief and reflect on the following questions: What do you notice? What commonalities and differences do you see among the five plans? How does one's perspective on distributive justice shape what one sees or does not see as a possibility? What changes or additions might you make to one or more of the plans? Which plans best align with your personal perspective on distributive justice? Why? Do possibilities expand when the question of distributive justice is considered from more than one perspective?

Critiquing Rawls and Considering Processes and Capabilities

Some scholars suggest that social work has been overly reliant on Rawls's view of distributive justice as the foundation for understanding social justice. For example, Iris Marion Young (2011) defines social justice as the elimination of institutionalized forms and practices of domination and oppression. She argues that the distributive justice framework is limited in that it does not address the underlying societal arrangements and practices that contribute to the unequal distribution of resources. Further, the distributive justice framework focuses on material goods to the neglect of nonmaterial resources such as rights and opportunities (Mullaly, 2010, pp. 44–45). Others argue that Rawls's approach to distributive justice focuses on outcomes to the neglect of perspectives that emphasize processes and human capabilities (Banerjee, 2005; Caputo, 2002; McGrath-Morris, 2002). They contend that social justice is also about *processes* of justice and ask us to consider these questions: Who has a say in the decision-making processes through which social goods and opportunities are distributed? Do those processes challenge or reinforce relationships between dominant and subordinate social groups? How are those processes embedded in social systems and organizations?

A number of contemporary scholars highlight the value of the capabilities perspective as a social justice framework for social work (Banerjee, 2005; Dessel, 2011; Gasker & Fischer, 2014; McGrath-Morris, 2002; Pogue, 2011). Based on the work of Indian economist and philosopher Amartya Sen and American philosopher Martha Nussbaum, the capabilities perspective starts with a few basic questions: "What are people actually able to do and to be? What real opportunities are available to them? What does a life worthy of human dignity require?" (Nussbaum, 2011, p. 29)? Rather than starting from abstract principles, the capabilities perspective starts with the individual and asks what the person is capable of being, doing, or becoming. Nussbaum (2011) puts forth a list of what she terms *central capabilities* that constitute the bare minimum of a life with dignity and thus the foundation for social justice (p. 32). Among these capabilities are the ability to live life and enjoy bodily health and bodily integrity; the ability to use senses, imagination, and thought; the ability to express emotions and engage practical reason; the ability to affiliate with others and to live with concern for and in relation to other species; the ability to laugh and play; and the ability to control one's environment in terms of political and material rights (Nussbaum, 2011, pp. 33–34).

Nussbaum asserts that each capability has intrinsic value and importance. Capabilities are not simply individual characteristics, but a combination of internal capacities and external environmental, economic, and political conditions that enable active realization of potential. Nussbaum argues that delivering these capabilities to all persons is a necessary condition of social justice, and she considers the capabilities approach to be closely aligned with a human rights approach to social justice. What image of social justice comes to mind for you when you consider a capabilities approach? On page 6 we asked you to imagine what social work might look like from the perspective of a person experiencing homelessness, a child entering foster care, an undocumented person whose child is in need of health care, or a person seeking service from your practicum agency. Now we ask you to imagine what social justice might look like from these perspectives. If you were to start from one of these perspectives and imagine social justice through a capabilities approach, how might it guide the possibilities for action?

LINKING SOCIAL WORK AND SOCIAL JUSTICE

In the exercises and discussion above, we asked you to think about the mean-ings of social work and social justice and to consider common ground and dif-ferences. Our bias is that social work should have a middle name—social *justice* work. Social justice work favors a vision of social justice that goes beyond redis-tribution of resources. It addresses the societal arrangements and practices that reproduce resource inequalities and attends to the conditions and processes that enable realization of capabilities, rights, and opportunities. In framing social work as social justice work, we place our commitment to social justice in the center of our practice. This frame locates social justice not only as a goal of social work, but also as the core of the relationships and processes that consti-tute the practice of social work. It demands that we critically address the inter-play between everyday human struggles and the structural arrangements that variably compromise or support human agency, dignity, capabilities, and rights. And it pushes us to look and think beyond local and national borders to under-stand how practices of economic globalization and the logic of free-market neoliberalism link us into complex systems of privilege and inequality with con-sequences in people's everyday lives (Abramovitz, 2012; Deepak, 2011; Finn, Perry, & Karandikar, 2013; Pyles, 2009; Whitmore & Wilson, 2005).

Some might say that giving social work *justice* as a middle name is hardly necessary. After all, social justice is a core professional value. For more than a century social workers have dedicated themselves to improving life conditions for vulnerable and marginalized individuals and groups and advocating for just social policies. Social workers have been champions of civil rights and activists for human rights. As Lena Dominelli asserts, "promoting social justice and human development in an unequal world provides the *raison d'etre* of social work practice" (2002, p. 4). However, Dominelli and others have also pointed to social work's long history of implication in systems of containment, control, and paternalism, arguing persuasively that social work is not a chaste profession in terms of perpetuating injustices (Briskman, 2008; Dominelli, 2008; Gray et al., 2008; Margolin, 1997). As Donna Baines (2011, pp. 4–5) suggests, social justice needs to be front and center in social work practice because both micro- and macro-social relations can generate oppression, and people's everyday experi-ences are shaped by multiple oppressions. Thus, we cannot assume that by doing social work we are engaged in social justice work. The everyday struggle for social justice demands ongoing vigilance, resistance, and courage. It demands ongoing critical reflection on our practice as social workers.

THE CHALLENGES OF PRACTICING SOCIAL JUSTICE WORK

The Daunting Realities of Injustice

We do not need to look far to see that much injustice persists in the world. The Universal Declaration of Human Rights is nearly sixty-eight years old, yet violations of human rights and struggles to recognize and realize these rights continue on many fronts. Those struggles force us to ask what conditions of humanity are necessary for people to claim the most basic of human rights— "the right to have rights "(Arendt, 1973, p. 296). Let's consider the reach of injustice that compromises human rights for so many. Poverty is ubiquitous and economic inequality is growing both nationally and globally. The World Economic Forum's *Global Risk Report* named inequality as one of the top global risks in 2013 (Oxfam, 2013, p. 1). Oxfam (2013), an international confederation of organizations dedicated to fighting poverty, reports:

> Over the last thirty years inequality has grown dramatically in many countries. In the U.S. the share of national income going to the top 1% has doubled since 1980 from 10 to 20%. For the top 0.01% it has quadrupled to levels never seen before. At a global level, [for] the top 1% (60 million people) and particularly the even more select few in the top 0.01% (600,000 individuals—there are around 1200 billionaires in the world), the last thirty years has been an incredible feeding frenzy. (p. 1)

Extreme wealth and inequality have profound costs and consequences. Again, according to Oxfam, inequality is economically inefficient, politically corrosive, socially divisive, environmentally destructive, and fundamentally unethical. But it is not inevitable.

Struggles for women's rights continue around the world in the face of persistent gender inequality, oppression, and violence (Finn et al., 2013). The Convention on the Rights of the Child was adopted by the United Nations in 1989, but children throughout the world continue to be viewed as less than full citizens and are exploited in families, factories, sex trades, and armed conflict (Finn, Nybell, & Shook, 2010). The distance between the principles of children's rights and their translation into practice was recently exposed in the massive containment and removal of children from El Salvador, Guatemala, Honduras, and Mexico who arrived at the U.S. border seeking relief from the violence and poverty that shape their everyday lives (United Nations High Commissioner for Refugees, 2014).

The rights associated with citizenship and home are denied to forty-three million people—twenty million of them children—displaced by war and its social, political, economic, and environmental devastation (Poverty Program, 2016). Millions more are caught in the push and pull of labor migration in response to economic globalization (Ho & Loucky, 2012). How can we speak of universal human rights when more than 2.2 billion people live in poverty, 842 million suffer from chronic hunger, 800 million adults are illiterate, and 2.5 billion people lack access to basic sanitation (Bread for the World, 2013; Oxfam America, 2014; United Nations Development Programme, 2014)?

Injustice and inequality persist at the national level as well, as evidenced in the rates of child poverty, particularly among children of color; violence against women; erosion of social safety nets, and deep inequalities in the U.S. justice system. The American Civil Liberties Union (ACLU) and Human Rights Watch have taken the United States to task for having the world's highest incarceration rate, further marked by the disproportionate imprisonment of people of color; the systematic sexual abuse of women prisoners; and the growing overrepresentation of the poor and people diagnosed with serious mental illness being held in jails and prisons around the country (ACLU, 2014a, 2014b, 2014c; Human Rights Watch, 2004). And as Ezekiel Edwards, director of the ACLU Criminal Justice Law Reform Project, writes, the 2015 U.S. Department of Justice report on the Ferguson Police Department is not just an indictment of racially biased policing practices in one community, but an indictment of American policing in general, "from the way law enforcement polices communities of color like an occupying army to how the court system sees its policing victims as a way to balance the budget on the backs of its most vulnerable citizens" (Edwards, 2015).

Thinking and Acting Globally and Locally

Given this bleak picture of injustice locally, nationally, and globally, some writers, such as Pyles (2009), and organizations, such as the IFSW, the International Association of Schools of Social Work, and the International Council on Social Welfare (2012), have called for social work to join in solidarity with global social and environmental justice movements in order to actively engage our professed commitment to social justice. These three organizations have put forth a global social work agenda to promote social and economic equalities, honor human dignity and worth, work toward environmental sustainability, and strengthen recognition of the importance of human relationships (p. 838). Loretta Pyles urges social workers to seize opportunities for transnational social justice through more global approaches to community organizing:

> We live in an era in which the largest social movement in history—the global justice movement—is transpiring (Hawken, 2007). This movement, though somewhat decentralized, includes people working for justice in the areas of labor, the environment, food security, health, and many other aspects of human well-being. Workers; farmers; indigenous people; people of color; lesbian, gay, bisexual and transgender people; women; and countless others are organizing for change at the community, national, transnational, and global levels (Shepard & Hayduk, 2002). . . . Because times of crisis open the doors for transformation, organizers have a chance to creatively frame their issues in solidarity with global justice activists. (p. 91)

We support the spirit of the global social work agenda and Pyles's vision of the possibilities for community organizing practice in social work. Even more fundamentally, however, we ask you to probe the possibilities for social justice in the most intimate spaces of social work practice. Social justice work occurs in the halls of government and in the streets. It occurs in family homes, schools, women's shelters, food pantries, nursing homes, youth centers, clinics, and prison cells. Social justice work also takes place in our social service agencies and organizations. Sometimes it is welcomed. More often, social justice work is met with resistance from administrators, policy makers, and funders who operate from a market-driven mind-set and value efficiency over efficacy, risk management over relationship, and diagnosis over dialogue. This resistance can be daunting but not determining. How, individually and collectively, might we imagine, create, and expand the pursuit of social justice in and from those most local and intimate spaces of everyday lives to the structures and forces that shape them? How might we envision and practice a social work of resistance that both questions and offers a viable alternative to the current emphasis on neoliberal, market-based, medicalized, and privatized approaches to personal struggles and social problems? In the following chapters we will not only explore this vision of social justice work, but we will also grapple with on-the-ground pragmatics of translating the vision into reality from engagement to planning, action, evaluation, and transformation. In the challenges of social justice work lie its possibilities.

Challenging Our Internalized Ways of Thinking

In addition to expanding our perspectives on practice, social justice work calls for challenging our ways of thinking. We must examine ways we have been taught to think and critically engage with perspectives that disrupt our *certainties*—our assumptions about what is right, true, and good. Drawing insight from an indigenous social work perspective, we must take up the hard work of decolonizing our ways of knowing, being, and doing. The ideas behind Just Practice have been shaped by a diverse range of scholars and activists who have challenged our thinking about diversity, difference, oppression, discrimination, domination, and privilege. They have challenged us to examine the social construction of reality, that is, the ways we as human beings use our cultural capacities to give meaning to social experience. They pose questions about the relations of power, domination, and inequality that shape the way knowledge of the world is produced and about whose view counts. Moreover, they call on us not only to question the order of things in the world, but also to be active participants in social transformation toward a just world. In the following section we will examine some of these challenges to our internalized ways of knowing, being, and doing. In chapter 4 we will examine in greater depth how these scholars and activists have shaped the theoretical premises of the Just Practice framework.

DIFFERENCE, OPPRESSION, AND PRIVILEGE

Beyond Diversity

The practice of social justice work and the complexities inherent in meanings of social justice call on us to examine questions of difference, oppression, domination, and privilege. We will do so throughout this book, and we encourage readers to do so in their everyday lives. We question superficial, celebratory notions of human diversity and address the historical, political, and cultural processes through which differences and our ideas about difference are produced. In addressing the concept of cultural diversity specifically, Flavio Francisco Marsiglia and Stephen Kulis (2015) note that the way we approach diversity has very real consequences: "When difference is defined broadly to encompass every imaginable factor that distinguishes one person from another, there is a risk of diluting key differences, overlooking their societal implications, and overemphasizing less critical factors" (p. 33). As Beth Glover Reed and colleagues (1997) argue,

> Recognizing and building on people's differences is important and necessary, but not sufficient for a practice that has social justice as a primary goal. For social justice work both *difference* and *dominance* dimensions must be recognized and addressed. Developing and using individual and collective critical consciousness are primary tools for understanding differences, recognizing injustice, and beginning to envision a more just society. (p. 46)

We have to look not only at differences, but also at the ways in which differences are produced and their relationship to the production, maintenance, and justification of inequality. We are challenged to recognize and respect difference at the same time that we question how certain differences are given meaning and value. We need to work collectively to critically examine connections among forms of difference, relations of power, and practices of devaluation.

Difference

Let's think for a moment about the concept of *difference*. How do we categorize human difference? What are the differences that make a difference, so to speak? What meanings do we give to particular forms of difference in particular contexts? What meanings do we give to the categories through which social differences are named and marked? How do we construct images of and assumptions about the *other*—a person or group different from ourselves? Too often, the marking of difference also involves a devaluing of difference, as we have witnessed historically and continue to see today, for example, in the social construction of race, gender, or sexual orientation.

Author H. G. Wells (1911) presents a classic example of difference and devaluation in his short story "The Country of the Blind." Nuñez, an explorer and the story's protagonist, falls into an isolated mountain valley and is rescued by the valley's curious inhabitants. Once Nuñez realizes that all of the residents are blind and have no conception of sight, he muses, "in the country of the blind the one-eyed man is king." He assumes that, by virtue of his sight, he is superior to the valley's residents. The residents, in turn, find Nuñez unable to respond to the most basic rhythms and rules of their society. They see him as slow and childlike, and they interpret his nonsensical ramblings about this thing called sight as another sign of his unsound mind. Wells skillfully illustrates the ways in which our constructions and (mis)understandings of difference are linked to assumptions about worth, superiority, and inferiority and ways in which they inform relations of domination and subordination.

In our social work practice we are called upon to be constantly vigilant about the ways in which ahistorical understandings of diversity—or calls for appreciating the *sameness* of our underlying humanity—may prevent us from recognizing the ways in which unjust structural arrangements and histories of exclusion and oppression shape the meaning and power of difference. In writing about the shortcomings of traditional social work models in the Australasian and Pacific region, Ingrid Burkett and Catherine McDonald argue that these models "have a tendency to blind practitioners to the particularities of, for example, Australia's colonial past in which racism and intolerance for difference figure highly" (2005, p. 181). They contend that a political rhetoric of multiculturalism contributes to a superficial understanding of diversity that may constrict rather than expand honest exploration of difference. Might their critique be relevant for social work practice in the United States as well? What might be an example of a rhetoric of multiculturalism or sameness that masks complex dynamics of difference? We will revisit these themes as we elaborate the foundations and possibilities of social justice work in the following chapters.

Positionality

We construct human difference in terms of cultural practices, gender identity and expression, racial/ethnic identification, social class, citizenship, sexual orientation, ability status, age, livelihood, education, and other forms of identification. Our *positionality*, or location in the social world, is shaped in terms of these multiple identifications. Our positionality is thus multidimensional, and it is a determinant of our relative power in a given social context (Perry & Kim, 2013, p. 128). It configures the angle from which we gain our partial view of the world. For some, that is a position of relative privilege. Privilege refers to "the sum of unearned advantages of special group membership" (Marsiglia & Kulis, 2015, p. 23). For others, it is a position of subordination and oppression. As Bertha Capen Reynolds (1951) reminds us, it is the mission of social justice workers to align themselves with those who have experienced the world from positions of oppression and to work to challenge the language, practices, and conditions that reproduce and justify inequality and oppression. To do so we must recognize and learn from our own positionality, consider how we see and experience the world from our positioning in it, and open ourselves to learning about the world from the perspectives of those differently positioned. As Reed and colleagues (1997) contend,

> Although some people suffer a great deal more than others, positionality implies that each and every one of us, in our varied positions and identities as privileged and oppressed, are both implicated in and negatively affected by racism, sexism, heterosexism, homophobia, classism, and other oppressive dynamics. The recognition of positionality, and of one's partial and distorted knowledge, is crucial for individuals of both dominant and subordinate groups, or we all contribute to perpetuating oppression. (p. 59)

Positionality is an unfamiliar word in our vocabulary. We hope you will find it to be a useful concept in thinking about the ways in which our understanding and worldviews are shaped by our various locations in the social world.

Oppression

Oppression may be defined as the unjust use of power and authority by one group over another. It is a systemic form of domination that may entail the denial of dignity, rights, and access to resources; silencing of voice; or the use of direct forms of violence (Dominelli, 2008, p. 10; Young, 2011). According to Donna Baines (2011, p. 2), "oppression occurs when a person acts or a policy is enacted upon an individual (or group) because of their affiliation to a specific group." Marsiglia and Kulis (2015) address the interdependence of oppressor and oppressed. For oppression to exist there needs to be a group or individual being oppressed and an oppressor who benefits. They point to the key role of power relations in understanding how oppression shapes lives both historically and currently (pp. 36–37). Bob Mullaly (2010) describes oppression as a systematic process that is group based, non-accidental, and perpetrated by dominant groups, though not necessarily intentionally. It plays out through everyday activities in which people contribute to maintaining systems of inequality without seeing themselves or their actions as oppressive (Mullaly, 2010, p. 145).

Dorothy Van Soest and Betty Garcia (2003, p. 35) argue that there are common elements in all forms of oppression, including the following:

- Oppression bestows power and advantage on certain people who are regarded as the norm against whom others are judged (e.g., white, male, heterosexual).
- Oppression is maintained by ideologies of superiority or inferiority and by threat (and reality) of both individual and institutional forms of violence.
- Oppression is institutionalized in societal norms, laws, policies, and practices.
- Oppression works to maintain the invisibility of those who are oppressed.

As Van Soest and Garcia (2003, p. 32) describe, racism is one form of oppression that is deeply entrenched in the United States. Racism as defined by Bulhan (1985, p. 13; also cited in Van Soest & Garcia, p. 32) is the "generalization, institutionalization, and assignment of values to real or imaginary differences between people in order to justify a state of privilege, aggression, and/or violence." Racism works through the complex interplay of psychological, sociopolitical, economic, interpersonal, and institutional processes. Van Soest and Garcia argue that a critical awareness of racism is the foundation for learning about experiences of oppression given the primacy of racism in American life (2003, p. 33).

Oppression is a complex concept, difficult to fully grasp, especially by people born into positions of privilege. Peggy McIntosh (1995) points to the invisible hand of oppression when she states,

> As a white person, I realized I had been taught about racism as something that puts others at a disadvantage, but had been taught not to see one of its corollary aspects, white privilege, which puts me at an advantage. I think whites are carefully taught not to recognize white privilege, as males are taught not to recognize male privilege. (p. 76)

Margaret Anderson and Patricia Hill Collins (2015) challenge us to form a new frame of vision, in which we think of race, class, and gender as intersecting systems of power that shape both oppression and privilege. From this new angle of vision we may come to see things differently, question assumed truths, and recognize the partiality of our perspectives. Fundamentally, they argue, "challenging oppressive race, class, and gender relations in society requires reconstructing what we know so that we have some basis from which to change these damaging and dehumanizing systems of oppression" (p. 3).

Reflection Moment:
Iris Marion Young, Five Faces of Oppression

Feminist philosopher Iris Marion Young identifies "five faces of oppression" to distinguish among various ways in which oppression is manifest in people's everyday experience (2011, pp. 34–65). We summarize them here:

1. *Exploitation*: Steady process of the transfer of the results of the labor of one group to benefit another group. Denial of the social and economic value of one's paid and unpaid labor. Examples include unsafe working conditions, unfair wages, and the failure to recognize the labors of whole sectors of a society, such as women's work as caregivers.

2. *Marginalization*: Creation of second-class citizens by means of the social, political, and economic exclusion of people from full participation in society, often resulting in their being subjected to severe material deprivation.

3. *Powerlessness*: Denial of access to resources and of the right to participate in the decisions that affect one's life and lack of power or authority even in a mediated sense to have a meaningful voice in decisions.

4. *Cultural imperialism*: Imposition of the dominant group's meaning system and worldview onto another group such that the other group's meaning systems are rendered invisible and other, thus marking them as different and deviant.

5. *Violence*: Systematic violation, both physical and structural, leveled against members of oppressed groups; unprovoked attacks, threats, reigns of terror, humiliation, often accompanied by a high degree of tolerance or indifference on the part of the dominant society.

Where do you see examples of these forms of oppression in your community? What are some ways in which you could interrupt and challenge these forms of oppression?

Class Learning Activity:
Faces of Oppression (Young, 2011)

Class members will be provided with a brief news article addressing a contemporary social justice issue, such as the overrepresentation of people with mental illness in jails and prisons. racial disparities in health and access to health care, or criminalization of homelessness. Divide into five groups, each assigned to explore one of the faces of oppression. In the small group, consider the social work and social justice issues. How might this face of oppression be manifest here? What are one or more strategies that might be used to address this face of oppression? After a fifteen- to twenty-minute conversation, each small group will give the class a brief summary of its discussion. Close with a full group reflection on ways oppression is manifest in people's everyday lives and possibilities for interrupting and challenging them.

Discrimination

Discrimination is a constitutive part of systems of oppression. Discrimination refers to unequal treatment of people based on their membership in a particular group. It is the "expression of a system of social relations and beliefs"

(Marsiglia & Kulis, 2015, p. 48). Discrimination is manifest in use of derogatory language and labels; in denial of access to social, political, and economic resources and opportunities; in organizational and institutional practices that constrain members of some groups while privileging others; and in acts of direct violence. It may play out at both individual and institutional levels. In the United States, for example, racial discrimination has been linked to a host of negative health outcomes for people of color and to continued health disparities between white people and people of color (Marsiglia & Kulis, 2015, p. 127). As Van Soest and Garcia (2003) describe,

> Discrimination represents an action intended to have a "differential and/or harmful effect on members" of a group (Pincus, 2000, p. 31). It has been characterized as responses that create distance, separation, exclusion, and devaluation (Lott, 2002). Pincus (2000) suggests that individual and institutional discrimination represent behavioral and policy actions that are intended to have a harmful effect, whereas structural discrimination refers to policies and behaviors that may be neutral in intent yet have negative, harmful consequences on target groups. When discrimination is buttressed by social power it represents racism and oppression. When not backed by social power, biased behaviors represent individual discriminatory actions. (p. 33)

Domination

Domination refers to the exercise of power or control over another individual or group. Patricia Hill Collins (2000) uses the concept of a *matrix of domination* to describe the complex interplay of positionalities in relations of privilege and oppression. Writing from her positioning as a black feminist woman, Collins argues that we cannot think of difference, oppression, and domination in additive terms. Instead, she challenges us to critically examine *interlocking systems* of oppression, such as those of racism, classism, and sexism; their systematic silencing of other voices and ways of knowing the world; and their power in determining and (de)valuing difference:

> Additive models of oppression are firmly rooted in the either/or dichotomies of Eurocentric, masculinist thought. One must either be Black or white in such thought systems—persons of ambiguous racial and ethnic identity constantly battle with questions such as, "What are you, anyway?" This emphasis on quantification and categorization occurs in conjunction with the belief that either/or categories must be ranked. . . . Replacing additive models of oppression with interlocking ones creates possibilities for new paradigms. The significance

of seeing race, class, and gender as interlocking systems of oppression is that such an approach fosters a paradigmatic shift of thinking inclusively about other oppressions, such as age, sexual orientation, religion, and ethnicity. (p. 224)

Collins asks us to think in terms of the matrix of domination:

In addition to being structured along axes such as race, gender, and social class, the matrix of domination is structured on several levels. People experience and resist oppression on three levels: the level of personal biography; the group or community level of the cultural context created by race, class, and gender; and the systemic level of social institutions. Black feminist thought emphasizes all three levels as sites of domination and as potential sites of resistance. (p. 227)

Collins challenges us to recognize the critical perspectives of those who have experienced the world from positions of oppression and to engage in dialogue and action to challenge and change relations of power and domination that reproduce social injustice. Similarly, Van Soest and Garcia (2003, p. 37) note that, given the complexity of our positionalities, we may simultaneously be targets of oppression and bearers of privilege. Therefore, we need to make privilege, as well as oppression and domination, talkable subjects.

Privilege

The concept of *privilege* too often "goes without saying" in examination of oppression. However, as Bob Pease (2010) asserts, privilege goes hand in hand with oppression. In conferring a sense of rightful place and positioning of superiority upon members of dominant groups, privilege keeps people from recognizing the realities of oppression and their complicity therein. Privilege, like oppression, is reproduced at the individual, institutional, and cultural levels. It is embedded in and plays out through everyday interactions, professional knowledge and discourse, policies, laws, and institutional practices (Pease, 2010). Privilege is insidious in that it becomes normalized and taken for granted. Its benefits are attributed to personal capacity and wherewithal rather than to one's place within a complex web of inequality.

Privilege is not a binary concept. Multiple factors and forces intersect in the structuring of systems of privilege and oppression. As part of our positionalities we may experience varying degrees of both privilege and oppression. However, experiences of oppression may be more readily recognizable than the unspoken benefits of privilege. Bob Pease (2010, p. 173) cautions people with privilege to avoid a "race to innocence" in terms of claiming their experiences of oppression while ignoring the benefits of privilege. Privilege itself can be a barrier to empathy when those with privilege fail to recognize their role in systems and practice of oppression (Marsiglia & Kulis, 2015, pp. 23–24). Fundamental challenges of social justice work include recognizing the workings and benefits of privilege as they variably play out in our own lives, in our organizations, and in our society and taking responsibility for change through listening, dialogue, and allying with those who have been denied these unearned advantages.

As social justice workers it is important to be mindful of the ways in which issues of difference, diversity, oppression, and privilege converge in our own lived experience and to be open to learning about the experiences of others. In order to meaningfully engage in social justice work, we must start by both honoring difference and critically examining its production. We need to recognize our own positionalities in the social world and the fact that our worldviews are always partial and open to change. We must "learn how to learn" about other people, groups, and their experiences (Reed et al., 1997, p. 66).

Ongoing attention to questions of oppression and privilege is both difficult and important. It is through confrontation with systems of domination, oppression, and privilege and their multifaceted effects that we open possibilities for *liberation*, the collective process of becoming free of dehumanizing conditions (Marsiglia & Kulis, 2015, p. 43). The practice of social justice work is envisioned as a liberatory practice. It involves development of critical consciousness through ongoing reflection on our values, positionality, and action; attention to historical forces, structural arrangements, and root causes of oppression; an integrated approach to practice; honoring human dignity and advocating for human rights; creation of new forms of alliance and solidarity; and a willingness to be transformed in the process.

JUST PRACTICE FRAMEWORK: MEANING, CONTEXT, POWER, HISTORY, AND POSSIBILITY

We close this chapter with an introduction to the key concepts of the Just Practice framework. In chapters 2 through 4 we will explore the history, values, and theories that have shaped the social work profession and our thinking about social justice work. In chapters 5 through 8, we will develop the core processes of Just Practice and show how the concepts and processes coalesce into an integrated approach to social justice work.

The Just Practice framework emerged from practice, reflection, and long-term dialogue with social work students, practitioners, and educators regarding the meaning of social justice work and the challenges of linking thought and action. The process of integrating social work and social justice to build a coherent understanding of social justice work revolves around five key concepts and their interconnections: meaning, context, power, history, and possibility. These key concepts are the foundation of the Just Practice framework.

Take a minute to consider the following questions: How do we give *meaning* to the experiences and conditions that shape our lives? How do structures and relations of *power* shape people's lives and their choices for individual and collective action? How might *history* and a historical perspective help us grasp the interplay between sociopolitical structures and human agency, the ways in which struggles over meaning and power have played out, and the human consequences of those struggles? What are the *contexts* in which those experiences and conditions occur, and how might context limit or expand possibilities for action? How might an appreciation of those struggles help us claim a sense of possibility for transformative social work practice? Although we will expand on these key concepts throughout this book, we will briefly introduce each concept here to provide a foundation for future reflection.

Meaning

Meaning is often defined as the purpose or significance of something. Humans are cultural beings, and as such we are meaning makers. Our social location and experiences in the world shape how we make sense of the world. We come to new experiences with a history that influences our ways of making sense of our circumstances. Sometimes we share meaning with others based on commonalities of social experience and life circumstances. Often, however, we differ from others in how we come to understand ourselves, others, and the events and circumstances surrounding our lives. Think for a moment about the partiality of our knowledge, the difficulty we have in fully understanding another person's experience or this person's view of happenings and circumstances. For this very reason, in social work practice it is essential that we attempt to understand how others make sense of their world and the commonalities, tensions, and contradictions this creates as we compare their meanings with our own. At the same time we need to stay mindful of the partiality of our own understanding. Just Practice means grappling with the ways in which we individually and collectively make sense of our worlds. Meanings can both constrain us and create new possibilities for thought and action.

Searching for meaning requires reflexivity. Reflexivity is both a theoretical concept and a somewhat circular process in which we examine our self-perceptions in relation to the perceptions of others and the influence of social context, thereby trying to see the world from multiple perspectives (Gardner, 2012, p. 107; White, 2006). It is a foundational skill upon which to build the knowledge base and skills for social justice work. Reflexivity goes hand in hand with critical reflection, which Fook and Gardner (2007, p. 21) describe as a practice of "unsettling" and examining dominant, taken-for-granted assumptions about the social world. It leads to critical dialogue with others about these assumptions and how they shape individual and collective understanding of causes of individual and social problems and possible solutions. Critical dialogue "is the encounter between . . . [people] mediated by the world, in order to name the world" (Freire, 1974, p. 76). It is a process of engagement with others to develop, recreate, contest, and affirm meaning.

Context

Context is the background and set of circumstances and conditions that surround and influence particular events and situations. Social work's legacy, and what distinguishes it from other helping professions, is its fundamental view of individuals, groups, organizations, and communities within a larger framework of interactions. These considerations include cultural beliefs and assumptions about reality and social, political, and economic relationships. Context shapes meaning and helps us make sense of people, events, and circumstances. We know this only too well when we take something (person or life event) out of context and attempt to understand it devoid of its surroundings. If we ignore context, our interpretation of a situation is myopic. We miss the intricate connections, patterns, and dynamic relationships. In sum, context shapes what is seen as possible or not possible (Locke, Garrison, & Winship, 1998, p. 14).

We often think of social work practice in terms of interpersonal, familial, organizational, community, and sociopolitical contexts. Although, for analytic purposes, we may focus on one at a time, our practice plays out in these multiple and mutually influencing contexts, which are embedded in and further shaped by broader social, political, cultural, and economic logics and forces. Consider for a moment the context of agency-based social work practice. Social workers work in organizations situated in communities and neighborhoods. The characteristics of communities and neighborhoods differ. Some have an abundance of resources and helping networks and others have to make do with little but their own ingenuity. Communities and organizations have distinct cultures that include spoken and unspoken rules and established patterns of interaction. Organizations, for example, are generally funded by state, federal, or private sources, each of which mandates funding allocations, types of services, who can be served, and the rules and regulations for receiving services. As we expand our contextual horizons, we discover that state and federal policies are linked to services, and these also are embedded with assumptions about what constitutes a social problem and how it should be addressed. Think for a moment about how these various contexts influence and shape both the worker and the work.

Power

Numerous scholars have investigated the concept of *power* and proposed interpretations ranging from the abstract to the practical. Dennis Wrong (1995, p. 2) defines power as the "capacity of some persons to produce intended and foreseen effects on others." Some have viewed power from a standpoint of exclusion, domination, and repression. However, Mark Homan (2016) argues that "power is not dominance. Dominance is the way some people use power. Collaboration is the way other people use power. . . . You can use your power to work with others to improve a condition. You can use your power to create. Power is both energy and influence" (pp. 202–203). Bob Mullaly (2010) describes power as both possessive and relational; people can both have power and exercise it. Philosopher Michel Foucault sees power as intimately linked to knowledge:

> What gives power its hold, what makes it accepted, is quite simply the fact that it does not simply weigh like a force that says no, but that it runs through, and it produces things, it induces pleasure, it forms knowledge, it produces discourse; it must be considered as a productive network which runs through the entire social body much more than as a negative instance whose function is repression. (1979, p. 36)

Some theorists describe power in social, political, cultural, and psychological terms. Isaac Prilleltensky (2008) has put forth the idea of psycho-political power as a relational form of power that refers to one's ability to influence macro-level forces in order to meet personal or collective needs. French sociologist Pierre Bourdieu (1979/1984) writes about the importance of symbolic power, which he describes as the power to impose the principles of a construction of reality on others. It is the power to name another's experience. He argues that this is a key aspect of political power. In contrast, resistance is also a form of power, and it may be exercised in the claiming and naming of one's own experiences. Others have pointed to the power of language and rhetoric, the power of emotion, and the power of collective memory as sources for resistance and motive forces for action on the part of people in less powerful positions (Foucault, 1980; Gramsci, 1957/1987; Kelly & Sewell, 1988; Moch, 2009; Portelli, 1991).

Through a workshop they conducted in Tapalehui, Mexico, Janet Townsend and her colleagues learned that poor, rural Mexican women had something to say about power (Townsend, Zapata, Rowlands, Alberti, & Mercado, 1999). The women, activists in grassroots organizations, joined academic women to discuss women's power, roads to activism, and possibilities for transformative social practice. Drawing from the women's on-the-ground experience, the authors identified four forms of power: (1) power over, (2) power from within, (3) power with, and (4) power to do. They describe *power over* as institutional and personal forms and practices of oppression that often serve as poor women's first reference point in discussion of empowerment. As women get out of their houses and come together to share their struggles and hopes with other women, they begin to discover the *power from within*. They discover *power with* others as they organize to address the conditions that affect their lives. They articulate the *power to do* in concrete, material terms, such as making money, designing projects, and getting funding. Through close attention to accounts of lived experience, Townsend and colleagues were able to present a nuanced view of the ways in which poor rural women give meaning to and negotiate the relations of power that affect their lives.

What meaning does power have for you? Who or what has the power to affect your own or another's behavior? How is power created, produced, and legitimized, and what are the varied ways in which it can be used? In social work practice, how might power influence the nature of the relationships you form with those with whom you work and those for whom you work?

History

History may be defined as "a chronological record of significant events, as of the life or development of a people or institution, often including an explanation of or commentary on those events" (*American Heritage Dictionary*, 2000). History has also been characterized as a composition of discrete facts, blended with the impression of the historian, to paint a "picture of the past" (Jenkins, 1995, pp. 20–21). Italian social historian Alessandro Portelli (1991) describes history as an "invention in which reality supplies the raw material" (p. 2). It is a complex amalgam of events, memory, interpretation, elaboration, and reconstruction of meaning over time. This definition gets at the socially constructed, mutually constituted nature of knowledge (Gergen, 1999), which suggests that, to understand history, it is important to know the storyteller. Although the historian may be able to accurately report chronology (that is, when a specific event occurred), location, and the players involved, the event is storied through the layered nuance of the historian's perspective. History, then, is at best a partial perspective.

Clearly these definitions indicate that history is much more than an objective reporting of the facts. Historian Howard Zinn (2003, pp. 7–8) illustrates the inescapable ideological presence of the historian in *A People's History of the United States*. For example, he recounts the European "discovery" of the Americas and the heroizing of Christopher Columbus that continues to be reproduced in history texts read by school children. Buried in these romanticized versions of a conquest story is reference to the genocide of indigenous people. Zinn writes that genocide is not omitted entirely, but given little attention as if to suggest an acceptance of atrocities as a "necessary price to pay for progress" (p. 8). Zinn argues for a critical understanding of history that considers whose story is being told and whose story is silenced. He sees history's potential for uncovering the stories of those whose voices have been silenced and whose experiences have been omitted or trivialized. When we illuminate these "hidden episodes of the past" (p. 11) we can better understand the actions, resistance, and occasional victories of the oppressed and find possibilities for the future.

Paulo Freire (Moch, 2009, p. 97) understands history as a critical factor in shaping the work of justice-oriented social workers. He envisions ordinary people as active players in its creation. Freire contends that we are historical beings, meaning that, unlike other species, we are conscious of time and our location in time. History is a human creation and we are continually making history and being shaped by history:

> As I perceive history, it is not something that happens necessarily, but something that will be made, can be made, that one can make or refrain from making. I recognize, therefore, the importance of the role of the subjective in the process of making history or of being made by history. And this, then, gives me a critical optimism that has nothing to do with history marching on without men, without women, that considers history outside. No, history is not this. History is made by us, and as we make it, we are made and remade by it. (Moch, 2009, p. 97)

This idea that we are all makers of history opens up spaces of possibility and hope as people engage with life to create history and be created by history.

Possibility

The concept of *possibility* asks us to consider what is historically possible and to move beyond the past and the present to contemplate alternatives for the future. A sense of possibility enables us to look at what has been done, what can be done, and what can exist. It engages us in reflection and helps us formulate a vision of something different. It is a way to get unstuck from deterministic, fatalistic thinking of "that which has been will always be." As historian E. P. Thompson (1966) reminds us, it is possible for people to make something of themselves other than what history has made of them.

Possibility challenges us to think differently about practices, people, and programs. It draws attention to human *agency*, or the capacity to act in the world as intentional, meaning-making beings, whose actions are shaped and constrained, but never fully determined by life circumstances. Australian social work educators Anthony Kelly and Sandra Sewell (1988) write about "a trialectic logic," or a logic of possibility, as a key part of community building:

> The task of a trialectic logic is to grasp a sense of wholeness which emerges from at least three sets of possible relationships among factors. . . . [It] is out of the context of their interdependent relationships that new insights into social realities can emerge, and hence new ways to solve problems. (pp. 22–23)

As we expand our possibilities for thinking, we may change the way a problem is perceived and envision new possibilities for action. Kelly and Sewell exemplify the logic of possibility with the title of their book, *With Head, Heart and Hand*:

> Knowing, feeling and doing describe three human capacities, each one important in itself. No one of these, by itself and without addition of the other two, is enough. Even taken in pairs, no two are sufficient without the third:
>
> - *head and hand* (without *heart*) is a familiar combination in public life—the politician or public administrator whose feelings are blocked, or considered irrelevant;
> - *heart and hand* (without *head*) leads to impulsive and undisciplined action;
> - *head and heart* (without *hand*) leaves us stuck with knowledge and good intentions, but with no action direction to pursue.

To bring all three together, in a piece of work or in a relationship or to an understanding of our context, is to expand a social reality to at least three factors. *Head, heart and hand* points to a quality of wholeness—even if an attempt at wholeness—in life and work. (pp. 23–24)

It is this spirit of hope and sense of possibility that we wish to infuse in the thinking and practice of social justice work. Throughout the text we will share the stories of courage and inspiration from people who have confronted contradictions and worked to transform oppressive life circumstances into spaces of hope, places of possibility, and bases for critical and creative action.

Class Learning Activity: Show and Tell

Over the course of a semester, class members will be invited to take turns bringing in Show and Tell items to demonstrate what the key concepts of meaning, power, history, context, or possibility mean to them. Each class session will start or end with a brief (two-minute) Show and Tell presentation by one or more class members on one of the themes. Show and Tell might involve an item—such as a photo, a personal memento, a news article, or a piece of art. Or it might involve a performance, for example, telling a story, reciting a poem, or performing a song. It is a chance to be creative and to make personal connections to the themes of Just Practice.

Putting It All Together

Meaning, context, power, history, and possibility and the ways in which they interrelate provide a framework for critical analysis (see figure 1.1). They provoke us to question our assumptions about reality and make us look at how certain assumptions gain currency at certain moments in time. As a foundation for social-justice-oriented social work practice, these key concepts invite us to question received truths. We use these concepts as a point of departure and a framework for reflection. How are certain ideas accepted as true? How have those ideas changed over time? What evidence is brought to bear to support their truth claims? What goes without saying in our assumptions and actions? How do rather arbitrary ideas about what constitute correct social relationships and behaviors, values, and concepts come to be seen as natural and true?

Think for a moment about some of the arbitrary concepts that shape the way we think and act in the world—for example, concepts of time and money, the side of the road on which we drive, or the people we consider to be family.

Figure 1.1
Key concepts of Just Practice

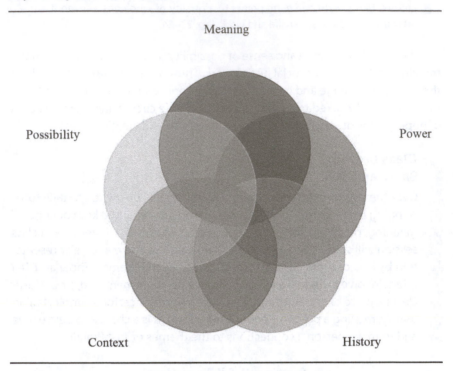

Over time, these arbitrary and variable concepts have become structured, insti-tutionalized, and rule bound in differing sociocultural contexts. They have become infused with meaning. We have been learning about and absorbing those meanings since infancy, just like the air we breathe. We have learned some of these rules so well that they seem natural, given, and absolutely true. They are so much a part of our experience that they go without saying. If we encounter someone who lives by a different set of rules, our response is often to think that those rules are wrong whereas ours are right. In other words, the deep meanings of these taken-for-granted certainties have become intertwined with our power of judgment and our valuing of good and bad or right and wrong.

Social justice work challenges us to examine the social construction of real-ity, that is, the ways we use our cultural capacities to give *meaning* to social experience. It guides us to look at the *context* of social problems and question the relations of *power*, domination, and inequality that shape the way knowl-edge of the world is produced and whose view counts. It forces us to recognize the importance of *history* and a historical perspective to provide a window into how definitions of social problems and the structuring and shaping of institutions and individuals are time specific and contextually embedded. Finally, social justice work opens the *possibility* for new ways of thinking about programs, policies, and practices. It helps us envision the people with whom we work and ourselves as active participants in transformation toward a just world.

Individual Learning Activity: Key Concepts Essay

In a three- to four-page essay, describe how you personally make sense of the five key concepts (meaning, power, history, context, and possibility). Provide an example of how you would apply these concepts in social work practice. Include an illustration that shows how you see the five key concepts and their interrelation. In the illustration, where would you locate yourself as social worker? Are there dimensions you would add to the framework? If so, describe them. Seth Quackenbush will describe how he made sense of these themes in the essay that follows.

SUMMARY

In this chapter we have examined the meanings of social work and social justice and the relationship between them. We have attempted to expand our thinking on the meaning of social work by looking beyond U.S. borders. We have argued that social justice work demands that we take seriously questions of difference, oppression, domination, and privilege. In so doing, we are challenged to probe the ways in which differences are produced and how they map onto values. We have introduced five key concepts that provide the foundation for the Just Practice framework, and we have offered opportunities for both action and reflection. In chapter 2 we will turn to questions of history.

ON REFLECTION

Just Practice: Making Sense of the Five Key Themes

Seth Quackenbush, MSW

Once every three or so weeks when I was a kid, I would ride a Trailways bus from my mom's place in Redmond, Oregon, across the high desert, through the Warm Springs Reservation, and over the Cascade Mountains to my dad's place outside of Portland to spend the weekend. My memories of these trips are vivid, and I remember being struck by the fact that the overall profile of passengers varied little from trip to trip.

In the back of the bus, a group of teenagers wearing Slayer or Iron Maiden t-shirts and ripped jeans would loudly vie for status, talking about whose ass they'd kicked or who was pregnant or how drunk they'd gotten last weekend; even as a kid, I could perceive the clanging insecurity under their veneer of toughness. There would be the young mom trying her damnedest to keep her baby quiet or toddler occupied; she'd always carry an air of desperation and twice as many bags as anyone else. A Vietnam vet, almost always in jeans and a camouflage jacket and sitting about a third of the way back, would hunch quietly against the continuous air vent spewing that chemically odiferous air. Finally, sitting in the first seat, there would be a lonely retiree or senior citizen intent on chatting it up with the driver during the duration of the three-and-a-half-hour journey. This was the profile with remarkable consistency.

The stories I overheard on these journeys offered a nerdy, awkward young me a look through a window into other people's lives, mostly folks who were poor or not far from it (my mom, whom I mostly lived with, landing in the latter category). In short, those trips branded me with an unsentimental, rugged compassion, and laid bare the deep currents of class that push beneath the surface of our world. Through those passengers, I'll explore my own conceptions of meaning, context, power, history, and possibility and how I hope to incorporate them into social work practice. Each of the five principles has both a personal and social component, which I will address in turn.

Faced with a reality that often appeared bleak on the surface, I came to appreciate the meaning fellow passengers drew from their circumstances. Through my eyes as a kid, the street-savvy teenagers at the back of the bus seemed, at first blush, rudderless, angry, and alone. And I imagine they often were, but that wasn't all; listening to them talk for awhile, I could discern their frustrations at home (the idea that things could and should be better there) and aspirations for the future, be they humble or grandiose, that fueled their days. We all need meaning like we need oxygen, and it is incumbent on me as a social worker to be explicitly aware of my own framework of meaning to maintain sincerity and passion and avoid burnout—and to know what that meaning is for those I work with so I can weave what I have to offer into that framework. Without that attunement, my work would be dissonant and ineffective.

When I think about context in relation to the bus, I think of the young mother and her child. Particularly in the state of vulnerability that is new parenthood, context is all-important. Multifaceted stressors that buffet young parents, from economic insecurity to the dissolution of traditional structures of familial and tribal support, are, at their root, problems of the rupture of the social context necessary for the optimal raising of children. As a social worker, paying attention to the context behind the problems people face seems crucial in determining the prospects for transformation or figuring out which elements of the context need to be addressed for transformation to take place.

The lonely senior citizen at the front of the bus illustrates how power, which I narrowly conceive here as economic in nature, plays itself out in America and increasingly in the rest of the world. The theme of many of the stories I heard seniors tell revolved around the status they had possessed when younger, working, and engaged with the life of society; these stories often seemed tinged with melancholy of something lost. And indeed I often felt that something was being lost in the relegation of the most experienced members of society to the margins once their economic output had ceased; their power, in the currency of wisdom, had been forsaken for power in the form of money. How, as social workers, do we help refocus the conception of power from the narrow confines of money to the more broad and nebulous, but ultimately far more enriching, products of cultural vitality such as the wisdom of old people?

The experience of emotionally or physically scarred Vietnam veterans is intimately intertwined with the idea of history when defined as one of the large-scale collective events that forever change the lives of people. Kennedy's hawk-ishness, Johnson and Nixon's obsession with credibility, and Kissinger's Machiavellian maneuvers all rippled into the deepest recesses of individuals and families throughout the United States and Southeast Asia. History, when ground into one's psyche through personal experience, ceases to be an abstract intellectual musing and becomes intimate and visceral. Social workers work in the wake of history and its effects, be they overt as in the case of a scarred Vietnam vet or subtle as in the legacy of the family molded by the effects of the Irish Potato Famine. They also work in the wake of the unrecorded history of endurance, resilience, and cooperation that characterizes the periods between the upheavals recorded in official histories, and they can draw on the well of strength these periods offer. To know the world in which they work, social workers need to stay consistently engaged with history, writ both large and small.

The bus itself, holding this unlikely, complex, eccentric collection of people barreling toward some future destination, symbolically embodies the idea of possibility through our shared needs as human beings. As a spindly, introverted kid sitting somewhere toward the middle of the bus, I was privy to the surprisingly candid and personal stories strangers would tell each other to pass the time or connect with another person. I remember many a time getting off the bus and being blown away by a moving story of human decency or enraged by some injustice someone had described facing at work or home (though, being shy, I never let on that I was intently listening). After hearing many such stories, something clicked, and cliché though it may sound, I realized that people need the same damn things at the end of the day, no matter how gruff their exterior or antisocial their presentation: dignity, relative stability, excitement, respect, and connection, to name a few. And, before I had ever heard of Crazy Horse or Angela Davis or Noam Chomsky or Franz Fanon, I asked the question "why can't we figure out a way to organize this world so it works for people?" That is a question about possibility, and it sits at the center of the vision of social work that most resonates with me.

QUESTIONS FOR DISCUSSION

1. What insight can be gained from an understanding of social work beyond U.S. borders?
2. What are some social justice issues affecting residents of your community? What understandings of social justice stem from these issues?
3. In what ways have you experienced the valuing and devaluing of difference? The unearned advantages of privilege?
4. What challenges does the Universal Declaration of Human Rights pose for social work? How will you bring human rights to bear in your social work practice?
5. How do you personally make sense of the key concepts of meaning, context, power, history, and possibility?

SUGGESTED READINGS

Freire, P. (1974). *Pedagogy of the oppressed.* New York: Seabury/Continuum. (Originally published in English in 1970)

Gil, D. (2013). *Confronting injustice and oppression: Concepts and strategies for social workers.* New York: Columbia University Press.

Marsiglia, F. F., & Kulis, S. (2015). *Diversity, oppression, and change* (2nd ed.). Chicago: Lyceum Books.

Mullaly, B. (2010). *Challenging oppression and confronting privilege* (2nd ed.). Oxford, UK: Oxford University Press.

Nussbaum. M. (2011). *Creating capabilities: The human development approach.* Cambridge, MA: Belknap Press.

Young, I. M. (2011). *Justice and the politics of difference.* Princeton, NJ: Princeton University Press.

Chapter 2

Looking Back

We are continually obliged to act in circles of habit based upon convictions which we no longer hold.

Jane Addams (1899)

History never really says goodbye. History says see you later.

Eduardo Galeano (Younge, 2013)

OVERVIEW

In chapter 2 we consider the importance of a historical perspective for the practice of social work today. We examine the roots of social work and explore the contexts, actors, institutions, and practices that shaped the emergence of social work as a profession. We pay particular attention to the roles of Charity Organization Societies and the Settlement House Movement in shaping social work in the United States. We explore some of the tensions and contradictions embedded in the profession's early history and trace their influences over time. We highlight key moments, challenges, and possibilities in social work's history so that we may learn from the past and use history as a tool for critical reflection on the present. We consider ways in which social work practice has both championed and jeopardized human dignity, rights, and well-being. We also point to the insights and actions that challenged the status quo and offered new ways for thinking about and engaging in practices of healing, support, and advocacy for change. We call attention to the contributions of legendary advocates and activists as well as those whose histories have been largely ignored. As we dislodge and examine embedded assumptions, we ask readers to probe the "circles of habit" that shape and constrain our present-day operating assumptions and practices (Addams, 1899).

CLAIMING A HISTORICAL PERSPECTIVE FOR SOCIAL WORK

Why Does History Matter?

Why look back? Why scrutinize our personal or familial history, revisit past trials and triumphs of the social work profession, or map out the evolution of a social problem? What can history teach us about today? What lessons can it offer to guide us to a just tomorrow? In this section, we present some reasons why a historical perspective is important to justice-oriented social work practice. We invite you to expand on these reasons.

History Serves as a Warning Device

A critical understanding of history can help us see where flawed assumptions, often reinforced by dominant ideologies about difference or about the nature of personal or social struggles, have led to ineffective and often harmful practices in the name of helping. Consider, for example, how beliefs about madness have led to inhumane treatments from bleeding, purging, and shackling to the infamous process of the lobotomy, an invasive procedure that "cured" mental illness by damaging the prefontal lobe of the brain. Critical hindsight regarding these practices and the beliefs that supported them can serve as a warning device that compels us to scrutinize present-day practices.

> **Class Learning Activity:**
> **"The Lobotomist"**
>
> As a class, view the PBS American Experience documentary entitled "The Lobotomist" (Goodman & Maggio, 2008). As described in the trailer to the film, "In the 1940s Dr. Walter Freeman gained fame for perfecting the lobotomy, then hailed as a miracle cure for the severely mentally ill. But within a few years, lobotomy was labeled one of the most barbaric mistakes of modern medicine" (http://www.pbs.org/wgbh/americanexperience/films/lobotomist). After you view the film, consider the following questions: How did prevailing understandings of mental illness inform ideas about treatment? What forms and relations of power seem to be in play here? How did the social and political context contribute to Freeman's success and the embrace of this form of intervention as a best practice? How might this account serve as a warning?

History Helps Us Create Linkages

A historical perspective helps us see patterns and threads of connection across time. For example, when we look back to the beginnings of the American welfare system dating to the colonial era, we discover deeply embedded ideas about who are considered the "worthy" and "unworthy" poor that persist in our welfare system today (Blau & Abramivtiz, 2010). We can further trace these connections to Elizabethan England and the Poor Laws put into force at the turn of the seventeenth century. Ideologies of racial superiority; patriarchal assumptions about marriage, family, and the proper roles of men and women; and political, economic, and religious beliefs regarding the nature and value of work have converged over time to inform moral judgments about who is deemed worthy or unworthy of support (Day & Schiele, 2012). Present-day debates about welfare are linked to this long and largely unexamined genealogy of beliefs about dependency, morality, and human worth (Fraser & Gordon, 1994). As we identify and examine these links to our past, we are better equipped to address how they might inform social justice work today.

History Permeates the Present

As we begin to trace the lineages of thought and practice, we find history always and everywhere intruding into the present. Within our arenas of social work practice, we are continually building on and responding to the ideas and practices that came before us. At times we may do this intentionally with a critical and appreciative eye to what we are building on and what we are challenging. Oftentimes, however, history permeates the present stealthily. It does so through what French sociologist Pierre Bourdieu (1984, p. 170) terms *habitus*—the implicit logic built into the operations of our organizations, the patterned ways of speaking about and relating to clients, and the everyday ways in which values and assumptions are translated into the action of social work. Jane Addams (1899), a legendary figure in U.S. social work history, refers to this simply as "circles of habit." History grooves our practice of the present with routines, with ways of being and doing through which we naturalize the arbitrary. When we take history seriously, we ask questions. How did we get here? What are we doing? Why are we doing it? Are there other possibilities?

History Helps Us Understand How Power Works

A historical perspective provides us the opportunity to see who has the power to name and frame what counts as a problem and to develop strategies and mobilize resources for action. For example, women reformers in the U.S. Children's Bureau used the combined power of systematic social investigation, social network mobilization, and public advocacy to document the widespread problems of maternal and infant mortality in early twentieth century America, to identify maternal and child health as a social issue, and to promote legislative action (Barker, 2003; Chepaitis, 1972). They engaged in *policy practice* by spearheading the passage of the first federal legislation for maternal and child health in the United States. The Promotion of the Welfare and Hygiene of Maternity and Infancy Act, more commonly known as the Sheppard-Towner Act, was passed in 1921. Their detractors, however, used the power of antifeminist and antisocialist rhetoric, coupled with the power of the American Medical Association, to eventually undermine their efforts (Lemons, 1969; Reisch & Andrews, 2001). A critical understanding of history can help us build our bases of power, frame the issues, anticipate sources of support and resistance, and respond effectively.

 A question to ponder: Why might the American Medical Association have opposed the Sheppard-Towner Act? Where might you turn to learn more?

History Inspires Us to Act

History reminds us that change is possible and that ordinary people, often in the face of tremendous adversity, can be powerful agents of change. It is through the stories of survivors and activists and the organizations and movements they have built and nurtured that we can find not only inspiration but also concrete lessons for practice. Clifford Beers (1904), a pioneer in advocating humane treatment of people with mental illness, used his personal experience of commitment to an asylum to launch a patient-centered mental hygiene movement at the turn of the twentieth century. Rose Schneiderman, a Polish-born Jewish immigrant to New York, translated her firsthand knowledge of poverty and gender oppression in the workplace into powerful advocacy as president of the New York Women's Trade Union League (Orleck, 2009). Ella Baker, one of the key architects of the U.S. Civil Rights Movement, believed that "strong people don't need strong leaders." Baker used her remarkable organizing skills, critical intellect, and belief in the power of participatory democracy not only to help build strong civil rights organizations such as the Southern Christian Leadership Conference, but also to nurture and empower grassroots leadership to sustain the movement on multiple fronts (Ransby, 2003; Ross, 2003).

History as a Tool of Inquiry

The importance of a historical perspective for social workers reaches beyond gaining an understanding of our professional roots. Reisch (1988b) claims that history is also a method, an essential tool of inquiry that "cultivates the development of a critical perspective—a problem posing approach" (p. 5). At all levels of social work practice, historical inquiry is a useful tool. It guides us in exploring meanings of individual and family histories; understanding organizational, community, and societal frames of reference; and considering the dynamic relationships among public policies, popular images, and people's everyday lives. Consider, for example, the stereotypic images and negative messages that have been constructed over time around the concept of welfare and those who receive welfare benefits. How are those images and messages mobilized and deployed in public policy debates? How, in turn, is the creation of public policy then informed by these images and messages rather than by understandings grounded in the complexities of people's everyday experiences with poverty, food insecurity, and lack of access to a living wage? How do those policies affect the everyday lives and life chances of people living in poverty (Kilty & Segal, 2006)? A historical perspective encourages us to unpack and examine the assumptions embedded in our present-day beliefs about personal and social problems, their causes, consequences, and solutions.

Marginalization of History in Social Work

Curiously, despite the importance of a historical perspective, an appreciation of history has been largely marginalized in U.S. social work. Social work scholar Michael Reisch (1988b) claims that we are an ahistorical culture. He contends that we have become accustomed to fragments of information, instead of what he refers to as the connective tissue, that is, themes that span time and integrate information across decades, centuries, and millennia. Too often we fail to question the fragments of information that we are presented with and consume each day. Instead, we accept them as the whole story. Context falls out along with history. Reisch (1993) comments,

> Unfortunately, our current cultural and political institutions perpetuate our ignorance of the past in order to sustain the perception of the present as a "given," and thereby limit the range of societal choices for the future. What makes this tendency so ominous is the absence of institutions of equal authority to critique the prevailing wisdom and present us with viable alternatives. Sadly, this is true for the field of social work as well. (p. 3)

In his critique of social work's neglect of history, Reisch (1988b) observes how the theoretical perspectives that guide social work practice rarely consider time as an essential factor. These include the person-in-environment and the ecosystems perspectives, two approaches to social work practice that we will discuss in chapter 4. History has been marginalized in social work education as well. For example, in the Council on Social Work Education standards for schools of social work, there is no requirement for competency in historical knowledge of social work and social justice. In short, historical consciousness has been effectively erased from the contemporary social work imagination. What might be the consequences of this erasure for current and future social workers? How might a loss of historical consciousness affect the future of social justice work? Whose interests are being served when we ignore certain aspects of our history?

Reflection Moment:
Thinking about the Multilayered Nature of Time

Carel Germain's (1994) work on family development provides an example of history as a tool of inquiry. Germain conceptualizes time in historical, social, and individual layers. *Historical time* refers to the effects of historic forces on groups of people born at particular points in time. *Individual time* reflects how people experience these circumstances, expressed through life stories. *Social time* merges the individual with the collective and intertwines development from one generation to the next. Social time supports the notion that parents and children develop simultaneously, thereby affecting one another's growth. These three conceptions of time help us think about human development in terms of synergistic processes instead of linear cause-and-effect patterns: "Human life is more aptly conceived as a moving spiral, manifesting predictable and unpredictable twists and turns along its track through physical and social environments" (Germain, 1994, p. 261).

Take a moment to think of your own family. What historic forces and social changes marked your development and that of your peers as children and as adolescents? Likewise, what historic forces and social changes affected your parents' generation? How did certain transitions you experienced affect and promote changes in other family members, and in turn, how did the transitions they experienced affect and change you? How might these notions about family and time inform your practice? In what other ways could you use historical inquiry to inform practice and policy decisions? How might reflection on the multilayered nature of time inform your thinking about your practicum site?

THE ROOTS OF SOCIAL WORK

Introduction

In this section we first take a look at social work's prehistory. We then turn to the emergence and development of the profession over the course of the twentieth century. We will respond to the following questions:

- Why did social work emerge when it did in U.S. history?
- What factors influenced its development?
- Historically, what has been the relationship between social work and social-justice-oriented practice?
- What key lessons can history teach us about social work's legacy of justice-oriented practice and people?

As you read this section consider questions of meaning, context, power, and possibility and how they bear on our representation of social work's history.

Social Work's Prehistory

Care for the Vulnerable

Practices of mutual aid, care for the vulnerable, and intervention into the lives of those variably labeled as different or deviant have much longer histories than the profession of social work. Likewise, those practices vary significantly across cultural as well as historical contexts. The profession of social work as we have come to know it in the United States has emerged from a complex genealogy of values, beliefs, and assumptions and a multilayered archaeology of institutions, policies, and practices built up over centuries (Foucault, 1969/1972, 1979; Rabinow, 1984). As the technological changes of the scientific revolution began to transform agrarian society throughout Europe, religious groups, rooted in Judeo-Christian traditions, were often the first responders to the growing ranks of the poor displaced from land and livelihood. Following the prevailing belief that problems of poverty were local responsibilities, church-based alms houses for the poor and "distressed" first appeared in Britain as early as the eleventh century. With the growth of textile production, workers began to join together to form guilds to protect their interests and provide mutual aid. However, with massive displacements of people due to both changes in production and widespread famine, practices of containment and control of the poor and dispossessed eclipsed those of charity and concern. By the mid-fourteenth century the number of alms houses and work houses was growing, and public laws began to be passed to classify and criminalize the poor (Blau & Abramovitz, 2010; Day & Schiele, 2012; Pound, 1986; Trattner, 1989).

Regulating the Poor

With dramatic changes in the organization of labor, including the shift to wage labor and a new understanding of workers as units of production, came a host of new laws to control labor. These changes were accompanied by equally dramatic shifts in religious ideology as the Protestant Reformation challenged the entrenched power of the Catholic Church. A new *work ethic* emerged, linking hard work and wealth accumulation as measures of one's closeness to God. Moral judgments about the poor were further infused with the power of religious conviction. Widespread poverty and growing unrest in England in the 1500s led to passage of further legislation to punish, classify, and contain the poor and to develop systems of taxation to pay for these practices. By the early seventeenth century, England had established a comprehensive set of poor laws addressing the categorization, placement, and differential treatment of the poor, children and adults alike, in work houses, poor houses, and prisons and as contracted labor (Day & Schiele, 2012; Hansan, 2011). This nascent system of welfare and the assumptions therein regarding the moral character of the poor, the need for local control of the poor, reliance on institutions of containment and control, and the belief that the poor should receive less than the lowest paid wage labor formed the basis of the welfare system in Colonial America as well (Blau & Abramovitz, 2010, pp. 239–241).

Welfare in Colonial America

The practices of social welfare—the concern for the well-being of the populace—have been fraught from the start with tensions between belonging and exclusion with regard to mutual aid and protection from others and *otherness* (Day & Schiele, 2012). Organized efforts to address the needs of the poor and vulnerable came with demands for conformity, containment, and control. This tension is clear in the formation of systems of indoor and outdoor relief for the poor practiced in Colonial America. Outdoor relief, which included the provision of basic resources such as food, clothing, and fuel that enabled the poor to stay in their homes, was provided to those who conformed to prevailing notions of worthy poor—generally whites who were elderly or disabled. Indoor relief, a curious euphemism for poor houses and workhouses, was the solution for those deemed less worthy, which encompassed any white person considered able-bodied, including children, those labeled as villains and vagabonds, and those who failed to conform to prevailing gender norms (Blau & Abramovitz, 2010; Trattner, 1989). Most fundamentally, the early welfare system was premised on assumptions of white superiority and racial exclusion. Native American people were subjected to systematic violence, displacement, and dispossession with regard for neither their welfare nor for the diverse systems and means of collective support developed and practiced within and among tribal groups. Enslaved blacks were denied the fundamental rights of personhood and any forms of aid. Arguably, their welfare was the responsibility of plantation owners. In reality, enslaved blacks forged individual and collective survival through clandestine efforts to preserve and protect kinship networks and through ongoing acts of subtle and overt resistance to oppressive conditions (Abramovitz, 1996). Free blacks were also excluded from the nascent welfare system, turning instead to development of self-help and mutual aid efforts to care for the poor, sick, and vulnerable and establishment of separate black churches as sources of material as well as spiritual support (Langhorne, 2000; Ross, 2003).

The Institutional Turn

In the early nineteenth century, America favored institutions as solutions for the problems of indigent and orphaned children; poor, sick, and criminal adults; and those deemed insane (Rothman, 2002). A veritable building boom of asylums, prisons, and poor houses was underway with both charitable organizations and states playing a role. Reformers, concerned by deplorable conditions in the growing number of asylums and by fears of the consequences of mixing children and adults, criminals and paupers, and the insane, called for separate institutions and better oversight. Activists such as Dorothea Dix drew attention to the inhumane conditions in asylums for the mentally ill and called for legislative reform (Brown, 1998).

By the mid-nineteenth century, some social reformers were coming to question the value of the institutional response to widespread social problems. They were also concerned with growing social unrest in response to economic inequality and poor labor conditions. Elite reformers began to develop new charitable organizations with a new social welfare strategy of home visits to better understand the living conditions and thus more systematically and assertively manage the lives of those living in poverty (Blau & Abramovitz, 2010). Their practice of *friendly visiting* would become a hallmark of early social work.

Rights, Claims, and Resistance

Social conditions of the mid-nineteenth century were also being shaped by powerful social movements demanding women's rights, labor rights, and racial justice. Abolitionists were challenging the institution and practices of slavery and making connections between the subjugation of blacks and other oppressed groups. For example, Frederick Douglass used editorials in his abolitionist newspaper *The North Star* to champion the rights of women and to critique the colonizing logic and classism of America's war against Mexico (Douglass, 1848a, 1848b). Sojourner Truth questioned the exclusion of women of color from the early suffrage movement by posing the question "Ain't I a woman?" (Mabee, 1995). Working-class people were forming trade unions to demand improved wages and working conditions and to protest growing economic inequality (Zinn, 2003).

As the United States emerged from the Civil War, the country experienced a volatile economy and the rapid expansion of large-scale industry. The Freedmen's Bureau, established by Congress in 1865 to provide material support, educational resources, legal aid, and land access to former slaves and poor whites in the South, marked a new direction in federal responsibility for social welfare (National Archives, n.d.). Funding for the Bureau was inadequate and short lived, however. Through the politics of Reconstruction and rise of the Ku Klux Klan as a social movement in the 1860s, new forms and practices of racialized violence and exclusion replaced the institution of slavery (Bryant, 2002). The doctrine of Social Darwinism and its claims regarding "survival of the fittest" proved to be a perfect ideological fit with the growth of monopoly capitalism (Blau & Abramovitz, 2010; Zinn, 2003). Labor organizations were growing more militant in response to entrenched inequality and exploitation, and capitalists were calling in support from the U.S. government in the form of military troops to suppress labor activism by any means necessary. It is in this crucible of social, economic, and political volatility that the new profession of social work took shape.

Reflection Moment:
Reformers and "Rescue" of Other People's Children

The early nineteenth century saw a proliferation of children's asylums, orphanages, and reform schools as solutions to growing problems of unsupervised children on the streets of the nation's rapidly developing urban centers. By midcentury, some reformers began to question the efficacy of this approach and the potential contagion effects of these institutions. Charles Loring Brace, the driving force behind the New York Children's Aid Society, led the charge for a new course of action—the "placing out" of children. His ingenious vision was to remove poor immigrant children from the squalor and dangers of urban life and to place them with rural farm families where he believed they would be inculcated in proper "American" values and an ethic of hard work. Brace (1872) argued:

Thus far, alms-houses and prisons have done little to affect evil. But a small part of our vagrant population can be shut up in our asylums, and judges and magistrates are reluctant to convict children so young and ignorant that they hardly seem able to distinguish good and evil. The class increases. Immigration is pouring in its multitude of foreigners, who leave these young outcasts everywhere abandoned in our midst.

These boys and girls, it should be remembered, will soon form the great lower class of our city. They will influence elections; they may shape the policy of the city; they will, assuredly, if unreclaimed, poison society all around them. They will help to form the great multitude of robbers, thieves, vagrants, and prostitutes who are now such a burden upon the law respecting community. (pp. 91–92)

Brace launched a bold initiative—taking groups of children by train to towns throughout the Midwest where they would be placed with rural farm families. This practice, which later came to be called the orphan train system, was promoted through elaborate marketing campaigns. It was, in effect, the nation's first foster care program. The charitable organizations and their benefactors supporting the effort were convinced by Brace and fellow reformers that the practice was a modern, efficient, and economical solution to the problem of troubled children and troubling youth on the streets of New York, Boston, and other urban industrial centers (Brace, 1872; Holloran, 1989). Between 1850 and 1929 nearly two hundred thousand children were shipped by train to fill the growing labor force needs of westward expansion. Few of these children were actually orphans. Many had parents who were simply unable to support or supervise them due to poverty and demands of work. For many children, contact with their families of origin was permanently severed.

During the same time period, another "solution" was promoted to address the "problem" of American Indian children. After the forced displacement and relocation of American Indian people to reservation lands, a new thrust in federal policy focusing on assimilation was launched. The boarding school system was designed to address what white leaders termed the Indian Problem. By 1890 there were over ten thousand children held in 140 federal boarding schools in the United States. Similar practices occurred with First Nations children across Canada, starting in 1883. Children were removed, often forcibly, from tribal culture, community, and family and placed in government- or church-run schools. They were systematically stripped of language and cultural ties so that they could then be filled, as if they were empty vessels, with values of individualism, hard work, and patriotic fervor, along with a continual message of cultural inferiority (Adams, 1995). As Commissioner of Indian Affairs, T. J. Morgan stated in 1889:

It is of prime importance that a fervent patriotism should be awakened in their minds. The stars and stripes should be a familiar object in every Indian school, national hymns should be sung, and patriotic selections be read and recited. They should be taught to look upon America as their home and upon the United States Government as their friend and benefactor. They should be made familiar with the lives of great and good men and women in American history, and be taught to feel a pride in all their great achievements. They should hear little or nothing of the "wrongs of the Indians" and the injustice of the white race. If their unhappy history is alluded to it should be to contrast it with the better future that is within their grasp. The new era that has come to the red men through the munificent scheme of education, devised for and offered to them, should be the means of awakening loyalty to the Government, gratitude to the nation, and hopefulness for themselves. (Morgan, 1889/1973, p. 434)

Routines were rigid, treatment brutal, and physical conditions deplorable. The practice of removal of Indian children to boarding schools came under critical scrutiny in the 1920s, but persisted in various forms over future decades (Adams, 1995; Szasz, 1974). The individual and collective trauma of the boarding school experience continues to reverberate through American Indian communities and families.

Consider the following questions:

- What do these accounts teach us about the importance of a histori-cal perspective?
- What relations of power and assumptions about difference are in play here? How are they shaping constructions of both problems and solutions?
- What lessons do you draw from these accounts to inform social work practice with children and families today?

To learn more about social justice action to address the history and conse-quences of boarding schools, visit the National Native American Boarding School Healing Coalition website (http://www.boardingschoolhealing.org). Importantly, the Canadian government has taken action toward healing and reparation. In 2006, class-action lawsuits on behalf of survivors resulted in the Indian Residential Schools Settlement Agreement. It called for inde-pendent investigation of the residential school history, payment to former students, support for the Aboriginal Health Foundation, commemoration of the residential school experience, and establishment of a Truth and Rec-onciliation Commission. In 2008 then Prime Minister Stephen Harper issued an official apology. The commission report, issued in 2015, found the board-ing school practice to be a form of cultural genocide (Truth and Reconcilia-tion Commission of Canada, 2015). In reporting on the Canadian government response, Julian Brave NoiseCat (2015) asks, "Why can't the U.S. do the same?"

THE EMERGENCE OF SOCIAL WORK

Pressures of Industrial Capitalism

Social work in the United States grew out of social turbulence around the turn of the twentieth century as the country experienced a period of tremendous change brought on by rapid industrialization, immigration, and urbanization (Day & Schiele, 2012). The expansion of industrial capitalism created new demands for laborers even as it concentrated wealth in the hands of a few (Zinn, 2003). Immigrants from Europe and China supplied the back-breaking labor demanded for industry and construction of a transcontinental railroad. At the same time, large numbers of people were leaving the rural South and seeking opportunities in the industrializing North. Workers not only faced dramatic changes in lifestyles, but they also faced fundamental changes in their relationship to work as they learned to incorporate new forms of workplace discipline and management into their lives. The nation's urban areas grew exponentially. Widespread poverty, the growth of slums, and the pressures for assimilating culturally different groups posed social, economic, and political challenges not only for big cities but for the country as a whole (Ehrenreich, 1985; Zinn, 2003).

> **Individual Learning Activity:**
> **Documenting Desperate Times**
>
> Jacob Riis (1890) was a photographer, police reporter, and author of *How the Other Half Lives*. His work chronicled tenement house life in New York City near the turn of the twentieth century and the human fallout of industrial capitalism, immigration, and urbanization. Riis used photographs to put a face on poverty for middle- and upper-class citizens and gave them indirect and therefore safe access to crowded housing conditions, disease, hunger, and the desperation of poor immigrants. On the one hand, Riis's photos provided a vivid window into the realities of late nineteenth century urban poverty. On the other hand, they tended to sensationalize poverty, reinforce notions of otherness, and perhaps contribute to negative beliefs about the moral character of the poor. Visit the Library of Congress website and view the gallery of Riis photos (http://www.loc.gov/pictures/item/2002710250). What strikes you about the photos? What do they suggest about the meanings of poverty? About the context of everyday life for poor and working-class immigrants in the late nineteenth century? About the power of the photographer's vision to construct a particular kind of story?

Organized Response

The profession of social work came about, at least in part, to mitigate the consequences of capitalism and to care for its casualties. Its professional foundation, goals, and ideology were profoundly shaped by the political and economic context and logic of industrial capitalism (Ehrenreich, 1985; Wenocur & Reisch, 1989). From the start, social workers were drawing on entrenched beliefs about the moral character of the poor and making distinctions between those deemed worthy or unworthy. They were also critically considering the impact of social conditions on people's lives and life chances and the need for structural as well as individual change. Two modes of intervention, Charity Organization

Societies (COS) and the Settlement House Movement (SHM), emerged in response to these conditions.

The COS tended to see social problems as the result of individual deficits, such as lack of moral character, training, discipline, or personal capacity. They sought to intervene through *scientific philanthropy*, that is, a systematic effort to identify personal struggles and shortcomings and provide proper support and guidance. The SHM, on the other hand, focused on conditions in the social environment that contributed to poverty and personal strife. The differences between them, however, were not so clear cut. Both approaches were experiments in human betterment that sought a systematic, scientific approach to their work, variably influenced by the emerging disciplines of psychology, sociology, psychiatry, and public health. The COS and SHM alike served as vehicles for young women, particularly educated white women, to enter the helping professions and engage in social investigation, education, and reform. Let's take a closer look at both.

Charity Organization Societies

Beginnings

Building on the model of the London Charity Organization Society founded in 1869, the COS movement was launched in the United States in 1877 by Samuel Humphreys Gurteen, a British minister who had been working in Canada before coming to Buffalo, New York, to do welfare work (Bartley, 2006). The movement emerged as a means to bring order to charitable efforts addressing problems of urban poverty. Proponents sought to apply methods of scientific investigation and business-like efficiency to charity work. Their practice of scientific charity blended moral judgment with provision of aid. The primary goal of charity was to "fix" the poor and make them independent, responsible, and self-reliant (Hansan, 2013).

A key feature of the movement was the use of friendly visitors, generally white women of relatively privileged backgrounds, who went to the homes of those seeking assistance to assess both their need and their worth. Their activities included teaching about the importance of thrift, household management, and basic nutrition. It was further believed that, through example, visitors would strengthen their clients' moral fiber. Linda Gordon (1988, pp. 61–64) describes how the COS defined pauperism as hereditary poverty "caused by loss of will, work ethic, thrift, responsibility, and honesty." The prevailing attitude of the COS is summarized in the popular motto: Help the worthy poor to help themselves (Finn, 2012, p. 112). John Ehrenreich (1985) uses an anecdote from a short story entitled "My Own People" by Anzia Yeziersha to illustrate the disconnect between COS goals and the realities of those living in poverty. The story's heroine, Hannah Breineh, cries out:

> [The friendly visitor] learns us how to cook oatmeal. By pictures and lectures she shows us how the poor people should live without meat, without milk, without butter, and without eggs. Always it's on the tip of my tongue to ask her, "You learned us to do without so much, why can't you yet learn us how to eat without eating?"(Ehrenreich, p. 39)

Expansion of the COS Movement

The COS movement expanded rapidly. Representatives of organizations for the oversight of charities and corrections were joining together to exchange ideas regarding scientific approaches to the social problems facing modern society. The National Conference on Charities and Corrections, convened for the first time in 1874, created a forum for addressing key social welfare topics of the day, including care of the insane, pauperism, children and delinquency, immigration, and the role of charities therein. By 1880 more than 125 representatives of public institutions and private charitable organizations were convening annually, and COS members played key roles in the conference. State boards of charity began to be established to ensure efficient oversight and management of systems of care, containment, and control (Bruno, 1948; Hansan, 2013).

The COS philosophy and practice were further developed by social work pioneers Edward Devine and Mary Richmond. They saw the need for professionalizing the practice of friendly visiting through formal training of caseworkers and developing systematic strategies for diagnosis and intervention in personal and social problems (Devine, 1919; Richmond, 1897, 1917). At the 1897 National Conference on Charities and Corrections, Richmond spoke to the need for training schools in what she termed applied philanthropy (Richmond, 1897). The New York School of Applied Philanthropy was started with a summer program in 1898. It shifted to a full academic year graduate program in 1904, under the leadership of Devine.

The Practice of Casework

Mary Richmond believed the project of human betterment was best carried out through the practice of casework focused on one individual or family at a time rather than through the work of social reform (Rasmussen, 2001). She reframed friendly visiting as the professional practice of social diagnosis and casework. Her groundbreaking text *Social Diagnosis* (1917) presented the casework method as a systematic approach to investigation that considers individual experience in a broader social and environmental context, thus foreshadowing the person-in-environment approach that remains central to social work today. Richmond saw the need to appreciate a person's history in order to get to the root cause of the problem. She envisioned social diagnosis as an interpretive as well as investigative process. Richmond was interested in potential sources of power available to clients via internal strengths, family resources, neighborhood and community networks, and formal agency supports (Social Welfare History Project, n.d.). She also infused her casework approach with a value stance that called for honoring the dignity, worth, and uniqueness of every human being, values still central to the practice of social work.

Exclusions

The COS and its casework approach focused on creating change within the confines of existing structural arrangements rather than challenging those arrangements (Reisch & Andrews, 2001). The COS offered little support to the growing numbers of African Americans who had migrated north. Although they investigated deplorable conditions in which African Americans were living, they directed little casework effort toward their amelioration (Gitterman & Germain, 2008, p. 13). Neither the friendly visitor nor the caseworker was equipped to address racism, discrimination, and their consequences and thus the organization "had little to offer this impoverished group" (Iglehart & Becerra, 2000, p. 99). African Americans drew on traditions of self-help and mutual aid to create systems of support and advocacy in their communities (Gitterman & Germain, 2008).

Settlement House Movement

Beginnings

The Settlement House concept can be traced to British social reformer John Ruskin, who put forth the novel idea of placing young college men in urban slums where they could learn firsthand about needs for reform and presumably use their privileged status as a resource to advocate for change (Davis, 1967). In 1884, a young clergyman named Samuel Barnett translated Ruskin's idea into action by opening a settlement house in East London, an area noted for its poverty and violence. This first settlement house was named Toynbee Hall, in memory of Arnold Toynbee, a young economic historian with a spiritual passion for social reform who had died at age thirty-one (Picht, 1916). The settlement house was a form of community center that created both space and opportunities for education, recreation, social support, and cultural engagement in poor urban slums. Settlement workers, generally well-educated young people moved by the spirit of the social gospel and possibilities of social reform, took up residence in urban neighborhoods where they could come to know their neighbors and their concerns and work in partnership to create community change (Addams, 1910, Davis, 1967).

Expansion of the SHM

The Settlement House idea soon traveled to the United States. The Neighborhood Guild, the first U.S. settlement, was founded by Stanton Coit in New York City in 1886. In 1889 Jane Addams and Ellen Gates Starr opened the door of Hull House in Chicago, which, thanks to the efforts of Addams and the remarkable cadre of women who lived and worked there, became the country's most well-known settlement house and the icon of the movement. By 1890 there were over four hundred settlement houses around the country, with the majority concentrated in major industrial centers (Harvard University Library [n.d.]). The movement spread across Canada as well. Evangelia Settlement, Canada's first settlement house, was opened in Toronto in 1902 by Sara Libby Carson and Mary Lawson Bell in collaboration with the Canadian Young Women's Christian Association (YWCA). Carson, who was from the United States, had previously helped establish a settlement house in New York City. Given her strong organizing and administrative skills, Carson was hired by the Presbyterian church to found or reorganize seven more settlement houses in Canada (Edwards & Gifford, 2003, p. 60). Canadian settlements tended to have more direct church affiliation, particularly Presbyterian and Methodist, than those in the United States (Lundy, 2011, p. 53).

The SHM both challenged and aligned with the COS approach. On the one hand, the SHM rejected the top-down charity model embraced by the COS. Settlement workers sought to work in partnership with community members to promote a spirit and practice of participatory democracy while attending to pressing problems of everyday life. They pioneered participatory approaches to the investigation of living and working conditions of the nation's urban slums. They used research as a tool to advocate for changes in public policies, programs, and practices. On the other hand, settlement house work was also informed and constrained by a white middle-class worldview, with settlement workers seeking to "enlighten" the poor and "Americanize" immigrants (Gitterman & Germain, 2008; Hounmenou, 2012; Park & Kemp, 2006).

Responding to Social Conditions

Settlement house workers embraced a more critical perspective than COS workers on the structural arrangements of political and economic power that contributed to conditions of poverty. Settlements supported labor unions and conducted social investigations that addressed issues such as child labor, unsafe working conditions, and wage inequality for women. In her descriptions of the settlement house, Jane Addams (1910) stated,

> It aims in a measure, to develop whatever of social life its neighborhood may afford, to focus and give form to that life, to bring to bear upon it the results of cultivation and training; but it receives in exchange for the music of isolated voices the volume and strength of the chorus. (p. 125)

The group work tradition in social work emerged from the SHM. Small groups were a context for action, a site for learning and practicing democracy, and an expression of the connection between the individual and the social (Schwartz, 1986). For this very reason Catheryne Cooke Gilman of the Northeast Neighborhood Settlement House in Minneapolis suggested that the motto of the settlements should be "Keep your fingers on the near things and eyes on the far things" (Chambers, 1963, p. 150). This motto expresses the twin emphases of group work: to pay attention simultaneously to individual need and social reform through the themes of shared control, shared power, and shared agenda (Schwartz, 1986).

Settlements served as bases for committed women to come together and forge strong personal and political relationships that sustained them in the work of community building and informed their collective approach to knowledge development, leadership, and advocacy (Addams, 1910; Deegan, 1988; Jabour, 2012). Together, these women advocated for woman suffrage, maternal and child health, industrial safety, juvenile justice, and consumer rights. Women such as Florence Kelley deftly combined skills in research and advocacy to seek social justice for the working classes. Kelley, a skilled researcher and powerful advocate for the rights of working women and children, used her investigations into working conditions not only to demand accountability of factory owners, but also to raise the consciousness of her sister settlement workers and engage them in legislative advocacy (Piott, 2006; Sklar, 2004).

Women in the SHM were also challenging the strictures of turn-of-century constructions of sexuality and gender identity as they forged new forms of family, developed close female friendships and intimate partnerships, and lived the connection of the personal and the political. For example, Jane Addams was in a committed relationship with Mary Rozet Smith, a major supporter of Hull House, for forty years. Deanna Morrow (2006, p. 9) writes,

> Jane Addams is frequently mentioned in social work textbooks as the "founding mother of social work." Yet seldom is she also noted to be a lesbian. It is time to recognize Addams for the whole person she was—activist, pacifist, feminist, author, and lesbian in a long-term committed relationship.

Exclusions

Settlement house work is noted for its vibrant engagement with community residents in efforts to change unjust social conditions. At the same time, settlement house workers could be blinkered by race and class privilege and influenced by implicit assumptions about difference and worth. Settlement house workers focused much of their energy on the needs of immigrant populations and neighborhoods of the nation's industrial centers. Despite their altruistic intentions, implicit moral judgments and notions of immigrants as other still filtered into their work (Park & Kemp, 2006). Anarchist and political activist Emma Goldman critiqued what she saw as the class-based biases of the SHM: "Teaching the poor to eat with a fork is all very well, but what good does it do if they have not the food?" (Ehrenreich & English, 2005, pp. 192–193). As Yoosun Park and Susan Kemp (2006) describe, settlement house workers and their fellow reformers at times reproduced notions of immigrant communities as both different and dependent, thereby reinforcing popular beliefs about immigrants as problems and justifying interventions to "educate, improve, and adjust immigrants to an American way of life" (p. 708).

The SHM also largely ignored the concerns of the growing numbers of black residents who had been migrating to industrial centers in the North since the late nineteenth century (Hounmenou, 2012). The prevailing assumption among white reformers seemed to be that African Americans would best be served through separate organizations of mutual aid and social support (Lasch-Quinn, 1993). The few settlement houses that were initially set up to serve black communities were generally under white leadership and were perceived more as agents of social control than social support. Institutional racism in the SHM is evident in the National Federation of Settlements' tradition of denying of membership to black settlement houses (Hase, 1994).

African Americans and the SHM

It was in this context that black club women took the lead in establishing settlement houses to support, educate, and empower African Americans facing everyday challenges of urban industrial life in the context of racial oppression. Charles Hounmenou (2012) argues that black settlement houses "were settings where a culture of resistance developed, with African American female activists and reformers in the vanguard role" (p. 647). Along with black churches, black settlement houses provided opportunities not only for education, recreation, and cultural enrichment, but also for activism and the development of oppositional consciousness (Carlton-LaNey, 2001; Hase, 1994; Hounmenou, 2012).

African American social workers and reformers engaged in both direct service and social change work as they confronted new forms of institutional and interpersonal racism. Their progressive efforts pushed against racialized assumptions and racist practices within the SHM. Some black women settlement house leaders, such as Lugenia Burns Hope of the Atlanta Neighborhood Union and Victoria Earle Matthews of New York's White Rose Mission, sought both to engage white reformers in constructive dialogue and to secure financial support and promote autonomous black leadership in social reform and community development work (Carlton-LaNey, 2001; Hase, 1994; Hounmenou, 2012). The White Rose Mission, for example, became one of the first settlements with an exclusively black leadership. The mission offered direct social services and education grounded in self-help principles and, importantly, a space where blacks could come together, talk about the oppressive conditions they faced, and build both oppositional consciousness and a base for collective action (Hounmenou, 2012).

Contributions of George and Birdye Haynes

Siblings George and Birdye Haynes were among the first African Americans to be professionally trained in social work. George graduated from the New York School of Philanthropy and Birdye from the Chicago School of Civics and Philanthropy during the Progressive Era, and both dedicated their careers to the cause of social justice. George was founder and first executive director of the National Urban League (NUL). As Iris Carlton-LaNey (1996, p. 32) describes, the

NUL was the most significant social service and action organization in the urban African American community in the United States. George Haynes also pioneered educational programs at Fisk University in Tennessee to prepare African American students to enter the social work profession. Birdye Haynes began her career in settlement house work and spent several years as the director of the Lincoln House settlement in New York, where she engaged in service delivery, program planning, advocacy, and community development. She navigated complex politics of sexism and racism as she grappled with building and sustaining her leadership role and advocating for the needs, dignity, and rights of community residents (Carlton-LaNey, 1996).

SOCIAL WORK IN THE TWENTIETH CENTURY: SNAPSHOTS OF HISTORY

We turn now to an overview of social work's development and maturation over the course of the twentieth century. We will highlight select historical moments and consider some of the forces influencing social work thought and practice. We ask readers to critically reflect on shifting notions regarding what constitute best practices, on the tensions between charity and justice, and on ways in which forms and mechanisms of oppression are incorporated and resisted.

Progressive Era

An Emerging Profession

Social work was emerging as a profession during the Progressive Era, a period of activism and reform spanning the years from 1890 to 1920 that emphasized the application of advancements of science, medicine, and technology to address social problems and promote human betterment (MacLeod, 1998). Schools of philanthropy, established initially in New York and Chicago, offered training in a scientific approach to social problems and began to formally define the profession. According to the bulletin of the New York School of Philanthropy:

> By social work is meant any form of persistent and deliberate efforts to improve living or working conditions in the community, or to relieve, diminish, or prevent distress whether due to weakness of character or to pressure of external circumstance. All such efforts may be seen as falling under the heads of charity, education, or justice, and the same action may sometimes appear as one or another according to the point of view. (Flexner, 1915, p. 584)

Both the COS and the SHM played influential roles in shaping the profession and its inherent tensions among charity, education, and justice. Edward T. Devine, who served as head of the New York COS and later directed the New York School of Philanthropy, firmly believed in the value of professional casework. Over time, however, he came to criticize the COS approach for its failure to attend to environmental conditions (Agnew, 2004). He teamed with prominent SHM leaders Lillian Wald and Florence Kelley to advocate for the establishment of the U.S. Children's Bureau, a federal agency that would oversee policy issues related to the well-being of children and youth. Former Hull House resident Julia Lathrop became the new bureau's first director and a tireless advocate for child welfare. Settlement house activists played key roles in a host of progressive efforts from the establishment of the first juvenile court to the founding of the National Consumers League and pioneering of mothers' pension programs. For example, Hull House resident Sophonisba Breckinridge helped establish the Chicago Women's Trade Union League and the Chicago chapter of the National Association for the Advancement of Colored People (NAACP). She founded the Immigrant's Protective League, served as vice president of the National American Women's Suffrage Association, and was instrumental in starting the School of Social Service Administration at the University of Chicago (Jabour, 2012). The work of these remarkable social workers spanned and linked local, state, federal, and international issues (Gitterman & Germain, 2008).

Reflection Moment: Discovering Lillian Wald

Robin Larrick Graham, MSW

I chose Lillian Wald as the subject of a research assignment for a course on the history of social work and social justice. At first, Wald's autobiographies and many of the early biographies I read about her discouraged a deep sense of intimacy, written as they were in the taut and wordy tradition of her time. Yet, I became increasingly drawn to her as I conducted my research. The rich stories of her social justice activism breathed life into the historical figure, and left an indelible impression on me. Her example of what it means to be an integrated practitioner fleshed out the core processes of engagement and teaching/learning that continue to influence the social worker I am becoming.

Born in the mid-1800s, Wald received training as a young girl to become a wife and mother—the only two vocations expected of her.

Desiring something more and disregarding society's narrow expectations, she later sought further education and became a nurse. Not long after Wald began working in her profession, a small girl led her to a tenement building on the Lower East Side of New York where her mother was hemorrhaging after giving birth. While on this journey to the ailing mother, Wald saw for herself the squalor and unsafe conditions in which people were living. This experience, described by Wald as a "baptism of fire" (1915, p. 7), brought to her an acute awareness of the plight of the poor and became the genesis of her idea to care for the ill in their homes and provide health education, a concept known today as public health nursing (Duffus, 1939). With the help of fellow nursing school friend Mary Brewster, Wald began the Visiting Nurse Service of New York and the Henry Street Settlement House where they committed to live in the neighborhood in which they served as nurses and identified socially with their neighbors (Wald, 1915), ideas similar in scope to those of Jane Addams, a personal friend of Wald.

In her capacity as neighbor, Wald sets for me an example of the type of engagement skills that I hope to emulate, entering the world of her participants as she did, not only metaphorically, but literally as well. Opening her own windows onto the streets of the Lower East Side, she bore witness to the lives being lived there, documenting and speaking out about the suffering her neighbors experienced. Wald exemplifies for me as well the art of the teaching-learning process. Though living in a time when women fought to be heard, and perhaps finding gratification in being viewed as an authority, Wald nevertheless recognized how necessary it is that "people learn to speak for themselves" and "that they become informed participants in the public debates" (Siegel, 1983, p 79).

Psychodynamic Influence

Throughout the early 1900s, social work practitioners were working hard to build the new profession. They were forming organizations, staking claims to a base of knowledge and skills, and expanding programs of professional study (Huff, 2006). Despite these efforts, the professional status of social work practice remained in question. In a 1915 speech to the National Conference of Charities and Corrections, Dr. Abraham Flexner posed the question "Is social work a profession?" His answer cast doubt on social work's professional status. He claimed that social work lacked both a systematic body of knowledge and theory and societal sanction to act in a particular sphere, characteristics he saw as fundamental to a profession (Flexner, 1915; National Association of Social Workers [NASW], 1977, p. 485; Specht & Courtney, 1994, p. 87). Flexner's pessimistic view fueled efforts to establish social work's credibility as a profession.

In response, social workers shifted their energies more toward person-changing approaches and diagnoses that informed those approaches. New thinking in medicine and the emerging fields of psychology and psychiatry was shaping their efforts. For example, Sigmund Freud's psychodynamic theories were coming into vogue and fundamentally reconfiguring ideas about the psychological nature of personhood, psychosexual development, and the inner world of psychic processes and their clinical applications (Browning & Cooper, 2004). In 1909 at Clark University, Freud gave a series of lectures on psychoanalysis that served as a springboard for popularizing his ideas. Within a short time his concepts of psychoanalysis were becoming part of popular culture, as evidenced in *Good Housekeeping* articles on the "diagnosis of dreams" and the human sexual instinct and its satisfaction (Browning & Cooper, 2004, p. 33; Macfarlane, 1915; McGerr, 2003, p. 261). They were readily embraced by social work as well.

Social Work and Eugenics

Along with interest in inner-psychic drives and processes there was a growing interest in scientific tests and measurements to identify and calibrate everything from intelligence to capacity for degeneracy and criminality (Gould, 1981). Couched in quasi-scientific language, these measures were embedded in and informed by ideologies of racial and class superiority and inferiority, thus linking ideas about difference to assumptions about deviance. This attention to the systematic investigation of markers of difference and deviance was closely aligned with growing support for eugenics in the Progressive Era. Eugenics, which refers to the science of improving hereditary qualities through controlled reproduction, was championed by statistician Francis Galton and others in the early twentieth century as a means to control or eliminate "undesirable" human traits and thus reduce traits believed to contribute to poverty, misery, or degeneracy.

As social work scholar Jeanne Anastas (2012) notes, both Jane Addams and Mary Richmond saw eugenics as a means to reduce poverty. Margaret Sanger, pioneer in development of contraception and champion of women's reproductive rights, also believed that limiting reproduction among the poor and those deemed less "fit" would contribute to overall societal betterment. In practice, the scientific logic of eugenics mapped onto racialized and class-based beliefs about difference, inferiority, deviance, and fitness for reproduction. Men and women of color, people labeled mentally or physically defective, and others such as immigrant groups and persons labeled as criminal or sexually deviant were targeted for practices of containment, sterilization, and exclusion (Stern, 2005).

For example, in California, social science researchers and social reformers at Whittier State School for delinquent youth believed delinquency to be caused by faulty genes and "feeblemindedness." They began using intelligence testing as a measure of delinquency. Disproportionate numbers of youth of color, primarily Mexican, Mexican American, and African American, were found to be feeble-minded and sent to state hospitals where they were routinely subjected to sterilization. Their "deficiencies" were more likely attributable to differences in language and literacy, as well as racist assumptions on the part of those determining their fate (Chavez-Garcia, 2007).

Racism and Mental Illness

Racist assumptions contorted the science regarding treatment of mental illness for people of color as well. For example, Vanessa Jackson (2003) details the treatment of African Americans in several state mental asylums at the turn of the twentieth century. She describes the use of hard physical labor as the primary "treatment" of incarcerated black men at the Alabama Insane Hospital. Nearby, at the Georgia Lunatic Asylum, Superintendent T. O. Powell reported alarming increases in rates of consumption and insanity among blacks since emancipation and attributed those increases to the loss of the "hygienic and structured lives" they had led under slavery (Jackson, 2003, p. 19).

Pemina Yellow Bird (n.d) offers a historical analysis of the Hiawatha Insane Asylum for Indians, built in Canton, South Dakota, at the turn of the twentieth century. The asylum, which operated for thirty-three years, served more as a prison than a place of care and healing. Indian people from across the country were sent there for many reasons, often unrelated to mental illness. Some suffered from physical illness; some were there for refusing to give up cultural traditions and spiritual practices. Some were committed for resisting the removal of their children to government-run boarding schools. Many were very young. All were defined as defective by virtue of their placement in the asylum and thus denied the right to procreate. For most, the asylum was a life sentence. We are left to critically reflect on the myriad ways in which practices of marginalization, exclusion, cultural imperialism, and violence in both structural and interpersonal forms shaped not only the broader social order of the Progressive Era, but also the practices of social service and social reform that emerged therein. Further, we must ask, what gets erased and obscured in naming this turn-of-century period the "Progressive" Era?

World War I and Its Aftermath

World War I marked a time of growing U.S. imperialism abroad and repression at home (Zinn, 2003). Early into the war, the women of Hull House took a stand for peace. Given their location in a neighborhood composed of European immigrants, they understood the ravages of war as these played out locally in the lives of their neighbors. During the fall of 1914, two feminist peace activists, Emmeline Pethick-Lawrence of England and Rosika Schwimmer of Hungary, visited Hull House to appeal to U.S. women to lead an international campaign for peace (Marchand, 1972, pp. 194–197). Hull House women responded by organizing the Women's Peace Congress in January 1915, attended by three thousand women. Jane Addams and Sophonisba Breckinridge cofounded the Woman's Peace Party (WPP) as a result of the Congress. The resolutions adopted at the Congress were novel at the time or would be novel at any time since: "The convention called for the limitation of armaments and the nationalization of their manufacture, organized opposition to militarism in the United States, education of youths in the ideals of peace, and removal of the economic causes of war" (Sullivan, 1993, p. 515). Representatives of the WPP traveled to The Netherlands in April 1915 to participate in the first international women's peace conference and draw up concrete proposals to bring an end to war. It was out of this gathering that the Women's International League for Peace and Freedom was formed, with Jane Addams serving as its first president.

Although war had been raging in Europe since 1914, President Woodrow Wilson did not come before Congress to request a declaration of war against Germany until April 1917. Montana representative Jeannette Rankin, the nation's first Congresswoman and a strong suffragist and pacifist who was trained at the New York School of Philanthropy, voted against war, stating, "You can no more win a war than you can win an earthquake" (Jeansonne & Luhrsson, 2006, p. 74). But imperialist forces prevailed. Once the United States entered the war, there was no tolerance for dissent. Those who questioned U.S. involvement were viewed as traitors. Speaking out against war became defined as an act of sedition, and there was widespread suppression of free speech. The silencing effects were powerfully felt (Punke, 2006; Zinn, 2003).

In the aftermath of war, casework methods and psychodynamic theories grew more popular whereas the more political voice of social work was countered with efforts to squelch it. Richmond's casework approach gained widespread acceptance when the Red Cross asked her to develop home services to address the trauma experienced by servicemen and their families (Figueira-McDonough, 2007, p. 119). Psychodynamic theory and the practice of psychiatric social work featured prominently in the curricula of schools of social work.

Following the war, dominant U.S. political sentiments and policies became more nativist and isolationist. Immigration policies grew more restrictive, requiring literacy tests and setting quotas to limit immigration from southern and eastern Europe and Asia (Koven and Gotske, 2010, pp. 131–133). Many of the advances made by labor organizations during the Progressive Era were retracted in the postwar era. Increasingly under corporate attack, union membership decreased (Ehrenreich, 1985, p. 45). This period also witnessed the first *Red scare* (fear of socialism and communist political ideology). Some of social work's most powerful voices for social justice and reform came under direct attack. Jane Addams's peace advocacy rendered her an enemy of the people in the eyes of the Daughters of the American Revolution (DAR). She, Lillian Wald, and others were labeled dangerous, undesirable citizens and subjected to investigation (Reisch & Andrews, 2001).

In 1922, a War Department librarian named Lucia Maxwell drafted a propaganda pamphlet claiming that a number of prominent feminists and social reformers were in fact subversive agitators. The pamphlet included a spider-web chart that accused several prominent women's organizations supporting feminist and pacifist causes such as the YWCA, the Women's Trade Union League, and the Women's International League for Peace and Freedom of subversive activities whose alleged main objective was to further the spread of international communism (Reisch & Andrews, 2001, p. 39). Women leaders with connections to the SHM were located at the center of the web (e.g., Jane Addams, Sophonisba Breckinridge, Florence Kelley, and Julia Lathrop). The pamphlet enjoyed wide circulation among powerful organizations with political clout, such as the American Medical Association and the DAR. Ultimately the pamphlet's message slowed the passage of legislative reforms, dampened social activism, and led social work further in the direction of professional casework. At the same time, many progressive social workers worked tirelessly to keep the reform impulse alive. Associations such as the National Consumers League, the Child Welfare League, the Children's Bureau, and the Women's Trade Union League continued to challenge unjust social conditions and advocate policy change (Jabour, 2012).

Hope in Hard Times? Social Work in the New Deal Era

Collapse

By the late 1920s signs of impending economic disaster were everywhere. Income inequality was growing, banks were failing, and unemployment rates and labor unrest were escalating (Zinn, 2003). By the time of the infamous stock market crash in October 1929, 40 percent of the country was not earning enough to cover basic expenses. People were growing angry and desperate, and strikes and riots spread across the country. Veterans and their families marched on Washington and set up a tent encampment—known as Hooverville—in front of the White House to demand attention to their rights to benefits. Soon there were hundreds of Hoovervilles across the country—shantytowns occupied by the homeless, unemployed, and dispossessed. By 1932, one of every four people formerly in the labor force was unemployed (Zinn, 2003). The economic situation was exacerbated by drought conditions that turned the middle of the country into a dust bowl. People of color were especially hard hit as they were often first to lose their jobs, and in the case of tenant farming, be evicted from their homes as well. Poverty rates skyrocketed, county poor funds were quickly drained, and state coffers could not make up the difference. A national response was needed.

Social Work and the New Deal

President Hoover was slow in responding, and when he did his initial legislation provided relief to corporations rather than the nation's growing numbers of poor and unemployed. Meanwhile, Franklin Roosevelt, then governor of New York, was turning to progressive social workers and reformers for help in addressing his state's pressing needs. In 1931 social worker Harry Hopkins, who had prior experience in charity organizations and settlement houses, with the American Red Cross, and in health and welfare administration, was selected to lead New York State's Temporary Emergency Relief Administration (Hopkins, 1999), which offered both direct relief and work programs to the state's unemployed.

Roosevelt appointed Frances Perkins as commissioner of the New York State Department of Labor and turned to her for guidance in navigating the labor crisis wrought by the Depression. Perkins came to the job with academic training in political science, sociology, and economics and practical experience as a Hull House resident and former director of the New York Consumer's League. She had also studied European welfare systems and sought to bring that knowledge to bear in the United States. As New York labor commissioner, Perkins advocated for a minimum wage, unemployment insurance, workplace safety, and restriction of child labor (Downey, 2009).

After Roosevelt assumed the presidency in 1933 he asked Hopkins to join him as head of the newly formed Federal Emergency Relief Administration (FERA) and Perkins to serve as secretary of labor, the first woman to serve in a cabinet position. Faced with crises of overwhelming proportions, Roosevelt encouraged his staff to "try something, try anything" to restore economic and social stability. Hopkins became the face of FERA, traveling the country, promoting work programs, and proclaiming his heartfelt desire to work himself out of his job. He went on to head first the Civil Works Administration and then the Works Progress Administration, which provided a wide range of government jobs for the nation's unemployed (Hopkins, 2011). Perkins kept the needs and rights of labor in the forefront, advocating for working people, with particular concern for the rights of working women. She played a key role in drafting New Deal legislation, proposing federal aid to states for unemployment relief, minimum wage and maximum hour laws, old age insurance, and an end to child labor (Social Welfare History Project, 2014).

Rank and File Movement

Many social workers and professional social work organizations actively supported Roosevelt's New Deal legislation to address widespread misery and regain a degree of economic stability. In fact, in 1934 Roosevelt claimed, "social workers and I have the same objectives in common—social justice for everyone" (Roosevelt, 1934; cited in Phillips, 1985, p. 267). There was also opposition on the part of those social workers who saw New Deal legislation as a means of stabilizing the capitalist system rather than challenging a system built on inequality and exploitation. For example, relief agency workers in New York began meeting to support one another, form study groups to learn about socialist and communist alternatives to capitalism, and confront their poor working conditions. These groups were the beginning of the Rank and File Movement. Rank and Filers recognized that they faced the same struggles affecting other workers and unemployed people around the country. They questioned the stance of professional social workers and organizations such as the American Association of Social Workers (AASW) who supported policies of adjustment to the economic and social crises rather than more radical change. They established their own newspaper, *Social Work Today,* and they began forming radical labor unions at relief agencies around the country (Leighninger & Knichmeyer, 1976). Rank and File numbers grew to exceed the membership of AASW by 1935.

Bertha Capen Reynolds (1992) became an active member of the Rank and File Movement. Reynolds had come to believe that the U.S. political economic system was an oligarchy of wealth. Those with economic power also held the political power and representation to control government. Reynolds called the poor "victims of economic disaster," a view that reframed beliefs about the causes of poverty from individual failings to structural deficits. In a telling quote, Reynolds speculated on what hindsight might reveal about the true nature of this period in U.S. history: "Was the meager provision for relief to be seen, in the long perspective of history, as just enough to keep alive without giving life—in reality as a preventive of really fundamental solutions?" (p. 77). Reynolds and other progressive social workers such as Mary van Kleeck positioned themselves as critics of New Deal social reforms for failing to address structural inequalities contributing to poverty.

Mary van Kleeck's Challenge

Former settlement house worker, social researcher, and social justice advocate Mary van Kleeck shared Reynolds's belief that government-supported relief programs such as the New Deal were a way to appease the masses so that the fundamental logic of the capitalist system could go undisrupted. Van Kleeck had dedicated much of her career to investigation and advocacy related to labor conditions and the plight of working people. At the start of the Depression she was director of the Department of Industrial Studies at the Russell Sage Foundation, where she honed her critical analysis of government, corporate, and labor relations. Van Kleeck accepted a position with the Federal Advisory Council of the U.S. Employment Service in 1933, but resigned after only one day on the job. The experience had solidified her critique of what she called the "three-cornered conflict of interest" among those who control the economic system; the government, which is allied with those who control the economy; and the workers struggling to have their rights recognized (Van Kleeck, 1991). In 1934, Van Kleeck presented her theory of conflicting interests and critique of government as an instrument of those with the most power to a largely receptive audience at the National Conference of Social Work. She remained a critic of the New Deal programs, arguing that they merely served to suppress revolt and squelch the possibility of more fundamental change in social institutions. Van

Kleeck remained dedicated to workers' rights and to the defense of human rights (Five College Archives and Manuscript Collections [n.d.]).

Social Security Act

The year 1935 saw the passage of the federal Social Security Act, which set up a federal system of responsibility for the well-being of the citizenry. The act included provisions for old age and survivors' insurance; unemployment compensation; public assistance programs for children, the elderly, and the blind; and maternal and child health and welfare. The Wagner Act, also passed in 1935, protected workers' rights to organize, and the Federal Housing Act (1937) provided federal funding for low-income housing. On the one hand, the package of social welfare legislation was far reaching in terms of recognizing federal government responsibility for people's social and economic well-being. On the other hand, the legislation failed to address long-standing structural barriers and served to reproduce embedded exclusions and inequalities along lines of race, class, gender, and ability status (Neubeck & Cazenave, 2001). Many social workers hailed the act as landmark legislation that established entitlement to certain social welfare benefits and protection. Others, however, critiqued it for failing to address underlying inequalities.

Historian Howard Zinn acknowledged both successes and shortcomings of New Deal programs and noted: "When the New Deal was over capitalism remained intact" (2003, p. 403). As we have seen, some social workers played key roles in developing and implementing New Deal policies while others were critical of those policies. Try to locate yourself in these debates. What position might you have taken as a social worker circa 1935? What policies would you have advocated? On what grounds?

Social Work at Midcentury

Diagnostic versus Functional Approaches

Social work of the late 1930s was characterized by increased professionalization, growing attention to models and theories of individual and family casework intervention, and expansion into the realm of public social services (Husock, 1993). More schools of social work were being established around the country. With the passage of New Deal social legislation, social workers expanded their professional domain into planning, management, and service delivery in public assistance programs as well as in private agencies (Howard, 1943). Although there was a revitalized interest in group and community work, an individualist ideology continued to dominate practice. However, within the practice of social casework itself, differing perspectives emerged. Proponents of the Freudian-influenced *diagnostic* approach, which had dominated practice thinking for two decades, were being challenged by the rise of the functional approach to social work practice.

Social workers Jesse Taft and Virginia Robinson of the University of Pennsylvania began to question the diagnostic approach, which framed social workers as experts and clients as in need of long-term treatment for psychic stress. (The contributions of Taft and Robinson are beyond the scope of this chapter. We refer readers to entries on Taft and Robinson at the Social Welfare History Project website [http://www.socialwelfarehistory.com].) Taft and Robinson were colleagues and life partners engaged in cutting-edge thinking and practice related to social casework and child and family services. They turned to the work of Otto Rank, a Freudian-trained psychoanalyst who took a more optimistic view of the human condition. Rank saw people as purposeful, growth-oriented, and able to seek out guidance as needed to address life's challenges. He proposed a time-limited therapy that encouraged clients to make conscious use of will (Dunlap, 2011).

Taft and Robinson embraced Rank's principles and reframed social work as a practice grounded in mutuality—done *with* rather than *to* clients (Howe, 1994, p. 20; Lloyd, 2008; Reisch, 2005). Their functional approach was characterized by a view of clients as self-determining and of the social work relationship as a helping process that releases the client's power for choice (NASW, 1977, p. 1554). According to proponents of the functional approach, the purpose of social work is

> the release of human power in individuals, groups, and communities for personal fulfillment and social good and the release of social power for the creation of the kind of society, social policy, and social institutions that make self-realization most possible for all men. (NASW, 1977, p. 1281)

Although the diagnostic approach remained a powerful influence, new theoretical space opened by the functional school was shaping the future of the profession. Bertha Capen Reynolds was one who supported this new direction. She too had become disillusioned with the psychodynamic emphasis in the profession. She found the functional approach to be in line with her thinking about the role of social service agencies, the collaborative nature of the helping process, and the capacities of clients as agents. Reynolds set forth the *five simple principles* she believed necessary to the practice of social work (1963, pp. 173–175):

1. Social work exists to serve people in need. If it serves other classes, it becomes too dishonest.

2. Social work exists to help people help themselves ... we should not be alarmed when they do so by organized means, such as client or tenant or labor groups.

3. The underlying nature of social work is that it operates by communication, listening, and sharing experience.

4. Social work has to find its place among other social movements for human betterment.

5. Social workers as citizens cannot consider themselves superior to their clients as if they do not have the same problems.

Reynolds also believed that this new thinking about the social-worker-client relationship was aligned with a broader critique of the existing political and economic system and the interests of social reform. She began to incorporate a Marxist critique of social conditions into her theory and practice. In so doing, she brought questions of power to bear forty years before the concept of *empowerment* was explicitly part of social work's vocabulary. By the late 1930s, however, her radical turn was the subject of sharp critique by her peers. In 1938 she was forced to resign from her faculty position at Smith College School of Social Work, where she had served for twenty years (Reisch & Andrews, 2001).

Debates between the functional and diagnostic approaches dominated much of social work's theoretical terrain into the 1940s. One of the foremost thinkers of the diagnostic school was Gordon Hamilton. As a casework practitioner and educator, she was an influential voice in social casework theory. Hamilton recognized Freud's contributions to casework and the power of psychodynamic processes. At the same time, she argued for social workers to retain a commitment to poor families and to the ways in which social and economic factors contribute to personal distress (NASW, 1977, p. 518). Hamilton was a strong advocate for linking social casework, social welfare policy, and social action. She described social work as a helping process that required an understanding of both the objective situation the client faced and the client's subjective interpretation of the situation. Her 1940 book *Theory and Practice of*

Social Casework (Hamilton, 1940) became a definitive text in articulating this broader diagnostic approach.

During this era, social group work and community organization became more broadly recognized as methods of social work practice (Alvarez, 2003). Social workers engaged in the development of theories and methods of group work as a means of effecting individual and interpersonal change. With the growth of human service bureaucracies, the 1940s also saw a growing interest in community organization to tackle larger scale or *macro* issues. The field and practice of social planning became a more recognized component of social work practice (Johnson & Yanca, 2007, pp. 22–24). The social work profession came to identify itself in terms of three key aspects of practice—casework, group work, and community organization—and to prepare practitioners with expertise in a particular field. However, the bulk of practice efforts continued to be directed toward person-changing interventions.

World War II and Social Work

World War II brought new challenges and opportunities for social work. As sixteen million men and women joined the armed forces, family life across the country experienced disruption (Mintz, 2004). A host of social service organizations developed programs in coordination with the U.S. military while others expanded child and family social services in response to wartime needs and demands (Kempshall, 1943).

Social workers were also directly implicated in facilitating injustices of wartime through their active participation in processes of internment of more than 120,000 Japanese Americans (Park, 2008). As Yoosun Park describes, "social workers vetted, registered, counseled, and tagged all Nikkei families, along with their accompanying luggage, at the many Wartime Civil Control Administration (WCCA) stations" (p. 448). They also staffed relocation camp offices and resettlement centers around the country where Nikkei were sent from the camps. Although some social workers registered disapproval and called for treating those in the camps with dignity, there was no organized resistance to the programs and practices of internment. Further, Park's careful review of reports and records reveals ways in which social work practice was powerfully influenced by workers' assumptions about Japanese Americans as other. Park concludes, "Good intentions notwithstanding, in its unwillingness to take a resolute stand against the removal and incarceration of the Nikkei and in carrying out these 'willingly accepted' tasks (DeWitt, 1942, p. 1) social work enacted and thus legitimized the bigoted policies of racial profiling en masse" (p. 474).

> **Reflection Moment:**
> **Densho: Sites of Shame**
>
> Visit the Densho: Sites of Shame website (www.densho.org/sitesofshame).
> Take time to learn more about the incarceration of Japanese Americans
> during World War Two and to reflect on the role of social work in this mass
> injustice. What social, political, and ideological conditions were necessary
> for this policy to be crafted and enacted? Why does an understanding of
> this history matter for social work practice today?

Postwar Social Work: Theory and Activism

In the post-World-War-II years, the social work profession was expanding its
influence into the fields of health and mental health, with continued emphasis
on casework. Professional social work organizations were also becoming solidified. The Council on Social Work Education was founded in 1952 from the
merger of two predecessor organizations. In 1955, seven professional groups
came together to form the NASW. These two organizations are the predomi-
nant social work professional organizations in the United States today. Social
work scholars were also seeking synthesis between the diagnostic and
functional approaches to practice. They explored the underpinnings of the
social-worker-client relationship and the principles, such as acceptance, individualization, promotion of client self-determination, and confidentiality, that
would promote growth and change (Biestek, 1957). Their work in articulating
principles of social work practice continues to guide the profession today.

In 1957, Helen Harris Perlman proposed a new conceptualization of social
casework that brought together the functional and diagnostic approaches. She
envisioned casework as a problem-solving process that reframed diagnosis as
a broader process of assessment and incorporated the functionalists' assumptions about the potential for human growth and competence. Her more encompassing approach not only had implications for social casework, but it also
provided a theoretical link among the multiple approaches to social work practice from casework to group work and community organization (Johnson &
Yanca, 2007, p. 24; Perlman, 1957). These theories, however, offered little in
terms of understanding the structural arrangements of society and the working of forms and mechanism of oppression therein.

At the same time, social workers like Whitney Young were turning their
attention to pressing human rights issues. Young earned his MSW in 1947 and
soon after began his career with the National Urban League as president of the
Omaha, Nebraska, chapter, where he challenged entrenched employment dis-

crimination against black workers. In 1954, the year the U.S. Supreme Court found school segregation to be unconstitutional, Young was named dean of Social Work at Atlanta University. As dean, Young expanded the school's base of support, and he backed alumni in a boycott of the Georgia Conference of Social Welfare in response to the organization's poor track record in hiring African Americans for decent jobs (Bevel, 2013, p. 159)

Social Work and Native American Families in the Postwar Era

Social work practice with American Indian families in the 1950s provided further evidence of ways in which racism had infiltrated the profession. Native Americans had suffered the historical and ongoing effects of public policies directed at their removal from traditional lands, forced relocation, and containment, as well as the termination of treaty rights and tribal sovereignty (Pevar, 2002). As discussed previously, the boarding school system played a key role in disrupting tribal integrity. In 1958, a new solution to the so-called Indian problem was conceived. Through a partnership between the Bureau of Indian Affairs and the Child Welfare League of America—the nation's flagship child welfare organization—the Indian Adoption Project (IAP) was conceived. The project was designed to "provide adoptive placement for American Indian Children whose parents were deemed unable to provide a 'suitable' home for them" (Mannes, 1995, p. 267). States received federal funds to remove Indian children from "neglectful" parents; the majority of the children were placed in non-Indian homes (Schiele, 2011). As anthropologist Laura Briggs described, the IAP intentionally sought to place Native children with white families "far from the reservation," as indicated by the revealing title of its outcome study (Briggs, 2012). As a demonstration project, the IAP set the stage for other child-placing agencies and services to follow suit (Briggs, 2012). Thus, the time-worn practice of breaking up Native American families continued under the direction of social workers and in the name of the best interest of Native children.

Social Work and the Second Red Scare

Those social workers who had held to progressive values and practices found themselves under attack in the 1950s as the second Red scare spread fear of communism across the country. Wisconsin Senator Joseph McCarthy led the anticommunist charge, sanctioned by passage of the Internal Security Act that authorized the president to declare an internal security emergency, permitting detention without trial of suspected dissidents and setting up a system of detention centers to hold those so detained (Ehrenreich, 1985). As Andrews and Reisch (1997) describe: "Thousands of workers lost their jobs and millions of others curtailed their political activities out of fear of being labeled a communist or a communist sympathizer" (p. 31).

McCarthyism, as it came to be called, had a profound effect on silencing the social action voice of social work. For example, a Department of the Army publication entitled *How to Spot a Communist* provided a list of words purported to be commonly used by communists and sympathizers such as progressive, colonialism, exploitation, civil rights, discrimination, and integrative thinking. (The text of the pamphlet, published in 1955, can be accessed at Northern Illinois University, Rosemary Feurer Labor Links [http://http://www.niu.edu/~rfeurer/labor/PDF%20Files/How%20to%20Spot%20a%20Communist.pdf].) Articles on how to spot a communist appeared in popular magazines as well. Those engaged in critical debates of the day risked being labeled Red. Many federal- and state-funded institutions and programs required their employees to sign loyalty oaths. Many social workers were fearful of taking a stand and distanced themselves from critical political issues. Those who did take a stand often paid a price.

Bertha Capen Reynolds spoke out, arguing that McCarthyism could be defeated if ordinary people would demand true democracy (Andrews & Reisch, 1997, p. 36). She found herself increasingly marginalized within the social work community. Jacob Fisher, a colleague of Reynolds from the Rank and File Movement, was similarly shunned by colleagues and coworkers. In 1954 his employers at the Social Security Administration charged him with being a security risk on the basis of his group affiliations and activities. Years later, through the Freedom of Information Act, Fisher learned that some of his social work friends and colleagues had informed on him (Andrews & Reisch, 1997, p. 36).

The silencing and censorship extended its reach to seemingly apolitical social work. For example, Charlotte Towle, a faculty member at the University of Chicago School of Social Service, had been working to craft a unified theory of social work committed to client-centered practice. Her most well-known book, *Common Human Needs*, was written as a training guide for the new cadre of public assistance workers employed as a result of expansion of the public welfare system. In the book Towle articulated the connection between an understanding of human behavior and the administration of social welfare programs and argued that psychological needs were connected to social forces (University of Chicago School of Social Service Administration, 2008). Interestingly, this text, originally commissioned by the director of the federal Bureau of Public Assistance, came under attack during the McCarthy era for promoting a socialist agenda. Towle had but one sentence in the book that referenced the value of social security and public assistance "for the attainment of the socialized state envisaged in democratic ideology" (Towle, 1945, p. 57). Nonetheless, the attack was fierce, and Towle eliminated the phrase "socialized state" in a revised edition of the book.

Similar instances of repression occurred in Canada. For example, Mary Jennison, a highly regarded social worker in Ontario, was a victim of an anti-communist witch hunt. Jennison was a member of the Canadian Association of Social Work (CASW) and editor and regular contributor to *The Social Worker*. She worked for a number of key social work organizations, including the Federation for Community Services in Toronto and the Central Volunteer Bureau in Montreal. She supported lifting the ban on the Communist Party, made illegal in 1940. In 1943 she moved to Hamilton, Ontario, to direct the Dale Community Center, which served a working-class community, offering support for children, youth, and the unemployed. In that capacity she supported a strike affecting steel workers and joined in solidarity with union families. In 1947 rumors about her Communist Party affiliation began to spread. When the Dale Community Center board approached her with a resolution to ban hiring of any known communist or sympathizer, Jennison refused. She was fired from her job, faced ethics charges, and saw her remarkable social work career come to an unexpected end. The firing prompted outcry from civil liberties and social justice groups, but not from the CASW, whose support of Jennison was reluctant at best. As a result of suspicions regarding her communist sympathies, her support of progressive causes, and her active involvement in peace work, Jennison's name remained on the Royal Canadian Mounted Police Red list until she passed away in 1970 (Jennissen & Lundy, 2011, pp. 120–125).

Claims for Political, Social, and Economic Rights

The 1960s saw pressures for change building on multiple fronts. The Civil Rights Movement was dismantling an entrenched system of American apartheid and demanding change through the courts at lunch counters, in schools, in the voting booth, and in the streets. Widespread poverty had been "discovered" hiding in plain sight in the land of affluence (Harrington, 1962). Mental health, juvenile delinquency, and the struggles of older Americans were recognized as matters of national public concern. Under the Kennedy and Johnson administrations key social legislation was passed recognizing the rights and concerns of disadvantaged and disenfranchised groups. For example, the 1961 White House Conference on Aging led to the passage of the Older Americans Act in 1965 to provide comprehensive community-based social and health services for older adults. Amendments to the Social Security Act, passed in 1962, expanded support to poor families and increased funding for social workers in public welfare systems. The Medicare and Medicaid programs were soon to follow (1965). The 1964 Economic Opportunity Act was the cornerstone of Johnson's War on Poverty. It provided funding for poverty relief, education, and training programs and launched new initiatives such as Head Start, Job Corps, Volunteers in Service to America (VISTA), and Community Action Programs to engage people with low income in planning and action for poverty elimination. The Civil Rights Act of 1964 formally outlawed discrimination on the basis of race, color, sex, religion, or national origin, and the Voting Rights Act of 1965 expressly prohibited racial discrimination in voting. Demands for change in the structures of society translated into demands for change within the profession of social work.

According to Mimi Abramovitz (1998) the upheavals of the 1960s rekindled social work's spirit of social action. She contends, however, that students, rather than seasoned professionals carried the banner of social change:

> Students charged that organizational maintenance interests overrode addressing clients' needs in agencies. They also lambasted rigid welfare bureaucracies, condemned school curricula as parochial and outdated, reproached social work's view of social problems as rooted in individual development or family dynamics, and protested social work's lack of response to the black revolution. (p. 517)

But change was not only student driven. African American social workers had been organizing to demand change from within the profession. They brought the philosophy and politics of the black liberation movement to bear by addressing the intersections of racism and poverty in U.S. society and by naming and challenging white supremacy in social welfare systems (Bell, 2014). The National Association of Black Social Workers (NABSW), founded in 1968, began as a movement within the National Conference on Social Welfare (NCSW) to challenge NCSW's failure to take a stand on racism within the profession. In its 1968 position statement (1968/1998), NABSW demanded representation on NCSW boards and committees; challenged misconceptions about the black community; and demanded that those who speak, write, and conduct research about the black community be members of and experts on the community. They called on all social workers to involve themselves in solving the problem of white racism, which they named as America's number one mental health problem (NABSW, 1968/1998).

During the mid-1960s welfare rights organizations began to emerge around the country demanding recognition of the rights and dignity of welfare recipients and the end to discriminatory, discretionary, and humiliating treatment in public welfare systems (Kornbluh, 2007; Nadasen, 2005). In 1966 this loose network of local organizations came together to form the National Welfare Rights Organization, whose grassroots leaders demanded a say in the policy decisions affecting the poor, particularly poor women. Some social welfare workers were joining the cause as well. Echoing the concerns of the Rank and File Movement of the 1930s, a cadre of radical frontline social workers, troubled by bureaucratic indifference in public welfare and conservatism in mainstream social work, formed the Social Welfare Workers Movement with the goal of gaining community-worker control of social welfare agencies and finding common cause with those they served (Reisch & Andrews, 2001, pp. 152–153). Although the movement was short lived, it revealed fault lines within the profession.

Directions and Challenges: 1970 to 2000

Emergence of a Systems Perspective

By the 1970s, mainstream social work practice was being conceptualized as a problem-solving process that could be applied at multiple levels, from the individual to the group, organization, and community. Some practitioners challenged the division of social work in terms of casework, group work, and community organization and called for a unified approach to practice that addressed social work's dual focus on individual functioning and social conditions (Bartlett, 1970). In 1973, Allen Pincus and Anne Minahan published *Social Work Practice: Model and Method*, which incorporated a systems perspective and put forth a model of social work as a process of planned change (see chapter 4 for further discussion of systems theory). Their work provided a foundation for what has come to be known and widely accepted as a *generalist* approach to social work practice.

Harkening back to the work of Mary Richmond, the generalist approach addresses the interplay of persons and larger systems in the process of assessment and intervention. It recognizes the centrality of relationships in the helping process and sees the process of change as patterned, sequential, and unfolding over time. Miley, O'Melia, and DuBois (2007) state that generalist social work provides an integrated and multileveled approach for meeting the purposes of social work. Generalist practitioners acknowledge the interplay of personal and collective issues, prompting them to work with a variety of human systems—societies, communities, neighborhoods, complex organizations, formal groups, families, and individuals—to create changes which maximize human system functioning. (p. 10)

Carol Meyer, professor of social work at Columbia University with a background in group work, casework, and family practice, played a key role in moving social work theory forward in the 1970s. Meyer sought to revitalize social casework by further developing the complex interplay between the individual and the social environment, with particular attention to what she termed the urban crisis of the 1960s (Meyer, 1970). Meyer drew from emerging directions in general systems theory and ecology theory to better understand complex human interaction in the social world (Healy, 2014; Hearn, 1969; von Bertalanffy, 1968). Meyers's *ecosystems perspective* provided a way of seeing the complex, multilayered interconnectedness of person and environment interactions (Mattaini & Meyer, 2002).

Critical Challenges

The systems perspective did not invite critical questions regarding structures and relations of power and conflicts of interests in society—questions that are at the core of radical thought. These questions were taken up by feminists addressing gendered relations of power in society and in social welfare systems. They were central to the work of the NABSW. And they sparked new directions in structural and radical social work, influenced by Marxist thought, which were emerging internationally and informing new directions in social work thought and practice in the United States (Bailey & Brake, 1975; Galper, 1975; Moreau, 1979; Mullaly, 2006). Structural and radical approaches to social work were grounded in a critique of capitalism. They challenged the structural arrangements of society that maintain and reproduce inequalities and injustices, which, in turn, contribute to human suffering. They called on social workers to engage in political struggle to transform society. Radical voices and views, however, remained largely on the margins of U.S. social work.

Survival of the Profession

The 1980s were characterized by the retrenchment of federal support for social welfare under the Reagan administration, growing anti-welfare sentiments, and the massive privatization of social services (Abramovtiz, 1996). In response, social work turned inward in an attempt to ensure the profession's survival. As the very fabric of the social safety net seemed to tear, the profession became increasingly preoccupied with professional licensure and credentialing for private practice (Reisch & Wenocur, 1986; Specht & Courtney, 1994). Graduate school enrollments expanded as the job market contracted. Many social workers were carving a niche for themselves in the clinical practice market and valuing the knowledge, skills, and professional accreditation that would secure these positions. Social work experienced a crisis of identity: There appeared to be no single organizing basis for unity (Ehrenreich, 1985). Common questions raised in the professional literature during this period included what is social work? Is it art? Or is it science? Are there any commonalities across what seem to be distinct fields of practice such as child welfare, school or hospital social work, social administration or clinical practice? Do social workers really share a common knowledge base, skills, and values?

While mainstream social work struggled with identity, critical voices continued to push the profession in the direction of its commitment to social justice. For example, Barbara Bryant Solomon's groundbreaking text, *Black Empowerment: Social Work in Oppressed Communities* (1976) explicitly addressed racism, oppression, and power and put forth a new model for social work practice based on empowerment as both process and goal. In the mid-1980s a cadre of feminist social workers came together to launch *Affilia: Journal of Women and Social Work* as a venue for critical feminist engagement with social work thought and practice. Throughout the 1980s and 1990s social workers of color were challenging the embeddedness of white privilege in the structures and practices of social work and demanding attention to race, racism, and diversity (Gutiérrez, 1990; Gutiérrez & Lewis, 1999; Lum, 1999). Lesbian, gay, and bisexual social workers were challenging the pervasive power of heteronormative constructions of identity and family in social work theory and practice and calling for changes in approach to research and education as well as practice (Reisch & Andrews, 2001, p. 181). In the late 1980s social work faculty at the University of Kansas School of Social Work began to develop the strengths perspective as a counter-approach to the problem-oriented, pathology-driven models that have defined so much of social work practice (Saleebey, 2006). These significant and ongoing efforts continue to inform and transform social work (see chapter 4 for further discussion of contemporary theoretical perspectives).

Eliminating the Social Safety Net

By the 1990s, "ending welfare as we know it" had become the mantra of U.S. social policy regarding the poor. The social safety net continued to be compromised by cuts in federal spending and the devolution of social costs to state and local governments and private charities (Kilty & Segal, 2006). Organized labor suffered tremendous losses. As welfare reform legislation moved toward passage, some social workers joined with welfare rights groups to challenge punitive social policy. Some worked within social work organizations to focus attention on the value of social justice. However, in August 1996, President Bill Clinton signed the Personal Responsibility and Work Opportunity Reconciliation Act. The goal of the legislation was ending "welfare dependency," not ending poverty. Media portrayals and policy debates regarding welfare dependency featured racist and gender-biased stereotypes of poverty and the poor, revealing once again the lasting power of ingrained beliefs regarding who is considered worthy or unworthy (Neubeck & Cazenave, 2001) The act dismantled the Aid to Families with Dependent Children program, an entitlement program for poor families in place since the New Deal. It was replaced by Temporary Assistance for Needy Families (TANF), a program with strict limits on eligibility and funding. By the turn of the century welfare rates had fallen dramatically, but poverty rates had not (Kilty & Segal, 2006). In fact, poverty rates increased to a fifteen-year high during the economic recession of 2008–09 (Eckholm, 2010).

Looking Back, Looking Forward

Social work in the second decade of the twenty-first century faces many challenges similar to those that confronted our predecessors. Social workers continue to struggle with the tensions between person-changing and systems-changing efforts. The role of social worker as psychotherapist remains a prominent and prestigious one in the profession. At the same time, a growing number of social workers engaged in clinical practice are further articulating the connections between social forces and personal struggles. This is exemplified in the growing attention to trauma and the cumulative impact of traumatic events and experiences that compromise individual and collective well-being (Caringi & Hardiman, 2011; van der Kolk, 2014). It is also demonstrated in critical attention to the pathological power of oppression in everyday lives (Blitz, Kida, Gresham, & Bronstein, 2013; Smith, Chambers, & Bratini, 2009).

The reform spirit of social work continues to be fueled by those addressing poverty and inequality; the costs and consequences of war; humane immigration policy; and the demands for human rights and racial, social, and environmental justice. The journey ahead is daunting, and each of us must determine what route we are going to take. Where will we position ourselves? For what will we take a stand? Will we, like Harry Hopkins, seek to work ourselves out of a job? At times, we may find ourselves prone to pessimism in the face of struggle. Yet historian Howard Zinn (1997) would encourage social workers to draw on history to shine a light on possibilities for the future:

> I can understand pessimism, but I don't believe in it. It's not simply a matter of faith, but of historical evidence. Not overwhelming evidence, just enough to give hope, because for hope we don't need certainty, only possibility. Which (despite all those confident statements that "history shows . . ." and "history proves . . .") is all history can offer us. (p. 656)

Class Learning Activity:
Reader's Theater: History as Inspiration

A reader's theater is a brief dramatization in which readers take on the roles of people in the scripts. The scripts are brief accounts written in the first person from the point of view of the historical figures. Each script highlights and personalizes the individual's life experiences, struggles, and contributions. This activity uses reader's theater as an approach to learn more about key players and accomplishments in the rich and dynamic history of social work's evolution.

We often hear about the remarkable work of Jane Addams at Hull House. There are so many more who have played influential roles, from the formative movements to more recent times, as chapter 2 suggests. As a class, decide on one or more particular eras of social work history that you wish to explore further. Work in small groups to identify some of the key figures in social work about whom you would like to learn more. Compile a master list with all of the names you have generated as a class. Assign each small group the responsibility to research the background and contributions of two or more historical figures and to write a first-person reader's theater narrative (about five hundred words) based on your research. Dedicate one or more class periods to reader's theater, in which class members perform these first-person scripts in character, using simple props or period-piece clothing to portray a sense of the person as well as the story. Consider including time for questions from the audience to see how much you were able to learn about the social workers who inspire you!

SUMMARY

In this chapter we have explored the reasons why history and a historical perspective are important to social justice work. We have summarized the prehistory and history of social work, focusing on its development in the United States. We have located the emergence of social work within a larger political and economic context. We have addressed moments of social work's complicity with injustice and highlighted the contributions of advocates and activists who challenged the status quo. We hope this history both challenges and inspires you. We close with a short essay by Sadye Logan, Distinguished Professor Emerita of Social Work, University of South Carolina, based on her recent book *The Spirit of an Activist: The Life and Work of I. DeQuincey Newman* (2014), which chronicles Newman's lifelong activism for peace and justice in South Carolina.

ON REFLECTION

Learning from History:
I. DeQuincey Newman, Servant Leader

Sadye Logan, MSW, DSW

I. DeQuincey Newman was born April 17, 1911, in Clyde Township, Darlington County, South Carolina. The son of the Reverend Melton C. Newman and Charlotte Elizabeth Morris, he attended public school in Williamsburg County and graduated from Claflin College in Orangeburg, South Carolina. He received degrees from Clark College and Gammon Theological Seminary, both in Atlanta, Georgia.

Newman was a born activist. At the age of six, he promised his mother on her death bed that he would become a minister like his father. He received his preacher's license at age nineteen and became an ordained minister in the Methodist tradition in 1931. While serving as a student pastor in Georgia, he met and married Ann Pauline Hinton of Covington, Georgia. The couple had one child, Emily Morris DeQuincey. The Reverend Newman served pastoral appointments in Georgia and South Carolina, founded two churches, and played a key role in bringing previously segregated conferences of the South Carolina Methodist Church into a single organization.

Reverend Newman was well known throughout the state and nation as a champion of the civil rights movement in South Carolina. Not only was he instrumental in 1943 in founding the Orangeburg branch of the National Association for the Advancement of Colored People (NAACP), but in 1944 participated in organizing the Progressive Democratic Party, which initiated full participation by Blacks in the South Carolina Democratic Party. He served in a number of offices in the South Carolina Conference of the NAACP and from 1960 through 1969 served as field director for the South Carolina NAACP. Through the use of multiple strategies such as nonviolent protest and effective use of the political and legal systems, the NAACP Legal Counsel won cases that changed the quality of life for all Americans, but especially African Americans, including where we lived, where and how we participated in recreation activities, our right to vote, how we ate, slept and studied, and how we interacted with each other.

As a nonviolent activist, Newman played a major role in helping South Carolina achieve a more peaceful transition from a racially segregated to an integrated society. His ability to work seamlessly in multiple ways over a lifetime is important in appreciating and understanding what it means to be in the struggle for a just and equal society. Newman's life and work are a true microcosm of the Civil Rights Movement covering this incredible arc of the twentieth century.

Newman was recognized by numerous civic and national organizations for his outstanding achievements in the progress of civil rights. He was also called on to serve at the federal level of government. For example, in 1977, he served as President Jimmy Carter's personal representative to Solomon Island independence celebrations, and in 1978 he was nominated to serve as the U.S. Ambassador to the Dominican Republic.

The Reverend Newman was a strong advocate of human services, particularly with regard to the needs of the elderly and of citizens in rural areas of the state. He served as executive assistant to the commissioner of the South Carolina Department of Social Services from 1972 to 1974. In 1975 he was named director of the Rural Regional Coordination Demonstration Project in the Office of the Governor. This project became the Division of Rural Development with Newman serving as its director until 1981. In this position, he developed and supported self-help economics and self-empowerment, especially for South Carolinians living in depressed rural areas.

Newman helped to organize the Statewide Homes Foundation to promote better housing and education for low-income families and the Senior Citizens Service Center to serve citizens of the Camden, South Carolina, area. His humanitarian service brought recognition from the South Carolina Congress of Parents and Teachers and the South Carolina Nursing Home Association. In 1982, he was named rural citizen of the year by the National Institute on Social Work in Rural Areas.

In October 1983, Newman was elected to the South Carolina Senate and became the first Black to serve in that body since Reconstruction. He received the distinguished alumnus award from Claflin College and was the recipient of the Order of the Palmetto, considered the highest civilian honor in the State of South Carolina. Senator Newman was cited for outstanding public service and civic leadership by the South Carolina legislature. In May 1984, upon recommendation of the College of Social Work, he was awarded the honorary degree of doctor of humane letters by the University of South Carolina.

Based on the life and work of Newman, the following questions are posed for reflection and further study:

1. Can we expect ever to live in a world free from the distinction of country, language, sect, and race; that is, based on love, respect for self, others, and the planet?
2. What has been your role in changing the racial climate in your state?
3. What do you see as the role of the state and federal governments in developing and supporting antiracist policy and practices?
4. What actions can you, as a social justice worker, take to promote antiracist policies and practices?
5. How might Reverend Newman's story inspire you to learn more about the dedicated activists who have engaged in the struggles for social justice in your community or state?

QUESTIONS FOR DISCUSSION

1. Why does a critical understanding of social work history matter for practice today?
2. What is an example from your social work experience that illustrates ways in which history permeates the present?
3. How might you use history as a tool of inquiry?
4. What are some of the contributions of the Charity Organization Societies and the Settlement House Movement to contemporary social work? What are some cautionary lessons they offer?
5. If you were a social worker in 2056 looking back at social work in 2016, what practices might you question? Why?

SUGGESTED READINGS

Addams, J. (1910). *Twenty years at Hull House*. New York: Macmillan.

Ehrenreich, J. H. (1985). *The altruistic imagination: A history of social work and social policy in the United States*. Ithaca, NY: Cornell University Press.

Reisch, M., & Andrews, J. (2001). *The road not taken: A history of radical social work in the United States*. New York: Brunner/Routledge.

Reynolds, B. C. (1987). *Social work and social living*. Silver Spring, MD: National Association of Social Workers.

Zinn, H. (2003). *A people's history of the United States: 1492–Present*. New York: HarperCollins.

Chapter 3

Values, Ethics, and Visions

The philosophy of social work cannot be separated from the
prevailing philosophy of a nation, as to how it values people and
what importance it sets upon their welfare.

Bertha Capen Reynolds (1951)

OVERVIEW

In chapter 3 we explore the concept of values, their formation, and their place
in our everyday lives. We develop a historical understanding of values, consider the concept of values in context, and address questions of power in the
practice of valuing. How are values and the practices of valuing shaped and
challenged over time? How are values entwined in our most basic assumptions about the world and how we relate to others? We explore the relationship
between values and ethics and address ways in which values are translated
into standards for ethical practice and frameworks for ethical decision
making.

In this chapter we also examine the value base of social work and introduce readers to the core values of the social work profession as described in
the Code of Ethics of the National Association of Social Workers in the United
States. We then address ethics and values in context, looking at the history of
social work ethics in the United States and changes in the code over time. We
consider the challenges and possibilities posed by alternative perspectives on
practice ethics in the United States, such as the Code of Ethics of the National
Association of Black Social Workers. Moving beyond U.S. borders, we explore
approaches to framing social work ethics in diverse national and international
contexts.

Returning to the grounded practice of ethical decision making, we critically consider frameworks developed in U.S. contexts for ethical decision making in social work. We then expand on those possibilities through consideration
of a human rights perspective and an ethics of participation.

WHAT DO WE MEAN BY VALUES?

Defining Values

Merriam-Webster's Collegiate Dictionary (2005) defines value as "a principle, standard, or quality regarded as worthwhile or desirable" (p. 1248). Values are often described as guides to individual and collective action. Values are not provable truths. Rather, they grow out of personal experience, they change with experience, and they evolve (Johnson & Yanca, 2007, p. 46). Some writers describe values as principles about what we ultimately hold as worthy and good, about desired ends, and about the means of achieving those ends. Frederic Reamer (2006) describes values as "generalized, emotionally charged conceptions of what is desirable; [they are] historically created and derived from experience; shared by a population or group within it; and they provide the means for organizing and structuring patterns of behavior" (p. 12). Attention to the emotional component is important. People feel deeply about that which they value, and value conflicts can provoke strong emotional responses. As sociologist Robin M. Williams, Jr. writes,

> Values merge affect and concept. Persons are not detached or indifferent to the world; they do not stop with a sheerly factual view of their experience. Explicitly or implicitly, they are continually regarding things as good or bad, pleasant or unpleasant, beautiful or ugly, appropriate or inappropriate, true or false. . . . All values have cognitive, affective, and directional aspects. Values serve as criteria for selection in action. When most explicit and fully conceptualized, values become criteria for judgment, preference, and choice. When implicit and unreflective, values nevertheless perform "as if" they constituted grounds for decisions in behavior. (1979, p. 16)

Our values "are not random" (Miley, O'Melia, & DuBois, 2013, p. 61); they have histories. They are learned through our experiences in families, communities, and other social groups. Values are emergent and dynamic, both shaping and shaped by our beliefs about and experiences in the world. We learn, internalize, and question our values in historical, political, and cultural contexts. We learn powerful lessons in values through participation in family, schooling, religious institutions, and workplaces as well as through media and broader social interactions.

Values and moral authority have long been the subject of study and debate by philosophers, religious and political leaders, and everyday people struggling to make their way in the world. Discourses regarding values reverberate throughout human history. As Frederick Ferré (2001) argues, fundamental questions of values came into play with the entrance of people into the world because humanity is the only species capable of acting irresponsibly toward other species and to the Earth. According to Simon Blackburn (2001) human beings are value-based animals, continually engaged in assessing, comparing, and judging our own and other's sense of worth.

Philosophers have pondered questions of values for millennia. Plato sought to identify moral values, or virtues as he called them, that guide both individuals and societies. For Plato, the morally virtuous person is wise, temperate, courageous, and just (Dobelstein, 1999, p. 27; Peterfreund, 1992, p. 10). In a similar vein, Confucius wrote, "wisdom, compassion and courage . . . are the three universally recognized moral qualities of men" (Seldes, 1985, p. 92) Scottish philosopher David Hume described benevolence and justice as the two great social virtues. French philosopher Denis Diderot saw the capacity for valuing and judgment to be fundamental to humanity. Echoing Diderot, German-born American political philosopher Hannah Arendt wrote: "Thinking, willing and judging are the three basic fundamental activities. They cannot be derived from each other, and although they have certain common characteristics, they cannot be reduced to a common denominator" (Seldes, 1985, p. 16). How would you define values? Do you agree that there are universally recognized moral qualities of human beings? How would you describe your personal philosophy of human values?

Some writers have sought to describe universal human values that remain constant through time and across human groups. For others, the very concept of value is socially constructed and imbued with multiple and contested meanings. Robin M. Williams, Jr. writes,

> Values operate as constituents of dynamic systems of social action because of their interconnectedness, their informational or directive effects, and their capacities as "carriers" of psychological energy. Values always have cultural context, represent a psychological investment, and are shaped by the constraints and opportunities of a social system and of a biophysical environment. (1979, p. 21)

One of the challenges of social justice work is to both appreciate diverse constructions of values and question the modes of power at work in the process of valuing. As Dobelstein (1999) describes, in the U.S. context:

[Values] have gradually become associated with nouns rather than verbs or adverbs, as if values were things rather than action. When objects are valued over actions, then much of the moral authority of the value is lost. . . . Turning values into things without concern for how the things are achieved empties them of much of their authority to guide morally relevant behaviors. . . . Thus, value has come to have a different meaning as it has become more closely associated with the goal-driven nature of economic rationality and less with a notion of virtue that guides individual and social actions. (pp. 26–27)

Dobelstein (1999) writes that values are based on ideologies, that is, our beliefs about what is true. As we saw in chapter 2, values are deeply embedded in our political, social, and economic institutions, creating an ideological foundation for institutional structures and practices that often go largely unquestioned. For example, in the United States freedom is broadly invoked as a fundamental value with the force of moral authority. The dominant concept of freedom in the United States is one grounded in liberalism, capitalism, and positivism and constructed in terms of individualism and individual rights (Dobelstein, 1999, p. 24). Discourses of individual rights often serve to limit reflection on other values, such as social responsibility and interdependence.

Class Learning Activity:
Reflection on Personal Core Values

This activity provides an opportunity to both reflect on values and practice skills of respectful listening.

Start with a few minutes of individual reflection. Think about your *core values*—the ways of being and doing that you hold to be good and desirable. What do these values mean to you? What are some of your life experiences and relationships that have played important roles in shaping your values? What role did your family play? Your community? What messages did you receive about values and valuing as you were growing up? What values have you embraced? What values have you resisted? Are there competing values that you continue to struggle with? Are there any current value-laden issues or debates that provoke an emotional reaction for you? How do your personal values relate to your pursuit of social work?

Now partner with another class member and take a minute to settle in comfortably. Take turns speaking about your values for three minutes each. While one of you speaks, the other will listen. As listener, simply try to be present as witness to your partner's story.

After each person has had a chance to speak, take a few moments to reflect with your partner on the experience—both process and content. How was it to talk about your values with another person? How did it feel to be a silent witness to another's story? What were you able to hear and appreciate? Take a few minutes to process the exercise as a group.

VALUES IN CONTEXT

American Values?

We often hear talk about American values, societal values, or middle-class values. Such sweeping notions of values suggest that these values are broadly shared and uncontested. They also assume that America, society, and the middle class are homogeneous groups that would readily agree on a set of shared values. Such value claims are often held up to be both correct and normative, that is, the standard by which *other* values held by other groups are to be judged. Such a view of values denies the complexities and conflicts of interests, beliefs, values, and practices within contemporary U.S. society. It creates boundaries between *us* and *them* and contributes to particular assumptions about difference and similarity. These all-encompassing notions of values may reflect the particular interests of dominant groups that wish to maintain the status quo; they neglect the possibility that others may share similar values but may be denied the resources and opportunities to realize them. Further, individuals and groups may give very different meanings to the same expressed value. Consider, for example, the many possible meanings of *success*. For some it may be measured in terms of individual achievement and monetary gain, whereas for those with a collectivist orientation, such a measure would be antithetical to their values.

Consider for a moment some of the values we commonly hear described as American values. A list of those values might include freedom, opportunity, individualism, enterprise, pragmatism, equality, progress, and democracy. What else would you add to the list? These values are deeply embedded in the discourses of our social, political, and economic institutions. And the values embedded in and expressed through these institutions have powerful effects that reverberate throughout our social relationships (Hugman, 2012, p. 91). They have evocative force. They are often paired with the value of patriotism and touted as values that others should embrace. And yet, as we look at this list, we can point to values that may be in conflict. Moreover, we can identify other values that are not part of the list, but that we can readily argue to be desirable in guiding human action, such as humility, generosity, belonging, creativity, stewardship, and spirituality. And we can describe a litany of examples that demonstrate the ways in which individual and institutional practices contradict the values they express. What are some contradictions that come to mind as you reflect on your list of American values? As you compare your list to your experiences of everyday life in the United States, what contradictions are most salient for you?

Thirteen American Values

In 1984, L. Robert Kohls, then director of International Programs at San Francisco State University, put together a list of basic values that Americans live by. Kohls (1984) argued that, although Americans see themselves as unique individuals who choose their values, these thirteen values are deeply ingrained in American life. Further, he contended that, by understanding these values, an international visitor would be better able to understand Americans and American culture. Would you agree that this list of values captures something typically American? Who counts as American here? Whose America might be missing from this list of values?

1. Personal control over the environment
2. Change
3. Time and its control
4. Equality and egalitarianism
5. Individualism and privacy
6. Self-help
7. Competition and free enterprise
8. Future orientation
9. Action/work orientation
10. Informality
11. Directness, openness, and honesty
12. Practicality and efficiency
13. Materialism and acquisitiveness

Now, imagine for a moment a first-time visitor coming to the United States with little prior knowledge of popularly expressed American values. She has an opportunity to travel, to visit cities and towns, to read newspapers, to watch television, and to participate in other activities of contemporary social life. Based on these experiences, how might she describe American values? Perhaps she would describe Americans as placing a high value on size, with bigger always seeming to be better. After a trip around the country she might note an American value for mobility, given the impressive amounts of pavement, cars, and trucks. A trip to a few supermarkets might leave her with the impression that Americans highly value choice, packaging, pets, and hygiene. A pass through the checkout stand would confirm suspicions about the valuing of sports heroes, diets, gluttony, political scandal, celebrities, greed, horoscopes, and pop psychology experts. She might be perplexed by reading a headline saying that a high court has upheld the fundamental separation of church and state and then paying for her groceries with money that claims "In God We Trust." A trip to a suburban housing tract might suggest that conformity is more highly valued than individualism. What other impressions of American values might our first-time visitor have? What sorts of contradictions might she encounter? If you were to take a visitor on an American value tour, where would you go? If you were to develop a list that reflected a more diverse perspective on American values, what might you include?

Values are also shaped in relationship to social class. How a person comes to value certain kinds of knowledge and forms of labor may be powerfully shaped by class-based experience. Those who have been involved in working-class struggles for the right to organize may value solidarity and mutual support over autonomy and assistance. People in different socioeconomic classes may also express values in common, such as the desire for a healthy environment, a comfortable home, and a good job. They may, however, give very different meanings to those values. And their differing access to resources will profoundly shape their possibilities for translating the visions of what they value into reality. Too often, helping professionals have taken a particular set of middle-class values to be the norm and have made faulty assumptions and judgments about other persons and groups based on those middle-class values. In our discussion of history in chapter 2 we saw how class-based assumptions about one's *worth* are deeply embedded in the ideologies shaping social work's emergence as a profession. Can you identify examples of where this continues to occur in social work practice today?

Family Values?

The concept of family values is another case in point. Although many people may value the concept of family, they may strongly disagree on the definition.

Family means different things to different people, and kinship is constructed in a remarkable variety of ways. The concept of family promoted in the family values discourse of recent years is based on one very particular family form—the heteronormative nuclear family, which is made up of two heterosexual parents and their children, with father as authority figure and mother as nurturer. It privileges marriage, presence of children, biological parenthood, gender-specific roles, and heterosexuality (Powell, Blozendahl, Geist, & Carr Steelman, 2010, p. 2). This model serves to both reinforce cultural imperialism (Young, 2011) and justify and maintain gender and generational inequality (Finn, 1998a, pp. 205–217).

The question of what constitutes family values depends on who counts as family. Rather than assuming the nuclear family as the norm, we can learn more about both family and values by appreciating the different ways in which we define and create families and practice family relations. Linda Nicholson (1986) defines family as a historically and culturally variable concept that connects positions within a kinship system and household. Kristine Baber and Katherine Allen (1992) describe families as powerful socializing institutions, arenas of affection and support and tension and domination between genders and across generations. Heidi Hartmann (1987) defines family as a locus of struggle and a location where production and redistribution occur. Take a moment to think about how you define family.

The Changing American Family

Natalie Angier (2013) of the *New York Times* describes the evolving definition of the American family. She writes,

Yet for all the restless shape shifting of the American family, researchers who comb through census, survey, and historical data and conduct field studies of ordinary home life have identified a number of key emerging themes.

Families, they say, are becoming more socially egalitarian over all, even as economic disparities widen. Families are more ethnically, racially, religiously, and stylistically diverse than half a generation ago—than even half a year ago. In increasing numbers, Blacks marry whites, atheists marry Baptists, men marry men and women women, Democrats marry Republicans and start talk shows. Good friends join forces as part of the "voluntary kin" movement, sharing medical directives, wills, even adopting one another legally. Single people live alone and proudly consider themselves families of one—more generous and civic-minded than so-called "greedy marrieds."

Class Learning Activity:
Family and Values

What does family mean to you? Take a minute and write down your definition of family. Get together with a small group of your classmates and
share your definitions. See if you can come to agreement on a definition of
family. Ask one member of each small group to write the group's collective
definition(s) on the board. Take time to read the definitions. What do the
definitions have in common? How do they differ? Is it possible to reach
consensus as a class on a definition of family? Do the definitions reflect values about what a family should be? Do the definitions reflect your own
experience of family? How do values shape our understandings of family?
How do our experiences in family shape values?

Our differing experiences in families shape the meanings we give to
family, which, in turn, shape our understanding of family values. Take a few
moments to reflect on your own experiences of family life. What were some
of the messages you received while growing up that indicated what attributes and actions were or were not valued? For example, what messages
did you receive about the value of family, work, education, religion,
achievement, money, relationships, or helping? From whom did you
receive those messages?

The expressions we pass down through families often serve as vehicles
for inculcating values (Nakanishi & Rittner, 1992). Consider the following
common expressions: a penny saved is a penny earned, time is money, and
children should be seen and not heard. What values are expressed here?
Think for a moment about the expressions you heard while growing up.
What did they teach you about family and values?

What messages did you receive about what it means to be male and
female in your family? What messages did you receive about race and
racism? About the valuing of whiteness? About social class? About sexual
identity and gender expression? From whom? Can you identify some values that you have incorporated? Values that you have resisted? Can you
identify changes in your values over time? What forces or experiences
prompted those changes (White & Tyson-Rawson, 1995)?

THE PRACTICE OF VALUING

Let's begin to think about *valuing* as a verb that describes the process by which
we make judgments about what is desirable and preferred. As cultural beings
constantly interpreting and making sense of the world, we are also engaged in

an ongoing practice of valuing. Learning to value is part of our broader experience of acquisition of cultural knowledge. Through our everyday interactions in the world—in families, schools, neighborhoods, communities, and cultural groups—we are subjects of, witnesses to, and participants in practices of valuing. Those practices are shaped by the political, economic, social, and historical circumstances of our lives. The lessons in valuing learned by a white boy growing up in an upper-middle-class Chicago suburb may be very different from those learned by an Assiniboine boy growing up on the Fort Peck Reservation in Montana or those learned by a boy surviving on the streets of Sao Paulo or Seattle.

When we shift our attention to valuing as a verb it helps us to think about the many ways that we learn which qualities and behaviors are considered desirable and by whom. As we discussed above, families are powerful arenas for learning to value. From our earliest social experiences we are enmeshed in the practices of valuing. Some of these practices, such as the ways in which resources of time and space are organized and managed in the context of family, are so deeply ingrained in our experience that they go without saying. Our *family paradigms* (Germain 1994, p. 261)—family members' shared implicit beliefs about themselves and their social world—profoundly shape our orientation to and patterns of action in the world. Through the everyday routines, the messages and silences, and the crises of family life many of us learn powerful lessons in valuing.

Families are not the only sources for lessons in valuing. Schools are particularly powerful sites of valuing. Public schools have played a prominent role in the inculcation of middle-class values and in the organization of working-class life (Apple, 2011). A number of critical education theorists have argued that public schooling works to socialize children to assume their class position in capitalist society at the same time that it promotes the myth of classlessness and equality of opportunity to get ahead (Apple, 2011; Shor, 1980). They argue that, in theory, public schools are democratic places of equal opportunity. In practice, they are places where differences play out and get reproduced, whether in the form of unequal funding for rich and poor school districts or in the everyday indignities and exclusions experienced by poor and working-class children, particularly poor children of color. Although schooling has created opportunities for some groups, it has served as a powerful form of discipline, containment, and social control for others.

In the history of Native American education in the United States, the boarding school system, addressed in chapter 2, offers a powerful example of the ways in which everyday practices served as lessons in (de)valuing of Indian children, families, and culture. Differential valuing of children by race, class, gender and gender expression, ability status, and sexual identity continues to play out in our educational systems. Poor children of color in the United States attempt to learn in underfunded unsafe schools where there are often not enough books, materials, or teachers to go around (Kozol, 1991). Meanwhile, children of the white middle and upper classes enjoy the safety of suburban schools equipped with the latest technology and resources. The result is a system of *apartheid schooling* (Kozol, 2005) with clear divisions among those who are valued and those who are not.

Longitudinal research by the Gay, Lesbian, and Straight Education Network (GLSEN) (Kosciw, Greytak,, Palmer, & Boesen., 2014; Palmer, Kosciw, & Bartkiewicz, 2012) documents the continued devaluing of lesbian, gay, bisexual, and transgender (LGBT) youth in U.S. schools. A 2012 study by GLSEN found pervasive use of homophobic, racist, and sexist language; verbal harassment; physical harassment; and cyberbullying in the school setting—with conditions even worse in rural than urban school settings. Moreover, LGBT youth were often reluctant to report their experiences given the overall failure of school personnel to respond effectively. In schools with supportive staff, active gay-straight alliances, inclusive curricula, and strong anti-bullying policies, LGBT youth experienced lower levels of victimization. Unfortunately, these supports are lacking in many schools, especially in rural areas. Thus, for many LGBT youth, schooling offers daily lessons in devaluation of personal safety, dignity, identity, and rights.

These examples from the context of schooling reveal how practices of valuing in our social and political institutions are inextricably linked to broader relations of power and inequality in society. Values are also embedded in the policies, practices, structures, and routines of social service organizations. Those values are not necessarily consistent with the stated mission of the organization. Consider, for example, ways in which staff of a human service agency might talk among themselves about clients. Are clients reduced to simply being a problem? Does office talk devalue client dignity? Imagine a person visiting a social service office where the waiting room is small, cramped, and crowded and the office receptionist is seated behind a protective barrier. The client must state the reason for her visit out loud, through a window, to be heard by the receptionist. Others in the waiting room now know the reason for her visit as well. What value is placed on this client's privacy and dignity?

Now let's think about the house rules at a youth home or women's shelter. Rules are often created over time and in idiosyncratic ways in response to perceived concerns for safety and control. What might the rules suggest to residents about the value of trust or the valuing of their capabilities? Might the values expressed in the rules contradict those stated in the organizational mission? Clients, residents, and service recipients are likely to have a much more direct experience with an organization's implicit values than its expressed values. Part of the challenge of social justice work is to strive for coherence between expressed values and values that are implicit in our organizational structures and practices. Think for a moment about your practicum site. What values are expressed in the physical space of the organization? What values are expressed in the rules or policies regarding the people served?

VALUING AND SOCIAL JUSTICE WORK

Valuing is a dialectical process. Our actions in the world are shaped in part by our valuing of the world. Our experiences in the world, in turn, shape our values. It is important to reflect critically on our values and the processes through which they have been formed and challenged. We continually bring our values and valuing to bear in the practice of social work. A commitment to social justice work demands a constant search for competence, an honest examination of our personal as well as professional values, and a commitment to making our actions fit our words (Moch, 2009). Are our actions consistent with our expressed values? Do our values form the basis for justice-oriented action? Our values can be thought of as screens through which we interpret actions and give meaning to experience. They are shaped by our power, positioning, and experiences. But our values are never fully determined or determining. There is always the possibility of new understandings and relations and thus alternative values and approaches to valuing.

In summary, valuing is a complex and contested process. We are social beings with interests, desires, and relations at stake. We incorporate, resist, reproduce, and change values over time through the dynamics of our life experiences. The process of valuing cannot be separated from the contexts of power and inequality in which it plays out. We grapple with value contradictions in our everyday lives even as we practice and resist the (de)valuing of others and ourselves. And in the struggle there is always the possibility of transformation.

THE CONCEPT OF ETHICS

Defining Ethics

The concept of ethics is closely linked to that of values. In a formal sense, ethics refers to the branch of philosophy that concerns itself with moral decision making and the principles that guide people in determining right and wrong.

Richard Hugman (2012) defines ethics as the "conscious consideration of our moral values" (p. 5). In everyday usage, ethics may be thought of as the translation of human values into guidelines for action. Loewenberg and Dolgoff (1996, p. 43) describe two major philosophical approaches that have historically informed ethical decision making—ethical absolutism and ethical relativism. Absolutists stress the importance of fixed moral rules and contend that actions are inherently right or wrong. Relativists argue instead that ethical decision making is contextual and may be judged on the basis of the results. Peterfreund (1992) summarizes two "great traditions" in ethics. The Greek tradition of ethics was centered around understanding the good life. Ethical inquiry was directed toward the nature of happiness and ways to achieve it. The Judeo-Christian tradition, in turn, emphasized righteousness before God and duty to God and neighbor. An emphasis on duty and rights tends to characterize contemporary approaches to codes of professional ethics.

Ferré describes ethics as a way of thinking, judging, and acting. As a way of thinking it requires adequate relevant data, a keen awareness that we will never have all the "facts," and an openness to the evidence while "seeking to integrate it in a pattern that does it no violence" (2001, p. 8). As a way of judging, ethics links thinking and feeling such that reason and emotion mutually shape moral sensibility and decision making. Finally, it is this interplay of feeling-laden judgments that makes coordinated action possible. As Ferré argues, "there is no ethical action without thought and feeling, no ethical thought without feeling and potential action, no ethical feeling without conceptual recognition and implications for behavior" (2001, p. 20). This sense of ethics encompassing thinking, feeling, and acting resonates with Kelly and Sewell's (1988) concept of *trialectic logic* addressed in chapter 1. Blackburn (2001) contends that ethics— dynamic processes of thinking, judging, and acting—play out in an *ethical environment*. He describes this as the "surrounding climate of ideas about how to live. It determines what we find acceptable or unacceptable, admirable or contemptible. It determines our conception of when things are going well and when they are going badly" (2001, p. 1).

Margaret Rhodes argues that dialogue is central to ethics:

> Only through sustained and open dialogue can we develop informed ethical positions. Dialogue of this sort assumes that (1) we can communicate across different views; (2) that we can be open to each other; (3) that we need other views in order to fully reexamine our own. Dialogue of this sort is itself an ethic, best exemplified in the early works of Plato, where Socrates questions the

actions and views of his fellow citizens and urges them to rethink what they are doing. The dialogues often end without a conclusion, the conclusion being that we must constantly reexamine our answers. (1986, p. 19–20)

ETHICAL THEORIES

As the preceding discussion suggests, a diverse range of ethical theories has been articulated and debated over the centuries. Jill C. Schreiber, Ruth E. Groenhout, and Cheryl Brandson (2014) summarize three main branches of ethical theory in terms of their focus on (1) consequences, (2) actions, and (3) agents. Utilitarian theories, exemplified by the thinking of English philosophers Jeremy Bentham and John Stuart Mill, focus on the consequences of ethical choices. They emphasize consequences that bring about the greatest good—and the least harm—for the greatest number. It is the outcome rather than the process that is central here. Duty-based approaches hold that actions are guided by fundamental principles of right and wrong. Thus, actions can be right or wrong in themselves regardless of their consequences. Duty-based theories, such as that articulated by Immanuel Kant, also focus on the fundamental respect and dignity owed to every human being. As Rhodes writes, duty-based theory "makes us focus on the value of every individual person and on the respect owed to a person, apart from that person's usefulness and apart from our own desires, a respect essential to human dignity" (1986, p. 32). Virtue-based approaches focus on the character of the agent, the person engaged in actions that have ethical consequences. Virtues are dispositions and habits, developed in the context of community, that, once acquired, become qualities of character, such as honesty, integrity, and compassion. According to virtue ethics, there are certain qualities and ideals of excellence we should strive for in order to promote the full development of our humanity and human potential (Rhodes, 1986; Velasquez, Andre, Shanks, & Meyer, 2014).

Scholars of ethics also address rights-based, fairness, and common good approaches to ethical thought and practice. *Rights-based theories* define rights as justified claims on others (Velsaquez et al., 2014). Fundamental here is the notion that human beings have a basic dignity and worth, grounded in free will, and the right to exercise that will through freedom to choose and through protection from encroachment by others. Ethical action is that which best protects the rights of all affected. *Fairness* approaches seek to ensure that all individuals are treated in the same way and view favoritism and discrimination as unjust. *Common good* approaches view life in community as a good in itself.

The good of individual members of society is inextricably linked to the good of the community. This approach considers both conditions and actions that are important to the welfare of all members of the community (Velasquez et al., 2004). According to Velasquez and colleagues, differing theoretical perspectives lead us to ask different sorts of questions regarding ethical decision making:

- What benefit or harm might result from a particular course of action?
- What action will lead to the best overall consequences?
- Does this course of action respect the dignity of another? Does it treat the person as an end and not as a means?
- What rights do the affected parties have? Which course of action best respects those rights?
- Which course of action treats everyone the same unless there is a morally justifiable reason not to do so? Which course of action avoids favoritism and discrimination?
- Which course of action promotes the common good? Which best contributes to the kind of society we want to be?
- Which course of action develops moral virtues? Which helps us realize the best of our human potential?

Although each of these questions may be important to guide action, it is equally important to recognize that each is informed by a unique theoretical viewpoint. Velasquez and colleagues (2014) make the case that we can engage more fully in debate by drawing from each perspective and posing all of these questions in our practices of ethical decision making. In the following section we will refocus on social work, explore the values that shape the profession, and consider the ways in which our ethical theories affect our practice.

VALUES, ETHICS, AND SOCIAL WORK

Social Work as a Value-Based Practice

Social work is a value-based profession. According to Reamer (2006), social work values shape the mission of the profession; relations with clients, colleagues, and members of the broader society; decisions about intervention methods; and the resolution of ethical dilemmas (p. 13). Writers in the field frequently describe social work's value base as a defining feature of the profession's uniqueness. Miley and colleagues (2013) write that values that shape thought and action in social work through practice principles include "acceptance, individualization, nonjudgmentalism, objectivity, self-determination, access to resources, confidentiality, and accountability" (p. 57). Social workers have developed ethical codes that translate expressed values into standards for professional practice. As Johnson and Yanca (2007) assert, "codes of ethics flow from values; they are values in action" (p. 48).

The Preamble to the Code of Ethics of the National Association of Social Workers (NASW) states in part:

> The mission of the social work profession is rooted in a set of core values. These core values, embraced by social workers throughout the profession's history, are the foundation of social work's unique purpose and perspective.

> - Service
> - Social justice
> - Dignity and worth of the person
> - Importance of human relationships
> - Integrity
> - Competence

> This constellation of core values reflects what is unique to the social work profession. Core values and the principles that flow from them must be balanced within the context and complexity of human experience. (NASW, 2008)

The complete Code of Ethics is available at the NASW website (http://www .socialworkers.org/pubs/code/code.asp). Virtually every contemporary U.S. social work practice text spells out the core values of the profession as articulated by the NASW. Writers often praise the uniqueness of a profession founded on these core values and encourage budding social workers to embrace them wholeheartedly in practice. Less attention is given to critical reflection on these values, their meanings, their relationship to the history of social work, the challenge of practicing them within contexts of unequal power, and the tensions among them and between this core set of values and one's personal values. Discussion generally sidesteps the practices of valuing within the field of social work. By providing a definitive list of core values and locating social justice as one among several values to be embraced, we may unnecessarily constrain a discussion of *possible* values that could illuminate a vision of a just world.

The NASW preamble states that the six core values listed above have been embraced by social workers throughout the profession's history. However, as we learned in chapter 2, the history of the social work profession reveals a rather awkward embrace of its core values. We need to examine the implicit and explicit values that guide social work practice, both past and present, rather than simply assuming that these core values are manifest. Take a close look at these six core values. It seems that they could have different meanings for different people in different situations. What do they mean to you? Are they meaningful outside of the context in which they are applied? Do they define a core of social justice work? Are there values you would add, delete, or question?

The History of Social Work Ethics

Becoming a Profession

As discussed in chapter 2, social work in the United States was coming to view itself as a profession in the early 1900s. Creation of frameworks and standards to guide practice ethics was a core part of social work's professional identity formation (Reamer, 2014). As early as 1919 there were attempts to draft professional codes of ethics for social work (Reamer, 2006, 2014). As noted in chapter 2, Mary Richmond furthered this work in the 1920s. During the 1940s professional ethics became a subject of study in its own right in social work (Johnson, 1955). In 1947 the Delegate Conference of the American Association of Social Workers (forerunner to NASW) adopted a code of ethics, thereby formally translating a value base into principles of practice and standards of professional conduct (Reamer, 1998). As discussed previously, the move toward professionalism was a move away from positioned advocacy and political critique.

> ### Reflection Moment:
> ### Professionalism and Activism
>
> In a 1957 article in *Social Work*, University of California professor Ernest Greenwood argued that social workers "might have to scuttle their social action heritage as a price of achieving the public acceptance accorded a profession" (1957, p. 55). What does it mean to say that activism undermines professionalism? Does a negation of activism suggest a political commitment to the status quo? What are the ethical implications here? Is activism antithetical to professionalism, or do we perhaps need to explore other possibilities for being professionals and activists?

Adopting a Code of Ethics

The National Association of Social Workers adopted its Code of Ethics in 1960 (NASW, 1960). That code consisted of fourteen proclamations, all in the form of first-person statements. It reads in part (p. 1):

> As a member of the National Association of Social Workers I commit myself to conduct my professional relationships in accord with the code and I subscribe to the following statements:
>
> • I regard as my primary obligation the welfare of the individual or group served which includes actions for changing social conditions.
> • I give precedence to my professional responsibility over my personal interests.
> • I hold myself responsible for the quality and extent of the service I perform.
> • I respect the privacy of the people I serve.

The historic events of the 1960s pushed social workers to reflect further on constructions of ethical practice in the face of the civil rights struggles and the War on Poverty. In 1967, the NASW Code of Ethics was amended to include the following statement on nondiscrimination: "I will not discriminate because of race, color, religion, sex, or national ancestry and in my job capacity will work to eliminate such discrimination in rendering service, in work assignments, and in employment practices" (NASW, 1967).

By the 1970s there was a growing interest in the study of applied and professional ethics and an increase in litigation regarding violations of ethical principles (Reamer, 2014). Some social workers sought a more prescriptive and proscriptive code to guide professional practice. A committee appointed by NASW in 1977 took up the task, and in 1979 a more substantive set of standards for ethical practice was adopted. The 1979 code, a nineteen-page document, included a preamble, six sections of standards, and eighty-two principles related to the social worker's responsibility to clients, colleagues, employers and employing organizations, the profession, and the broader society. It also introduced the idea of the code as not only a guide but also an enforcement tool regarding standards of professional conduct (NASW, 2015b).

Ethical Challenges

Some social workers, dissatisfied with the direction the profession was moving, embraced a more radical approach to social work practice and challenged an ethical stance that was disconnected from a political stance. As noted in chapter 2, the National Association of Black Social Workers (NABSW), formed in 1968, was challenging racism and Eurocentrism in the social work profession, social welfare systems, and the broader society. It sought to make social welfare organizations more accountable to the black community and to develop delivery strategies that both reflected and respected black experience (NABSW, 1968/1998, 2015). In 1971 NABSW crafted its Code of Ethics (NABSW, 1971), which challenged the limits of the NASW code and addressed the inextricable link between an ethical stance and a political stance:

> In America today, no Black person, except the selfish or irrational, can claim neutrality in the quest for Black liberation nor fail to consider the implications of the events taking place in our society. Given the necessity for committing ourselves to the struggle for freedom, we as Black Americans practicing in the field of social welfare, set forth this statement of ideals and guiding principles.
>
> If a sense of community awareness is a precondition to humanitarian acts, then we as Black social workers must use our knowledge of the Black community, our commitments to its determination, and our helping skills for the benefit of Black people as we marshal our expertise to improve the quality of life of Black people. Our activities will be guided by our Black consciousness, our determination to protect the security of the Black community, and to serve as advocates to relieve suffering of Black people by any means necessary.
>
> Therefore, as Black social workers we commit ourselves, collectively, to the interests of our Black brethren and as individuals subscribe to the following statements:
>
> - I regard as my primary obligation the welfare of the Black individual, Black family, and Black community and will engage in action for improving social conditions.
> - I give precedence to this mission over my personal interest.
> - I adopt the concept of a Black extended family and embrace all Black people as my brothers and sisters, making no distinction between their destiny and my own.
> - I hold myself responsible for the quality and extent of service I perform and the quality and extent of service performed by the agency or organization in which I am employed, as it relates to the Black community.
> - I accept the responsibility to protect the Black community against unethical and hypocritical practice by any individual or organizations engaged in social welfare activities.

- I stand ready to supplement my paid or professional advocacy with voluntary service in the Black public interest.
- I will consciously use my skills, and my whole being as an instrument for social change, with particular attention directed to the establishment of Black social institutions.

The code calls for workers to commit to the welfare of black individuals, families, and communities as their primary obligation and to work as instruments for social change. The code challenges the value of *professional distance* between worker and client and rejects notions of social worker neutrality. The impassioned tone of the code sets it apart from that of the NASW. Importantly, this powerful document has remained unchanged over the course of nearly forty-five years.

The 1970s also saw what Reisch and Andrews (2001, p. 174) refer to as an explosion of radical theory in social work. Social workers who embraced a structural approach, informed by a Marxist critique of capitalism and vision of societal transformation, also sought to challenge the dominant social work paradigm. Radical social workers held that the NASW Code of Ethics contained a conservative bias that did not serve the best interests of clients or workers. In response they put forth the Code of Ethics for Radical Social Service, built on fourteen planks (Galper, 1975) that include the following:

- I will work toward the development of a society that is committed to the dictum, "From each according to his or her ability, to each according to his or her need."
- I will struggle for the realization of a society in which my personal interests and my personal actions are consistent with my interests and actions as a worker.
- I will consider myself accountable to all who join in the struggle for social change and will consider them accountable to me for the quality and extent of work we perform and the society we create.
- I will use information gained from my work to facilitate humanistic, revolutionary change in society.
- I will use all the knowledge and skill available to me in bringing about a radically transformed society.

(For full text, see Galper [1975], pp. 224–227.)

> **Reflection Moment:**
> **Codes of Ethics and Commitments**
> Take a moment to reflect on the first NASW Code of Ethics (1960), the NABSW Code of Ethics (1971), and the Code of Ethics for Radical Social Workers. Consider the meaning and power in the use of *I* statements. What personal and professional commitments do the codes expect of social workers? How do they compare to the language of the current NASW Code of Ethics?

Conceptualization of a Professional Value Base

Despite the radical challenge, the service-oriented model of social work continued to largely dominate the change-oriented approach, and the development of ethical standards reflected this dominance. In 1976 Charles S. Levy published *Social Work Ethics*, a foundational text that sought to articulate the philosophical and conceptual basis for social work ethics. Levy (1973) classified social work professional values in three categories: preferred conceptions of people, preferred outcomes for people, and preferred instrumentalities for dealing with people. Levy's classification of social work values is summarized in table 3.1.

Table 3.1
Levy's classification of social work values

Preferred conceptions of people	Preferred outcomes for people	Preferred instrumentalities for dealing with people
Belief in:	Belief in society's obligation to:	Belief that people should:
• Inherent dignity and worth	• Provide opportunity for individual growth and development	• Be treated with dignity and respect
• Capacity for change		• Have the right to self-determination
• Mutual responsibility	• Provide resources and services for people to meet basic needs	• Be encouraged to participate in social change
• Need to belong		
• Uniqueness		• Be recognized as unique individuals
• Common human needs	• Provide equal opportunity for social participation	

Source: C. S. Levy, "The value base of social work," *Journal of Education for Social Work, 9* (1973), pp. 34–42.

Levy's conceptualization is frequently cited in social work texts as the classic formulation of social work values. Levy's schema brings together humanitarian values and a sense of societal obligation to create conditions in which these values can be expressed. He recognizes and articulates the fundamental linkage of the personal and the social, or *person-in-environment* perspective as it is commonly called, that has been central to dominant depictions of social work's professional uniqueness (we will elaborate on this in chapter 4). Levy implies that society has an obligation to the poor and that people should participate in the decisions that affect their lives. Importantly, Levy also speaks to questions of power in the social work relationship and the need to be mindful of that power and its ethical implications: "The social worker's power is a function of the client's vulnerability, and the client's vulnerability is a function of the social worker's power" (1976, p. 70).

However, Levy does not develop a political and ethical critique of the *conditions* of poverty, inequality, and exploitation and of the arrangements and relations of power that create and maintain those conditions. He speaks of common human needs, but does not address basic human rights. He speaks of opportunities for social participation but not of struggles for social justice. In contrast to the NABSW, which challenged a professional ethics of neutrality and named the pathologizing power of racism, and radical social workers, who argued the need to confront structural as well as interpersonal contradictions, Levy's schema stops short. How is it that Levy's formulation has become central to values discussions in social work whereas the principles articulated by those speaking with a critical political voice have remained on the periphery?

Values and Survival of the Profession

By the 1980s, with the retrenchment of federal support for social welfare under the Ronald Reagan administration, the growing anti-welfare movement, and the massive privatization of social services, social work seemed to value professional survival more than anything. The profession was preoccupied with professional licensure and credentialing for private practice (Reisch & Wenocur, 1986; Specht & Courtney, 1994). Many social workers were carving a niche in the clinical practice market and valuing the knowledge, skills, and professional accreditation that would secure their positions. The NASW Code of Ethics, as revised in 1979, detailed attention to professional-client relations, confidentiality, access to records, payments for services, and responsibilities to professional colleagues. The revised code reflected the *medical model* of social work, that is, the social worker as professional expert engaged in client treatment focused on change at the personal and interpersonal level. Social workers were not ethically obliged to combat conditions of violence, inequality, and exploitation, nor were they obligated to make the concerns of people living in poverty their priority. It was not until 1983, as the U.S. social context grew bleaker, that the Council on Social Work Education (CSWE), the profession's academic accrediting body, called for the study of oppression and injustice as part of the social work curriculum (Gil, 2013).

Feminist Interventions

Feminist social workers were also bringing a critical perspective to social work, addressing the connection of the personal and political, and posing questions regarding conceptualizations of ethical practice (Dominelli & McLeod, 1989; Hanmer & Statham, 1989). In 1986 *Affilia: Journal of Women and Social Work* was launched to create a venue for feminist social work critiques, theoretical analyses, practice research, and ethical reflection. In 1989 Jalna Hamner and Daphne Statham (1989, pp. 139–143) proposed a Code of Practice for Non-sexist Woman-Centered Social Work. The code is built around principles for personal awareness, such as awareness of one's own biases and the pervasiveness of interpersonal and institutionalized sexism, recognition of the role of social definitions in causing women's problems, and understanding of the nature of women's survival strategies—and strategies for intervention—such as establishment of nonhierarchical working relationships, use of all-woman groups, and validation of women's strengths. Feminist scholars and practitioners also engaged in sustained critical analysis regarding the underlying assumptions of notions of justice that inform ethical stances and the workings of power that shape interpersonal relationships and institutional arrangements (Figueira-McDonough & Sarri, 2002). They made questions of power central to ethical inquiry, examined gender as a central axis of power and inequality, and considered the intersection with other axes such as race, class, and sexual identity (Boris, 1995; Dujon & Withorn, 1996). Feminists explored the need to problematize women's relationship to both the state and "expert" models of diagnosis and treatment (Gordon, 1994; Rossiter et al., 1998). Some called for an ethics of care as a corrective to what they saw as an overemphasis on a rights-based ethics (Bubeck, 1995; Gilligan, 1982; Held, 2006). Others, such as Amy Rossiter and colleagues (1998), called for an "ethics of resistance" that challenges the assumptions and practices of the dominant disciplines and institutions of helping. Their voices, too, spoke to the connection between ethical and political concerns.

These critical voices within the profession, along with continued cutback in public spending to support a social safety net, brought questions of injustice and oppression to the fore. In 1992, CSWE put forth a curriculum policy statement that made it the responsibility of schools of social work to teach more explicitly about social justice and approaches to overcoming oppression. However, as Gil (1994) notes, "the 1992 revision reflects the fallacious assumption that discrimination, oppression, and injustice affecting women, minorities, and other discrete social groups can be overcome without eradicating their sources in the occupational and social class divisions of contemporary capitalism" (p. 259).

SOCIAL WORK ETHICS AT THE TURN OF THE TWENTY-FIRST CENTURY

The political realities of the late twentieth century and the accompanying tensions and debates among social workers prompted serious reflection on the profession's ethical direction and responsibilities. In 1993 the Delegate Assembly of NASW formed a task force to craft a new code of ethics. Its efforts reflect concern over the mechanisms and consequences of discrimination, oppression, and injustice. In addition, a new scholarly field of applied ethics had emerged over the previous decade, and this, along with the emergence of the field of bioethics, also shaped the direction of the new code (Reamer, 2014). In August 1996, the Delegate Assembly adopted a revised code of ethics that went into effect in January 1997. (It underwent minor revision again in 1999.) In contrast to the earlier code, which summarized social work values to include "the worth, dignity, and uniqueness of all persons as well as their rights and opportunities" (NASW, 1979, p. iii), the revised code spelled out the mission of social work: "to enhance human well-being and help meet the basic human needs of all people, with particular attention to the needs and empowerment of people who are vulnerable, oppressed, and living in poverty" (NASW, 2008, p. 1).

The revised code provided a pronounced shift in attention to questions of poverty, oppression, and injustice. It also called on social workers to take social justice seriously. The ethical standards spelled out social workers' responsibilities to the broader society. For example,

- Social workers should promote the general welfare of society, from local to global levels, and the development of people, their communities, and their environments. Social workers should advocate for living conditions conducive to the fulfillment of basic human needs and should promote social, economic, political, and cultural values and institutions that are compatible with the realization of social justice.

- Social workers should promote the conditions that encourage respect for cultural and social diversity within the United States and globally. Social workers should promote policies and practices that demonstrate respect for difference, support the expansion of cultural knowledge and resources, advocate for programs and institutions that demonstrate cultural competence, and promote policies that safeguard the rights of and confirm equity and social justice for all people.

- Social workers should act to prevent and eliminate domination of, exploitation of, and discrimination against any person, group, or class on the basis of race, ethnicity, national origin, color, sex, sexual orientation, age, marital status, political belief, religion, or mental or physical disability. (NASW, 1999)

In 2006 NASW convened an Ethics Summit to examine the relevance of the code of ethics. The Summit found no need for substantial revision, but encouraged further support of ethics education (Hobdy, Murray, & Morgan, 2006). In 2008 the NASW Code of Ethics was further revised to incorporate sexual orientation, gender identity or expression, and immigration status in its statements on anti-discrimination and respect for diversity.

The Challenges Ahead

These are daunting standards. They pose challenges and opportunities as social workers make the commitment to translate them to practice. However, as Gil (1994) notes with regard to the CSWE curriculum standards, we cannot overcome the oppression, exploitation, and discrimination experienced by discrete groups without confronting the underlying systemic inequalities. Further, social workers in both the United States and abroad have reported on the insidious damaging effects of market-driven thinking, managerialism, and fragmentation of social welfare systems and social work practices in the era of neoliberal globalization (Clarke, Gewirtz, & McLaughlin, 2000; Harris, 2005; Jones, 2005). According to Ferguson, Lavalette, and Whitmore (2005), these forces have contributed to a "'dumbing-down' of social work education and practice, with theory often seen as subordinate to a set of technical skills suited for employer-driven interests." Karen Healy (2005, p. 220) warns about the trend toward "reprivatization of public concerns, such as poverty" and the implications for a critical practice of social work. Healy (2002) has expressed concern that social workers face increasingly stringent demands for efficiency and evidence from funders and administrators that may serve to distance practice from the profession's core values. Similarly, Dominelli (1996) has voiced apprehension about the "commodification of social work" that moves the focus of practice away from concern about people and relationships toward a "product that is being purchased from a contractor" (pp. 163–164).

Rossiter (2005) asks us to think specifically about the clinical, legal, and ethical implications of social work within the neoliberal global order. What happens when private, profit-oriented interests overshadow professional values? What are results when human rights and human needs are subordinated to market values, profit margins, and bottom lines? Where do you see this occurring in social work and social welfare today? What may be the consequences? These are serious questions that challenge our values and the integrity of value-based practice.

The rapidly shifting terrain of technology poses further challenges for ethical practice. What constitutes ethical social work in the digital era? What does ethical use of social media entail? These questions have captured the attention of contemporary scholars of social work ethics. Reamer (2013) describes the ethical complexities of current practices such as online and video counseling, websites for "self-help" interventions, digital record-keeping, and the blurring of personal and professional boundaries in the use of social media by both social workers and clients. Issues of privacy, confidentiality, and consent are often at stake, and the guidelines for ethical practice are far from clear. Elizabeth Voshel and Alia Wesala (2015) raise similar concerns, noting that codes of ethics are behind the times in providing meaningful guidelines for practice. They call for further research and dialogue regarding the ethical use of social media as well as the establishment of clear, ethically sound, agency-based guidelines. Additionally, they argue that, given the global nature of social media, social work practice needs to take international ethical principles into account.

Interestingly, current discussion of ethical use of new media tends to focus on the implications for the *social worker as therapist* model of practice. Less attention has been paid to the ethics of social media in advocacy and activism. Medhi Gharbi's (2014) notes on social media and the Arab Spring is an exception. Gharbi describes *Tunisnews*, an online newsletter that served as a platform for information access and freedom of expression for people of Tunisia during a time of extreme repression. The newsletter served as a concrete expression of human rights and nonviolent resistance, seeking to break the authorities' control over news and provide people access to information about the reality of what was occurring in the country. It illustrates the potential power of social media as a key instrument of ethical practice in struggles for social justice.

Social Work Values and Ethics: Beyond U.S. Borders

We turn now to an international perspective on social work as a value-based profession and locate the subject of ethics in a global context. There is a rich history of social work engagement with the struggles to meet human needs and champion human rights on an international scale that both parallels and challenges the domestic social work story we have addressed. A thorough discussion of that history is beyond the scope of this chapter. We refer readers to Lynne M. Healy's *International Social Work: Professional Action in an Interdependent World* (2008) for an excellent overview of social work history from an international perspective. We highlight moments in that story here, with particular attention to the evolution of standards of ethical practice.

Social work as a profession and the modern social welfare state were emerging across Western industrialized societies in response to the contradictions and fallout of industrial capitalism at the turn of the twentieth century. Schools of social work education were forming around 1900 in London, New York, Berlin, and Amsterdam. By 1920 concerted efforts were underway to bring social work knowledge and practice to bear on a broader global audience. European and U.S. "experts" began to introduce social work theories and methods as correctives to concerns over modernization and development in parts of Asia, Africa, and Latin America. For example, the first Latin American school of social work, established in Chile in 1925, was strongly influenced by the medical model of practice. A similar pattern characterized the emergence of social work in Argentina, where the first prototype of social work was the "hygiene visitor." South Africa and Egypt hosted the first schools of social work on the African continent, and students were tutored in a charity model borrowed from the United States and Europe (Healy, 2008).

The International Association of Schools of Social Work was founded in 1928, along with the International Permanent Secretariat of Social Workers (IPSSW). These professional entities emerged from the first international social work conference, held in Paris in 1928. An aim of the Secretariat was to promote the professionalization of social work through establishment of ethical standards. The IPSSW was the predecessor to the International Federation of Social Workers (IFSW), which was founded in 1956. The IFSW has served as a vehicle for representing social work perspectives and positions on significant global issues before the United Nations, and it has played a role in human rights advocacy (Healy, 2008).

IFSW Declaration of Ethical Principles

The IFSW adopted the first international code of ethics in 1976. The code was substantially revised in 1994 and again in 2004. Human rights and social jus-tice are guiding beacons of the IFSW Statement of Ethical Principles (2012) (http://ifsw.org/policies/statement-of-ethical-principles). It stands as a con-certed effort to position social work as a profession committed to the realization of these values in practice in a global context. However, the legitimacy of an international code of ethics for social work is not without question and criti-cism. There have been intense debates regarding the universality of social work values and the predominance of individualistic Western values that leads to the marginalization of other perspectives, especially those that might claim a more communal worldview (Healy, 2008; Ife, 2010, 2012; Ife & Fiske, 2006). The fun-damental debates between absolutism and relativism that resonate through the long history of human values discourse play out here as well in the tensions between universal human rights and cultural relativism. Healy argues that there is a continuum between universalism and cultural relativism, and she sees the IFSW Statement of Ethical Principles as a valiant effort to position itself in the middle ground.

These discussions of universalism and relativism are challenging. Drawing from Donaldson (1996, p. 48), Healy (2007, p. 13) raises the question "When is different just different and when is different wrong?" Healy does not pose facile answers, but contends that social workers in a global context face the ongoing challenge of "negotiating spaces of moral ambiguity discerning value tensions from intolerable practices that cause harm" (Rao, 1995, cited in Healy, 2008, p. 241). Healy brings a dynamic concept of culture to bear in discussing these tensions and the ethical implications for international social work. She defines culture as "a series of constantly contested and negotiated social practices whose meanings are influenced by the power and status of their interpreters and participants" (Healy, 2008, pp. 244–245). She poses four questions for eval-uating cultural claims (p. 244):

1. What is the status of the speaker?
2. In whose name is the argument of culture advanced?
3. What is the degree of participation in culture formation of the social groups primarily affected by the cultural practices in question?
4. What is culture anyway?

In the effort to craft a set of practice principles that meaningfully crosses and bridges complex boundaries of difference, the tension between universalism and relativism continues. This tension is not the only focus of the critique of the IFSW statement, however. Some have expressed concern over its language of professionalism and implicit assumptions of a client-oriented model of practice. (See the website of the School of Social Work, University of Costa Rica, San Jose, Costa Rica, at http://www.ts.ucr.ac.cr/decla for an archive of declarations and debates regarding the definition of social work.)

Some critics contend that the IFSW Statement of Ethical Principles favors an expert model of social work practice over one that promotes participation and social transformation. For example, during the revision of the IFSW declaration, the Committee of Professional Social Work and Social Service Organizations of the Southern Cone of Latin America (in Argentina, Bolivia, Brazil, Chile, Parguay, and Uruguay) argued that the understanding of social work embraced by the IFSW is disconnected from the social realities and pressing concerns of people in different countries and regions of the world.

Members of the Southern Cone organizations developed their own statement of ethical and political principles to guide social work practice. Their statement recognized their differing social realities and their common concerns regarding social exclusion, violation of human rights, conditions of widespread poverty, and erasure of collective memory. They specifically identified social work's responsibility to "contribute to maintaining the collective memory of the people." They called for respect for self-determination, not only of individuals but also of groups, organizations, and popular movements. They directly voiced concern over globalization and its effects on cultural identity in Latin America. They criticized the neoliberal economic model of late capitalism, the concentration of economic and political power in the hands of the elites, and the barriers to democratization throughout the region. These forces, they argued, have severely limited social work's historic commitment to social justice. They pointed to the urgent need for social workers to assume a *political-ethical* position in the face of these forces and to engage in the struggle for social transformation.

They embraced human emancipation, liberty, social justice, solidarity, and participation as core social work values. (For the full text of the statement of political and ethical principles see Escuela de Trabajo Social [2000].)

Take a moment to reflect on their critiques and their articulation of ethical and political principles. What challenges do they pose to the IFSW Statement of Ethical Principles? To the scope and nature of ethical practice put forth by NASW? To your own thinking about social work ethics?

Social Work Ethics in Differing National Contexts

Let's look beyond the IFSW Statement of Ethical Principles to a few examples of ethical standards for social work practice in different national contexts. Many social work organizations in diverse parts of the world have adopted standards of ethical practice regarding professional obligations, competence, and responsibilities to clients, the profession, and society that closely resemble those of NASW. Others address the importance of ethically responsible behavior by social workers but do not standardize those value expectations in a code of ethics. We find interesting and important variations in the ways values and expectations are expressed. For example, the Canadian Association of Social Workers Code of Ethics, along with accompanying guidelines for practice, was revised in 2005 (CASW, 2005). It closely resembles the NASW Code of Ethics in terms of its attention to core values. In contrast to the NASW code, however, the CASW code makes explicit its commitment to the Universal Declaration of Human Rights (United Nations, 1948).

Challenges to an individualist view of ethics are reflected in some national contexts. For example, social workers in India "have questioned the relevance of clinical, individualist-oriented Western codes and prefer the term 'declaration' of ethics for people-centered work" (Desai, 1987). The Indian Declaration of Ethics for Professional Social Workers prioritizes social work's responsibility to advocate for oppressed groups. It emphasizes family, community, capabilities, and holistic, wisdom-oriented, duty-based cultural values. It is written in the language of first-person pledges. It specifically names honesty, personal integrity, solidarity with marginalized people, participation, self-determination, cooperation and collaboration, and peace and nonviolence in resolving conflicts as core values guiding social work (Hill & Jones, 2003). In contrast to other ethical statements we have considered, the Indian Declaration of Ethics pays specific attention to the environment in which humans are but one life form. In so doing it locates social work ethics within a broader context of *environmental* ethics. It begins:

> As a professional social worker, I pledge to inculcate and promote the following values, in myself, in the profession, in the organisations I work with, and in the society.

> 1. I pledge to perceive and accept people as having inherent worth and dignity, irrespective of their attributes and achievements, having the capability of change and development; and I pledge to perceive people as part of the scheme of nature, needing to live in harmony with other life forms. (Hill & Jones, 2003, p. 176)

Some social work organizations have embraced a union role and stance rather than the model of professionalism dominant in the United States. For example, the Danish Association of Social Workers describes itself as a professional organization and trade union with an interest in both working conditions and working methods. More than 90 percent of social workers are members, and the association is a powerful voice of advocacy, not only for members but also for broader social justice agendas (Karger, & Lonne, 2010, p. 38). This model is reminiscent of the Rank and File Movement in the United States, discussed in chapter 2. The association practices a strong commitment to international cooperation and solidarity. Similarly, social workers in Norway and Finland are organized in trade unions and professional associations and maintain a strong international focus.

A key feature of Aotearoa's/New Zealand's colonizing history was the 1840 Treaty of Waitangi, negotiated between Maori chiefs and occupying British leaders. The treaty "established the foundation of biculturalism in the country and entrenched rights of Maori people as *Tangata Whenua* (a Maori term meaning people of the land)" (Staniforth & Noble, 2014, p. 178). When a 1986 government-commissioned review of social welfare practices in the country revealed deep institutional racism, social workers responded by reconfiguring education and practice models and approaches to be more in line with Maori culture, history, worldviews, and practices. For example, Maori models of well-being have been incorporated into social work education. In 1993 the Aotearoa/New Zealand Association of Social Work (ANZASW) adopted a bicultural code of ethics and practice as a concrete commitment to anti-oppressive practice that honors the identity, history, and rights of Maori people. A bilingual code of ethics was adopted in 2007. Social workers are called upon to advocate for policies and practices that honor the treaty and the rights of Maori people. The code also recognizes the right of Maori clients to have access to Maori social workers and culturally appropriate resources and services (Aotearoa/New Zealand Association of Social Workers, 2015; Birkenmaier, Berg-Weger, & Dewees, 2014, p. 48; Staniforth & Noble, 2014).

In sum, these alternative conceptualizations of social work values reflect the intimate linkage between ethics and politics. They suggest the importance of understanding values in context. And they remind us of the dynamic nature of codes of ethics. Perhaps we can best think of codes of ethics as living, evolving documents, shaping and shaped by the historical, political, social, and cultural context of practice.

Class Learning Activity:
Applying Codes of Ethics

As a class, visit the National Center for Child Poverty website (http//www
.nccp.org) and review the Center's publication entitled "Basic Facts about
Low Income Children: Children under 18 Years." Divide into four groups to
apply an ethical framework to the issue of child poverty in the United
States. Each group will consider the issue through the lens of a specific
social work code of ethics:

• Group 1: NASW

• Group 2: IFSW

• Group 3: NABSW

• Group 4: Radical Social Worker code

Each group will then develop a position statement—or platform—and a
five-point plan for addressing the issue of child poverty in America. Imagine that this statement and plan will guide the actions of your organization. Imagine that it is a statement that representatives of the organization will make publicly and include on the organization's website. The
statement should embrace the values, commitments, and ethical stance
of the organization as expressed in its code of ethics. Each group will then
present its position and plan to the class, followed by a full class discussion
and debriefing. Consider the following questions in the discussion:

1. How does the code guide your thinking?

2. Does the code help focus your priorities? How?

3. What ethical questions does it raise for you?

4. What direction does it offer in terms of ethical course of action?

5. Which code is most in line with your own professional stance? Why?

FRAMEWORKS FOR ETHICAL DECISION MAKING IN SOCIAL WORK PRACTICE

Our preceding discussion of values and ethics in social work speaks to the complexity of ethical issues that we confront in our practice. How then should we

proceed in the process of ethical decision making? What frameworks might guide us? These questions have been the subject of study and debate by social work ethicists and practitioners over the course of the profession's development. The key questions that stem from the differing ethical perspectives discussed on p. 108 may be a starting point for the process of ethical decision making in social work. However, we are still left with fundamental questions regarding which of these perspectives takes priority in guiding our actions.

Ethics and Step-by-Step Decision Making

Some students of social work ethics argue that there is, in fact, a clear order of priorities that should guide our decision making. For example, Loewenberg, Dolgoff, and Harrington (2000) have put forth the "Ethical Principles Screen" and argue that seven core principles can be rank ordered in guiding decision making: (1) protection of life, (2) equality/inequality, (3) autonomy and freedom, (4) least harm, (5) quality of life, (6) privacy and confidentiality, and (7) truthfulness and disclosure. At first glance this hierarchy may have a common sense appeal. On closer examination, however, it seems to be informed by an implicit set of values that may be at odds with those of the individuals and communities with whom we are engaged as social workers. Think for a moment of a situation where you might apply the Ethical Principles Screen. Where might it help guide your decision making? Where might it prove problematic?

Social work scholars and practitioners have also outlined specific steps for ethical problem solving. For example, NASW (2003, based on Reamer & Conrad, 1995) offered a six-step process to guide ethical decision making:

1. Determine whether there is an ethical issue or dilemma.
2. Identify the key values and principles involved.
3. Rank the values or ethical principles which, in your professional judgment, are most relevant to the issue or dilemma.
4. Develop an action plan that is consistent with the ethical priorities that have been determined as central to the dilemma.
5. Implement your plan utilizing the most appropriate practice skills and competencies.
6. Reflect on the outcome of this ethical decision-making process

Fossen, Anderson-Meger, and Zellmer (2014), building on the work of Elaine Congress (2000), offer the ETHICS-A Model as a means of preparing social workers for ethical decision-making. The ETHICS-A Model (p. 68) provides a mnemonic device to facilitate the process, which entails the following steps:

- **E**xamine the situation to determine if there is an ethical dilemma and examine personal and professional values.
- **T**hink about ethical principles, standards, or laws that may be relevant.
- **H**ypothesize possible options and decisions.
- **I**dentify possible consequences of each option.
- **C**onsult with supervisors and colleagues.
- **S**elect a course of ethical action.
- **A**dvocate for change on appropriate system level.
- **D**ocument the process, decisions, actions, and outcomes.

These step-by-step models may hold appeal for helping us think through ethical issues. However, they also suggest that complex, multilayered ethical situations can be reduced to and resolvable through clear-cut, linear, technical processes and principles. Moreover, they suggest that there is a shared understanding of the issue at stake among the parties involved. Finally, they seem to assume that the practice of ethical problem-solving happens outside the worker-client relationship and is then *applied to* rather than emergent through that relationship.

Ethics and Dialogue

Merlinda Weinberg and Carolyn Campbell (2014) contend that the real world ethical issues social workers grapple with every day are not so neatly understood or resolved. They propose that "what is identified as an ethical issue is not the same for every professional. There is not clear, objective truth 'out there' to which we all subscribe" (p. 38). They draw attention to the contextual, relational nature of social work, and they, like Margaret Rhodes, speak to the importance of dialogue and the place of feelings in the process. They challenge us to think of ethical practice as open, emergent through collaboration and dialogue, and situated in "context, culture, community, history, and time" (p. 45). They consider the possibilities that may emerge when we listen with genuine openness and curiosity to another's worldview. They encourage us to let go of the faulty assumption that we must (and can) make the "right" ethical decision and remind us that the ripple effects of our actions are at once endless and unknowable. They direct our ethical gaze to the macro level of societal inequalities and call on us to assume moral responsibility as active change agents willing to question and resist the prescriptive, rule-based modes of operation that support the status quo. Finally, they invite us to learn from our own experiences through self-reflexivity and humility and bring that knowledge to bear as ethical practitioners (p. 47).

Marcia Abramson (1996) has similarly argued that we as social workers must know ourselves ethically in order to engage in meaningful ethical decision making with others. She sees self-examination as an ethical responsibility for professional practice. To this end, Abramson has developed a framework for ethical self-assessment that challenges us to look inward and see where and how our personal values, beliefs, and experiences filter into our professional ethical stance. In so doing, she has drawn from diverse ethical perspectives to pose a series of critical questions to practitioners. Take time to assess yourself in light of Abramson's framework. How might your ethical stance shape your approach to decision making regarding a social work issue such as transracial adoption or end-of-life care?

Knowing Yourself Ethically: A Framework for Self-assessment
Adapted from Marcia Abramson (1996)

- *Prejudgments*: What do you bring from your own personal and cultural history in terms of attitudes, biases, stereotypes, and agendas?

- *Character and virtue*: What is your image of a morally good person, a good social worker, a good member of society? What generates self-esteem or self-approval for you? How might that affect your practice as a social worker?

- *Principles*: How do you use and prioritize ethical principles? When they come into conflict, which ones take precedence over others? For example, how do you weigh safety issues against self-determination?

- *Ethical theories*: Do you believe that correctness of action needs to be weighed against context or outcome? Or do you hold that certain acts are intrinsically good or bad, regardless of consequence?

- *Free will versus determinism*: Do you see human beings as free agents, able to choose courses of action, or as determined by their life circumstances? Or as somewhere in between?

- *Spirituality*: What is the place of religion and spirituality in your world-view and in your understanding of the human search for meaning and purpose?

- *Individual-community*: Where do your values fall in the balance between individual rights and social responsibility? Are you guided more by an ethics of individualism or communalism?

- *Voice*: How would you describe your moral voice? Is it a voice of rights and justice? A voice of relationship, care, and connection? Another voice?

EXPANDING THE POSSIBILITIES FOR ETHICAL DECISION MAKING

Human Rights as a Foundation for Ethical Practice

Let's return to the question of social work and human rights. A number of scholars have called on social work to use the United Nations Universal Declaration of Human Rights (UDHR) as a foundation for ethical practice (Ife, 2010, 2012; Mapp, 2007; Reichert, 2011; Witkins, 1998). The UDHR is a remarkable document crafted in the aftermath of World War II. It recognized human rights as "those rights that are inherent in our nature and without which we cannot live as human beings" (United Nations, 1987). The framers of the UDHR concluded that "recognition of the inherent dignity and of the equal and inalienable rights of all members of the human family is the foundation of freedom, justice, and peace in the world" (United Nations, 1948). These rights were recognized as universal, inalienable, indivisible, and interdependent. They address the social, cultural, political, economic, personal, spiritual, and environmental dimensions of human experience (Ife & Fiske, 2006). The UDHR was endorsed in 1948 by member states of the newly formed United Nations who explicitly recognized its principles as the "common standard of decency."

The UDHR is a product of the historical and political moment in which it was crafted and ratified. It has been criticized for its privileging of Western conceptions of personhood, individual rights, and citizenship (Healy, 2008; Link, 1999; Lyons, 1999). However, as Stanley Witkin (1998) notes, the declaration is significant for articulating the idea of universal rights that cannot be separated from political, social, and economic arrangements (p. 197). A fundamental implicit principle was that less powerful people and groups needed protection against those with more power, especially the state (Nagenast & Turner, 1997,

p. 269). The UDHR addresses *positive rights*, such as freedom of thought and religion and the right to recognition as a person before the law, and *negative rights*, such as protection from arbitrary arrest and detention. Its very existence provides a basis for grappling with complex questions of national sovereignty, cultural relativity, collective rights, the nature and extent of rights, the right to have rights, and the myriad tensions therein.

"In Our Hands"

Eleanor Roosevelt, 1958 speech delivered on the tenth anniversary of the UDHR

Where, after all, do universal human rights begin? In small places, close to home—so close and so small that they cannot be seen on any maps of the world. Yet they ARE the world of the individual person; the neighborhood he lives in; the school or college he attends; the factory, farm, or office where he works. Such are the places where every man, woman, and child seeks equal justice, equal opportunity, equal dignity without discrimination. Unless rights have meaning there, they have little meaning anywhere. Without concerted citizen action to uphold them close to home, we shall look in vain for progress in the larger world.

Eleanor Roosevelt served as chair of the UDHR drafting committee of the UN Commission on Human Rights. Take a moment to reflect on her words. Does her vision of human rights offer of vision for social justice work as well? How might the UDHR serve as a framework for social justice work? What might be some reasons for the lack of attention to human rights within social work in the United States?

The UDHR and its supporting declarations, conventions, covenants, and treaties inform the ethical and practical framework for social work in many parts of the world. This is not the case in the United States. In fact, most social workers, like the larger public, have little working knowledge of human rights in general and the UDHR in particular. Many of us have not been exposed to the UDHR during elementary, high school, or even college education. Popular discourse about human rights in the United States tends to focus on violations of rights perpetrated by persons and states outside the United States. The UDHR is less likely to be used as a framework for critical reflection and analysis of the foreign and domestic practices of U.S. government and social and political institutions. When human rights are addressed in the U.S. context, those discussions often focus more on political and civil rights than on social, cultural, and economic rights. As a result, we are generally ill equipped to think in terms of human rights in our everyday lives and in our social work practice.

Elizabeth Reichert (2011) argues that social work in the United States has avoided specific integration of human rights documents into the study and practice of social work for too long. Stanley Witkin (1998) points out that the values articulated in the declaration are central to social work. He contends, however, that a true commitment to human rights is neither visible in social work practice nor integrated into social work education in the United States. He argues that U.S. social work's continued emphasis on individual change and psychological explanations for complex human concerns and noncritical acceptance of capitalism and Western individualism obscure the view of broader human rights issues (pp. 199–200). He calls on social workers to challenge individualist medicalized explanations of people's pain and troubles and to make human rights a part of all aspects of practice, from assessment to intervention and evaluation criteria (p. 201).

We must start from a position of not knowing and create opportunities for learning about human rights before we can meaningfully bring them to bear to guide our practice. Listed below is a plain language version of the thirty articles of the UDHR (Cho et al., 2004, pp. 160–161). (The complete text of the UDHR can be accessed at http://www.un.org/en/universal-declaration-human-rights). We will provide examples of human-rights-informed practice in the chapters that follow.

Universal Declaration of Human Rights: Plain Language Version

Article 1:   Right to equality
Article 2:   Freedom from discrimination
Article 3:   Right to life, liberty, and personal security
Article 4:   Freedom from slavery
Article 5:   Freedom from torture and degrading treatment
Article 6:   Right to recognition as a person before the law
Article 7:   Right to equality before the law
Article 8:   Right to remedy by competent tribunal
Article 9:   Freedom from arbitrary arrest and exile
Article 10:   Right to fair hearing
Article 11:   Right to be considered innocent until proved guilty
Article 12:   Freedom from interference with privacy, family, home, and correspondence
Article 13:   Right to free movement in and out of the country

Article 14:   Right to asylum in other countries from persecution in other countries
Article 15:   Right to a nationality and the freedom to change nationality
Article 16:   Right to marriage and a family
Article 17:   Right to own property
Article 18:   Freedom of belief and religion
Article 19:   Freedom of opinion and information
Article 20:   Right of peaceful assembly and association
Article 21:   Right to participate in government and in free elections
Article 22:   Right to social security
Article 23:   Right to desirable work and to join trade unions
Article 24:   Right to rest and leisure
Article 25:   Right to adequate standard of living
Article 26:   Right to education
Article 27:   Right to participate in the cultural life of a community
Article 28:   Right to a social order that articulates this document
Article 29:   Community duties essential to free and full development
Article 30:   Freedom from state or personal interference in above rights

Australian social work scholar Jim Ife (2012) examines human rights in the context of ethical decision making. He suggests that ethics and rights are two sides of the same coin. He argues, however, that traditional social work discourse on ethics and codes of ethics have tended to focus on the worker and the decisions she or he must make, with no clear role for the client in the process. This focus emphasizes the power and expertise of the worker and can render the client powerless in the process. In contrast, a human rights approach brings the focus to the client—that individual or group with whom the social worker is interacting—as an active participant in the decision-making process. This, Ife suggests, is a more empowering approach to recognizing, realizing, and protecting rights (Ife, 2012, pp. 165–167). Further, he contends, a human rights approach can prevent social workers from "drowning in a sea of moral relativism" (2012, p. 170).

Reflection Moment:
Rights, Values, and Social Justice Work

Take some time to read and reflect on the Universal Declaration of Human Rights. What are some of the core values it addresses? What challenges might you face in taking a human rights approach to social work? What possibilities might a human rights approach provide? Consider the following situations from a human rights perspective. What rights may have been denied or violated? How might your knowledge of human rights inform your response to the situation? How might your response differ from that of a social worker taking a more "traditional" approach?

- A person experiencing homelessness who is turned away from a full shelter for the third night in a row
- A nine-year-old child in a receiving home awaiting temporary placement in a foster home
- An undocumented resident of the United States whose young child, born in the United States, is in need of emergency health care
- A person seeking the services of your practicum agency

Has your engagement with the UDHR prompted you to think differently about yourself as a social worker or the possibilities for social work practice? If so, how? How would you describe the relationship between human rights and social justice work?

Incorporating Human Rights in Practice

It is easier to talk about human rights than to actively incorporate them in our practice and struggle with the tensions and contradictions therein. One of the implications for social work in the United States is that we must move beyond the safety of local and national boundaries and consider the potential political and ethical ramifications of our privileged positioning in the Global North and the action generated from that positioning. Rosemary Link (1999, p. 85) develops the idea of an "ethics of participation," which may serve as a guide.

An ethics of participation demands, most fundamentally, that the people affected by particular issues or circumstances and events need to be present in the process of decision making. Discussions need to take place in these people's first language. And people need to have a legitimate voice in all decisions that affect them (Link, 1999, pp. 85–86). Link proposes a number of universal principles for social justice work. She organizes the principles into three broad categories. The first principle, "widest perspective for assessment," asks us to consider how we as social workers are influenced by the problem and issues; how we explore the values, histories, and cultural perspectives of others involved; and how we question the power of *geocentrism* and the effects of our location on the process.

The second principle, "inclusion of the service user in dialogue and decisions," calls on social workers to address questions of language and power, to respect others' *right to reality*, and to consider how the immediate situation may be shaped by broader structural arrangements. The third, "joint evaluation," frames ethical decision making as a collaborative, dialogical, and critically reflective practice with careful attention to process and outcomes (Link, 1999, p. 90).

Let's return for a moment to the Indian Declaration of Ethics for Professional Social Workers. As noted previously, the declaration makes specific reference to environmental ethics. Social workers are called upon to "perceive people as part of the scheme of nature" and to assume responsibility to "live in harmony with other life forms" (Hill & Jones, 2003, p. 176). Take a moment to consider the principles of an ethics of participation and those of environmental ethics. What possibilities do they pose for the ethical practice of social justice work? How might they challenge or expand your thinking? Using these questions as guidelines, take time to reflect on an ethical dilemma you have faced as you have engaged in social work practice. Do you see alternative possibilities for understanding the problem, building relationships, and developing courses of action? We will return to specific questions of values, ethics, and participation as we explore the core processes of social justice work in the following chapters.

SUMMARY

In this chapter we have examined the concept of values, their place in our everyday lives, and their role in shaping social work thought and practice. We have considered values in political, historical, and familial contexts, and we have addressed the practice of valuing. We have considered the core values of social work, the relationship between values and ethics, and the emergence of codes of ethics. We have challenged the ethical boundaries of social work in the United States by examining alternative constructions of values and standards of ethical and political practice in diverse organizational and national contexts. We have outlined approaches to ethical decision making and the challenges therein. Finally, we have considered the relationship of social work and human rights and put forth ethical and political principles that may guide us in the pursuit of social justice work. We close this chapter with an individual learning activity and an essay by social worker and ecologist Katherine Deuel, who addresses the everyday challenges and hopes of putting ethical principles of social, environmental, and economic justice into community-based practice. In chapter 4, we will turn our attention to theory, the dialectics of understanding and action, and the Just Practice framework and processes.

> **Individual Learning Activity:**
> **Applying Codes of Ethics**
>
> Draw from a practice-related experience, an example addressed in class, or an issue currently in the news to describe (in one page or less) an ethically challenging situation you have faced or may face as a social worker. Select two of the codes of ethics or statements of ethical principles addressed in this chapter and compare them in terms of how they might guide your process of ethical decision making in this situation. Which course of action aligns best with your personal values? How? Develop your comparative analysis in a three- to four-page essay.

ON REFLECTION

Practicing Social and Environmental Sustainability

Katherine Deuel, MSW

I am an ecologist, a social worker, and a mother. I serve as the executive director at a building materials reuse center in Montana. The young male founders created the organization in response to the waste produced by the building industry—construction and demolition waste are reported to make up 40 percent of the United States' solid waste stream. They worked the magic, shed the tears, and sweated the gallons that go into starting a nonprofit and succeeded, producing along the way a mission statement that not only directs this organization to reduce waste but also to help build a vibrant and sustainable local economy.

The ecologist in me is familiar with this now ultra-hip concept of sustainability. From an ecosystem perspective, it implies that inputs and outputs roughly balance and that whatever is being used in the moment will still be available and productive in the system later (though maybe not in the same form). I was attracted to the organization by the powerful climate impacts mitigation of reducing waste (saves energy, keeps materials local, and reduces resource extraction) and the organization's triple-bottom-line business model that puts social and ecological profit on equal footing with its economic profit.

The social worker in me is less familiar, but intrigued, with how sustainability plays out in the social and economic milieu. For example, when I worked in wildlife conservation, the trend was to include people. Environmentalists were struggling with the historic shift from rugged individuals saving a species to collaborative efforts that teach coexistence with the entire arc of native wildlife.

I made the shift to social work because I was discouraged by the rampant conflict over practical means to achieve philosophical ends and because I was hungry to find a way to meaningfully include people, the vast and glorious diversity of us, in the effort to keep the natural world that sustains us all functioning. I quickly came to understand why environmentalists, myself included, were labeled elitists because we champion a cause that extends far into a future that many don't have the resources to even imagine and promotes benefits, like solitude in wild nature, which many will never enjoy.

The urgency of many social needs drives a sense that social and environmental sustainability are in tension. It's widely believed that attention to one of these worthy goals—long-term conservation or social justice now—inherently reduces the resources available to the other. My experience at our building materials reuse center has proven the opposite. Our story turns that implied zero-sum mind-set of people versus the environment on its head. Here, the more waste we keep out of the landfill (currently about four tons a day), the bigger our positive environmental impact. And the more work we have sorting, cleaning, moving, and revamping, the more customers come through our business, the larger and more diverse staff we employ, the more people learn about reuse, the more money and materials stay in the local economy, and the more people feel connected and engaged in powerful, positive cultural change.

One of the programs that strengthens this sustainable loop is our work program, which hires and offers green-building-skills training to people who are experiencing barriers to employment such as mental and physical disabilities; histories of incarceration, addiction, or trauma; and issues that frequently tumble them into (or arise out of) a cycle of poverty that would break the best of us. This leading edge of sustainability looks gritty and rough—the work is dirty and tiring and rather endless. From a management perspective, the pluses and minuses of daily hugs, random lectures, no-shows, devilish humor, fierce loyalty, and bitter heartbreak are incalculable. But at the end of the day we provide meaningful work with dignity that comes with genuine belonging to a tough and inclusive community. Many of our participants have previously gotten the message that they don't have value, that they are the throwaways of the human world, and that they don't belong and have no power. There can be no more foolish or significant waste than not keeping each precious individual secured within and contributing to the human ecology loop.

I mentioned that I am a mother. The mother in me will always worry about my children's future—and, if not mine, then yours. I carry a load of grief (about loss of natural systems, war, and systemic human degradation) and fear about how today's challenges will unfold tomorrow. The mother in me is determined to use my power to alchemize the zero-sum mind-set that grief and fear dispatch into a bounty of hope and connection that propels itself forward. And our building materials reuse center provides some of that hope and connection. Social workers, like you, who are reading this text do too.

Ultimately, this is about possibility. Sustainability is not about how we manage waste once we create it, but about not accepting the concept of throwaways, human or material, in the first place. As we recreate our food, waste, energy, and transportation systems to be sustainable in the currently accepted sense of that word, we must also recreate our power systems to make them socially sustainable—just—in their very design. We need to start with a closed system, where no one falls off the precipice of dignity, caring, and ability to support themselves. Getting there is not a choice—it is an imperative; one that asks us to work like mad dogs for whatever good we can do in our day jobs and then open ourselves to the songs the stars sing on the darkest nights of a long, sustainable, and just vision. We will recognize the tune. We just need to take it up and sing.

QUESTIONS FOR DISCUSSION

1. If you were to organize a value tour of your community, where would you go? What values would you highlight? What impressions might participants take away from the tour?

2. What life experiences have posed the greatest challenges to your values? What institutions beyond the family have shaped your values? How have your values evolved or changed as a result?

3. Based on your review of a number of codes of ethics, what would you include if you were to write a code of ethics for twenty-first century social justice work?

4. What insight or inspiration do you take from the ethical principles and standards that guide social work in diverse national contexts outside the United States?

5. Is it possible to be an ethical social worker without being political?

SUGGESTED READINGS

Healy, L. (2008). *International social work: Professional action in an independent world* (2nd ed.). New York: Oxford.

Hugman, R. (2012). *Culture, value and ethics in social work*. London: Routledge.

Ife, J. (2012). *Human rights and social work: Towards rights-based practice* (3rd ed.). Cambridge: Cambridge University Press.

Rhodes, M. (1986). *Ethical dilemmas in social work practice*. London: Routledge.

Vosel, E. H., & Wesala, A. (2015). Social media and social work ethics: Determining best practices in an ambiguous reality. *Journal of Social Work Values and Ethics, 12*, 67–76.

Chapter 4

Just Thinking: Theoretical Perspectives on Social-Justice-Oriented Practice

I came to theory because I was hurting—the pain within me was
so intense that I could not go on living. I came to theory desperate,
wanting to comprehend—to grasp what was happening around
and within me. Most importantly, I wanted to make the hurt go away.
I saw in theory a location for healing.

bell hooks (1994)

OVERVIEW

In chapter 4 we define and discuss theory and the practice of theorizing in social work and in everyday life. We consider theorizing as a fundamental human activity through which we work to make sense of our worlds, experiences, and relations. We present a brief overview and critique of several theoretical perspectives that inform contemporary social work including medical/psychological, ecosystems, structural, strengths, and empowerment approaches.

We introduce readers to a range of critical theoretical contributions that have been developed by people both within and outside of social work who are concerned with questions of social justice and social change. They have addressed questions about the social construction of reality; the politics of knowledge development; the interplay of social structures, relations, and actions; workings of forms and mechanisms of oppression and domination; and possibilities for liberatory action. They have explored the *intersectionality* of race, class, gender identity and expression, sexuality and sexual orientation, citizenship, ability status, and age in systems of oppression; they have considered the centrality of language, meaning, and narrative in the crafting of human experience. We reflect on their contributions and the ways they have informed our thinking about the Just Practice framework.

We return to our key concepts—*meaning, context, power, history,* and *possibility*—and argue their relevance for social justice work. We then introduce the seven core processes—*engagement, teaching/learning, action, accompaniment, evaluation, critical reflection,* and *celebration*—through which the concepts are translated into practice.

139

WHAT IS THEORY?

Challenge of Defining Theory

Theory is ever present in our practice. Nevertheless, say the word *theory* to many social work practitioners and be prepared to hear of its irrelevance outside the classroom. Theory is often thought of as academic and abstract. In school we often learn about theory without using theory, and we learn theory without recognizing that we have been using theory all of our lives. The irony here is that theory is always in play in our work, whether we take the time to think about it or not. It underscores every action we take as social workers. It informs our thinking, the choices we make, and the interventions we plan and carry out. When we decide a course of social work action, we are doing so with the assumption that our actions will make a difference, a particular kind of difference. That means we have a theory about what will and won't work to create a desired change. In order to practice social work with intention and integrity we need to think critically and explicitly about the theories that guide our practice.

So what is theory? How does it work? Theory may be defined in various ways. Malcolm Payne (2014) has defined theory as a "generalized set of ideas that describe and explain our knowledge of the world in an organized way" (p. 3). Theories have been described as formal knowledge structures, subject to systematic evaluation, or as personal knowledge structures (McCracken & Rzepnicki, 2010, p. 211) that help us organize and understand the phenomena we encounter in our social work practice and our broader life experience.

Theorizing is something we all engage in every day of our lives as we act in and reflect on the world. In our work, play, and relationships we use theories to interpret our experiences. We gather data from the trial-and-error experiences of everyday life, sometimes changing our practices and sometimes changing our thinking along the way. We apply our folk theories about body, health, and illness as we take our family cures for hiccups or the common cold or as we adopt and invent new remedies. Parents apply and develop theories of child rearing as they put personal and cultural knowledge into practice each day. Likewise, children develop their own theories about the meaning of adulthood and the practice of parenting based on their experiences. Their respective theories of childhood and adulthood may be sharply contrasting, given their very different positionalities or locations in the social world.

Perhaps, by recalling the constant curiosity of children, we can better appreciate theorizing as a fundamental human activity. Let's think for a moment about that favorite phrase of toddlers: "But why?" With those two words, children enter into theorizing about the world and their experience in it. They are seeking explanations and trying to grasp cause and effect. They are trying to understand the rules and figure out the way things work. For example, a friend recalled a time when she was caring for her preschool daughter who had a bad case of the flu. Stroking her daughter's feverish forehead, she said, "Honey, you just feel miserable, don't you?" Her little girl looked up and asked, "Mommy, what makes 'mizzuhble' happen?" Her daughter's question was about theory—about trying to understand her misery and give meaning to her experience. She was trying to construct a theory of health and illness.

Philosopher Terry Eagleton (1990) contends that "children make the best theorists, since they have not yet been educated into accepting our routine practices as 'natural,' and so insist on posing to those practices the most embarrassingly general and fundamental questions, regarding them with a wondering estrangement which we adults have long forgotten" (p. 34). How might we bring that "wondering estrangement" to bear in reflecting on theories that inform social work practice?

Reflection Moment:
Theory: A Child's Eye View

Take a moment to remember some of the theories you developed as a child to make sense of something you experienced or observed in the world around you. What were you trying to understand? What data did you draw on to develop your theory? Did you try to test your theory? If so, how? Did you share your theory with others? Did they concur with your theory or did they have a different explanation? Did your theory change over time as you gathered more information? What might your childhood experience teach you about theories and theorizing?

Making Theory, Making Sense

Before taking a closer look at the place of theory in social work, we offer alternative perspectives on theory that we will keep in mind throughout this chapter. First, we consider the concept of *grounded theory*, or theory built inductively, from the ground up, in contrast to the positivist tradition. Then we address the *urgency* of theory and the idea of theory as a survival skill (Lemert, 2004). Finally, we consider the potentially oppressive force of theory and why that matters for social work.

Grounded Theory

A positivist approach to theorizing assumes that there is a distinct, knowable, and predictable world that can be objectively studied by value-neutral researchers. Theory is built by generating hypotheses and designing experimental methods to test those hypotheses (Guba & Lincoln, 1994). Grounded theory, in contrast, does not start with a hypothesis to be tested but with systematic, ongoing processes of data gathering, analysis, and interpretation. Grounded theory is built bottom-up, from the concrete, empirically grounded realities of people's lives, experiences, and narratives, rather than top-down, from general abstract principles (Glaser & Strauss, 1967; Lengerman & Niebrugge-Brantley, 1998, pp. 40–43). The researcher starts with a question and uses methods such as participant observation, interviews, and collection of artifacts of material culture to try to grasp the phenomenon in question. The process of *constant comparative analysis* leads to the next question and further investigation (Corbin & Strauss, 1990; Glaser & Strauss, 1967). Grounded theory is a means of building knowledge about the world through concrete engagement with people's experiences in the world. The following example illuminates the concept of grounded theory.

Grounded Theory:
Janet's Story

In the early 1990s, I spent three years tacking back and forth between two copper mining towns, Butte, Montana, and Chuquicamata, Chile. The towns had been the copper-producing hubs for the Anaconda Copper Mining Company for the better part of the twentieth century. I wanted to learn how residents imagined and built community together with and in resistance to a powerful corporation. Most accounts of mining towns and their histories focus on men's experiences. I was especially interested in learning about community history and practices from the perspectives and experiences of working-class women—the wives, mothers, and daughters of miners—many of whom were workers themselves. I spent time living in both towns, talking and working with women, visiting their homes and families, and recording their stories of community support, struggles, and survival. Women in Butte told stories about the temporal structuring of their lives around three-year labor contracts as they maintained a vigilance over family and community life during times of employment and mobilized networks of friendship and kinship to hold the "body and soul" of community together during strikes.

> In contrast, women in Chuquicamata told stories of the spatial struc-
> turing of their lives as they got up at dawn to stand in line at the company
> store every day in order to provide for their family's needs. The lines shaped
> the social space of women's lives, where they came together, shared their
> stories, and built solidarity and support. Their critical consciousness of their
> positionings as women and of the possibilities for collective action was
> honed through their everyday struggles for family and community survival.
> Drawing from their stories, I began to develop a theory of gendered social
> practice grounded in women's experiences of "crafting the everyday."
> Women crafted a sense of the ordinary to hold family and community
> together during hard times. They used their material and emotional
> resources to create community and a sense of the possible. They were
> craftswomen, using the tools and supplies at hand to create new mean-
> ings and purpose (Finn, 1998b, p. 176).

The Urgency of Theory

Black feminist scholar bell hooks, whose quote begins this chapter, speaks to
the urgency and necessity of making sense of life experiences and conditions.
Her sense of desperation in the face of intense struggle and of urgency to grasp
and give meaning to the power and pain of her experience contrasts sharply
with more traditional definitions of theory. She described her lived experience
as a child trying to make sense of her world and to make the hurt go away. She
found healing in theory as a place to "imagine possible futures, a place where
life could be lived differently" (1994, pp. 60–61).

There are obvious parallels between hooks's understanding of theory and
that of Antonio Gramsci, the Italian Marxist philosopher who theorized about
culture, power, history, and Fascism from his prison cell. Gramsci spent the last
eleven years of his life—1926 to 1937—in prison for his participation in working-
class movements and his promotion of the dangerous idea that poor and working-class people were capable of critically understanding and collectively
changing the conditions of their lives (Gramsci, 1957/1987). Like hooks, Gramsci
wrote about theory with a sense of urgency, filling notebooks from his prison
cell. He asked how it was that the poor and working classes accepted societal
arrangements that served elites' interests, and he developed critical theories
about the role of ideology in the production of common sense. Gramsci lived
and wrote of the inseparability of theory and practice. He described theorizing
as an impassioned back-and-forth movement from knowing to understanding

to feeling. He held that there is no true understanding devoid of feeling (Forgacs, 1988, p. 349; Gramsci, 1957/1987, p. 67).

The sense of urgency expressed by hooks and Gramsci resonates with Charles Lemert's (2004) depiction of theory as a basic survival skill. Lemert argues that ordinary people create theory every day to understand and survive their life circumstances. Lemert uses an example from Alex Kotlowitz's book, *There Are No Children Here* (1991), where Kotlowitz tells the story of a young boy trying to survive in Chicago's most dangerous public housing project. This ten-year-old child says, "If I grow up, I want to be a bus driver." Think for a moment about what the word *if* means in this context. Contrast this with the common phrase of a privileged child: "When I grow up." In the story, the boy's mother adds her own theoretical perspective as she states, "But you know, there are no children here. They've seen too much to be children." Lemert tells us this is social theory. The boy and his mother are theorizing about their experience in the world. What theories of children and childhood do this boy and his mother express? How do they test out these theories every day? What are other examples of everyday theorizing to understand and survive in life circumstances that diminish one's dignity, identity, and well-being? How, in these circumstances, does theory serve as a basic survival skill as bell hooks recounts in the quotation at the beginning of this chapter? Have you witnessed theory as a survival skill in your social work experience?

Theory as a Form of Oppression and a Tool of Liberation

Although theory can serve as a survival skill in the face of oppression, it can also serve as a form of oppression. Writing from an indigenous perspective, Maori scholar Linda Tuhiwai Smith notes that theory is a word that can provoke a broad range of feelings, values, and attitudes. She addresses ways in which indigenous peoples have been oppressed by theory. Outsider understandings and assumptions have guided the probing into "the way our origins have been examined, our histories recounted, our arts analysed, our cultures dissected, measured and torn apart" (1999, p. 38). Smith recognizes the power of theory in crafting social reality and making claims about that reality. She reminds us that theory is not made in a vacuum but in the context of cultural understanding and social and political relations. She calls on indigenous people to participate in the theory making that shapes understanding of their histories and experiences:

> The development of theories by indigenous scholars which attempt to explain
> our existence in contemporary society (as opposed to the "traditional" soci-

ety constructed under modernism) has only just begun. Not all these theories claim to be derived from some "pure" sense of what it means to be indigenous, nor do they claim to be theories which have been developed in a vacuum separated from any association with civil and human rights movements, other nationalist struggles or other theoretical approaches. What is claimed, however, is that new ways of theorizing by indigenous scholars are grounded in a real sense of, and sensitivity towards, what it means to be an indigenous person. As Kathie Irwin (1992) urges, "We don't need anyone else developing the tools which will help us to come to terms with who we are. We can and will do this work. Real power lies with those who design the tools—it always has. This power is ours." (Smith, 1999, p. 38)

Smith not only addresses the oppressive power of theory, but she also speaks to the potential for theory to serve as a tool of liberation. Theory informed by the knowledge and expertise of those who have experienced oppression can open new possibilities for making sense of an individual's or group's experiences. Smith's discussion of theory and the experiences of indigenous peoples resonates with experiences of other groups who have been viewed as objects of study without having a meaningful voice in the making of theories about their lives.

Patricia Deegan, in her powerful documentary *The Politics of Memory*, makes a similar argument about the history of mental illness. She demonstrates the ways in which theories about madness have contributed to the construction of persons with mental illness as *other* and justified their subjugation to oppressive forms of intervention. Deegan also points to the liberating potential of theory in which those affected by mental illness have come together to name their experiences and realities and make claims for their knowledge to be valued and their voices heard. Let's think for a moment about theory in the context of your current social work practice. Have you witnessed examples of the oppressive power of theory? If so, how has theory worked in oppressive ways? What have been the consequences? Have you witnessed examples of theory as a tool of liberation? If so, how did theory work in liberating ways? What were the consequences? How might you use theory as a tool for liberation in your social work practice?

Theorizing is a critical and creative process of making sense of and giving meaning to the world and our experience in it. Theorizing is part and parcel of our social practice. We have attempted to bring the process of making theory to light in order to systematically reflect on it and examine the relationship between theory and practice. We turn now to consideration of the social construction of theory and questions of positionality and standpoint therein.

> **Class Learning Activity:**
> **The Politics of Memory**
>
> Arrange a viewing of Patricia Deegan's documentary *The Politics of Memory* (https://www.youtube.com/watch?v=U09S7k4phY). As Deegan describes, official accounts of psychiatric history have left out the voices and stories of those subjected to treatment. She argues that a *politics of memory* for people with psychiatric disabilities is key to challenging the oppressive weight of theories that have defined their reality without hearing their voices. After viewing the film, consider the following questions:
>
> - What does Deegan mean by a politics of memory?
> - How might this concept help in understanding forms and mechanisms of oppression embedded in our theories and shaping our practices?
> - What does the film suggest about the liberatory potential of theory?

The Social Construction of Theory

Our discussion of the history and development of social work thought and practice presented in chapter 2 helps us see theory as socially constructed (Robbins, Chatterjee, & Canda, 2006). This means that our ideas about the social world are shaped by our experiences in the world. We are born into an existing social context and immersed in a complex system of cultural norms, schemas, and patterned practices of behavior that shape our ways of seeing, knowing, and engaging with the world around us. From generation to generation, notions of social reality are transmitted and internalized (and at times resisted) through socialization processes. This socially and culturally transmitted knowledge that we acquire from infancy equips us with systems of language, screens of meaning, patterns of practice, and shared assumptions through which we engage in the world and from which we come to question, explore, and theorize about the world. Our more formal theories about human behavior and processes of change are intimately linked to these broader systems of values, meanings, assumptions, and practices that shape our worldviews. This tacit knowledge that surrounds the larger context of our theories goes largely unquestioned.

Social Construction of Disability

Romel Mackleprang and Richard Salsgiver's (2015) description of the social construction of disability provides a powerful example of theory as socially constructed. They start by situating meanings of disability in historical context.

Ancient beliefs in many societies associated disability with a form of spirit possession. In early Judeo-Christian beliefs, disability was constructed as a form of punishment from God. Moral and spiritual theories prevailed into the Middle Ages throughout Western culture. The Enlightenment brought a new interest in rational thought, scientific inquiry, and the application of mathematical models to social questions. Statistical concepts about normal distributions could be applied to human beings, thus framing new theory around what was considered normal and abnormal. By the mid-1800s moral models were merging with medical models of disability; both framed disability as an undesirable condition. Social Darwinist thought of the nineteenth century further reinforced beliefs about persons with disabilities as deviant and unfit. As Mackleprang and Salsgiver describe, Social Darwinist theory gave rise to the eugenics movement, which remained popular well into the twentieth century.

A medical model with moral undertones dominated much of twentieth century theory and practice related to disabilities. Michelle Fine and Adrienne Asch (1988) have argued that these constructions of disability have become embedded in widely held myths and stereotypes about persons with disabilities, such as a belief that disability defines a person's life and identity and reduces him or her to the status of victim. Further, they argue, these myths have been incorporated into much of the research on disabilities and have shaped the assumptions researchers make and the sorts of questions they ask. Their research informs theory, which may further reinforce very "disabling" perspectives on disability.

These constructions of disability have been subject to challenge, particularly by scholars and activists whose work is informed by the lived experience of disability. An emerging disability rights movement, led by persons with disabilities resisting discriminatory treatment, was gaining strength alongside the Civil Rights Movement. The medical model of disabilities was being challenged by a social model of disability (Davis, 1997; Jessup, 2009). The social model locates disability as external to the person and addresses the ways in which disability is socially constructed through language, everyday interaction, media representation, social institutions, and public policies that limit full social participation.

The social model provides a framework for critiquing *ableist* assumptions about the inferiority of persons with disabilities (Mackleprang & Salsgiver, 2015). The focus shifts from the deficits of an individual to the individual's experiences in the context of family, community, and the broader society and to the disabling effects of "physical, attitudinal, and policy barriers" (Jessup, 2009, p. 244). A social theory of disability makes a profound shift from thinking about individual deficits to thinking about rights claims and reducing barriers that limit one's rights. This brief summary illustrates how theories about disability have been constructed over time, how theories are embedded in broader social and political ideologies of a particular historical moment, and how new theory may emerge through struggle informed by those with different positionalities and standpoints. In this case, our example also shows how concepts of social construction have transformed disability theory.

Positionality and Standpoint

From a social constructionist perspective, our theories about the social world are shaped by our location in (*positionality*) and perspective on (*standpoint*) that world. As engaged human beings we bring our histories and experiences with us as we act in and make sense of the world. Our positionalities are shaped through ongoing processes of identification. By this we mean that, as social actors, people are at once claiming identities, being labeled by others, and experiencing the world in terms of those multiple intersecting identities such as race, gender, age, class, citizenship, ethnicity, and sexual orientation. As Reed and colleagues (1997) note,

> Some of these identities give us, almost automatically, and certainly at times unconsciously, certain privileges and stakes in power; alternatively, some of these identities work to produce us as oppressed. . . . Positionality underscores the necessity that each of us locate himself or herself along the various axes of social group identities. We must begin to articulate and take responsibility for our own historical and social identities and interrogate (challenge or question and work to understand in an ongoing way) how they have helped to shape our particular world views. (p. 58)

Proponents of various standpoint theories argue that people with different positionalities acquire differing standpoints, positions from which they view and experience reality and from which alternative views may be obscured. Standpoints, in turn, shape the perspectives from which they theorize about the world and social experiences therein (Collins, 2000; Swigonski, 1994). According to some standpoint theorists, people in oppressed social positions experience a different reality from those who enjoy positions of privilege. As W. E. B. DuBois (1903) has argued, oppressed people develop a critical consciousness as part of their survival strategy. They must be attuned to the dominant rules and vigilant in their social practice. As a result, people in positions of oppression develop a more critical and complex view of social reality, a "double consciousness" in DuBois's words.

Similarly, Patricia Hill Collins (2000) argues that group location within a context of unequal power relations produces common challenges for individuals in those groups. Further, those shared experiences shape similar angles of vision leading to group knowledge or standpoint that is essential for informed political action. These theorists contend that theory making from the standpoint of the oppressed is not simply an intellectual exercise but a matter of survival (Collins, 2000; hooks, 1984; Moraga & Anzaldúa, 1983). Let's take a moment to consider some questions regarding standpoint in relation to theory. What are the implications for social justice work here? What are the risks of making universal theoretical assumptions based on research that provides only a partial view of human experience? What are the risks of theorizing about others when their voices and views are not part of the process? What is at stake when the other who is the object of theorizing is in a position of unequal power vis-à-vis the theorist? How might theorizing about the other lead to theory as a form of oppression?

Summary

Theories are not facts. As tools of inquiry, theories aid in the study of human behavior, provide us with ways in which to explain how the world works, and help us build frameworks, models, and guidelines for practice. Theories, however, are much more. They are value-laden social constructs, the process and products of our search for meaning, and part of our human repertoire of survival skills. Theories emerge in and are shaped by particular social, political, and historical contexts. Thinking of theory in these ways reminds us that we must search for the meanings others create and make no assumptions regarding how others construct their worldviews. It also compels us to look critically at our own thinking and practice.

THEORY AND CONTEMPORARY SOCIAL WORK

Critiquing Theory

Contemplating and engaging with theory require the use of critical thinking skills. They demand *complexity thinking*. Robert Adams and colleagues (2005, pp. 6–7) describe complexity thinking as a skill set that blends critical self-awareness and the ability to contextualize and problematize our work.

Complexity thinking calls for *reflexivity*, or the ability to observe and act from both inside and outside the situation, thus allowing for the identification of implicit assumptions concerning the way things work. In the following discussion we will present an overview of several dominant social work theories and consider both their contributions and critiques. We invite you to practice the skills of complexity thinking as you explore and critique these theoretical perspectives. We present eight questions (adapted from Schriver [2004] and Robbins et al. [2006]) to guide your complexity thinking as you read about theories that inform social work practice and assess their contributions and limitations:

1. What contextual aspects or forces does this theory address (individual, relational, familial, organizational, communal, political, cultural, economic, environmental)?

2. How congruent is this theory with the values and ethics of social work practice?

3. Does this theory support or promote particular values or assumptions about human behavior, human nature, and how the world should be?

4. At what particular point in time is this theory historically situated? When did it develop and what was its contextual surround?

5. Does this theory contribute to preserving and restoring human dignity and rights?

6. What is the power of this theory to define, explain, and interpret reality?

7. Does this theory address human diversity? Does it reflect the experiences of diverse social identities and positionalities?

8. Does this theory assist us in transforming our society and ourselves?

Medical Model

Overview

Let's start our consideration of social work theory by revisiting the medical model that became central to social case work at the turn of the twentieth century. The *Social Work Dictionary* (Barker, 2014) defines the medical model as "an approach to helping people that is patterned after the orientation used by many physicians. This includes looking at the client as an individual with an illness to be treated, giving relatively less attention to factors in the client's environment, diagnosing the condition with fairly specific labels, and treating the problem through regular clinical appointments" (p. 264). *Medical model* is an umbrella term for a range of theoretical and therapeutic approaches that focus on problems, symptoms, or deficits of the individual and their possibilities of amelioration through treatment aimed at the individual. The model pays limited attention to the broader social, political, and economic context in which individual struggles take shape. Although the bulk of social work theorizing over the last century has sought to locate people and their problems in a broader context, the individualizing pull of the medical model remains powerful. This power is evidenced in the significant interest in clinical social work and the role of social worker as psychotherapist and in the expanding use of diagnostic labels of psychopathology as a basis for access to and funding for social work treatment.

Operating within a medical model, the social worker is in the role of expert, charged with gathering the data needed to make an informed diagnosis and direct treatment. The client is cast in a more passive and less powerful role as the target of intervention. Change may be measured in terms of improved physical, emotional, or social functioning of clients, with little attention to the context shaping their experience. Rather, the medical model suggests that finding a diagnosis of client pathology and treating it is the essence of social work (Mattaini & Meyer 2002).

Key Contributions

The medical model of social work has value. Human suffering is real. A systematic approach to the diagnosis and treatment or management of human suffering, whether physical, cognitive, or emotional, can bring relief and improve quality of life. A diagnosis can be very helpful in giving meaning to one's experience of suffering. A diagnosis of *illness* can provide a powerful counter narrative to moral judgments of an individual's being or behavior as bad or somehow morally flawed (Bosk, 2013). The use of a disease model approach to addiction is a case in point. Likewise, processes of treatment and recovery can lead to profound life changes that go beyond the level of the individual. Historically speaking, we saw how the medical model formed the basis of *social diagnosis* and the practice of social casework, which was foundational in the framing of social work as a professional practice. The ability to work within a medical model has enabled social workers to contribute to multidisciplinary professional teams that share a common understanding of a diagnosis/treatment approach.

Critiques

The medical model also has significant limitations. As Ann Weick describes (1983), the medical model of social work, which frames problems in the context of disease, has fundamentally shaped thinking about how human beings grow and change (p. 467). Weick contends that the medical model operates on a mechanistic-static view of human behavior in which there is a specific cause, with a specific effect and concomitant cure. Power is in the hands of the professional who is seen as the agent of change with specialized knowledge to bring about both diagnosis and cure. Moreover, Weick argues, the medical model is "deeply rooted in notions of individual fault and deficiency" as remnants of old thinking surface when one's body or mind "falls from perfection" (p. 468). In addition, the medical model focuses diagnosis and intervention at the level of the person, thus bracketing out consideration of broader systemic forces that are contributing to personal struggles and that could be targeted for change efforts.

Systems

Overview

For the past forty years, social systems or ecological (ecosystems) perspectives have had a prominent place in social work theory in the United States. The approach argues that individuals are complex living systems and that human behavior needs to be understood in its broader systemic context. A system is defined as "an organized whole made up of components that interact in a way distinct from their interaction with other entities and which endures over some period of time" (Anderson & Carter, 1990, pp. 266–267). Systems theory emphasizes reciprocal relationships among individuals, groups, or communities and their interaction in a broader environment (Barker, 2014, p. 423). Systems maintain boundaries that give them their identities, and they tend toward homeostasis, or equilibrium, which means that they try to maintain a balance between sameness and change. Systems theorists view systems holistically and consider the dynamic transactions and relationships among larger systems and their various subsystems. Proponents contend that the systems perspective provides a means for considering the total social situation and intervening accordingly. Systems theories focus on the present and the possibilities for creating change, with little attention to the past.

Systems theories attracted support in social work for their fit with a person-in-environment perspective. The work of Pincus and Minahan, introduced in chapter 2, provides a classic example of the systems perspective as applied to social work. They outlined an integrated approach to problem assessment and planned change that addressed the role of systems as well as people in the helping process. They put forth a conceptual model for social work practice that identified four systems—change agent system, client system, target system, and action system—as central to the change process (1973, p. 63). Systems theories were readily adopted into social work understandings of human behavior in the social environment and practice with families, groups, and communities.

Building on the work of Carol Meyer and others, systems theorists began to incorporate the language of human ecology with that of general systems theory in order to conceptualize more specifically the dynamics of exchange between people and their social and physical environments (Gitterman & Germain, 2008; Mattaini & Meyer, 2002; Meyer, 1970, 1983). In 1980, Carel Germain and Alex Gitterman published *The Life Model of Social Work Practice*. They embraced an ecological approach, promoted the person-in-environment language and perspective, and identified both persons and social systems as contributing to the problem-solving process.

Key Contributions

Systems theories construct human interaction with the social environment in terms of resources, niches, carrying capacity, adaptation, and competition. They emphasize the integrated nature of human behavior, the interplay of multiple systems, and the fit between people and their environments (Mattaini & Meyer, 2002). Systems approaches provide a theoretical basis for social work's professional uniqueness, which is predicated upon the grasp of this relationship. Systems and ecological approaches challenge understandings of social problems that emphasize individual problems or deficits. They look beyond the individual person in crafting solutions and they point to social work's historic concern for the broader context of personal and social experience. The popularity of an ecosystems perspective prompted James Whittaker, Steven Schinke, and Lewayne Gilchrist (1986) to proclaim that social work had a new *paradigm*— the ecological paradigm. Paradigms refer to worldviews, ways of thinking, or systems of belief that shape practice (Lincoln & Guba, 1985, p. 15).

Critiques

Despite its continued prominence in the field, the ecosystems perspective has also been criticized on a number of fronts. Some critics see the perspective as so vague and general that it can be broadly applied yet gives us very little specific guidance for practice. Its focus on the here-and-now situation and possibilities of intervention has resulted in a neglect of history. Critics also argue that the emphasis on fit tends to support the status quo rather than question underlying relations of power. Ecosystems perspectives emphasize strategies for adaptation to, rather than transformation of, existing structural arrangements. Amy Rossiter (1996) argues that the ecosystems perspective incorporates an uncomplicated view of both person and environment, assuming that both are stable, knowable, and non-problematic concepts. Furthermore, the perspective assumes a fundamental distinction between the person and society rather than seeing the relationship as mutually constituting (Rossiter, 1996). In their more recent writing on the ecological or ecosystems perspective, Gitterman and Germain (2008) have responded to some of these concerns and called for consideration of power, history, and life course development in the definitions and dynamics of person-environment transactions.

Structural Social Work

Overview

The structural approach, as Merlinda Weinberg describes, "is part of a critical, progressive tradition that has been concerned with the broad socioeconomic and political dimensions of society, especially the effects of capitalism, and the impact of these influences in creating unequal relations among individuals" (2008, "What is structural theory?" para. 1). Social workers in the United States (Galper, 1975), Great Britain (Bailey & Brake, 1976), and Canada (Moreau, 1979), challenged and inspired by Marxist critiques of capitalism and social movements of the 1960s and 1970s, began articulating radical approaches to social work practice. They drew attention to structures of society that perpetuated inequalities and called for change at the structural level. Maurice Moreau and colleagues in Canada played key roles in further articulating what became known as a structural approach to social work. Structuralists view the problems that confront social work as a fundamental, inherent part of the present social order in which social institutions function in ways that systematically work to maintain social inequalities (Carniol, 1990; Moreau, 1979; Mullaly, 2006). Oppression, and its elimination, is a main focus of structural social work (Mullaly, 2006; Payne, 2014). Informed by Marxist theory, structuralists place questions of conflict and exploitation at the center of social work theory. They see personal problems as resulting from structural injustice and the resulting unequal access to means and resources of social and economic production. Institutions of the state, including social welfare systems, are implicated in structural inequalities. Structuralists raise questions about the historical and material conditions through which inequalities are structured and experienced. Structural social workers direct their energies toward working both within and against the system and outside and against the system (Mullaly, 2006; Payne, 2014, p. 340).

Key Contributions

Structuralists have placed questions of power and inequality at the center of theory and practice. They have challenged social workers to see personal problems as resulting from structural injustice and have advocated for systems-changing interventions. Structural social workers have engaged in a critique of the relationship between social work and capitalism and have contended that the goal of social work practice is the transformation of the social structure to a new order grounded in social justice, egalitarianism, and humanitarianism (Bailey & Brake, 1976; Coates, 1992; Galper, 1975). They have addressed oppression as group based and relational, working to bolster the interests of more powerful groups and to maintain disadvantage of subordinate groups (Mullaly, 2006; Payne, 2014). From a structural perspective, social workers must go beyond amelioration of problems at the individual level and address the arrangements of power and inequality that produce and perpetuate personal struggles. Such an endeavor would challenge a case work approach, which focuses on individual pathology to the neglect of structural arrangements (Weinberg, 2008). Weinberg argues that a structural approach offers a moral theory "because it suggests what type of society we wish to have and how we ought to behave to create it" (2008, "Not Discarding the Baby with the Bathwater," para. 1).

Critiques

Although structural social work played a significant role in Canadian, Australian, and British social work theory and practice, it has largely been marginalized in the United States. Structural social workers have been criticized for being too political in their sympathies with a socialist alternative to the dominant political order. Structural theory has been criticized for creating a binary division between people and structures and for reifying the concept of structure as something that exists outside the individual (Weinberg, 2008). The structural approach has also been critiqued for a tendency to see people as victims of structural inequalities rather than as actors capable of participation in processes of personal and social change. Further, some critics contend that structural social work focuses power as a finite resource and emphasizes "power over" rather than more constructive possibilities of power (Weinberg, 2008).

Strengths Perspective

Overview

Over the past twenty years a strengths perspective has gained attention in social work in the United States. The strengths perspective emerged as a corrective to social work's problem-focused approach, arguing that, to be true to the value base of the profession, we need to begin by recognizing people's capacities and the potential of their circumstances. As Dennis Saleebey describes it, the strengths perspective "presents a shift from an emphasis on problems and deficits defined by the worker to possibilities and strengths identified in egalitarian, collaborative relationships with clients" (2006, p. 38). It "requires an accounting of what people know and what they can do, however inchoate that may sometimes seem. It requires composing a roster of resources existing within or around an individual, family, or community" (Saleebey, 1996, p. 297). Social workers are encouraged to attend to the resource potential of the environment and appreciate human resiliency, creativity, and capacity for survival in the face of adversity. The basic premises of the strengths perspective (Saleebey, 2006, 2011) are as follows:

- Individuals, families, groups, and communities have many strengths.
- Client motivation is based on fostering client strengths.
- The social worker is a collaborator with the client.
- Any environment is full of resources.
- A focus on strengths poses a challenge to a victim mind-set.
- Taking people's aspirations seriously precludes setting limits on their potential to grow.

Key Contributions

Working from a strengths perspective, the social worker seeks to identify, facilitate, or create contexts in which people who have been silenced and isolated gain an understanding of, a voice in, and an influence over the decisions that affect their lives. The strengths perspective promotes belonging, healing, and relationship building through dialogue and collaboration. Rather than asking "What's wrong?" the social worker operating from a strengths perspective asks "What's possible?" (Cowger, 1994; Saleebey, 2006). The strengths perspective recognizes the power of expectancy and hope as well as the power of narratives of resilience and strength in the change process (Saleebey, 2011). It challenges social workers to believe and to believe in the client and to bring strengths to bear by accounting for, appreciating, affirming, and acting on them (p. 484). It recognizes clients as agents of change and it recognizes the transformative potential of the change process.

Critiques

Proponents of the strengths perspective point to its compatibility with an ecosystems approach. Rather than challenging the fundamental tenets of the ecological model, the strengths perspective is generally seen as offering an enhanced lens through which to view the person-in-environment nexus. The strengths perspective has been praised for recognizing human capacity and agency. It has been criticized for underplaying constraints and the often overwhelming struggles that poor and oppressed people face in their everyday lives (Coates & McKay, 1995). Further, as Malcolm Payne (2014) writes, "Clients face real difficulties, and agencies' social order roles require practitioners to manage difficult behavior and tackle serious social problems. Whether the focus on being positive allows for that is debated" (p. 243). A focus on strengths may underestimate the oppressive power of structural inequalities on individuals and their environments.

Empowerment Perspective

Overview

The empowerment approach in social work was first articulated by Barbara Solomon (1976) and has gained prominence over the past twenty-five years. In her construction of an empowerment model, Solomon specifically addressed power and powerlessness in the context of black communities in the United States. She addressed the pervasive damaging effects of racism on minority individuals and groups. She presented an approach that made power a central theme of social work practice, addressed the effects of negative images and valuation on people of color, and described skills needed for social work practice that resisted racism. She outlined steps toward empowerment, which included establishing rapport, crafting new understandings of worker and client expertise, assessing client strengths, and recognizing the client as the agent of change (Solomon, 1976).

Judith Lee (2001) further articulated an empowerment approach as a method of social work that integrates personal struggles and political issues. She described empowerment as both a clinical and community approach and as both process and product in which healing and liberation are intertwined. Lee (2001, p. 34) outlined three interlocking dimensions of empowerment: (1) development of a more powerful sense of self; (2) development of knowledge and capacities to better address political realities affecting one's environment; and (3) development of resources, knowledge, and skills to attain personal and collective goals.

In developing an empowerment approach to social work with women of color, Lorraine Gutiérrez and Edith Lewis (1999, pp. 18–20) call for practice that addresses power at the personal, interpersonal, and political level. They identify education, participation, and capacity building as the key methods for empowering practice. Following Freire (1974), they see education as a critical process of raising consciousness. To develop critical awareness, one must engage in a power analysis of the situation in which connections are made between the immediate practice context and the distributions of power in society as a whole. From the perspective of empowerment theorists, power cannot be given to people; instead the role of the social worker is to work in collaboration with individuals and groups to help them grasp the relations of power affecting their lives, identify and build their capacities and confidence, and take action to claim power on their own behalf.

Key Contributions

Empowerment theory and practice are premised on recognition and analysis of power, group work practices of consciousness raising and capacity building, and collective efforts to challenge and change oppressive social conditions (Gutiérrez & Lewis, 1999; Lee, 2001; Simon, 1994; Solomon, 1976). Theorists clearly recognize the power of the group in the process of empowerment. Empowerment is grounded in the idea that personal, interpersonal, and structural change can occur when people have decision-making power over the issues affecting their lives and are able to recognize and exercise their individual and collective power to challenge social and personal barriers (Payne, 2014). This approach makes linkages between the personal and the political. It builds on the traditions of self-help, mutual support, and collective action.

Some empowerment theorists, such as Gutiérrez and Lewis (1999), draw on both feminist and critical race theories in critiquing the limitations of competing approaches and articulating an alternative direction for social work. Further, they contend that social work can work toward greater social justice by simultaneously building on individual and social transformation through an empowerment approach. Thus, both the practices and goals of an empowerment approach align with social work's stated value and goal of social justice. Empowerment approaches attend to the importance of self-determination and client participation in the decisions that affect their lives (Beckett, 2006; Payne, 2014).

Critiques

Empowerment perspectives have been praised for bringing questions of power to the center of social work theory and practice and for recognizing the mutual constitution of individual and society. Concepts of empowerment have been criticized for being so broadly applied to such diverse practices that the term itself has become meaningless. Some have argued that, in practice, empowerment approaches may focus more on increasing power and control at the individual level and less on social or structural change (Beckett, 2006; Payne, 2014). Although an empowerment approach may help people critically examine barriers that constrain their lives, there is often less attention to sustained efforts to remove those barriers.

We have also seen the appropriation of the term empowerment to describe punitive practices. For example, time limits imposed by welfare reform under Temporary Assistance for Needy Families Program have been described by proponents as incentives that empower poor people to get off welfare. This use of the term masks the power relations in play in the politics of welfare and represents poverty as a personal problem that can be ameliorated through self-help without structural change. Critics have argued that social workers may be more likely to embrace the language than the practice of empowerment. Leslie Margolin (1997) contends that most empowerment perspectives fail to fully acknowledge social work itself as a type of power, a way of seeing things. He suggests that a language of empowerment may mask practices through which social workers use their own power (p. 5).

Summary

Let's take a moment to think about these five theoretical perspectives. What do you see as their strengths and limitations? How might you apply the skills of complexity thinking in assessing the common ground and important differences among these perspectives? Do the eight questions on critiquing theory help you gain a better understanding of these approaches, their common ground and their difference? How?

Class Learning Activity:
Applying Theoretical Approaches

Take a few minutes to read the following case vignette. It is based on a 2011 PBS special entitled "Minds on the Edge," which explored public policy issues related to mental illness. (View the full documentary at http://www.pbs.org/newshour/bb/health-jan-june11-mentalhealth_01-18). James's story draws directly from a case presented to a panel of experts in the documentary.

James is thirty-two years old. He has heard voices off and on for years. The voices tell him that he is no good. James has been on and off medication for several years. When he heard these voices in the past, he would turn to his mother as a source of support. But a few months ago, his mother died. Then the voices started coming back in a very serious way. James lives with a diagnosis of schizophrenia. This is an illness that may result in a person experiencing delusions (i.e., beliefs that are not supported by external realities) and hallucinations (sensory experiences that do not correlate with external events). According to psychiatric specialists, these alterations in thought and logic can create a somewhat internally consistent way of looking at the world that does not correlate with the outside world.

James might describe his experience of delusions and hallucinations as a waking nightmare in which things are confusing and frightening. He may feel very alone. He has been staying in his apartment and has recently lost his job. In a moment of clarity, he seeks help and goes to the emergency room (ER). The ER is crowded. James is given a prescription refill and an appointment to an outpatient mental health clinic. The next available appointment is in three weeks. James leaves the ER disoriented. A few days after his visit to the ER, James is arrested for public urination and is charged with a misdemeanor.

James's situation is one of many that have come to public attention in your community in recent months. A community task force is being formed to address practice and policy concerns related to persons diagnosed with mental illness who become involved in the criminal justice system. You are asked to provide the task force with a social work perspective.

Divide into five groups, each of which will approach the task from a different theoretical perspective (medical, systems, structural, strengths, and empowerment). Take twenty minutes to discuss and develop your assessment and action plan. Select one representative from each group to present the group's assessment and action plan as part of a five-member panel. Each panel member will have three minutes to present. After the panel presentation, engage in a full group discussion.

How do differing theoretical approaches lead to different understandings of the problem and directions for intervention? How does your theoretical perspective shape what you do and do not see? What theoretical approach do you find most helpful in this case? Why? What approach or combination of approaches might best serve James? What approach or approaches engage James as a participant in the process?

EXPANDING THE THEORETICAL POSSIBILITIES

In contemporary U.S. social work, ecosystems, strengths, and empowerment constitute the field's most widely taught theoretical perspectives. At the same time much of our practice continues to be guided by the medical model. We contend that our dominant theoretical repertoire is limited in helping us grapple with the complexities of contemporary social work. We turn to concepts and insights being developed across a range of critical social thought to help us challenge the limits of social work theory and realize the possibilities of social justice work. In this section we explore possibilities for expanding our thinking and practice.

Social work is not alone in struggling with questions about the production and application of knowledge. Over the past several decades there has been considerable attention to the crises of theory throughout the social sciences (Agger, 2006). Social theorists operating from various critical and interpretive perspectives have questioned notions of determinist universal social laws and pointed to the subjective nature of knowing in which knowledge is understood as culturally and historically situated. A number of these theoretical contributions have filtered into social work (Adams, Dominelli, & Payne, 2009; Allan, Pease, & Briskman, 2009; Chambon, Irving, & Epstein, 1999; Gray & Webb, 2013; Payne, 2014). We will highlight some of these theoretical contributions and point to ways in which they have informed development of the Just Practice framework. These rich, and at times difficult, theoretical contributions have shaped our thinking behind the five key concepts of Just Practice: meaning, power, context, history, and possibility.

Understanding Critical Social Theory

We start with the concept of *critical social theory*, which, as used here, encompasses a range of perspectives, including postmodern, post-structural, feminist, and critical race theories. The significant differences among these perspectives are beyond the scope of this chapter, and have been addressed elsewhere (see, for example, Agger, 2006; Lemert, 2004; and Payne, 2014). We introduce them only briefly in this discussion. Critical social theories challenge positivist assumptions that knowledge is a reflection of a world that is ultimately knowable through objective, value-free inquiry (Agger, 2006). This is a key aspect of postmodern thought, which expresses skepticism regarding universal truths and presumptions of scientific certainty. Critical social theories are concerned with questions of power, difference, and domination, and they attend to the structural dimensions of power and their roles in the production of difference and inequality. They argue that people's consciousness and everyday life experiences are shaped and constrained by structural forces. Critical social theories are *political* in that the goal of theory is to inform transformative action (Agger, 2006). They attend to the connections between everyday life and large-scale social structures and consider how people can participate in their own liberation from oppression. Critical social theorists address the mutual constitution of forms of knowledge and relations of power, that is, the ways in which what we take as knowledge is shaped by relationships of power and, in turn, how knowledge acts in powerful ways in the world (Rabinow, 1984).

Concepts of critical social theory have been challenging and reshaping social work theory and practice. The role of social worker as expert has come under scrutiny as theorists and practitioners have critically examined the ways in which social work encounters are shaped by power and authority in the helping relationship as well as in the larger world. Some theorists have pointed to the partial and socially located nature of the social worker's knowledge of another's experience in the social world and the inseparability of forms of social work expertise and forms of power. They have questioned the ways in which *master narratives*—overarching accounts that structure how we explain social reality in terms of difference, pathology, and intervention—have become deeply embedded in social work thought and practice (Allan, Pease, & Briskman, 2009; Chambom, Irving, & Epstein, 1999; Sakamoto & Pitner, 2005). They have asked social workers to examine the *certainties*—those implicit, unspoken truths we hold about how the world works—that underlie our practice (Sarri & Finn, 1992). They challenge social workers to critically examine and deconstruct the forms and relations of power and inequality that infiltrate both the helping process and the broader social context in which it is embedded. These insights are key to informing the practice of social justice work.

Power, Hegemony, and the Making of Common Sense

Some critical theorists have returned to the insights of Antonio Gramsci in order to better grasp workings of power in society. At the beginning of this chapter (p. 143) we introduced Gramsci and his interest in understanding how popular *consent* to the class structure of capitalist society is *produced* and accepted as common sense. Gramsci wanted to understand how people in less powerful positions came to participate in systems of domination and exploitation that conflict with their interests. He was interested in the "distinction between coercion and consent as alternative mechanisms of social power" (as cited in Stoddart, 2007, p. 200). He asked difficult questions: What is the role of economic systems in producing particular kinds of social and cultural subjects? What, in turn, is the role of cultural systems and social institutions in supporting a particular political and economic order? Through posing and reflecting on these sorts of questions, Gramsci (1957/1987) put forth his concept of *hegemony* to describe processes of nonviolent domination and the ways in which people become participants in systems that continue to oppress them. He explored the ways in which everyday social action within capitalist systems worked in shaping people's dispositions and desires as workers, consumers, and citizens. He concluded that the "social action of everyday life produces hegemonic effects" (Stoddart, 2007, p. 201).

We have found Gramsci's work helpful in thinking about questions of meaning, power, and history in the making of social problems and interventions. He reminds us that we are never outside of the political, cultural, and economic systems that shape our experiences, interpretations, and actions. He challenges us to question received common sense and to pose questions that may help us come to an alternative common sense regarding root causes of social problems and the words and actions that both mask and support structured inequalities. For example, how might our social service systems work to support and maintain structures of race and class privilege, and how might we as social workers be complicit therein? How is it that market-based models of health care and mental health care that provide people with the care they can afford, rather than models of health care as a human right, have become accepted as common sense in U.S. society? How has the concentration of older people into age-segregated congregate care become a broadly accepted common sense model for aging? How has massive incarceration of people of color become accepted as the common sense of criminal justice? How has the widespread use of Ritalin become accepted as the common sense approach to management of children's attention and behavior issues, such that the United States consumes 90 percent of the world's Ritalin supply (Transit, 2004)? Gramsci's critical thinking about the concept of hegemony encourages social workers to probe these sorts of questions.

Post-structural Theory and the Concept of Discourse

Post-structural theorists have also unsettled implicit assumptions about the social world and the place and practice of social work therein. Post-structuralists challenge the notion of universal truths and argue that social structures do not exist apart from meaning systems and social relations. They too raise questions about notions of a knowable and stable reality, and they invite critical deconstruction of the operating assumptions and certainties that implicitly and explicitly inform action. They have also attended to interpretive processes through which people give meaning to, navigate through, and contest the social world. Post-structural theorists have put forth nuanced understandings of power as multifaceted, fluid, relational, and productive (Foucault, 1980; Rossiter, 2005; Wendt & Seymour, 2010). They have drawn attention to the place and power of discourse in the shaping of social reality.

The concept of discourse as used here is about more than language and talk. It draws attention to language as a "medium of social power" (Stoddart, 2007, p. 192). Adrienne Chambon (1999) writes: "More than ways of naming, discourses are systems of thought and systematic ways of carving out reality. They are structures of knowledge that influence systems of practice" (p. 57). For example, if the medical model structures one's knowledge of what social work is, the system of practice that follows is one of expert diagnosis, use of labels to name and classify disorders, and person-changing interventions. Thus, the concept of social work discourse brings critical attention to the mutual constitution of systems of knowledge—what counts as "truth"—and systems of practice—what count as problem and intervention. Leslie Margolin (1997) describes the power of social work discourse in constructing both clients and their problems through the written words of case records. In effect, the social worker's language in the case record "creates" the client as an object of investigation and intervention. Margolin notes that it is generally the social worker, not the client, who has control of the record and of the naming and framing of the client's problems:

Because written words are more easily controlled than speech, fine distinctions can be drawn between those who should have access and those who should not, between those who can make additions and corrections and those who cannot. Recordkeeping, in other words, is the mechanism that assures the differential distribution of power. (p. 37)

The concept of discourse helps us think more specifically about the ways in which knowledge is constructed and the power relations therein. It allows us to move from a more abstract level of theoretical, political, and ethical concerns to the concrete realities of the power of language and the ways we carve out the terrain of the "talkable" and that which goes without saying. For example, how is it that only certain kinds of social benefits are construed as welfare? How did welfare come to be thought of as a dirty word, associated with the dependency of the poor (Fraser & Gordon, 1994)? And how is it that dependency is constructed as a bad thing, pitted against the correctness of independence? What are the social and political consequences of omitting discussion of interdependence and social as well as personal responsibility from the welfare debates? These are questions of discourse.

Let's pause for a moment and think about the power of discourse in the context of your own social work practice. Where do you see language taking on particular power to name a client or frame a problem? Where might forms of professional language have the power to exclude service users from the conversation? Where do you see examples of inclusive language? Is language used in shorthand ways that reduce people to labels? How does the particular language used to name an issue or problem shape the social work response?

Bourdieu and the Concept of Habitus

We have also gained critical insight from the work of French sociologist Pierre Bourdieu, who studied the workings of power in society. Bourdieu (1986) paid particular attention to the subtle ways in which power is brought to bear in everyday interactions such that a larger social order is produced and maintained over time. Bourdieu, too, argued that social structures do not exist outside of human action. Rather, it is through the patterned practices of individual and collective action that we produce and maintain a broader social order.

In chapter 2 we introduced Bourdieu's concept of habitus, which refers to the processes through which people internalize and embody habits, tastes, dispositions, and skills through their everyday social and cultural experience—the processes that allow us to navigate in our social environments (Bourdieu, 1990). Habitus is the process through which we are socialized to norms that guide our thinking and action. It is the process through which we internalize the external and naturalize the arbitrary in ways that generally go without saying (Bourdieu, 1990; Wacquant, 2005).

The concept of habitus is helpful in thinking about the social environment not merely as a site of individual and social experience, but also as a constitutive part of social identity. Bourdieu's insights provide us a more complex and nuanced way to think about context and a person-in-environment perspective. In addition, his insights help us to think more critically about our socialization as social workers within the contexts of the agencies and organizations in which we work. When we bring the concept of habitus to bear in relation to our professional practice, we are challenged to reflect on the ways in which we come to embody particular habits, ways of working, and patterns of practice that may implicitly encode assumptions about clients, problems, and interventions that may be faulty or problematic. Bourdieu's work challenges social workers to think about how our patterned practices in sites of social work, such as child welfare offices, homeless shelters, or mental health clinics, play out. How might these patterned practices that go without saying contribute to the *production* of particular kinds of clients (and workers) who are socialized to respond in particular kinds of ways in order to demonstrate (and document) therapeutic progress or (give and) receive material resources (Carr, 2010; Desjarlais, 1997)?

Take a moment to think about your social work practicum experience. As a newcomer to an agency or organization, you likely encountered unspoken rules, implicit assumptions about the way things work, and practices that go without saying as part of the work. What were some of the patterned practices you observed? How might those practices implicitly shape what it means to be a social worker or a service user within your practicum site?

Meaning Making and Narrative

Social constructionist and constructivist theorists have also expanded social work thought and practice regarding meaning making and the power of language (Witkin, 2012). The terms *constructionist* and *constructivist* overlap and are at times used interchangeably in the literature, so for simplicity's sake, we will refer to *social constructionist* thought in this section. As part of the post-structural move, social constructionism is the term for a range of approaches that argue that the social world is not an objective, knowable, reality; rather the social world is viewed as constructed through language and human interaction in meaning-making processes. Human beings are viewed as actively engaged in the construction and interpretation of the social world and in rendering experience meaningful and communicable through narratives (Mahoney, 1995).

A social constructionist approach to social work draws attention to the language that shapes social work practice and how language is used in the construction of what we see as social problems and in giving meaning to our interventions (Witkin, 2012). There is clearly overlap here with our previous discussion of discourse. What we emphasize in this section is the importance of narrative and meaning. The work of Michael White and David Epston (1990) brought social constructionist thought to bear in social work practice through their pioneering work in narrative therapy. Narrative approaches focus on meaning making, the power of narratives, and the ways in which people tell the stories of their social realities in order to make sense of their experiences. Narrative approaches consider how stories develop a sense of coherence, what stories gets told, and what gets left out. They attend to constructions of meaning within complex social contexts in which relations of power play into the telling, silencing, amplifying, and distorting of narratives (Nybell, 2013). They are concerned with the ways in which *problem-saturated* stories—those that emphasize problems, deficits, and barriers over possibilities—are co-constructed, often with adverse consequences for the narrator. Their work helps us think critically about the interplay of meaning and power in the narrative construction of people and problems and about the possibilities that emerge in the deconstruction of problem-saturated narratives and the reconstruction of narratives of hope and liberation (Kelly, 2011).

Reflection Moment:
Crime and Punishment

Below is the mission statement for Critical Resistance, an organization dedicated to challenging the "justice" behind the burgeoning prison population in the U.S. criminal justice system. Take a moment to read the mission statement and reflect on the questions that follow:

Critical Resistance seeks to build an international movement to end the Prison Industrial Complex (PIC) by challenging the belief that caging and controlling people makes us safe. We believe that basic necessities such as food, shelter, and freedom are what really make our communities secure. As such, our work is part of global struggles against inequality and powerlessness. The success of the movement requires that it reflect communities most affected by the PIC. Because we seek to abolish the PIC, we cannot support any work that extends its life or scope. (Critical Resistance, 2015)

Think about the term *prison industrial complex*. What images does it bring to mind? What questions might it spark regarding the production of crime, criminals, prisoners, and "justice"? How is it that U.S. prison populations have exploded in recent years? How is it that people of color are vastly overrepresented in prisons? What common sense is at work here? How does the discourse of crime and punishment work to construct not only a certain common sense but also an economic industry of the keepers and the kept? What *alternative common sense* is suggested by the work of Critical Resistance? What alternative narrative of criminal justice does Critical Resistance offer?

Thinking about Globalization

Our thinking about social work and social justice has also been shaped through critical engagement with the concept of globalization and its often very local effects in people's everyday lives. Global economic shifts have exacerbated economic and social inequalities and have changed the nature of work and family life for many people. Moreover, the logic behind economic globalization has pushed social services to become more market driven, posing significant challenges for social justice work. In order to engage in effective social justice work we need to grapple with the processes and consequences of globalization.

First, let's consider meanings of globalization. Journalist Thomas Friedman (1999) defined globalization as

the inexorable integration of markets, nation-states, and technologies to a degree never witnessed before in a way that is enabling individuals, corporations and nation-states to reach around the world farther, faster, deeper and cheaper than ever before . . . the spread of free-market capitalism to virtually every country in the world. (p. 7)

Drawing from the work of a number of writers, we characterize globalization as "complicated transnational political and economic processes that have (a) restructured relations and alignments of nations and regions of the world; (b) stimulated new linkages, flows, and disruptions of people, ideas, cultures, and politics; and (c) contributed to shifting patterns of migration, forms of labor, and relations of power and inequality" (Finn, Perry, & Karandikar, 2013, p. xviii).

Some writers have pointed to the potential for globalization to produce new opportunities for technological advance, cultural engagement, and development of a new global consciousness. Others have been less optimistic in their assessment, pointing to rising rates of poverty and inequality, accelerated rates of social and environmental degradation, growing transnational corporate power combined with a weakening of labor protection, and increasing violence and militarization (Harvey, 2007; Korten, 2001; Scholte, 2008; Stiglitz, 2002). Some social work scholars have suggested that we are experiencing a rapid globalization of the economy without an accompanying globalization of citizenship, thereby jeopardizing basic human dignity and human rights (Ife, 2012). Others have argued that social workers, through critical engagement with issues of globalization, have the opportunity to expand their work in collaboration with broader movements challenging social exclusion and promoting global social and environmental justice (Hessle, 2014; Munck, 2005; Pyles, 2009; Whitmore & Wilson, 2005). Critical understanding of and attention to these processes are essential to social justice work, even in its most local and personal forms.

At first glance, forces of globalization may seem removed from the everyday practice of social work. Let's pause to think about possible consequences and ramifications of globalization close to home. Perhaps your community has experienced a shift in its economic base in recent years, either through loss of extractive and manufacturing industry or the loss or expansion of service industry, producing changes in both work and family life. Perhaps you or members of your community have migrated intranationally or internationally as a result of the push and pull of global political and economic forces. Perhaps you or members of your family have served in the military and have direct experience with global issues and their human consequences. Where do you see connections between global forces and local issues in your community? How might these issues have implications for social work practice?

From Globalization to Neoliberalism

Many theorists of globalization have critically addressed neoliberalism as a driving force in the production of new forms of social exclusion and political conflict (Harvey, 2007; Polack, 2004; Reisch, 2013). Neoliberalism can be described as the "logic of market rule on a global scale" (McMichael, 2000, p. 149). As Cabezas, Reese, and Waller (2007) describe,

> [Neoliberalism] privileges the expansion of the "free" (without regulation or tariff) market and the global integration of economics. It proposes the abolition of government intervention in economic matters and radical cutbacks in social services, including education, health care, housing, agricultural subsidies, and nutrition. (p. 6)

Governments worldwide, either voluntarily or under pressure to reduce national debt, have undertaken structural reforms to reduce taxation; scale back social, health, and educational supports and services; and reduce labor and environmental protections. The social burdens of these cutbacks fall on communities, families, and individuals, often women, who carry out the majority of social care work. Meanwhile, private entities profit from reduced taxation and lower costs of doing business.

An understanding of neoliberal logic and practice matters for social work. Neoliberal approaches have resulted in the dismantling of social safety nets and the erosion of rights for basic social and economic protection. Public welfare institutions and services have been cast as costly and outdated. Notions of citizen rights have been displaced by discourses focused on consumer "choice," with a loss of critical attention to structural constraints imposed by employment, housing, education, health care, and the fundamental opportunity to live and work with dignity in one's home country. Neoliberal practices have exacerbated existing social inequalities, leaving historically marginalized groups all the more vulnerable (Cabezas et al., 2007; Ferguson et al., 2005; Finn et al., 2013; Kilty & Segal, 2006)

Critical theorists such as Loic Waquant (2009, 2010) have pointed out that neoliberalism is not merely an economic logic, nor has it simply called for limiting the role of the state. Rather, the state plays an active *facilitating* role for market-based interests, for example, by *limiting* barriers such as safety standards, environmental protections, and workers' rights to organize. At the same time, the state plays an active *social control* role through use of coercive policies and practices, such as expanded state surveillance power, increased militarization of borders, expansion of immigration enforcement and border patrol powers and resources, and continued growth of the prison system. These coercive practices unequally and harmfully affect groups who are already on the margins of social and economic power. In short, Wacquant argues that under neoliberal rule the state "plays a crucial role in disciplining and controlling those who do not 'achieve' based on the dictates of the market" (Finn, Shook, & Nybell, 2013, p. 1161; Wacquant, 2009, 2010).

These are challenging ideas. Let's pause again to think about how they relate to the everyday practice of social work. Can you point to examples of a *neoliberal logic* working within your practicum agency or other agencies within your community? Do market-based outcomes take precedence over relationship-based best practices? Does a language of choice overpower a language of rights? Are there workplace practices that limit the potential of both social workers and service users? Do you see examples of the expansion of social control to the neglect of social support?

Feminist Perspectives

Feminist movements have challenged the political, social, and economic marginalization of women and the systems of thought and practice that have informed and justified women's marginality and inequality. Feminist theorists and activists have sought to raise consciousness of the many forms of women's oppression, whether in the home or workplace, in schools or on the streets. Feminists have made gender an issue and have examined the workings of patriarchy in the family and larger society that systematically structure women's subordination (Donovan, 2012; Smith, 1990). They have addressed the connection of the personal and political and critically examined the politics of everyday life that have contributed to women's oppression.

In social work, feminist scholars have explored assumptions about gender, marriage, and family that have informed and continue to inform social welfare policies (Abramovitz, 1996; Figueira-McDonough, Netting, & Nichols-Casebolt, 1998; Gordon, 1994). They have critically addressed the interplay of gender and oppression by considering how dominant societal and cultural assumptions regarding gendered identities and relations become embedded in social institutions, relations, and practices (Finn et al., 2013, p. xxv). For example, Susan Kemp and Ruth Brandwein (2010) have described the interlocking history of feminism, social work, and activism from early social reform to women's suffrage, policy making, institution building, and the fueling of social movements linking struggles for gender equality with other liberation movements. Feminists have also addressed the burden of social support work carried out by women and have challenged the devaluation of women's care work (Hess, 2013).

Let's pause to consider the connections between feminist thought and your social work practice. Do you see issues regarding gender and gender oppression manifest in the context of your practicum experience? How are they addressed? Are the problems that service users experience connected to their everyday experiences of gender oppression? Have you witnessed or experienced the devaluation of "women's work"? In contrast, have you witnessed or experienced the valuing and empowerment of women and girls, resistance to gender oppression, and possibilities for transformative gender relations?

Feminism and Globalization

Critical feminist scholarship has also taken a global perspective in understanding and addressing gender oppression. Feminists have considered the gendered dimensions of poverty and food insecurity, the global scale of systematic violence against women and girls, the health consequences of gender inequality, and both the central role of women in the global economy and their gendered vulnerability (Cabezas et al., 2007; UN Women, 2011, 2012). They have explored the workings of *global care chains*, through which women are linked together in unequal relations of paid and unpaid caregiving around the world (Hochschild, 2012; Orozco, 2009). They have challenged the ways in which women have been variably represented and rendered invisible in the development paradigm promoted by institutions such as the World Bank (Drolet, 2010). Feminist scholars have critically explored the consequences of militarization and political conflict on women's lives (Enloe, 2000, 2004). They have pointed to the increasingly globalized nature of social, political, and economic disparities and structured inequalities of power that silence women's voices and threaten their well-being and to the responsibility of social work to address these concerns as they play out in our practice (Gringeri & Roche, 2010; Mehrotra, 2010; Moos-Mitha & Ross-Sheriff, 2010). Do you see connections between these global concerns and the everyday struggles of vulnerable women in your social work practice or community?

Intersectionality and Critical Race Theory

Women of color have challenged universalist assumptions about women that informed much of feminist social thought into the 1980s. They have drawn attention to power in the lives of women, to the intersecting dimensions of identity and oppression, and to the significance of differences as well as commonalities among women (Kemp & Brandwein, 2010; Gutiérrez, 1990; Ross-Sheriff, 2007; Solomon, 1976). The work of feminists of color has been critical in naming and addressing *intersectionality*, a concept that speaks to the power of intersecting forms of oppression based on gender, race, ethnicity, class, sexuality, and other dimensions of identity (Hurtado & Cervantez, 2009). For example, Patricia Hill Collins (2000) speaks to intersectionality in her discussion of matrices of domination, which we explored in chapter 1.

An intersectionality perspective challenges us to address connections among macro-level issues of oppression and to the complex ways in which people navigate social identities in everyday relations and interactions (Villarreal

Sosa & Moore, 2013, p.160). Olena Hankivsky (2012) has outlined core tenets of an intersectionality perspective (Sethi & Hankivsky, 2013, p. 217):

1. People cannot be reduced to single characteristics, nor can human experience be understood by considering only a single dimension of experience.
2. Social categories such as race, ethnicity, class, gender, and sexuality are socially constructed.
3. One's location in the social world is inseparable from the surrounding social structures and processes that shape and are shaped by interactions over time and place.

Further, an intersectionality perspective draws attention to the complex interplay of privilege and oppression and the tensions and contradictions of lived experience therein.

Theories of intersectionality build on and contribute to critical race theory, which is both an interdisciplinary framework and a movement focused on the "dynamics of race, racism, and power" (Crenshaw, Gotanda, Peller, & Thomas, 1995; Delgado & Stefancic, 2012, p. 3). The key assumptions of critical race theory (Delgado & Stefancic, 2012, p. 10) include the following:

1. Race is a social construction.
2. Racism is a central feature of American society.
3. Racism serves the material interest of white elites and the psychic interests of working class whites.
4. Identity is intersectional in nature.
5. People of color have a presumed competence to speak about race and racism due to their unique histories and experiences of oppression.

Critical race theory challenges us to address intersecting forms of oppression, honor the expertise that those who experience oppression in their everyday lives bring to understanding oppression, and engage in action to end all forms of oppression.

Let's pause for a moment to think about the implications of intersectionality and critical race theory in your everyday practice of social work. Do you see intersecting forms and mechanisms of oppression shaping the lives and life chances of service users in your practicum setting? How are these manifested in clients' everyday lives? How are everyday experiences of poverty connected to and exacerbated by experiences of racism and gender oppression? Is there an overrepresentation of people of color among your agency's service users? How is that overrepresentation understood and addressed? For example, children and youth of color are disproportionately represented in out-of-home care and juvenile justice systems. How might theories of intersectionality and critical race theory inform thinking and practice related to youth of color in systems of care and control?

Queer and Transgender Theory

Queer and transgender theorists are further challenging social work thought and practice by disrupting deeply embedded binary thinking about gender upon which so much of social work theory, policy, and practice is based (Burdge, 2007; Hicks, 2008; McPhail, 2004; Nagoshi & Brzuzy, 2010). Queer theory has both challenged binary categories of male/female and destabilized the very notion of categories that have shaped the ways in which we name and locate people. Transgender theory has emerged from feminism and queer theory; it explores the intersection among social identities, forms of oppression, and the physical embodiment of identity. As Nagoshi and Brzuzy (2010) describe, transgender theory pushed critical thinking further in questioning how concepts of gender get socially constructed, reproduced, and reinforced. Transgender theorists contend that identity is at once fluid, contextually and socially constructed, and embodied and internalized (Nagoshi, Nagoshi, & Brzuzy, 2014). We are simultaneously shaped by the structures, relations, and discourses of our everyday experiences; interpreters and embodiments of our experiences of personhood; and shapers of our personhood in relation to our experience in the social world (Nagoshi & Brzuzy, 2010; Nagoshi, Nagoshi, & Brzuzy, 2014).

How might you draw on insights from queer and transgender theory in your social work practice? For example, does male/female binary thinking structure the organization and delivery of services within your practicum site? How? Are there embedded assumptions about the needs or capacities of males and females? Does a heteronormative worldview permeate the organizational space and practices? If so, how is it manifest? In contrast, does your organization challenge binary categories and create a different kind of social space and practice? Is it a welcoming space for people who do not conform to a dominant heterosexual or *cisgender* (persons whose gender identity corresponds to their assigned sex) identity? How might we think about gender outside the binary box?

Anti-oppressive Theory and Practice

The range of critical theories addressed above furthers our complexity thinking about oppression and the possibilities for engaging in anti-oppressive practice. Social work theorists in Canada, the United Kingdom, and elsewhere have utilized these theories to develop models of anti-oppressive practice (AOP), which "draw attention of social workers to the more focused objective of challenging structural power dynamics in order to eradicate various forms of oppression" (Sakamoto & Pitner, 2005, p. 437). Anti-oppressive practice locates social work in a broader social context of multiple oppressions and deep structural inequalities. It "attempts to integrate the search and struggle for social change directly into the social work experience" (Baines, 2011, p. 4). In the spirit of structural and empowerment approaches, AOP seeks to both address personal struggles and redress societal inequities by engaging in social as well as individual action. Baines (2011, pp. 4–7) describes core principles of AOP social work practice, which reflect a melding of diverse critical theoretical perspectives addressed above:

- Oppression is generated through both micro and macro social relations.
- Everyday life experience is shaped by multiple oppressions.
- Social work is not neutral but a contested and political practice.
- Social-justice-oriented social work both supports individuals in participatory and transformative processes of change and challenges unjust social arrangements that contribute to individual struggles.
- Social work seeks to build alliances with other liberatory movements.
- Social work theory and practice are informed by and responsive to the needs and struggles of persons who are oppressed and marginalized.
- Social work supports participatory approaches to individual and social change.
- Social work involves the ongoing interplay of self-reflexivity and social analysis.
- Social work draws on a variety of critical approaches to inform practice.

In many ways, AOP incorporates and is informed by the dimensions of critical theory that we have addressed. In building the Just Practice framework, we have embraced the principles of AOP and have attempted to integrate the rich and complex insights from the critical theories that we have highlighted in this discussion. We now turn to a new way of thinking about practice that informs the framework.

A Different Way of Thinking about Practice

The Just Practice framework we develop here is also grounded in a reconceptualization of practice informed by critical social and cultural theory. The term *practice* in contemporary social theory does not have the same meaning as practice in the traditional social work sense of a series of planned interventions. Rather, according to anthropologist Sherry Ortner (1989, 1994), practice refers more broadly to social action carried out in the context of unequal power relations. According to Ortner (1994, p. 403), a fundamental premise of practice theory is "that society is a system, that the system is powerfully constraining, and yet that the system can be made and unmade through human action and interaction." Practice theorists have attempted to place human agency and social action at the center of new social theory. As Linwood Cousins (2015) describes,

> This theoretical orientation seeks to explain what people do as thinking, intentionally acting persons who face the impact of history and the restraints of structures that are embedded in our society and culture. It asks how social systems shape, guide, and direct people's values, beliefs, and behavior. But it also asks how people, as human actors or agents, perpetuate or shape social systems. (p. 273)

Practice theorists pay close attention to the complex interplay among historical forces, social structures, and human agency. As discussed in chapter 1, people make history, but they do so within the constraints of their social, political, economic, and environmental contexts. Our lives and contexts are structured by cultural meaning systems; cognitive, emotional, and behavioral frames of reference; and the social, political, and economic systems that order social life. These social structures are variably reproduced, internalized, acquiesced to, resisted, and transformed through human agency. In explaining the concept of human agency, Albert Bandura (2006) states,

> To be an agent is to influence intentionally one's functioning and life circumstances. . . . People are self-organizing, proactive, self-regulating, and self-reflecting. They are not simply onlookers of their behavior. They are contributors to their life circumstances, not just products of them. (p. 164)

People's behavior is never fully determined by circumstances. "Rather, human functioning is a product of a reciprocal interplay of intrapersonal, behavioral, and environmental determinants" (Bandura, 2006, p. 165). Practice theorists are responding to what they see as overly deterministic structural approaches that ignore human actors, and overly actor-oriented approaches that neglect attention to the structural forces that shape and constrain human action (Giddens, 1979). They draw our attention not only to large-scale evidence of people resisting seemingly overwhelming structural forces in social movements such as civil rights, women's rights, disability rights, and immigrant rights, but to everyday forms of resistance in which people assert their human agency.

Although the language of practice theory may sound unfamiliar to social work, we argue that the issues practice theorists are grappling with go to the theoretical and practical heart of the profession. The practice perspective attends to the mutual constitution of the person and society; points to the irreducible connection of structure and practice; and addresses the power of discourse in constructing the terrain of the thinkable, talkable, and doable. Practice theorists are concerned with the interplay of culture, power, and history in the making of social subjects and in the processes of social reproduction and change (Dirks, Eley, & Ortner, 1994). Working from a practice perspective, we are challenged to consider the cultural and political *processes* and historical *contexts* in which we construct social problems; imagine clients, helpers, and their respective roles and relationships; and develop social policies and intervention technologies. Importantly, then, a practice perspective makes power, inequality, and transformational possibility foci of concern, thus offering a theoretical bridge between the concept of social justice and the practice of social work.

We have covered much conceptual ground in this chapter. This abbreviated discussion does not do justice to the richness of the theoretical terrain. Our journey across this terrain continues. Our purpose in this section has been to point to some of the important influences on our thinking and to offer readers some theoretical benchmarks to guide their own journeys.

We turn now to the Just Practice framework, which we have developed through ongoing engagement with critical theory. In the following section we will provide an overview of the framework, linking the five key concepts and seven core processes.

JUST PRACTICE FRAMEWORK: AN INTEGRATED APPROACH

These critical social theories have posed challenges to dominant modes of social work thought and practice. Concerns over questions of meaning, power, and knowledge in social work have been variably addressed by empowerment, narrative and social constructionist, and postmodern approaches. Some of these approaches have emphasized questions of meaning, others have addressed relations of power and inequality, and a few have attended to questions of history. However, none of these has articulated an *integrated approach* to social work that theoretically and practically links concepts of meaning, power, and history to the context and possibilities of justice-oriented practice.

We organized the Just Practice framework around these five key concepts: *meaning, power, history, context,* and *possibility*. We posed these questions: Could these five concepts be the necessary and sufficient elements for a foundation? As we hold these five independent concepts in relation and explore their interconnection, what new possibilities for thought and practice may emerge? We began to explore those possibilities.

In articulating the Just Practice framework, we have attempted to incorporate the insights of critical theorists and bring forth the meaning and power of transformative possibility. As we have argued above, the challenge of social justice work calls for challenging ways of thinking and disruption of our certainties about the world. The Just Practice framework offers a model for critical inquiry that enables us to disrupt assumed truths, explore context, and appreciate ways in which social location may shape interpretation.

To recap, the five key concepts provide the basis for posing questions to inform and shape the practice of social justice work. How do people give *meaning* to the experiences and conditions that shape their lives? What are the *contexts* in which those experiences and conditions occur? What forms and relations of *power* shape people and processes? How does *history* make people and how do people make history as they engage in struggles over questions of meaning and power? How might an appreciation of those struggles help us imagine and claim a sense of *possibility* in the practice of social justice work? These questions are translated into action through seven core processes that link theory and practice: *engagement, teaching/learning, action, accompaniment, evaluation, critical reflection,* and *celebration*. In this section we will address each of the core processes and consider how it works with the five key themes of the Just Practice framework. This foundation will provide the theoretical and practical support for the subsequent chapters in which we will develop the processes and present concrete skills and exercises that help us think about and engage in social justice work.

Table 4.1 links the five processes and the seven key concepts of the Just Practice framework.

Table 4.1
Just Practice matrix: Critical questions linking concepts and processes

Concepts	Engagement	Teaching/Learning	Action and Accompaniment	Evaluation, Reflection, and Celebration
			Processes	
Meaning	What is the significance of the encounter and relationship? How do the parties involved interpret the experience?	What and how do we learn from one another's interpretations? Create new meanings and understandings?	How does partiality of knowledge shape action? How do differing meanings constrain or promote differing courses of action?	How do we appreciate meaning via reflexivity? How do we validate the meaning of our work? Give meaning to social justice?
Context	How do interpersonal, organizational, and social contexts shape relations and trust building? How can the context be changed to facilitate engagement?	How does context inhibit or facilitate possibilities for mutual learning? How does the teaching/learning process challenge the interpersonal, organizational, and social context?	How does context shape the pathways for action, access to resources, patterns of practices, social work roles, and nature of partnerships? How do our actions expand contexts for social justice work?	What is context specific about the process? What can be applied to other contexts? How can reflection on the context be a catalyst for contextual change? What forms of celebration fit the context?
Power	How do differing positionalities of participants shape engagement? What forms of power need to be addressed in the engagement process? How do we use the power available to promote justice in a relationship?	What can we learn from a power analysis of the situation? How can the process of teaching/learning challenge power inequalities among participants and promote social justice?	What access is there to power and resources? How do we remain mindful of power differences in the change process? How do they challenge accompaniment? How do actions contribute to empowerment of participants?	How do we evaluate redistribution of power in the change process? How do we measure individual, organization, and community empowerment? How do we both appreciate and celebrate new forms and practices of power?

Table 4.1
Just Practice matrix: Critical questions linking concepts and processes—(Continued)

Concepts	Processes			
	Engagement	Teaching/Learning	Action and Accompaniment	Evaluation, Reflection, and Celebration
History	How do past histories and experiences of participants shape the encounter and process of relationship building? What prior knowledge and assumptions might promote or inhibit the process?	How do we teach/learn from and about our histories? How do our histories shape the ways that we know and experience the world? How do we learn from those who came before? How do we learn from what is historically possible?	How do histories become resources and catalysts for action? How does historical consciousness inform future action? How do we bridge differences of history and forge an alliance for action? How do actions challenge inscriptions of historic injustice?	How do we evaluate change over time? How do we account for historical conditions? How does reflection on where we have been inform where we are going? How might celebration of our histories animate future efforts?
Possibility	What are the possible relationships that can be formed and strengthened in this change effort? What spaces of hope can be opened?	What can I learn from this other person/group? What can I contribute? What new ways of knowing might emerge from this experience? How can this learning promote other possibilities for social justice work?	How might I expand my repertoire of roles and skills? What possible courses of action are available? How can our efforts enhance future possibilities for empowering action?	How do we select among the possibilities at hand? Assess possible courses of action? Expand the terrain of the thinkable, talkable, and doable? Reflect on decisions made and opportunities lost? Celebrate creativity?

The Core Processes

The theory, politics, and ethics of social justice work are translated into practice as participants in the change process engage in the *praxis* of action and reflection for personal and social transformation. It is possible to think of the core processes as a series of actions or steps that, when taken together, move us toward this goal. However, the seven core processes do not necessarily imply linear sequential movement. It may be helpful to envision them as overlapping and mutually informing processes, like waves, shaping and washing over one another. It is in this sense of nonlinear movement that we can better grasp the dynamics of change produced through the ebb and flow of ideas, reflections, and actions (Smith, 1999, p. 116). In the following paragraphs we outline the core processes.

Engagement

Engagement is the process through which the social worker enters the world of the participant(s) in the change process and begins to develop a working relationship. It entails entry into both context and relationship. It is a process of listening, communication, translation, and connection that seriously addresses questions of trust, power, intimacy, difference, and conflict. Social workers begin from a place of openness and curiosity and acknowledge the partiality of their knowledge. Through the engagement process social workers anticipate the work ahead by reflecting on the participant(s) in the change process and coming to an appreciation of the other's situation. Engagement also calls for critical reflection on one's own positionality and the ways in which it may shape the relationship and the process of change.

Teaching-Learning

Teaching-learning is a participatory process of discovery and critical inquiry. In part, it entails data collection, assessment, and interpretation and reframes them as collaborative activities. Teaching-learning connotes a two-way street and a relationship of interchange among participants. We teach at the same time that we are taught. We engage in mutual question posing, use various means to collaboratively collect information, identify resources and supports, discuss root causes of presenting concerns, teach and learn skills of assessment, and discover personal and collective capacities for our own critical practice and that of others.

Action

Action is the process of carrying out plans and sustaining the momentum. Action consists of recognizing and activating, brainstorming, decision making, planning, organizing, and putting these efforts in motion. It includes animating, facilitating, maintaining impetus, awakening the spirit and sense of possibility, advocating, and taking responsibility to speak for the values of social justice. Action is informed by reflection. It demands vigilance and a commitment to the ongoing search for one's own competence (Moch, 2009). Action calls for critical and respectful attention to resistance.

Accompaniment

Accompaniment refers to the actual people-to-people partnerships through which action is realized. In its simplest sense, accompaniment means to go with, to support and enhance the process. It reflects a commitment to being part of the journey over the long haul. The process entails ongoing critical dialogue regarding difference, power, and positionality among participants. It keeps us mindful of the challenges of collaboration and the need for conscious work in building alliances, mediating conflicts, and negotiating power.

Evaluation

Evaluation is an ongoing process consisting of stepping back, taking stock at different moments in the change process, and assessing the effectiveness of our efforts. Evaluation is interwoven with reflection and teaching/learning. In evaluation, we systematically examine the process and outcomes of our efforts. Evaluation is a collaborative process done *with* rather than *to* others. It is a process of documenting, scrutinizing, and sharing the results of our efforts so that we can learn from one another and produce the changes that we have envisioned.

Critical Reflection

Critical reflection is a dialogical process of learning together from our experiences. It is a structured, analytic, and emotional process that helps us examine the ways in which we make sense of experiences and circumstances. Through critical reflection, we systematically interpret our individual and collective experiences, question implicit assumptions, and reframe our inquiry to open up new possibilities. Critical reflection enables us to challenge common sense, make connections, and explore the patterns that connect.

Celebration

Celebration is the act of commemorating the successes, big and small, in the process of change. It consists of the activities and performances that allow us to have fun with and in the work. Celebration is a process of bringing joy to the work and honor to the participants. Celebration, as a process, is rarely examined or practiced, but it is a fundamental way in which we can give voice to the beauty and power of our work. We borrow this process from other cultural contexts in which people integrate work and play and see celebration as an essential component of a just world and the struggle to achieve it.

Putting It All Together

We envision the Just Practice framework as a guide for critical question posing throughout the change process. It enables us to structure the process of being, doing, and becoming in light of the values and principles of social justice. As we engage in each moment and facet of the change process, the Just Practice framework keeps us critically mindful of the interplay of forces that are shaping the process. In the matrix on pp. 179–180, we illustrate the possibilities for question posing and critical reflection that emerge as the Just Practice framework is brought to bear in carrying out the core processes. The questions we pose are not exhaustive. Rather, we offer them as a starting point for your own critical reflection and action.

SUMMARY

In this chapter we have taken a close look at the concept of theory and the making of theory. We have explored the dominant paradigms that have shaped contemporary social work practice in the United States. We have drawn from a range of critical social and cultural theory to pose challenges to the dominant paradigm and suggest alternative possibilities for thought and action. Critical engagement with social work's theoretical history, contemporary theory, and new theoretical directions has shaped the Just Practice framework outlined here. We close with a case example that illustrates the interplay of meaning, context, power, history, and possibility in the practice of community-based social justice work. In chapters 5 to 8 we will develop each of the seven core processes and address the skills needed to carry them out.

ON REFLECTION

Resident Engagement during Public Housing Redevelopment

Laurie A. Walker, MSW, PhD, assistant professor of social work at the University of Montana

Cities and housing authorities often use large-scale change strategies to transform areas with concentrated poverty into areas that increase tax generation via home ownership and business development. Planning to change places often involves top-down social planning in communities with existing patterns of relating both within the community and between the community and other systems. Planners working in low-income communities need to take into account the historic and present experiences of power dynamics within these communities.

Social workers, community organizers, and other professionals working within these communities often have a better understanding of the meaning, context, power, and history in interactions among planners, community leaders, and residents. Professionals who take a teacher/learner stance can partner with community residents and leaders to envision models of engagement that create more genuine partnerships to envision a future for the community.

The Sun Valley neighborhood in Denver, Colorado, is the neighborhood with the lowest income in the state. More than half of the residents are children, more than 70 percent of the neighborhood has an income below the poverty level, and about 90 percent are people of color. The community has decades of history with community development, community organizing, and social planning processes. The neighborhood has experienced previous planning processes as patronizing despite their experiences with several projects. The planning processes have included an interstate, the widening of nearby streets, two professional football stadiums, riverfront recreational amenities, public transportation improvements, and public housing redevelopment.

Traditional planning processes involve planners from outside the neighborhood that focus on rational solutions. Large-scale change initiatives that receive federal funding are often required to engage the public in a feedback process. Public engagement typically takes the form of workshops that solicit feedback on several possible directions that the planning/development could take. Feedback is collected via individual written and verbal comments that are synthesized into formal plans.

Residents of the Sun Valley neighborhood regularly expressed that public workshops and design concepts did not take into account their values, needs, priorities, or knowledge. In Denver, Colorado, public workshop attendance and engagement in low-income neighborhoods had been limited and ineffective. In response, a collaboration formed among foundations funding resident engagement, planners, the housing authority, and the office of economic development to form Resident Advisory Councils (RAC) in the La Alma/Lincoln Park and Sun Valley neighborhoods.

The RAC was made up of a fifteen-person planning committee of professionals that consulted with the facilitator to plan meetings conducted with the professionals and thirty-nine additional RAC participants total from both neighborhoods. Although each of the two neighborhoods had its own RAC, the professionals informed the RAC process for both neighborhoods.

The La Alma/Lincoln Park neighborhood recently experienced the redevelopment of the North Lincoln public housing site and expected the redevelopment of the South Lincoln public housing site soon. The RACs played a critical role in the process by engaging with residents, building trust, and developing a priority list of key focus areas for change. The La Alma/Lincoln Park RAC influenced the direction of the Redevelopment Steering Committee and helped the housing authority provide proactive and transparent information to key community leaders regarding the redevelopment process.

In contrast, Sun Valley residents saw the redevelopment process as something in the distant future and wanted to address more immediate concerns, as well as the failings of past processes. In both neighborhoods the RAC became a venue to discuss resident meaning and experiences in the context of their neighborhood, as well as a means to debrief historically painful experiences with city structures. The Sun Valley residents utilized their community organizing meetings to formulate collective requests that addressed both past promises that had not materialized (as a form of evaluation/critique of previous planning processes) and current resident needs. They presented their collective requests verbally in formal planning workshops and followed up with written requests to targets of change, such as public works, city planning, and the regional transportation system, with specific timelines for expected responses. As a result the community secured millions of dollars of improvements that met community needs and desires, including sidewalks that had been promised in a previous football stadium planning process.

The typical planning processes in the Sun Valley neighborhood engaged adults and did not take into account half of their community's population, which consisted of children and teenagers. In fact, when members of the Sun

Valley Youth Coalition attended a public workshop, the planners attempted to send them to childcare. In response, the community organizer working with the Sun Valley residents before and after the RAC accompanied these residents as they made requests of the housing authority and city planners to engage the community in a more inclusive participatory planning process. Many neighborhood adults and more than sixty children/youth were engaged in a second planning process that included public workshops and meetings with participatory techniques such as photovoice, listening sessions, and discussions regarding neighborhood identity. As a result, many of the formal speakers at the City Council meeting adopting the neighborhood plan were children in support of the proposed changes. The City Council acknowledged and validated the residents' experiences of historically fighting for basic amenities, which was likely a result of the RAC dialogues. (For more information see the City and County of Denver [2013] and Walker and East [2014].)

QUESTIONS FOR DISCUSSION

1. What do the concepts positionality and intersectionality mean to you? How are they related to theory and theorizing?
2. In what ways might theory function as a form of oppression? As a form of liberation?
3. What are the most prominent social work theories used at your practicum site? What do you see as their strengths and limitations? How might alternative theoretical approaches expand practice possibilities?
4. Where do you see examples of critical social theory informing social work practice in your community? How does the theoretical perspective shape practice?
5. Where would you begin to build your own theory of social work? What key principles would guide your theory?

SUGGESTED READINGS

Gray, M., Coates, J., & Yellow Bird, M. (2008) *Indigenous social work around the world: Towards culturally relevant education and practice.* Burlington, VT: Ashgate.

hooks, b. (1984). *Feminist theory from margin to center.* Boston: South End Press.

Nagoshi, J., Nagoshi, C., & Brzuzy, S. (2014). *Gender and sexual identity: Transcending feminist and queer theory*. New York: Springer.

Payne, M. (2014). *Modern social work theory* (4th ed.). Chicago: Lyceum Books.

Reynolds, B. C. (1987). *Social work and social living*. Silver Spring, MD: NASW Press.

Smith, L. T. (1999). *Decolonizing methodologies: Research and indigenous people*. London: Zed.

Chapter 5

Just Get Started: Engagement

When social workers enter helping relationships, they enter with their own biases and prejudices. It is these biases and prejudices that can, and often do, affect how they listen to the problems of their service users and, ultimately, how they proceed to address them.

Izumi Sakamoto and Ronald Pitner (2005)

OVERVIEW

In this chapter we develop the meanings and contexts of engagement; consider power, history, positionality, and participants in the engagement process; and explore associated skills and practices and address their challenges and possibilities. Engagement provides the entrée to social justice work in cultural-political, community, organizational, and interpersonal contexts. It requires attention to the interplay of privilege and oppression and the physical as well as social worlds in which people's everyday struggles and social work practice are located. In addition, effective engagement brings attention to human rights and calls on social workers to strengthen their understanding of human rights. We build on the process of human rights education begun in chapter 3. We then explore skills central to engagement: anticipatory empathy; observation, noticing, and bearing witness; body consciousness; listening; and dialogue. We return to questions regarding power, difference, and resistance that may pose challenges for engagement. Finally, we attend to the place of group work and popular education in expanding the possibilities of engagement for social justice work.

Throughout this chapter we ask you to try to imagine the intertwining and mutually informing relationship between engagement and teaching-learning. One image that may be helpful is that of a dance with partners responding to one another as they execute complex patterns and improvise new possibilities of form and expression. Through engagement, we bring both preparedness and openness to bear on the teaching-learning moment. As we learn more about one another and our social realities, we construct shared meanings and histories and reshape the nature of our relationships and the processes of engagement. The *dance* of engagement and teaching-learning may grow more intimate, confident, and creative and the pacing and rhythms may shift over time. Likewise, we may make mistakes, stumble, and need to regroup and reflect on the limits of our engagement and learning. What might be another image that captures the dynamics of engagement and teaching-learning?

THE MEANING OF ENGAGEMENT

Engagement has multiple meanings. The word may refer to a mutual promise, a pledge or obligation, an emotional involvement or commitment, an arrangement to meet or to be present at a specified time and place, or a conflict encounter. The process of engagement in social work may reflect these aspects and more. Social work texts generally describe engagement as a process of establishing rapport; creating an environment of genuineness, empathy, and warmth; forming partnerships; and establishing a basis for trust and collaboration (Altman, 2008, p. 555; Miley, O'Melia, & DuBois, 2013, p. 133). These descriptions are helpful but partial. They do not speak to the biases and prejudices with which social workers enter the relationship or to the broader dynamics of power that may impinge upon that relationship (Sakamoto & Pitner, 2005).

The Just Practice approach asks us to think of engagement as both an intentional *process* and an ongoing *commitment*. Engagement is a socio-emotional, practical, and political process of coming together with others to create a space of respect and hope in which we can learn from and about one another. It is an iterative process. As we engage, we begin building a base of knowledge and a place of trust from which to discover, reflect, and act. Engagement is shaped by critical curiosity, humility, compassionate listening, and respect. It is also shaped by the histories and worldviews of the participants. It requires a commitment of our energies to be present, open, and willing to struggle with our own worldviews, biases, and prejudices so that we can allow space for alternative possibilities. It calls our attention to power relations both within the immediate encounter and in the larger social context shaping the encounter. It is about being fully present and open to another's story; doing the communicative, critically reflective, and relationship-building work; and becoming transformed through the cocreation of relationship.

Importance of Relationship

Relationship, a core social work value, is a key aspect of engagement. Human experience and identity are constituted through relationships (Christens, 2012). Jane Addams sought to build meaningful, lasting relationships with the residents of the Hull House neighborhood. As Sharon Berlin describes (2005), a practice of "relational acceptance," blending compassion and self-determination, was exemplified in Addams's work. Bertha Capen Reynolds believed that social work operates by communication, listening, and sharing experiences—the building blocks of relationship. Helen Harris Perlman (1979) described relationship as the heart of social work, characterized by a special kind of love. Felix Biesteck (1957) saw relationship as social work's soul.

Social workers have drawn on the humanistic psychology of Carl Rogers in promoting relationships based on three qualities: empathy, genuineness, and unconditional positive regard (Rogers, 1951). Rogers and his colleagues held that these core qualities facilitate a climate in which a relationship of dignity and respect can develop and in which challenging work can be tackled (Rogers, Gendlin, Kiesler, & Truax, 1967). Building a relationship grounded in love, dignity, and respect is not something to be taken lightly. Our own humanity is deepened as we engage in what philosopher Martin Buber terms an "I-thou" relationship; through compassionate connection to mutual personhood an "I-thou-we" relationship is created (Buber, 1937; Kelly & Sewell, 1988).

When we fail to engage with love, dignity, and respect, we not only risk diminishing the humanity of another, but we also find that our own personhood begins to atrophy (Deegan, 1996, p. 7). The result, as Patricia Deegan (1990) describes in her work on professional helpers and mental illness, is a breaking of the spirit that robs both clients and helpers of their full humanity. Deegan criticizes approaches to engagement in which professional expertise eclipses the expertise of the person living with mental illness. In contrast, she invites us to think about engagement as entry into a "conspiracy of hope" in which we "refuse to reduce humans beings to illness"; challenge radical power balances between professionals and those labeled as clients, patients, or consumers; and craft relationships marked by "true mutuality" (1996, p. 2, 3). What has your experience in social work thus far taught you about the importance, challenges, and possibilities of relationship?

Participants and Positionalities

A social-justice approach to engagement calls on us to honor the dignity and full personhood of all participants in the change process. In so doing, we must think critically about the ways in which concepts such as client, service user, patient, consumer, or member are used in our social work practice. These are questions of *discourse*. How does the naming of participants shape perceptions of personhood, competence, and capacity to participate in decision making?

Each term carries a certain cultural valence and suggests particular kinds of relationships. At times, a language of participation and collaboration may mask relationships of unequal power. There is a fundamental politics of naming at work in our practice, and it is important to explore and acknowledge the ways in which the language used to name social work relationships and activities shapes practice from the first moment of engagement.

The labels of helping systems may keep social workers from seeing the full personhood of those with whom they work. This, in turn, may lead them to make assumptions about a person's capabilities, thereby limiting his role from the moment of engagement. The very definition of who counts as part of the change process from the start is informed by theoretical, organizational, political, and practical factors. As critically reflective practitioners we need to continually consider the ways in which assumptions about the nature of the social work relationship and about who participates in the relationship often go without saying—as part of the unspoken rules of a particular context of practice. This requires critical curiosity from the start regarding the meaning of client, problem, and intervention. Think for a moment about your practicum context. How are clients referred to? How are they talked to and about by staff members? Are they ever reduced to labels or problems? Is there a tone of respect? Do you see ways in which the naming of participants shapes relations and interactions?

Effective engagement also demands attention to positionality and recognition of the complexity of social locations on the part of social workers as well as service users. Our positionalities are shaped by the multiple identities through which we experience the world and through which we acquire or are denied certain privileges and stakes in power. Social workers are a heterogeneous lot. We approach the engagement process from diverse points of entry and through multiple lenses of identity. A social worker who comes from a particular position of privilege may struggle to grasp the reality of her client's lived experience of poverty or racism. In turn, a social worker who has lived experience of racism, ableism, or heterosexism may have a different point of entry for engagement and find different possibilities for connection. We are not claiming that successful engagement depends on a common social location between worker and client. Rather we emphasize the complexity and heterogeneity of social location on the part of both workers and clients who come together in the engagement process. Moreover, we need to be critically attuned to ways in which institutional systems of privilege and oppression may distort or constrain the engagement process for both workers and clients, especially those from historically disadvantaged groups. We must continually confront questions of power in the social work process.

Let's consider an example. Stephen Rose (2000) writes of his positionality and power as a white middle-class social worker struggling to engage with Michael, a black teenager identified as having anger issues. Rose describes his personal epiphany when he realized that his social work training had taught him strategies for distancing himself from Michael, drawing on his expertise to interpret the meaning of Michael's anger, and using his professional power to name Michael's experience. Rose recalls,

> I was trained not to share power in constructing or producing what we worked on together, in not perceiving him worthy or capable of partnership with me. . . . In other words, my professional status included the illusion of ownership of meaning of another person's experience through the delegated power to interpret it. Professional knowledge was built into my packaged identity, the medium through which domination reigned. (p. 404)

Once Rose opened himself to listen to and learn from Michael, he faced a personal and professional crisis: "I knew that my reality and my identity—place, position, and privilege—were being challenged" (p. 405). Rose describes his encounter with Michael as a transforming learning experience in which Michael became the teacher who turned Rose's safe, knowable world into an "active contradiction." Michael taught Rose that authentic communication could not happen in the confines of the agency. Rose had to enter Michael's lived reality. Rose states: "We existed in relation, Michael and me; we were not discrete entities linked in a linear equation, but relationally connected parts of a larger social world whose requirements created both Michael's suffering and rage and my position to respond to it" (pp. 405–406).

As Rose reworked his assumptions, not only was his relationship with Michael transformed, but so was his relationship with social work. His account speaks to both the challenges of engagement and the possibilities that emerge when we take power, positionality, and participation seriously.

Individual Learning Activity:
Reflecting on Positionality

This activity provides an opportunity to critically reflect on your positionality and consider how it might shape what you bring to the engagement process. Positionality comprises many dimensions of social identity. For the purposes of this activity, the dimensions include:

1. Race/skin color/ethnicity/nationality/first language
2. Gender and gender expression

3. Socioeconomic class

4. Age

5. Sexual orientation

6. Religion/spiritual belief system

7. Ability/disability

8. Sense of place

In a six- to eight-page essay explore each of these dimensions to gain a deeper understanding of what they mean to you personally, how these meanings developed, how your life has been shaped by larger social interpretations of these dimensions, and how these meanings might impact your stance toward difference. In sum, the purpose is to answer the questions "Who am I?" and "How does this affect how I relate to others, especially those who are different from me?" These are complex questions, and the answers are ever changing.

In order to make the task more doable, there are four components of the assignment. First, write a brief description of seven of the eight categories. Second, include a more in-depth discussion of the remaining category. Your choice of category for in-depth reflection should be based on what you feel has been the most important influence on your personal or professional development or the dimension that has been the most invisible and thus perhaps the most taken for granted. Third, describe how you see the interplay of these dimensions. Finally, describe any new insights or implications for your future practice that you gained from this activity. If you wish, you can include photographs, documents, or stories from family members and ancestors or other personal artifacts.

Power in the Process

Power relations are in play in any relationships formed for the purpose of creating personal, social, or political change. As part of the engagement process we need to consider the contextual and structural arrangements; the conditions in which people come together; the nature of our social work practice; and the social, political, environmental, and organizational forces that shape our roles as social workers and the lives of those with whom we work. Structural inequalities can permeate the engagement process in complex ways that often go unquestioned.

For instance, in the United States we live in a society characterized by deeply embedded racism. The reality of racism is revealed in what Ta-Nehisi

Coates (2015c) refers to as the *carceral state*, in which our prison and jail population has increased sevenfold, from 300,000 to 2.2 million from 1970 to the present and in which one in four black men born since the 1970s has spent time in prison. It is revealed in the repeated police killings of unarmed black men, women, and children and the subsequent acquittals of those responsible. Economic inequality is on the rise, with 20 percent of U.S. households controlling 84 percent of the wealth and the bottom 40 percent controlling a mere 0.3 percent (Fritz, 2015). The staying power of gender oppression is reflected in continuing high rates of violence against women and the economic vulnerability of women, especially women of color. Heteronormativity remains an unspoken operating assumption that informs dominant social policies, practices, and discourse related to couples, families, and parenting. Interpersonal and institutional practices of ableism persist, even though it has been more than a quarter century since the passage of the Americans with Disabilities Act.

Structured inequalities have real, material effects in people's everyday lives. For example, poverty is not distributed equally; it maps onto other forms of inequality (Goodman et al., 2007). The "insistent daily struggles" with deprivation, violence, marginalization, and stigma associated with poverty have detrimental health and mental health consequences. Further, mental health research has pointed to the *pathogenic* power of racism and other intersecting forms of oppression in compromising health and well-being. Poverty and racism are not merely contextual factors. They are also direct causes of both emotional and physical trauma (Belle & Doucet, 2003; Bryant-Davis & Ocampo, 2005; Smith, Chambers, & Bratini, 2009, p. 160).

Reflection Moment: "Letter to My Son"

In July 2015, journalist Ta-Nehisi Coates published an article in *The Atlantic* entitled "Letter to My Son" (2015b), which was developed further in the book *Between the World and Me* (2015a). We include a brief excerpt and ask that you read the full article (http://www.theatlantic.com/politics/archive/2015/07/tanehisi-coates-between-the-world-and-me/397619).

I write you in your 15th year. I am writing you because this was the year you saw Eric Garner choked to death for selling cigarettes; because you know now that Renisha McBride was shot for seeking help; that John Crawford was shot down for browsing in a department store. And you have seen men in uniform drive by and murder Tamir Rice, a 12-year-old child whom they were oath-bound to protect. And you know now, if you did not before, that the police departments of your country have been endowed with the authority to destroy your body.

There is nothing uniquely evil in these destroyers or even in this moment. The destroyers are merely men enforcing the whims of our country, correctly interpreting its heritage and legacy. This legacy aspires to the shackling of black bodies. It is hard to face this. But all our phrasing—*race relations, racial chasm, racial justice, racial profiling, white privilege,* even *white supremacy*—serves to obscure that racism is a visceral experience, that it dislodges brains, blocks airways, rips muscle, extracts organs, cracks bones, breaks teeth. You must never look away from this. . . .

After reading the article, take time to sit with your thoughts and feelings. What responses does the essay evoke? How does Coates challenge or affirm your perceptions and experiences? Does Coates provide a context for what it means to be a fifteen-year-old black male in the United States that is missing from Stephen Rose's account of his work with Michael? What are our responsibilities for engagement as social justice workers?

As Stephen Rose's example suggests, social work's professional training schema has not necessarily prepared practitioners to critically consider the power of structured inequalities, such as racism, and its relationship to the specific situated experiences of people's everyday lives (Sakamoto & Pitner, 2005). Our dominant theories and models, at least within the U.S. context, have equipped us to look for signs and symptoms of individual pathology or family dysfunction as the entry point to our work (Waldegrave, 2005). Too often we remain silent on the subject of racism itself as a pathogen (McCabe & Davis, 2012). This silence is potentially harmful not only to the clients and communities served but also to social workers and their agencies. When racism is unacknowledged and under-standings of *difference* are filtered through a lens of white privilege, dominant meaning systems and practices go unquestioned (Briskman, 2008).

Linda Briskman argues that this "white lens" has shaped fundamental thinking and practices of much of the social work profession. Social workers who experience the world through the lens of white privilege may remain unwittingly complicit in practices of oppression in their work as they follow the path of least resistance. In turn, social workers and clients alike who identify as racial, ethnic, gender, or sexual minorities may face everyday experiences of oppression as a result of their social identities not only in the outside world, but also in the context of social service systems, agencies, and relationships. Take a moment to consider your own practicum experience. Do you see ways in which systems of privilege are at work? Ways they are resisted or transformed? Given your positionality, how do you experience the professional training schema of your practicum organization? Is it filtered through a white lens or does it offer a different lens? Might our perceptions and experiences as workers differ significantly here depending on our differing social identities? How might this organizational lens affect the process of engagement?

The National Association of Social Workers (NASW; 2007) describes the subtle forms of racism that play out in society at large and in the context of social work practice as "silent obstacles" that maintain and reinforce barriers to human dignity and fulfillment of human potential. NASW addresses *symbolic racism*, through which traditional values of the dominant group are imposed on groups who do not share those values; *aversive racism*, in which those who see themselves as non-racist will do racist things or avoid people deemed different without explicit racist intent; and *micro-inequities*, those "tiny damaging characteristics of an environment," perhaps communicated in a comment, tone of voice, or failure of acknowledgment, that provide continual negative messages regarding respect and belonging (p. 9). These practices filter through social welfare systems and social work agencies, they affect both workers and clients, and they may shape the engagement process in both subtle and profound ways. As social justice workers we need to engage in candid dialogue about our complex experiences of privilege and oppression so that entrenched systems of privilege and institutional discrimination can be recognized and redressed rather than reproduced. Let's turn to an example of institutional racism and consider possible responses.

Reflection Moment:
Engagement and the Power of Institutional Racism

The NASW has developed several scenarios to raise consciousness and promote dialogue regarding the workings of racism in the profession. Consider the following:

A senior woman of color, employed by a state agency to monitor mental health programs, finds that assessments of black families and children do not adequately consider the social context and family strengths. When she raises such concerns with white program leaders she is frequently told that she is missing the clinical aspects of what is involved, even though she is an experienced clinician herself. (NASW, 2007, p. 13)

What does this scenario suggest about the power of racism to shape agency practice? What might be the consequences for the senior woman of color, the black families served, and other agency staff and clients? How might the organizational stance affect engagement with families of color? How might program leaders perceive efforts to change the organizational stance initiated by a white social worker? How might change efforts initiated by a social worker of color be perceived? Have you witnessed or experienced a similar situation? What did you see as your responsibility and possible response? How did your positionality affect your response? What was at stake for you? As a worker of color, you may risk being subject to further symbolic and aversive racism as well as micro-inequities. Allies in the process of consciousness raising, resistance, and change are essential. And yet, for racism and other forms of oppression to continue requires only that people of privilege not notice, remain silent, and do nothing (Johnson, 2006; Mullaly, 2010, p. 295).

The Challenge of History

Let's return to the question of history and consider those who have historically been excluded from the processes of making decisions about their lives. Think about the ways in which oppression has systematically silenced some voices— children, women, people with disabilities, the poor, people of color, and immigrants—and legitimated the voices of the more powerful to speak for or about them. Histories of marginalization and exclusion have profoundly shaped and constrained practices of engagement. In chapter 4 we saw how historical constructions of disability filter through contemporary perceptions that continue to focus on limitations. These perceptions may also intrude on the engagement process. In a qualitative study of individuals with disabilities and their experiences with social workers, Stephen French Gilson, John Bricout, and Frank Baskind (1998) found that social workers treated respondents as if they had categorically fewer aspirations and rights than people without disabilities. Social workers tended to make prejudgments about capacity based on their personal assessment of the level of visible disability. They tended to establish an instant one-way familiarity while failing to really listen, recognize the uniqueness of the individual, or seek the expertise of individuals with disabilities themselves. Overall, the respondents characterized social worker engagement as demeaning and paternalistic (Gilson, Bricou, & Baskind, 1998). Their "expertise" limited their capacity to engage.

Reflection Moment:
Eli Clare on Ableism

Eli Clare is a writer, activist, and educator who confronts issues of disability, ableism, and the power of intersecting forms and practices of privilege and oppression. Clare (2015a, 2015b) has cerebral palsy and identifies as a white, genderqueer, trans man. In describing his experiences with ableism and being reduced to *other*, Clare reveals how histories of prejudice and stereotype reverberate in the present:

Complete strangers offer me Christian prayers or crystals and vitamins, always with the same intent—to touch me, fix me, mend my cerebral palsy, if only I will comply. They cry over me, wrap their arms around my shoulders, kiss my cheek. Even now, after five decades of these kinds of interactions, I still don't know how to rebuff their pity, how to tell them the simple truth that I'm not broken. Even if there were a cure for brain cells that died at birth, I'd refuse. I have no idea who I'd be without my tremoring and tense muscles, slurring tongue. They want to make me normal. They take for granted that my body-mind is wrong, bad, broken.

Complete strangers ask me, "What's your defect?" To them, my body-mind simply doesn't work right, defect being a variation of broken, supposedly neutral. But think of the things called defective—the mp3 player that won't turn on, the car that never ran reliably. They end up in the bottom drawer, dumpster, scrap yard. Defects are disposable, body-minds or objects to eradicate.

Complete strangers pat me on the head. They whisper platitudes in my ear, clichés about courage and inspiration. They enthuse about how remarkable I am. They declare me special.

Oh, how special disabled people are: we have special education and special needs. That word drips condescension. It's no better than being defective. It's simply another way to declare some body-minds bad. (Clare, in press)

What does Clare's narrative suggest about the infiltration of history into present-day thinking about disability? What are possible implications for engagement?

Hilary Weaver speaks powerfully to the challenges of history as part of contemporary practice with American Indian people. As Weaver describes, social work in its early years had little interaction with American Indian people. When social workers did become involved, it was in the form of coercive practices that included removal of children from family and tribal communities and promoting sterilization of Native American women (Weaver, 2008, p. 73; see also Lawrence, 2000). At the same time, social workers ignored long-standing indigenous ways of helping that incorporate ceremony, spirituality, and collective participation in community well-being (Weaver, p. 74). Weaver notes the irony of social work's stated focus on the "person in environment" and the profession's overall failure to grasp the complexity of environment in terms of indigenous people's experiences.

Weaver describes historical trauma and unresolved grief resulting from genocide as legacies that many American Indian people continue to struggle with today (1998, p. 205). She details the forced relocation, land dispossession, and breakup of families that characterized nineteenth and twentieth century federal policies and practices toward American Indian people in the United States. Weaver writes:

> Suspicion and mistrust are natural outcomes and important survival skills for people who have experienced attempts at genocide. Many interactions with the dominant society have had dire consequences for Native Americans. Practitioners and program planners who seek to work with Indian people must realize that their helping interventions may be viewed within this context. (1998, p. 206)

As Clare's and Weaver's discussions suggest, history cannot be bracketed out of the engagement process. Instead, we as social workers must be mindful of the ways in which personal, political, and cultural histories shape our positionalities as well as those of the people with whom we work. "Helping" systems of the state or dominant culture have served as institutions of power and control over oppressed groups. Distrust and resistance are often healthy responses to such systems, and social workers within these systems need to approach the engagement process with sensitivity to the palpable presence of history and an appreciation of resistance as both a right and a survival skill. Furthermore, social workers and service users frequently enter as participants in the engagement process with little shared history. Those histories cannot be assumed. Rather, the art of engagement entails making space and time where experiences can be shared, stories told, and trust built in the process of cocreating relationship.

THE CONTEXT OF ENGAGEMENT

Engagement is embedded in context. Participants come together in a specific time and space that is shaped by personal experiences, historical and political influences, and current social circumstances. The process of engagement plays out in cultural-political, community, and organizational contexts that serve as both resources and constraints. In this section we address the cultural-political, community, and organizational contexts of engagement. We then locate engagement as an interpersonal process that is shaped powerfully by the contexts in which it plays out. At the same time, through the dynamics of engagement, participants encounter and create possibilities for transforming the very contexts in which their relationships emerge. As we consider contexts of practice, we ask you to consider these contexts in terms of your own positionality and the implications for practice.

Cultural-Political Context of Engagement

Reconsidering Cultural Competence

We refer to the *cultural-political* context here to emphasize the point that culture is inseparable from forms and relations of power. We first address the concept of *cultural competence* and then consider the interplay of cultural and political dimensions of context. The NASW Code of Ethics calls on social workers to engage in culturally competent practice. The profession has struggled over time with the challenge of both defining and realizing cultural competence. Much of the early work on cultural diversity focused on characterizations of and intervention strategies for presumably discrete groups viewed as culturally different (see, for example, Atkinson, Morten, & Sue, 1989). These approaches often relied on understandings of cultures as homogeneous entities identifiable by common history, language, customs, values, belief systems, and practices. The audiences for the early writings on ethnic sensitivity and diversity in U.S. social work were generally assumed to be members of the dominant white majority who needed tools for working with the ethnic other. Over time, these limited perspectives have been questioned as the profession has come to appreciate a more complex understanding of culture and its interplay with history and power (Dean, 2001; Healy, 2008; Sakamoto & Pitner, 2005).

Considerable attention continues to be focused on the question of cultural competence and to the preparation of social workers to engage in culturally competent practice (Lum, 2011). At the same time, understanding of cultures as homogeneous entities identifiable by common history, language, customs, values, belief systems, and practices persists. For example, the *Social Work Dictionary* (Barker, 2014) defines cultural competence as "possession of the knowledge, attitudes, understanding, self-awareness, and practice skills that enable a professional person to serve clients from diverse socioethnic backgrounds." The NASW Code of Ethics (section 1.05) states that cultural competence and social diversity have three components: (a) that social workers should understand culture and its functions and the strengths that exist in all cultures, (b) that they should have knowledge about their clients' cultures and differences among cultural groups, and (c) that they should seek out education and understanding about the nature of social diversity and oppression for all cultural groups.

This understanding of cultural competence speaks to the importance of self-awareness and active engagement in learning about both diversity and oppression. At the same time, it operates from a modernist notion of culture as a discreet, neutral, bounded collection of "customs, habits, skills, technology, arts, values," and ideologies of a group of people (Barker, 2014, p. 103). It does not address the importance of historical context, power relations, or community and intergenerational dynamics in understanding people's strengths and struggles (Sakamoto, 2007) nor does it capture the interplay of structural forces and cultural processes, which we will explore below. Some have argued that this framing of cultural competence in social work not only operates from an outmoded understanding of culture, but that it also essentializes culture, constructs "whiteness" as the default norm and in effect, operates as a new form of racism in constructing others as those who differ from the standard of whiteness (Pon, 2009). In contrast, Lynn Nybell and Sylvia Gray (2004) place questions of power front and center in addressing what cultural competence entails in the context of child welfare agencies. They contend that "achieving cultural competence in a predominantly white social service organization requires redistributing power toward clients, toward programs that disproportionately serve the most disenfranchised clients, to workers of color, and to representatives of communities of color" (p. 25).

From Cultural Competence to Cultural Humility

Some social workers have challenged the assumption that one can attain cultural competence. They suggest a more humble appreciation of the ongoing struggle to grasp another's experience. Cultural engagement entails opening ourselves not only to hearing another's story, but also to appreciating very different systems of meaning and values and ways of organizing and making sense of basic concepts—such as personhood, family, health and illness, faith, and social organization. For example, Ruth Dean (2001) writes persuasively about the *myth* of cross-cultural competence and encourages social workers to recognize their "partiality of knowledge":

> The concept of multicultural competence is flawed. I believe it to be a myth that is typically American and located in the metaphor of American "know-how." It is consistent with the belief that knowledge brings control and effectiveness and that this is an ideal to be achieved above all else. I question the notion that one could become "competent" at the culture of another. (p. 624)

Rather than assuming cultural competence as an achievable goal, Dean and others encourage social workers to practice from a place of *cultural humility* and to take responsibility for ongoing learning about difference and about one's own cultural story (Dean, 2001; Hohman, 2013; Laird, 1993; Zayas, 2001). Cultural humility calls for acknowledgment of the limitations of our knowledge and recognition of the unconscious stereotypes we employ in attempting to understand or explain cultural difference (Ortega & Faller, 2011).

Linking Meaning and Power

Given the centrality of cultural competence in contemporary social work debates, we want to probe further into the concepts of culture that inform our thinking regarding the cultural context of engagement. We draw from cultural anthropologists who have helped us to see culture not as a fixed set of traits and customs, but as a dynamic and contested process of meaning making embedded within relations of power. Anthropologists have critiqued the concept of culture as a shared system of order, a unified whole of the customs, practices, language, symbols, and institutions of a group. Instead, they call attention to the permeation of power relations, forms of resistance, the contested and contingent nature of culture, the role of hegemony, and the active practice and resistance of cultural agents (Rosaldo, 1989). For example, anthropologist James Clifford contends that culture is historically produced, actively contested, temporal, and emergent. He describes culture as "always relational, an inscription of communicative processes that exist, historically, *between* subjects in relations of power" (1986, p. 15).

From this point of view, the process of engagement invites us to start from a place of not knowing and to open ourselves to the ethnographic experience of "learning from other social worlds" (Davies, 1999, p. 77). It is a process of entering into "another history of interactions," and can pose for the social worker what Charlotte Aull Davies calls "the problem of memory"—we enter without a shared history and without being privy to the collective memory of which other participants are a part; therefore, we have to have a heightened sensitivity to the limits of our knowing and the dangers of facile interpretation. We are, in many ways, having to learn a new language of relationship that both draws on the language of the other party(ies) and that is co-constructed through the relationship. When we put cultural engagement in the frame of learning another language it helps us keep that sense of humility about the limits of our knowing and the possibilities for making "cultural mistakes."

When we speak of the cultural context of engagement, we speak to the dynamic interplay of meaning and power among the worldviews of the social worker and the other participants in the process. It is helpful to think of the engagement process itself as a cultural encounter in which the participants struggle to hear and be heard, to understand and be understood. We start from recognition of the partiality of our knowledge, we bear witness to another's experience, we continually examine our own cultural freight, we seek to cocreate meaning, and we remain ever vigilant to the workings of power and privilege and the possibilities for mitigating the effects of past and present inequalities.

The work of anthropologist/physician Paul Farmer is instructive here. Farmer warns against the danger of confusing structural violence and cultural difference. Too often, he argues, those in positions of privilege invoke notions of culture to explain difference without acknowledging the underlying structural inequalities that shape so much of human experience. He cautions us to be wary of simplistic explanations of difference as "part of one's culture" or "in one's nature." According to Farmer such explanations reflect a cultural essentialism "used to explain away assaults on the dignity and suffering" of others. Farmer states that "culture does not explain suffering; it may at worst furnish an alibi for it" (2003, p. 49). One of the challenges of engagement, then, is to be at once attentive to cultural context, sensitive to cultural difference, and mindful of the role of structural forces in shaping both.

Cultural and Political Dimensions of Engagement

This brings us back to the inseparability of cultural and political dimensions of engagement. The work of Michael Reisch and Jayshree Jani (2012) on the new politics of social work is instructive here. Working from a postmodern perspective, they address ways in which the social construction of social service institutions, relations, language, and practices reflect and sustain broader power arrangements of society that affect both workers and clients. They argue that social workers need to confront the political dimensions of practice and critically attend to ways that power shapes (1) allocation of rights, resources, status, access, and opportunities; (2) inter- and intra-organizational dynamics; and (3) implicit operating assumptions about needs, helping strategies, and evaluation of interventions (p. 1137).

Reisch and Jani (2012) point to the significant increase in numbers of involuntary clients, the rise in prescriptive interventions, the role of outside funders in determining agency priorities, and the linkage of outcome measures to funder rather than client requirements as examples of the contemporary cultural politics of social work. They call for a *repoliticizing* of social work and for approaches to practice that respect difference and recognize common human needs and culturally based means of addressing them. Their analysis reminds us of the importance of complexity thinking as a practice skill. How might a client's involuntary status and limited choice in seeking services shape the engagement process? How might the mandates of outside funders and policy makers limit the social worker's range of choices as well? How might critical consciousness of these factors better prepare us to confront and address the political nature of social work practice from engagement forward? What are some of the questions you might ask to better understand the cultural-political context that shapes engagement in the context of your practicum?

Community Context of Engagement

The process of engagement also calls on us to be cognizant of our personal and organizational location within a larger community. The concept of community itself has multiple meanings. Community may refer to a political entity, a circumscribed and identified social and geographic space, or a group of people with common interests or concerns. Although geographic proximity may be a key feature in defining community for some, others develop and sustain community through extended social networks, shared social identities, or common political commitments (Hardina, 2013; Homan, 2016; Pyles, 2009). Early studies of community focused on place-based relationships, a sense of belonging and connection, and the ways in which people developed structures and functions to sustain social life (Redfield, 1960; Toennies, 1957). Systems theorists have framed communities as complex social systems that fulfill multiple functions

for members, including socialization, social control, social support, social participation, and economic production (Warren, 1963).

Communities have also been characterized as sites of struggle over forms
and relations of power, access to resources, and demands for justice (Homan,
2016; Hunter, 1953; Phillips & Pittman, 2009). Intersections of poverty and
racism leave not only individuals and families but also entire communities at
risk, as evidenced in studies of education inequities (Tough, 2009), food deserts
(Whitacre, Tsai, & Mulligan, 2009), and environmental racism (Taylor, 2014).
Dorcetta Taylor (2014) examines the disproportionate industrial toxic exposure
experienced by poor African American and Native American communities in
the United States and the compounding of community risk as a result of severe
constraints on resident mobility. Her work unveils the history, practices, and
consequences of environmental racism as well as the power of poor and minority communities to build and sustain movements for environmental justice.
Taylor speaks to the importance of engaging in community struggle as a part
of social justice work.

New forms of transnational community are emerging as people navigate
labor, family, and caregiving across borders (Cho, Chin, & Shin, 2010; Nicholson,
2006). For some, technological advances have opened the way for creation of
countless virtual communities of engagement that transcend cultural, political, and geographic borders. For others the relentless downward pressure of
structural adjustment policies and the consequences of free-trade agreements
have contributed to the dissolution of long-standing ties to land and place, loss
of sustainable life ways, and movement into precarious circuits of global labor
migration (Ho & Loucky, 2012; Yan, 2004). Traditional notions of communities as
stable, homogeneous, place-based entities are becoming anachronistic as more
and more people negotiate complex global circuits of interaction and obligation just to survive (Ho & Loucky, 2012; Zayas, 2015). Despite and because of
this complexity, community still matters to people.

As Jim Ife (2000) asserts, community is still an important buffer to the
effects of globalization on people's lives. We have a responsibility to learn how
people define and practice community, cultivate a sense of belonging, meet
social obligations, negotiate barriers, and stake claims to their rights as community members. Engaging with others as members of communities is a measure of respect for their full personhood and for the power of relationships. In
sum, communities are sites of struggle and support, conflict and connection.
Social justice work challenges us to bring to the engagement process a
permanent critical curiosity about the dynamics of community in which our

practice is located. Patterns of social relations, structures of power, and the cultural politics of community are not necessarily forces of constraint; they are also sources of possibility for transformative engagement. Think for a moment about the communities of which you are a part. Do they support and sustain you? What responsibilities do you have in return? What happens when you are separated from community, when communities are fractured, or when communities are toxic and threatened rather than safe and sustaining? How will you bring a consciousness of community to the process of engagement?

Organizational Context of Engagement

The process of engagement also calls for reflection on our location as social workers in an organizational context. Most social work practice is carried out under the auspices of state-based human service systems; voluntary not-for-profit organizations; community- or neighborhood-based associations; or with increasing frequency, for-profit corporations. Despite the centrality of organizations to social work practice, social workers often lack what Ed Silverman (2015) terms *organizational awareness*—an understanding of their purpose, culture, operating systems, and social relations. Engagement requires critical reflection on the organizations in which we work. What can we learn by reflecting on our positioning within organizations and the ways in which organizational context may variably constrain and enable our social justice work?

Organizations have long been a subject of inquiry. Early theorists focused on organizational structure and function, rules and roles, and resource allocations (Netting & O'Connor, 2003; Weber, 1922). Attention then shifted to human relations and the power of individuals and groups in shaping organizational structure and function (Argyris, 1970). Systems theorists have characterized organizations as complex systems of information, control, and decision making navigating the demands of changing environments (Hutchison, 2015, pp. 426–427). Conflict theorists have taken power as a central theme in organizational analysis and have addressed the importance of informal power and politics within organizations (Netting & O'Connor, 2003, p. 45).

Theorists of organizational culture and sense making have brought questions of meaning to the fore. Organizational culture theorists emphasize the shared experiences among organizational members that merge over time into a shared pattern of beliefs, values, practices, language, and everyday rituals. They argue that these patterns eventually become internalized and adhered to, even though individuals are not consciously aware of them. Closely related to theories of organizational culture are theories of sense making in organizations, which explore the ways in which people within an organization seek to understand the organization. Weick (1995, p. 13) describes sense making as an active process through which people "generate what they interpret" as they try to bring a sense of order and manageability to organizational ambiguity. Theorists have examined ways in which organizational power intersects with meaning making and the ways in which those with power are able to privilege their versions of organizational reality and marginalize others' realities (Hutchison, 2015, p. 431).

Feminist theorists have brought a gender lens to bear in understanding formal and informal organizational structures and practices. They have critiqued the power relations embedded in traditional bureaucracies and probed the possibilities of nonhierarchical organizational structures and consensus models of organizational leadership and decision making (Ferguson, 1984; Iannello, 1992; Kanter, 1977). Organizational theorists have also drawn insights from thinking regarding intersectionality and framed organizations as sites of multiple oppressions wherein hierarchical arrangements and practices produce complex matrices of domination and subordination (Hutchison, 2015, p. 432).

We find these ideas about structure, power, culture, and sense making useful in developing awareness of ourselves as organization-located actors and in engaging with others in the organizational context. From a practice theory point of view, we must be mindful of the interplay of these aspects of organizations to understand how we shape and are shaped by the organizational context of practice. Reisch and Jani (2012), for example, remind us that broader political processes and economic arrangements are never external to the workings of our organizations, but are intimately involved in the production of particular kinds of organizations, workers, and clients. They challenge us to engage critically and politically with the practice environments of our organizations and to challenge a status quo that sustains unequal power arrangements.

In chapter 6 (Table 6.1, pp. 270–271) we will present a guide to "Getting to Know Your Organization" that provides a starting point for critical organizational awareness. Take a moment to think about your workplace or practicum organization. Are there a clear mission and guiding principles? Do organizational practices align with principles? Who holds formal and informal power? How are decisions made? To whom is the organization accountable? What voice do service users have in organizational decision making? What voice do social workers have? How might answers to these questions affect the engagement process?

Learning from Experience:
Janet's Story

Janet Finn offers an example from her social work experience to illustrate ways that organizational context shaped the practice of engagement and ways in which she was both constrained and transformed by her experiences:

One of my first paid social work positions was as a group life counselor in a state institution for girls and young women who had been adjudicated "delinquent." I was twenty-one years old and fresh from college when I took the job. The institution resembled a country boarding school, with several residential cottages, a cafeteria, gymnasium, and school. Underneath its welcoming façade was a tightly controlled system of discipline, rules, and surveillance. I was a shift worker charged with overseeing cottage life in the afternoons and evenings, one of the least powerful staff positions in the institution. I was barely older than many of the young women under my "supervision." In many ways, it was by not-so-simple twists of fate that I was the one with the keys. But with those keys came power and responsibility. Those keys marked my privileged position as a well-educated white woman. They symbolized a boundary of difference between me and young women who had used the resources at hand to escape violent homes and abusive parents and partners, who had survived on the streets by plying their wits and selling their bodies, and who had sought comfort or oblivion in glue and booze and dope. The keys gave me access to everything from deodorant and hairspray to cigarettes and aspirin—all securely locked away from my young charges. They symbolized my everyday power to withhold privileges and offer rewards—"Yes, you can call home this weekend. . . . No, you cannot leave campus with your aunt on Sunday." They symbolized the power of my voice in decisions about life beyond the institution.

In effect, the job was an ongoing negotiation of the nuances of power, trust, and intimacy. I worked to build trust and to be clear about my responsibilities and the limits of my authority. But the institution's policy manual did not prepare me for the everyday challenges that negotiation posed. There was so much I did not know—about myself, the young women, and the structural inequalities of justice systems. I made lots of mistakes, usually when my own lack of confidence and fear of failure pushed me to wield my authority and restrict possibilities when what I really needed to do was listen more carefully. I felt my own sense of powerlessness as a young woman in a male-dominated system. And yet the young women in my cottage saw the many sources of power at my fingertips that separated me from them. I came to appreciate my privileged positioning as one with potential to advance in the system due to my degree while my coworkers often had more limited options.

With time, I learned to suspend my disbelief, tether my precarious authority, and listen more carefully and respectfully to the young women's stories. Their stories of tenacity, survival, courage, and longing were their gifts to me. As I became more cognizant of both the limits and possibilities of my position, I sought ways to push the boundaries of the possible. I began to find my own voice as I learned to advocate on behalf of the young women in staff meetings and court reports where their voices were too often silenced. When I left my position after two years, I did not know enough to thank them for all they had taught me. Thirty-five years later, I continue to draw lessons for engagement through critical reflection on the organizational context of that profound experience.

Reflection Moment:
Engagement with Human Rights

Social justice work calls for ongoing recognition of and advocacy for human rights. How might human rights be brought to bear in the engagement process? This question challenges us to think critically about the relevance of human rights to our everyday social work practice and to continued ongoing knowledge development related to human rights. Revisit the plain language version of the Universal Declaration of Human Rights (UDHR) on p. 131. What human rights do you see as most salient in the context of your current social work practice? What human rights does your organization or program seek to protect? What human rights violations have service users possibly experienced? Are human rights a talkable subject within your agency? How might you address questions of human rights concretely in this organizational context? How might critical consciousness of human rights shape your approach to engagement?

The United Nations Convention on the Rights of the Child (CRC) was adopted by the UN General Assembly in 1989. It consists of forty-one articles that address children's rights to survival, development, protection, and participation. In general it calls for "freedom from violence, abuse, hazardous employment, exploitation, abduction, or sale; adequate nutrition; free compulsory primary education; adequate health care; equal treatment regardless of gender, race, or cultural background; the right to express opinions and freedom of thought in matters affecting them; and safe exposure/access to leisure, play, culture, and art" (Amnesty International, 2015).

The CRC is the most widely and rapidly ratified international human rights treaty (UNICEF, n.d.). As of 2016, the United States is the only UN member country who has yet to ratify the CRC (American Civil Liberties Union, 2015). In a growing number of countries, the CRC provides the framework for child welfare and protection services. (The full text of the CRC is accessible at http://www.unicef.org/crc, and a simplified version of the CRC is accessible at http://www.everychild.ca/uncrc) Take time to review the CRC. How might implementation of the CRC affect approaches to children's services offered by agencies in your community? How might it shape the engagement process with children and families?

Engagement as an Interpersonal Process

The interpersonal process of engagement cuts across all facets of social justice work. As Donna Hardina (2013) described, the skills of interpersonal practice are also essential to effective community work, and that starts with engagement. Person-to-person relationships provide the foundation of social justice work. Regardless of whether we work with communities, families, neighborhoods, groups, or organizations, we are called upon to build and maintain interpersonal relationships. Bertha Capen Reynolds (1951), for example, challenged us to get close to people and honor the inseparability of social work and social living. This closeness implies a relationship that respects the whole person, encourages a sense of belonging, and recognizes people as much more than "bundles of problems and needs."

In recognizing the central place of relationships in social justice work, we acknowledge that relationships have value in themselves; they are not merely means to an end. Rather, relationships are the bedrock of our humanity. As we discussed earlier in the chapter, we are likely to be confronted with differences in our power and positionalities and with the limits of our partial worldviews as we work to build meaningful productive relationships. Dynamic change-oriented relationships create possibilities for shifting our positions and expanding our views. This is hard work that demands humility, commitment, and reflection. Most fundamentally, it requires that we are *present*, physically, mentally, and emotionally. In the following section we will address the skills of engagement that enable us to form partnerships and alliances, develop trust through dialogue, build and share power, and create an interpersonal context that contributes to justice-oriented practice.

SKILLS AND PRACTICE OF ENGAGEMENT

In this section we develop a range of skills to draw from in the process of engagement. These include (1) anticipatory empathy; (2) observation, noticing, and bearing witness; (3) body consciousness; (4) listening; and (5) dialogue. This is not a definitive list of techniques to be mastered but an entry point into building genuine relationships. We draw from the practice knowledge of social work and communication studies, the teachings of social justice workers who have challenged and expanded our thinking, and our own practice experience. We invite you to add to and refine these skills as you create your personal tool kit for social justice work.

Skills of engagement are fundamentally about communication. Floyd Matson and Ashley Montagu (1967) describe communication as dialogue through which participants seek to find and create common ground. They assert that "the end of human communication is not to *command* but to *commune*. . . . Knowledge of the highest order is to be sought and found not through detachment but through connection, not by objectivity but by intersubjectivity, not in a state of estranged aloofness but in something resembling the act of love" (pp. 3, 6). In every communication process, the attitudes, feelings, and positionalities of both receiver and sender are vitally important. As Gregory Baum (1971, p. 42) writes, "we are created through ongoing communication with others." Differences in social identities, experiences, and expectations affect the communication process. Awareness of these differences and relations of power inherent in them is crucial to effective communication.

Anticipatory Empathy

Engagement calls for *anticipatory empathy*—a process of preparation through critical reflection on the possible situations, concerns, and interests of the participants in the change effort. In this process we are mindful of the question "What is the significance of this encounter and relationship—what does it mean to me and to the other participants?" It is a process of readying ourselves for an encounter with others, focusing our energies and attention, and opening ourselves to new learning. In many ways it is a time of transition when we move away from the phone calls and e-mail and other demands of our work and create a space for intentional reflection. We start from a place of not knowing and uncertainty and allow ourselves to wonder. What information do we have thus far? What sort of partial picture is beginning to emerge? Who has provided us with the information? How might the people we are about to encounter tell their story? It is through storytelling that people recount how they have been affected by a problem or issue (Hardina, 2013). How can we best open ourselves to hearing their stories and receiving them as gifts? What might the other person (people) be feeling or thinking? How might our differing histories and positionalities influence the encounter?

Anticipatory empathy may entail very concrete preparation for a specific encounter or meeting. It creates time and space to think about the *purpose* of our engagement and our *role* in the process. It provides an opportunity to consider our own expectations and those of others. Who will be present? Who else should participate? What resources are available? What may be some of the constraints? What do we hope to accomplish? What might others hope to take away from the meeting? It is a time to consciously reflect on the cultural-political, community, and organizational contexts in which we are coming together with others and to think about the ways in which these forces might infiltrate the emergent relationship. Returning to the insight of Ruth Dean (2001), anticipatory empathy entails reflection on the cultural, political, and historical forces that may have shaped our own and another's experience. It is a time to take stock of the cultural baggage we carry with us so that we enter the encounter from the humble position of not knowing. It is a time to think about the multiple and complex intersections of privilege and oppression that may have left and continue to leave their marks on the participants, ourselves included. It is a time to reflect on the ways in which our differing locations within broader community and organizational contexts may come into play.

Anticipatory empathy is also a time to consider the possibilities, capabilities, and strengths of people and communities and to resist the pull of problem-saturated preconceptions (Saleebey, 2006). As we open ourselves to new learning from and with participants, it is important to think not only in terms of struggles, but also in terms of capacities, resilience, and creativity. Because we often see only that which we are conditioned to see, part of the process may involve preparing ourselves to "see" in different ways and learning to recognize social, emotional, and material resources that may be outside of our own experience. It is helpful to ask ourselves these questions: What new knowledge and understanding might I take away from this experience? How might I be changed by my participation in this process and relationship? Too often, we assume change is about others. In social justice work, we recognize that change is also about *us*.

Anticipatory empathy is also a time for getting in touch with our own feelings and biases. The structural violence confronting people in unsafe housing, poverty-stricken neighborhoods, and communities endangered by toxic waste; the human drama of a hospital emergency room; the dank air of a jail cell— these sensory realities can tap into our histories and memories in a visceral way that is beyond words. They pummel our emotions and wrench our guts. Anticipatory empathy requires time and space to feel and to be honest with ourselves about what we feel, especially difficult emotions such as fear, anger, or outrage. Even as we prepare to approach what we anticipate to be comfortable encounters, it is important that we allow space for feelings of uncertainty, anticipation, and perhaps discomfort. Recognition of the emotional context of the work prepares us to engage with our hearts as well as our heads and hands.

The practice of self-reflection in anticipation of the encounter is a crucial component of the engagement process. Unfortunately it is often neglected in practice. As the demands for efficiency, productivity, and the overall businessing of social work increase, anticipatory empathy is too often construed as a luxury. We often hear social workers lament, "Who has time to sit and think . . . I have too much work to do!" We argue that reflection is a necessary part of the work, but organizational constraints are real and they impose barriers to reflection. How do we carve out spaces for contemplation in our work places? What organizational changes might be necessary to legitimize the importance of reflection time? These are essential questions to pose, especially as we consider the linkage between reflection and anticipatory empathy.

Anticipatory empathy puts us in touch with both pain and possibility. It is through genuine connection to our own humanity that we open ourselves to tap into and engage the dignity and worth of others. It situates us in a mutually informing process of being, doing, and becoming. Anticipatory empathy is not a one-time exercise carried out before engaging with a person or group for the first time. Rather, it is a process we engage in as we move in and out of particular contexts of communication and action. It prepares us to enter the world of the participant(s) and develop and strengthen the working relationship. Each participant in the change process approaches the encounter from the complex context of everyday life and brings the weight of history and memory to bear in crafting a new context.

Observation, Noticing, and Bearing Witness

Observation

A fundamental communication skill is that of observation. The social work setting, whether it is a kitchen table, community hall, hospital room, or boardroom, presents both possibilities and constraints that shape the process of relationship building. It is important that we be tuned in to the immediate context of practice so that we can best appreciate and address both limits and possibilities. Our initial observations give us a very partial sense of context, but it is a beginning. In addition to taking in the physical context of our work, the communication process is shaped by our observations of the social context. How do other participants in the change process initially respond to us, to one another, and to their surroundings? How do we interpret the mood or tone of the setting? What sorts of patterns of social interaction are in play? What unspoken rules seem to govern people's social relations and actions?

In our everyday interactions we are observers of people and social groups. We give meaning to social interactions as we take in content; "read" nonverbal expressions; and interpret feelings, attitudes, and intentions (Brill & Levine, 2002). We hone our observation skills as we become cognizant of the aspects or levels involved and systematically attend to them.

In the context of social justice work, however, observation is not a detached process. Observation is a connecting two-way process, shaped by relations of power. We are both observers and observed in any social work relationship. Our initial and ongoing observations provide us with data from which we can engage in dialogue for co-learning. We also provide other participants with "data" regarding our comfort level and preparedness in the situation. As our impressions and understandings become more textured and detailed, we may find that interpretations based on initial observations were faulty. Careful, respectful observation is a skill that we can hone through practice.

Noticing

Noticing is the practice of critical, compassionate observation in which we are probing the connections between personal struggles and public issues (Witkin, 1998). Noticing entails attention to time as well as to people and place. Barry Locke, Rebecca Garrison, and James Winship (1998, p. 18) use the Greek concepts of time, *chronos* and *kairos*, to capture a distinction that social workers need to keep in mind. *Chronos* refers to chronological time, and *kairos* refers to readiness or timeliness. Mindfulness of an individual's or group's readiness to engage in a process of change is critical. Readiness is not simply a matter of individual motivation, but a complex phenomenon shaped by levels of trust, structural constraints, available resources, levels of acceptance, and cultural norms in addition to individually or collectively felt need for change. Attention to readiness draws on skills of empathy as well as analysis.

Martha Dewees (2006, p. 48) describes noticing as "both a political and pragmatic act" wherein we pay attention to everyday indignities of racism, sexism, homophobia, and other forms of violation and exclusions; to the subtleties of our own practice, from tone of voice to sense of time and style of dress; and to the myriad barriers large and small that can block participation—lack of gas money or public transportation, child care, or confidence. Noticing may also entail the practice of bearing witness.

Bearing Witness

Engagement also entails bearing witness. We are present in the moment, witness to another's story and experiences. Paul Farmer suggests two ways of bearing witness, and he sees both as essential to the process of social justice work. One is to observe, document, and speak out about the suffering of others that we have seen with our own eyes. In this sense one bears witness by making the connections between personal pain and structural violence. A second way is to stay present with what Farmer terms the "surface silence"—a silence perhaps conditioned by poverty, oppression, exclusion, and concomitant distrust—and respect the "profound eloquence" that lies beneath it (2003, p. 26). We may be tempted to probe that silence, and at times that may be helpful. At other times it may be more respectful to bear witness through honoring the silence and engaging in pragmatic solidarity to address the immediacy of that suffering and its consequences (Farmer, 2003). Barbara Levy Simon (1994) writes that as we bear witness to the misery of people with whom we work we have an ethical obligation to step forward and speak truths about the issues we observe. We will return to the practice of bearing witness as a form of action in chapter 7.

Lessons for Engagement from Street Outreach with Youth Sex Workers

Kennedy Saldanha and Derek Parenteau (2013) provide powerful insights into the challenges and possibilities of engagement through their examination of street outreach with young sex workers on the streets of Toronto. They describe outreach as an "active form of waiting" in which workers demonstrate commitment through their consistent presence:

Waiting communicates respect towards the individual. It acknowledges that street youth are on their own stage of the journey and will not be ready or able to make changes in their life just because we want them to or because we happen to have room in our program for them at that time. Waiting shows people that outreach workers care about them, not just about helping them; while we wait we spend time with people just as they are. When doing outreach, workers get really good at talking about the weather, about their pets, about everything other than what the young person's struggles might be. When workers combine waiting with a consistent presence in the community, they establish a basis for trust and engagement for when the time finally comes to "do your job." Some people will take a long time to be ready and others may never be ready to change. Even then, actively waiting is not a waste of time. A consistency in their lives helps keep the desire to change alive and gives them hope. Relationship and connection honor dignity in the here and now. Outreach workers who remember the names and stories of those they meet demonstrate a genuine desire to connect and to respect dignity. (pp.1278–1279)

How does the concept of *active waiting* inform your thinking about engagement? Might we think about active waiting as a form of anticipatory empathy? How might you make use of active waiting in your practice?

Body Consciousness

Honest, respectful communication starts from a place of openness, curiosity, and readiness. We convey that readiness through our bodies and physical presence as well as through our words. Our responses and emotions are coded on our faces and bodies and through our carriage and gestures, as well as through our spoken and written words and silences. As Brill and Levine (2002) describe:

> Nonverbal messages are conveyed through the person and the setting. Age, sex, color, speech, personal appearance—physique, posture, body odor, dress, tension, facial expressions, behavior, silence or speech, tone of voice, gestures or movements, eye contact, touch, body sounds—all convey messages to the receiver, as does the physical setting—its appearance, aesthetic quality, comfort, and privacy (or lack of them), and general climate. The ways in which we convey nonverbal messages about ourselves are endless. Once workers know where to look and what to listen for and to sense in both self and client, their sensitivity and ability to understand will increase. (p. 92)

Take a minute to think about conversations when you have felt as if the other person was really listening to you. How did she convey that attentiveness? How did she position herself? How did her body indicate openness? What were the cues that indicated this person was paying attention and that what you said mattered? Take a minute to become aware of your own body and practice that physical attentiveness. How would you describe your posture? Do you feel comfortable? Try taking a deep breath in and out, relaxing and opening yourself to the person and situation as you do so. How would you describe your posture now? Do you feel ready to listen and engage?

Now take a moment to think about conversations when you have felt shut out and ignored. How did that person's body convey his inattentiveness or resistance to your words? Take a minute to practice that physical inattentiveness. How would you describe your posture? Your breathing? Do you feel comfortable? Take a deep breath in and out and then return to your posture of openness. How would you describe the difference between the two?

Each of us brings particular sociocultural knowledge and patterns of practice to the communication process. The process is a complex one of expression, reception, translation, and interpretation through screens of cultural meaning. The process is fraught with possibilities for misunderstanding. However, we can become more critically conscious participants in the process as we learn to appreciate the communicative power of our own bodies. When we are uncomfortable in the process, our bodies become physical blocks to effective communication. Therefore, the first, basic rule for respectful communication is *remember to breathe*! As we remind ourselves to breathe we create the possibility of releasing the block and opening ourselves once again to respectful listening. Yes, we will make mistakes and misinterpret even when we are attending as best as we can. But as we come to better understand our capacities for communication we can better address the mistakes and craft a space of understanding.

Class Learning Activity: Mirroring Exercise

Get together with one of your classmates. Arrange your seats so that you are facing one another and a comfortable distance apart, as if you were going to engage in conversation. Sit facing one another in silence for three minutes (use a cell phone timer). Take time to observe one another without words. Be mindful of breathing. Try to mirror the rhythm of your partner's breathing without forcing it. At the end of three minutes, talk to your partner about your response to the exercise. Did three minutes seem like a long time? Did the exercise make you feel uncomfortable? What were some of your observations? How did it feel to focus attention on breathing? If you do this exercise as a class working in pairs, you probably found it hard to maintain three minutes of silence. Most likely, bursts of laughter

> rippled through the class a time or two. Many of us lack experience or comfort in being present with another person without words. What reflections on communication could you draw from this exercise? What insights for engagement do you gain from this exercise?

It is also important to keep in mind that the concept of body consciousness goes beyond awareness of body language. From a social justice perspective, we are called on to be mindful of the ways in which forces of oppression insinuate themselves and shape our physical as well as psychological beings. The author recalls her group work with young survivors of sexual abuse. One girl had virtually no memory of her life without violation of her body as a part of it. She had learned to curl into herself, rarely standing or sitting erect. At age twelve she had the curved posture of an elderly woman. Although her experience of violence and survival was deeply personal, it also played out in a society that maintains high tolerance for violence against women and children and in a nation that still refuses to recognize children as bearers of rights. We need to continually examine the relationship between structural violence and individual experience. In the words of Paul Farmer (2003, p. 30), we need to keep asking, "By what mechanisms, precisely, do social forces ranging from poverty to racism become *embodied* as individual experience?"

Listening

Perhaps the most important skill of communication is listening. It is a skill we have been developing since birth, and, as a result, we often take our listening skills for granted. For example, in various communication situations we may find ourselves tuning out what others say or busying ourselves thinking about what we would like to say next. Or we may find ourselves listening to those whose knowledge we value and failing to hear alternative views. Listening is a powerful skill, one that takes considerable discipline and a willingness to set aside our own needs. Listening gives voice, affirmation, and confidence to those individuals and groups who have been typically ignored, marginalized, and oppressed. It is through respectful listening that a group develops a sense of belonging and community and members see themselves as participants worthy of voice (hooks, 1994, pp. 148–150). As bell hooks describes, teaching people how to listen is part of a pedagogy of liberation. We have to learn how to hear one another, suspend disbelief, and take what another person says seriously.

People often use the term *active listening* to describe the focused, intentional process of listening. In active listening we use words and gestures to show the speaker that we are attending to her words. A nod of the head may indicate that we are understanding, or perhaps encouraging the speaker to continue. We may reflect feelings we have been picking up back to the speaker or summarize the content of the story to both demonstrate that we are listening and see if we are grasping the speaker's intended meaning (Shulman, 2012). We may ask the speaker to tell us more so that we have a better grasp of the context. However, beneath all of the techniques that demonstrate that we are actively listening, we need to be honestly listening. If we are busy thinking about what we will say or do next, we often fail to listen deeply and fully to the other person's words.

Martha Dewees (2006) describes listening skills as those needed to truly hear another's story. She encourages social workers to engage through the practice of *radical listening*, which recognizes clients as experts on their own lives (p. 94). Dewees (2006, pp. 94–95) addresses radical listening in terms of four processes and skills: attentive listening, deconstructive listening, perspectival listening, and listening to bear witness.

Attentive listening "requires the social worker to listen for and hear the client's story, not for symptoms or insight, but rather for the experience and what it meant to the client" (Dewees, p. 94). Deconstructive listening is a process through which the social worker helps the client consider alternatives to his or her understanding of the story. Perspectival listening is a circular process in which worker and client uncover and explore ways of viewing the situation from the perspectives of the other. In listening to bear witness, the social worker allies with the client in "recording and taking a stand on the experience of hardship, discrimination, or violence (for example) that she or he has endured" (Dewees, p. 95).

A Short List of Interpersonal Communication Skills (adapted from Brill & Levine [2005]; Miley et al. [2013]; Shulman [2012])

- *Listen for meaning and feeling*: Try to grasp both the message and the associated emotions.

- *Listen for history and context*: Attend to the ways in which the personal story provides insights into a broader social and historical story.

- *Clarify*: Check in with the other person to make sure you are understanding what he is telling you. Invite the other person to seek clarification from you.

- *Paraphrase*: Restate the other person's story in your own words to make sure you are grasping the content.

- *Reflect*: Check in with the other person regarding the feelings associated with what she is telling you.
- *Encourage elaboration*: Invite the other person to tell you more about his situation or experience.
- *Reach for feelings*: Invite the other person to share her emotional response to what she is telling you.
- *Validate feelings*: Acknowledge and honor the other person's emotional response.
- *Check in*: Take a moment to reflect on the here and now. How is the other person doing? Does he have questions or concerns?
- *Allow for silence*: Give the other person time and space to collect her thoughts and feel emotions.
- *Summarize*: Take a minute to highlight both the content and feelings that have been expressed.
- *Acknowledge mistakes and ask for feedback*: Remember that you are human and will make mistakes. Take responsibility and apologize. Give the other person a chance to tell you how you are doing.
- *Respect resistance*: Remember that change is not easy and honor ambivalence.
- *Point out contradictions*: If you are picking up discrepancies between what someone is telling you in words and what you are reading in nonverbal communication, respond directly and encourage reflection.

What other skills would you add to this list? What skills are needed for bridging possibilities of communication across boundaries of difference?

Dialogue

Engagement calls for dialogue. Whether working in one-to-one situations or in the context of groups and communities, social workers need skills in listening and dialogue in order to build a sense of safety, trust, and hope. As Anne Hope and Sally Timmel (1984/1999, vol. 2) write:

> Building trust and dialogue in society cannot be done by pronouncements nor by some "magical waving of a wand." Dialogue begins at the local level, in small units and thus in groups. . . . Dialogue is based on people sharing their own perceptions of a problem, offering their opinions and ideas, and having the opportunity to make decisions or recommendations. (p. 3)

Paulo Freire reminds us that dialogue "requires an intense faith in man, faith in his power to make and remake, to create and recreate, faith in his vocation to be fully human, which is not the privilege of an elite, but the birthright of all people" (1974, p. 79). Freire believed that honest, genuine dialogue is founded on love, humility, and faith. It cannot exist without hope. Nor can it exist without critical thinking and the possibility of transformation. Dennis Saleebey (2006) has drawn from Freire in articulating his beliefs about dialogue and collaboration that inform a strengths perspective in social work:

> Humans can only come into being through a creative and emergent relationship with others. Without such transactions, there can be no discovery and testing of one's power, no knowledge, no heightening of one's awareness and internal strengths. In dialogue, we confirm the importance of others and begin to heal the rift between self, other, and institution.

> Dialogue requires empathy for, identification with, and the inclusion of other people. Paulo Freire (1974) was convinced, based on his years of work with oppressed peoples, that only humble and loving dialogue can surmount the barrier of mistrust built from years of paternalism and the rampant subjugation of the knowledge and wisdom of the oppressed. "Founding itself upon love, humility, and faith, dialogue becomes a horizontal relationship of which mutual trust between dialoguers is the logical consequence" (pp. 79–80). A caring community is a community that confirms otherness, in part by giving each person and group a ground of their own, and affirming this ground through encounters that are egalitarian and dedicated to healing and empowerment. (Saleebey, 2006, p. 14)

It is this understanding of dialogue that creates the possibility for social justice work.

Introductions and Openings

Dialogue is the basis for building and sustaining relationships. We need skills in initiating dialogue. Whether we are meeting with a single individual, a family, or a group, we need to address basic questions of why we are here and what each of us hopes to accomplish. The change process is structured and purposeful, and it requires that each participant have a voice in defining the purpose and creating the structure. The social worker can take responsibility for initiating the process by (1) introducing himself and his organizational position, (2) clearly stating his understanding of the reason for coming together and inviting others to do the same, and (3) asking questions and seeking clarification. It is a process of *welcoming* and *naming* ourselves, our concerns, and our hopes. Together, participants seek to establish a common understanding of purpose. The process of getting started in face-to-face meetings is often easier said than done. It is a tentative process of feeling one another out and trying to get a sense of where others are coming from.

It is important that we pay attention to the physical surroundings of the meeting and try to make the context conducive to dialogue. For example, does the seating arrangement encourage open communication? Do others know the layout of the space and facilities available to them? If we are meeting in someone's home, how can we be sensitive to issues of space and privacy? If the meeting space poses challenges—too hot, too cold, too big, or too small—can we make adjustments before the meeting gets underway? If not, how might we address the limitations of the space and be cognizant of the ways it may affect people's participation?

Part of the social worker's responsibility is to set the stage and the tone and facilitate the process of opening dialogue. We can begin by acknowledging that first meetings can be difficult, especially if the participants do not share common knowledge or histories. We can encourage people to ask questions and seek clarification, and we can do the same. As facilitators of communication, we help others recognize and express their understandings, attitudes, and feelings and put them into words. We do so by encouraging elaboration of experiences, perceptions, and context. Our job is to create opportunities for participants to tell their own stories in their own words, let people know that they have been heard, and seek clarification to build mutual understanding. The process of storytelling is vital for individual, group, and community work, and a key component of engagement is setting the stage for telling and listening to people's stories.

Reflection Moment:
Engagement and Child Welfare

Think for a minute about the process of engagement in child protection services (CPS). What must the worker know about the limits and requirements of her role? How and what does she need to communicate in order to begin to build trust and set the stage for future work? What might be some qualities and skills needed for effective engagement? Tamara Fuller and Megan Paceley (2011) sought answers to these questions through interviews with parents who had been involved in CPS investigations. Parents described how important it was to have social workers who openly listened to their story; explained the CPS process; shared power; and actively communicated honesty, respect, and genuine concern rather than judgment. They appreciated reassurance and recognition of their roles and capacities as parents and caregivers. Workers who made themselves available, advocated for the parents and the children, and followed through on commitments fostered positive engagement with parents and outcomes for families over time. As one parent summarized, "They treated me like a real person." Their perspectives speak to the power of seemingly basic skills of engagement.

In turn, parents recounted how difficult the experience was when workers were rushed, judgmental, poorly prepared, inflexible, and nonresponsive. What might be some of the contextual factors that work against effective CPS involvement with families? What contextual factors must be in place to support positive and productive engagement with families? How might organizational commitment to culturally competent practices as described by Nybell and Gray (2004, p. 25) strengthen the possibilities of engagement (see p. 201)?

Closings and Transitions

Each meeting and encounter, whether it is a first meeting with a teenager in a youth shelter or with a newly forming advocacy group at a homeless shelter, becomes a micro context in which questions of meaning, power, history, and possibility are in play. Part of the communicative work of engagement is to value that context, acknowledge what has been accomplished in it, and prepare participants to move beyond it at its close. To do so, we need to be able to summarize both the content and process of the encounter and seek feedback from participants. What did we accomplish? Where are our points of agreement and difference? What are people thinking and feeling about the process? Where do we go from here? Who takes responsibility for what?

It is important to recognize people's participation, to thank them for their presence, to honor their silences as well as their words, and to address the challenges posed in getting started. Just as we emphasized the importance of creating time and space to prepare for engagement, it is important to give time and space to disengagement and transition. That may entail acknowledging the emotions people express and creating an opportunity for both letting go of and holding onto those feelings as participants move out of this context and into other spaces of their work and lives. It may mean giving participants the last word. It may involve giving yourself a few minutes to absorb and reflect on the process and the responses it evoked for you. What do you take away from this closing that will inform the next opening? What did you learn about yourself, others, and the possibilities for social justice work in this encounter? Thus, the basic skills of communication provide us tools for tacking back and forth between action and reflection.

CHALLENGES OF ENGAGEMENT: POWER, DIFFERENCE, AND RESISTANCE

Effective social justice work requires us to be able to acknowledge and address issues of trust, power, and difference in the relationship-building process with individuals and groups. Given their differing past histories and experiences, participants often have reason to be distrustful of "helpers" and processes of change. We need to start from the point of distrust and work to build trust rather than assuming that it exists. For example, Lorraine Gutiérrez and Edith Lewis (1999, pp. 25–26) address the troubling history of misdiagnosis and mistreatment of people of color by professional helpers: "This mistrust has been exacerbated by the lack of attention to gender, ethnicity, race, economic status, and environment as variables influencing the engagement process for both service providers and service consumers" (p. 26).

We need to honestly and directly speak to mistrust and invite participation in determining ways to build trust and understanding. In order to do so we need to make power, authority, and difference talkable themes. Too often, these are taboo subjects that we shy away from even as they play out in and shape the dynamics of a meeting or relationship. We can facilitate this conversation by speaking honestly to our own power and authority and its limits in the context at hand. For example, if, in our social work capacity, we have the authority for particular types of legal or social sanction that others do not have, it is important that we speak honestly about our power, invite questions from other participants, and respond candidly to their concerns. We can also initiate a discussion of power and engage in an analysis of power as part of the process of co-learning. Finally, we need to acknowledge difference as an issue and create space for dialogue about differences that shape our meanings, interpretations, and actions.

How do we respond when our authority and assumptions are challenged? It is one thing to talk about power, trust, and difference. It is another to honestly reflect on our ability to open ourselves to challenge, especially if we come from positions of privilege where dominant views have been part of our common sense. How do we stay open to listening and learning when faced with differences of experience and perspective that disrupt our certainties? What happens when we respond defensively, asserting our authority in the face of challenge and attempting to discredit or dismiss the challenger? Communication across and about differences that disrupts our comfort zones is a key part of the labor of social justice work. Yuk-Lin Renita Wong (2004) encourages us to befriend feelings of discomfort as opportunities for openness, learning, and growth.

Honoring Difference

As we have discussed throughout the text, issues of difference and power profoundly shape our experiences and positionalities in the world and the perspectives from which we see, make sense of, and act in the world. Operating from our particular locations and partial views of the world, we give meaning to new experiences and interpret new information in differing ways. Thus, each person engaged in a relationship and process for change has a somewhat different experience of the process. We hear things in different ways. We grant importance to some information and interactions and discount or ignore others. As a facilitator of open dialogue and effective communication, the social worker has a teaching responsibility to help other participants see that differing meanings and interpretations will emerge. Effective communication depends on helping participants seek clarification of one another's interpretations, respect differing meanings, and recognize common ground. This is a socialization process that the social worker can initiate by speaking directly to difference, acknowledging the ways difference shapes trust and dialogue, and making respect for difference and the negotiation and clarification of meaning part of the change process in which all participants are engaged.

These issues are particularly challenging in cross-cultural and multilingual contexts. We quickly run into barriers to understanding when attempting to bridge differing meaning and belief systems or interpret a discussion to speakers of different languages. For example, people from different cultural backgrounds may have very different assumptions regarding fundamental issues such as the meaning of family, decision-making authority, and privacy. Our cultural meaning systems shape our beliefs about fundamental issues such as the nature of the body and bodily integrity, causality, and health and illness. Further, our linguistic systems are rich in nuances of expression that are often not directly translatable. Readers who have had experience in multilingual settings know that it takes very skilled interpreters to ensure that meanings, not just words, are communicated. Such is the case in professional groups as well in which use of technical jargon may lead to confusion and misunderstanding.

We can think of a multidisciplinary planning team as a multilingual context in which representatives of different professions may require an interpreter so that they are not talking past one another as they speak in the jargon of their respective professions. Professional language is a source of power that can exclude those who do not speak that language. Part of the challenge of social justice work is to interrupt practices of exclusion and advocate for skilled interpretation that promotes open, intelligible communication across multiple "languages" and boundaries of difference.

Engaging with Resistance

People in less powerful positions and people who have experienced oppression and discrimination may have very little reason to put their trust in helpers and helping systems and have very good reason to be suspicious and guarded about becoming participants in the process. As social justice workers we need to be both mindful and respectful of resistance.

Let's think for a moment about the meanings of resistance. In systems theories resistance is described as a force that helps systems and organisms remain stable in the face of other forces. In a psychological sense resistance is viewed as a defense mechanism that we use to avoid and cope with stress and change (Wade & Travis, 2007). It is often more popularly interpreted as a deficit—a person's refusal to open up, admit to personal difficulties, and engage in the work of personal change. In literature on oppression, resistance describes the many subversive and often indirect strategies through which oppressed people assert their agency in the face of dehumanizing circumstances (Scott, 1985). In literature on privilege, resistance connotes a person's or group's reluctance to reflect critically on the benefits of their positionality (Fine, Weis, Powell, & Wong, 1997; McIntosh, 1995). What other meanings and images of resistance come to mind? In the practice of social justice work, it is important to consider the many facets of resistance and to consider resistance as a skill for personal and cultural survival.

In social work, a great deal has been written about resistant clients, referring to those who are unwilling to open up in the engagement process, acknowledge particular definitions of the "problem," or participate in prescribed courses of action. Resistance is often the defining feature of the involuntary client, one who is required to participate in an intervention and treatment effort as a result of legal order or other institutional sanction. Often, the person's resistance becomes defined as pathology, a symptom of his inability or unwillingness to make prescribed changes. Judi Chamberlin (1998) in her provocative essay "Confessions of a Non-compliant Patient" offers a powerful critique of the ways in which resistance becomes framed as a symptom rather than a right to refuse. She poses a challenge to professional expectations of compliance and the assumptions behind them.

Let's consider alternative views regarding the meaning and power of resistance. For example, psychotherapist and pioneer of hypnotherapy Milton Erickson (1954) saw resistance as a source of energy to be acknowledged and validated (Cormier, Nurius, & Osborn, 2013). Resistance, Erickson contended, can stem from the worker's failure to recognize and use a person's uniqueness. From a cultural-political perspective, resistance may be seen as a survival strategy invoked when powerful forces threaten to invade, invalidate, or erase one's history, knowledge, and experience. Beverly Bell (2001) has documented the lives and words of Haitian women living in contexts of extreme violence and deprivation. She describes survival itself as a form of resistance, a determined claim to the fundamental right to life, and a "purposeful act of defiance" of the destruction of body and soul. Bell offers the testimonies of Haitian women to illustrate their many forms of resistance, including "maintaining survival and psychological integrity; enacting personal, political, and cultural expression; battling for political and economic justice; fighting gender oppression; and transforming the nature and application of power to create a new civil society and polity" (2001, p. 7).

A person resisting participation in the change effort may not be demonstrating pathology but may be actively asserting her right to protect herself, lay claim to her experiences and fears, and challenge those threatening to misinterpret her experience and silence her voice. There is a rich array of cultural and historical literature that examines the creative resistance of less powerful people and groups to the oppressive forces of dominant cultural systems (e.g., Guzman Bouvard, 1994; Ong, 1987; Scott, 1985). We have also seen evidence of resistance to social work interventions on the part of people who have very different understandings of what constitutes a problem and for whom. The policies, procedures, goals, and expectations of social service agencies are often culturally foreign and at times antagonistic to the values, beliefs, and practices of those they serve. Resistance to intervention is born of a struggle to retain one's autonomy and beliefs in the face of powerful countervailing forces.

We must also examine the other side of the coin—the resistance of individuals and institutions ensconced in relations of power and privilege. Rather than thinking of resistance as a marker of the pathology of an individual, we may find it more instructive to examine the resistance of those invested in their particular worldviews, expertise, theories, and practices. Consider the brief

vignette on p. 196 regarding white program leaders' resistance to consideration of the social context and strengths of black families. What does this example suggest about the power of resistance on the part of professionals involved
in the engagement process?

As social justice workers we need to *notice* how resistance is talked about
in our work. Does the label of resistance become another form of violence perpetrated against people in positions of vulnerability? How might we draw on
our knowledge of context in exploring how resistance is identified and
addressed? In locating resistance in an individual, what other forms and practices of resistance remain invisible and unaddressed? Think for a moment about
your own work or field site. Where have you seen resistance in the organizational context? How has it been addressed? How has it been experienced by
workers? By clients or other organizational participants? What have been the
consequences? Who has borne the burden of resistance?

Recognizing and Respecting Resistance

The Just Practice framework provides a guide for recognizing and respecting resistance through posing critical questions regarding meaning, context, power, history, and possibility. Consider the following questions:

- *Meaning*: Are the policies, practices, goals, and language of your organization meaningful to the person with whom you are working? How
  do you know? What have you done to check this out?

- *Context*: What is the context of your encounter? Under what circumstances did you come together? How do those circumstances, as
  well as the physical context of your meeting, contribute to or reduce
  resistance?

- *Power*: What are the relations of power that affect the encounter?
  What forms of power do you as the social worker bring to bear? How
  might the other person perceive your power and his own in relation
  to you? Have you explored the issue of power as it affects the
  encounter? Are there alternatives open to you that could shift the
  balance of power? Might specific attention to the rights of service
  users create a shift in the balance of power?

- *History*: What prior history with the organization or with "helpers"
  does the other person have? How might this history, along with other
  experiences and feelings of powerlessness, contribute to resistance?
  What are the nonnegotiable aspects of the relationship (e.g., a person

may be required to participate in a court-ordered treatment plan in order to regain custody of a child, avoid incarceration)?

- *Possibility*: Where are the spaces of possibility for negotiating a process that recognizes and respects the other person's values, beliefs, and interests? How might the plan not only acknowledge but also challenge and change the power differences among agency, social worker, and clients?

EXPANDING THE POSSIBILITIES: ENGAGING GROUPS

In this section we turn to the practice of group work and its significance for social-justice-oriented practice. Breaking with the individual-focused, person-changing approaches to intervention, social justice work emphasizes the power and possibilities of collective effort to produce change. The basic communication skills outlined above apply to both one-on-one and group contexts. In this section, however, we further develop issues, skills, and possibilities for engagement with groups. We conclude with an overview of popular education as a practice of group work.

The Power of Groups

Social work has a rich history of group work beginning with the Settlement House Movement. Jane Addams (1910) envisioned groups as helping people learn about democracy through participation in democratic group dynamics. People came together in groups to address mutual concerns, gain support from others when they faced overwhelming personal problems, and teach and learn skills to improve the quality of their lives. Through practices of shared control, power, leadership, and agenda, group members create support systems whereby they empower themselves to take collective action to address personal, interpersonal, and social concerns (Schwartz, 1986). Social workers have recognized the importance of group work and the beneficial dynamics and processes groups help to support. Some of these dynamics and processes are outlined below (Freire, 1974; Gutiérrez & Lewis, 1999; Schwartz, 1986; Shulman, 2012):

- Groups provide the milieux in which the social worker becomes one of many helpers.
- Groups create opportunities for developing critical consciousness.

- Group dialogue challenges cultures of silence and helps people gain confidence and find their voices.
- Groups provide people with the opportunity to become conscious of power relationships, the differing effects of social inequalities on different social groups, and their own location therein.
- Groups offer spaces for mutual support and collective problem posing, action, and reflection.
- Groups help people structure the time and space of co-learning and unite change efforts.

As social justice workers we need to develop our capacities as group workers and to teach skills of mutual aid and collective action to others.

Creating a Climate for Group Work

In order to engage people in a group process, we need to create a welcoming learning climate. Issues of trust and intimacy, power and authority, and difference and commonality are at the very heart of group work (Shulman, 2012). We need to start by honoring feelings of distrust and ambivalence and recognizing that people in marginalized or vulnerable positions have good reason to be suspicious of helpers. Reflect for a moment on your own experiences in a group context. How did you feel at the first meeting of the group? What questions and concerns did you have? What did you know about or wonder about other members of the group? Did you have a sense of common purpose? Perhaps you felt exposed or resistant. Perhaps you felt wary, not knowing what was going to be expected of you or what you could expect of others. Perhaps you had concerns about how others would respond to you and whether they would respect your contributions to the group. Reflection on our own experiences provides a helpful entry point for engaging other people in the process of working in groups. What sorts of concerns can we anticipate? How can we address those concerns honestly and openly?

We can begin building trusting relationships among group participants by starting from a place of not knowing and acknowledging distrust. As group members share knowledge, histories, and experiences, they develop a basis for trust. Similarly, as people begin to trust that others are committed to respectful participation, they are more likely to offer more of themselves and their experiences to the process. As engaged participants, they are better able to recognize and respect differences and seek possibilities for common ground. Over time, a sense of collective wisdom and intimacy emerges. As facilitators, we also have the responsibility of engaging with questions of power and authority as they play out in the group. How does our organizational position shape our role in the group process? How do others perceive our power?

If we are in the position of primary facilitator of a group process, how do we both acknowledge and share the power of that position? What forms of power do other group members bring to bear in the process and how do we acknowledge them? For example, a member may use the power of silence or silencing in ways that inhibit communication. Others may use the power of blocking, which is finding reasons to stall or stop the progress of the group. Members may draw from outside or intimate knowledge related to the group as a source of power. These various means of bringing power to bear are not inherently wrong or right. Rather they are part of the group dynamics that facilitators must address openly.

Class Learning Activity: Developing Group Ground Rules

As members of a social work practice class, you are being asked to participate in a group learning process, take risks, and develop your repertoire of skills. The experiences may leave you feeling exposed and vulnerable. What sorts of ground rules do you want to have in place that will help create a context of safety in which you can take risks? Think about the difference between *safety* and *comfort*. The risk taking associated with new learning may create discomfort. Risk taking in a group setting may also expose challenges of difference in the classroom. By virtue of positionality some class members may enjoy a greater degree of taken-for-granted safety and comfort in the classroom than others. Some class members may find unacknowledged comforts of privilege challenged by those who have been denied those comforts. Questions of difference may play out in very personal and emotional ways.

How can the classroom become a safe enough place to be uncomfortable and to learn through that discomfort? Prepare your own list of ground rules for group learning that would allow you to take risks. Get together with a small group of classmates and share your lists. See if you can agree on a set of ground rules. Now get together as a class and consider each group's ground rules. Where are the points of agreement? Where are the differences? See if you can reach consensus as a large group on the ground rules for group process.

A key part of the engagement process is the socialization of group members about the dynamics of group work. By preparing people for what lies ahead—inviting candid dialogue about trust, power, and difference and modeling openness—we help them become committed partners in the process. In order to engage meaningfully in a group process, members need to have a sense of belonging and a voice. They need to feel that their experiences and perspectives are valued despite differences and disagreements with other members. And they need to feel both a sense of responsibility and a sense of possibility in the process. The principles of popular education outlined below will provide a valuable base for engaging groups in the process of personal and social transformation.

POPULAR EDUCATION

Popular education has been defined as a strategy for social change in which people struggling under conditions of oppression come together in small groups to critically reflect on the conditions of their lives; become conscious of the social, political, and economic contradictions in which their social experience is bound; and utilize the power of the group as a resource for transformative action (Freire, 1974; Weiler, 1988). Through dialogue with others, people connect their personal troubles to broader structural problems in society and strive to rectify these conditions through collective action. The National Network for Immigrant and Refugee Rights (NNIRR) has published *BRIDGE—Building a Race and Immigration Dialogue in the Global Economy—A Popular Education Resource for Immigrant and Refugee Community Organizers* (Cho, Paz y Puente, Louie, & Kjokha, 2004). The NNIRR summarizes beliefs and principles of popular education (Cho et al., 2004, pp. 9–10):

What do we believe is popular education? We believe that:

- Popular education *draws on the direct lived experiences* and knowledge of everyone involved—including participants and facilitators.
- Popular education encourages *active participation* to engage people in dialogues, fun, and creative activities, and it draws on the strength of our diverse cultures. We learn in many ways—by seeing hearing, talking, doing, creating, or a combination of these modes. We include dialogues and learning experiences that engage all of our senses, emotions, perceptions, and beliefs.
- Popular education draws on these *multiple modes* of learning. Discussion, drawing, writing songs, making sculptures, or acting out a

skit gives us tools to express ourselves and communicate at all levels of our human experience.

- Popular education creates spaces for *trust and participation*. All education takes place within a larger context of behaviors, attitudes, and values. The ways in which we feel "safe" in a space depends on our own circumstances—our class, our race, gender, sexual orientation, age, immigration status, disability, and many other variables. As facilitators, we cannot remove these differences, but we can acknowledge their existence in order to open a space of more direct dialogue.

- Popular education is clear about its *agenda*. All education reproduces a set of values, ideologies, and attitudes. Popular education is not neutral, but holds a commitment to liberation from oppression at its ethical cores.

- Popular education is *accessible* to all participants, and actively works to explore and challenge ways that create unequal access to participation, such as language barriers, disability, and group dynamics.

- Popular education *connects our lived experiences to historical, economic, social, and political structures of power*. When our personal experiences are placed in larger contexts and patterns of power, our personal realities are transformed.

- Popular education *explores our multiple identities and experiences* of inclusion and exclusion, oppression and privilege. The underlying truth of popular education is the existence of oppression: Racism, classism, sexism, homophobia, heterosexism, and transphobia are a reality in all of our lives. Popular education is not about building tolerance, but about building respect, acceptance, equality, and solidarity.

- Popular education *empowers individuals and groups to develop long-term strategies* to transform structures of power and to build a more just society. Popular education and organizing should not be reduced to short-term campaigns, mobilizations, or events but rather realized as a democratic process based on values, connected and accountable to concrete needs of a community.

- Popular education *develops new community leaders* to build movements for social change. Popular education is a way to develop new leaders who will in turn develop other leaders. This kind of leadership will be based upon concrete experiences of collective action and organizing.

- Popular education *results in action* that challenges oppression and helps develop political spaces that are democratic and equal.
- Popular education *affirms the dignity* of every human being.

SUMMARY

In this chapter we have explored the many facets and dynamics of engagement. We have considered the significance of cultural-political, community, and organizational context in the process of engagement. We bring our histories with us to each new relationship, further shaping the possibilities and limits of engagement. We have addressed the interpersonal context of engagement and the importance of anticipation, observation, respectful listening, and dialogue in building mutual knowledge and trust. Social justice work calls for strong skills in interpersonal communication and the ability to engage people in teamwork. We have considered both specific skills and the larger questions of meaning, power, difference, and resistance that we need to bring to bear simultaneously in the practice of engagement. The process of and commitment to engagement prepares us for the work of teaching-learning that we will address in chapter 6. We close with a case example by Bonnie Rae Buckingham, MSW, which illustrates the power and possibility of community engagement, followed by questions for discussion and suggested readings.

ON REFLECTION

Promoting Social, Economic, and Environmental Justice through a Community Food System

Bonnie Rae Buckingham, MSW, Co-founder and Executive Director, Community Food and Agriculture Coalition, Missoula, MT

The Community Food & Agriculture Coalition (CFAC) began in 2004 to revolutionize the way our community thinks about, produces, and accesses our food. Over the past eleven years, CFAC has collaborated with a multitude of businesses, organizations, students, and stakeholders to realize a vision of our community where houses, farms, and ranches thrive together, people are well fed and food secure, family farms are supported within a community food system, and beginning farmers and ranchers access vital farmland to feed the rest of us—including those most vulnerable.

The Community Food & Agriculture Coalition operates as a grassroots group of dedicated volunteers, a very small staff, and meaningful partnerships with other organizations and agencies. As we've grown, these partnerships have strengthened our collective vision of a regional food system that is sustainable, just, and economically robust. Throughout all our work is a dedication to ensuring that everyone is invited to the local food table, regardless of income. What began as a future dream has become a very tangible food and farm system that builds upon itself and is changing the norm of how people access food within our region.

One of the initiatives that CFAC uses to ensure inclusion of low-income people in this vital movement is the Farmers Market SNAP Initiative (Supplemental Nutrition Assistance Program of the U. S. Department of Agriculture— formerly known as food stamps). Several years ago, CFAC helped launch a program at the farmers' markets to bring SNAP benefits to the markets. The program's benefits are numerous. It allows everyone who attends the markets to access locally grown food, it benefits the vendors by increasing their sales, and it benefits the local economy by keeping federal dollars from the Food Stamp Electronic Benefits Transfer (EBT) program within Missoula. Before the program was initiated, people who used SNAP did not have the choice of shopping at the markets because vendors did not have the technology to use the swipe cards. Now, everyone has the option of purchasing food from the farmers' market and supporting local producers! Not only does it provide much needed healthy food, it also creates inclusion in one of our community's most vibrant social connections.

To make this program even stronger this year, CFAC is partnering with several organizations and markets to increase participation and help make local food even more affordable through a Double SNAP Dollar program. For every SNAP dollar used to purchase local food, the program will provide two dollars' worth of produce. This has been expanded beyond farmers' markets to include produce purchased directly from farms, as well as a community cooperative market. Additionally, CFAC will be working with a corps of SNAP Ambassadors to promote the program through a targeted marketing campaign designed by and for low-income participants. This initiative will not only create greater awareness of the program and its benefits, but it will also develop leaders within the community and promote healthy eating, better nutrition, and community health.

Ultimately, CFAC's goal is to democratize our food system and create a more just and sustainable food future, building avenues of inclusion developed by those most directly affected by our current industrial food systems. To build lasting change, we must recognize the value of each citizen and create new paradigms to encourage inclusiveness within the fabric of that system.

QUESTIONS FOR DISCUSSION

1. Describe anticipatory empathy in your own words. In what situations have you made use of this skill? How would you describe the relationship between anticipatory empathy and social justice work?

2. What challenges have you faced in the engagement process? What lessons have you learned in those challenging situations that inform your current practice?

3. Where have you encountered resistance as a survival skill? As a manifestation of power and privilege? As a form of cultural expression?

4. Where have you experienced or witnessed subtle or overt forms of oppression in the context of your social work practice? How have they been addressed? How might you address them in the future?

5. What does the practice of cultural humility entail? How does it differ from cultural competence? How do these concepts relate to your social work practice?

SUGGESTED READINGS

Coates, T. (2015). *Between the world and me.* New York: Spiegel and Grau.

Dean, R. (2001). The myth of cross-cultural competence. *Families in Society, 82,* 623–630.

Hardina, D. (2013). *Interpersonal social work skills for community practice.* New York: Springer.

Hope, A., & Timmel, S. (1999). *Training for transformation: A handbook for community workers* (Vol. 1–4). London: Intermediate Technology Publications. (Originally published in 1984)

Kelly, A., & Sewell, S. (1988). *With head, heart, and hand: Dimensions of community building* (4th ed.). Brisbane, Australia: Boolarong Press.

Chapter 6

Teaching-Learning: Reframing the Assessment Process

For apart from inquiry, apart from the praxis, individuals cannot be truly human. Knowledge emerges only through invention and re-invention, through the restless, impatient, continuing, hopeful inquiry human beings pursue in the world, with the world, and with each other.

Paulo Freire, *Pedagogy of the Oppressed* (1974)

OVERVIEW

In chapter 6 we reframe the social work process of *assessment* as a process of teaching-learning. We challenge the one-way flow of information that characterizes conventional social work approaches to assessment. We frame the assessment process as one of co-learning in which the social worker and other participants come together to share knowledge; pose questions; raise consciousness; seek out new information; assess needs, strengths, and resources; and draw on collective wisdom to inform action. We start by problematizing dominant notions of assessment and show how the teaching-learning process challenges more top-down or expert approaches. We frame teaching-learning as a collaborative practice of developing critical consciousness that may entail both new learning and unlearning. We provide concrete examples of a teaching-learning alternative to conventional assessment.

The teaching-learning process is also shaped by power dynamics. We examine power in the process and provide strategies for engaging in analyses of power. The teaching-learning process pushes us beyond a problem focus and draws attention to capabilities and rights. We explore specific examples of teaching-learning situated in a human rights framework. We highlight skills of teaching-learning in community, organizational, familial, and interpersonal contexts and provide examples of practice possibilities. We pay particular attention to the skills of group work that are often central to the teaching-learning process. In addition, we examine a variety of assessment strategies, including both classic social work tools and alternative approaches. We ask you to apply

237

your critical thinking skills to evaluating the assessment tools and to constructing and modifying assessment approaches to reflect understandings of
social justice-oriented practice.

PROBLEMATIZING ASSESSMENT

Questioning Conventional Approaches

Most guides to social work practice speak of assessment as a key phase in the
change process that follows initial engagement. Assessment refers to the collection and interpretation of information needed to inform change-oriented
action. Although assessment processes make up part of the teaching-learning
process, the term does not capture the sense of collaboration and co-learning
that is fundamental to social justice work. Assessment has often been construed
as a neutral, objective, one-way process directed by the social worker. The
assessment process has also been largely problem focused, resulting in a discourse of deficits, with little critical analysis of the ways in which the very notion
of problem gets constructed (Iverson, Gergen, & Fairbanks, 2005). Further, conventional understandings of assessment operate from the assumption that
there is a knowable problem to be discovered and that discovery will lead the
way for intervention. We want to *problematize* conventional thinking about
assessment by questioning underlying assumptions and opening new spaces
of thought and practice.

Let's consider what it means to problematize conventional approaches to
social work assessment. First, we are often guided by engrained ideas, beliefs,
and assumptions embedded both in our own worldviews and in the theories
that guide our practice (Gil, 2013). Those underlying assumptions and beliefs
shape what we see and what we miss in the assessment process. If our theoretical lenses focus on problems located in individuals, our assessments follow
suit. They fail to attend to the broader social, historical, political, and economic
contexts and the prevailing inequalities therein that shape people's everyday
encounters (Gil, 2013). We thereby risk *decontextualizing* people's struggles, that
is, developing an understanding that is devoid of the context of meaning
systems and power relations in which problems in living are produced and
maintained.

Second, if we consider our assessment processes as neutral and objective,
we fail to account for our own positionality and the ways it may shape how we
see, experience, and account for one another's social realities and struggles
therein (Marsiglia & Kulis, 2015). Third, we may fail to consider how our profes-

sional *habitus*—those unspoken assumptions, routines, and ways of knowing and doing shaped by our professional training, organizational context, and social identity—become internalized and part of what we simply take for granted in the assessment process (Bourdieu,1979/1984; Briskman, 2008). Fourth, we risk imposing meaning on another's experience, misinterpreting symptoms as root problems, unwittingly colluding with unjust systems, and taking action that may do more harm than good (Waldegrave, 2005).

Missing: Attention to Structural Inequalities

If a social worker assesses only the biopsychosocial aspects of a low-income woman presenting with symptoms of depression, she may miss the relentless everyday struggles and stressful life conditions that result from the intersections of poverty, gender oppression, and depression in many women's lives (Goodman et al., 2007). As a result, these forces will become normalized and their effects become interpreted through an individualizing lens. The social worker's assessment, then, may lead to interventions that support the woman in coping with the status quo rather than engaging in change to improve the everyday conditions of her life. The social worker may offer therapeutic strategies for relief of symptoms of depression, but may fail to provide material support or engage in gender and welfare rights advocacy as part of the social work intervention (Krumer-Nevo, Weiss-Gal, & Monnickendam, 2009).

As we discussed in chapter 5, there is a substantial and growing base of research documenting the pathogenic effects of racism and other forms of oppression in people's lives. However, if we bracket out attention to racism, sexism, heterosexism, classism, ableism, and other forms of oppression from the assessment process, we will miss opportunities for alternative framing of the issues and courses of action. Moreover, social workers and the organizations we represent may be complicit in their perpetuation.

Conventional child protective service (CPS) assessments, for example, focus primarily on assessing the child's safety in the immediate context of the referral (Clarke, 2012). Unnoticed in the assessment are the structural inequalities that shape the child's and parent's everyday experiences. The assessment will likely lead to a narrow set of interventions focused on psychological counseling, parenting classes, substance abuse treatment, and anger management rather than on real material needs such as adequate housing, basic income, education, employment, transportation, and daycare (Clarke, 2012, p. 237). Further, the CPS assessment of safety and risk considers the immediate context of the child and family's experience but does not take into account broader concerns such as the disproportional representation of youth of color in child welfare systems and the failure of those systems to meet the needs of children of color when underlying policies and practices ignore race and perpetuate racism (Kolivoski, Weaver, & Constance-Huggins, 2014).

Limits of the *DSM*

Another example of the problematic nature of conventional assessment is seen in the growing reliance on the *Diagnostic and Statistical Manual of Mental Disorders* (*DSM*) as the primary basis for making assessments in direct social work practice. The *DSM* is a system for classification of mental disorders produced by the American Psychiatric Association and widely used by mental health professionals in the United States and elsewhere. Eileen Gambrill (2014) offers a strident critique of the dehumanizing effects of this narrow diagnostic approach to assessment. She addresses the rapidly expanding "medicalization of everyday life" that is drawing more people into the "widening net of mental illness." She points to the power of such classification systems to label, categorize, and mark those who bear labels as *other*. And she points out that there is no clear connection between diagnostic labels and approaches to treatment. Further, she contends that this labeling process shifts the blame for complex, intractable problems to the individual (p. 20).

Dennis Saleebey (2001), pioneer of the strengths perspective in social work, offers similar critiques of the *DSM*, noting that it carries extraordinary influence even though it "provides an insufficient and hard-to-operationalize conceptualization of mental disorder" (p. 183). As an example, he critiques the framing of attention deficit and hyperactivity disorder (ADHD) by the *DSM*, which, he argues, fails to offer alternative explanations for children's "over-active" behavior. Others have made similar critiques, noting the steady rise in the popularity of ADHD diagnoses over the past thirty years, particularly in the United States. Further, Saleebey contends, the *DSM*'s pathologizing focus fails to account for the assets, capacities, and survival skills that people may possess both in spite and because of their life difficulties (2001, p. 184).

Questioning Standardized Tools

Conventional assessments often utilize standardized tools. The term *standardized* refers to instruments that have been tested on large numbers of people and that provide practitioners guidelines for diagnosis. Most standardized tools used by social workers focus on the individual and not on the context of the individual's life experience. Most are administered by the practitioner, who then interprets the results and uses them to inform action. Further, standardized assessment tools tend to be normative; that is, they include assumptions about what is considered "normal," which may not be universally applicable. Standardized measurements may not take into account the social reality of the person being assessed (Gutiérrez & Lewis, 1999, p. 31).

Let's consider a few examples. Community development workers in England wanted to assess community readiness to support mental health at the community level (McCabe & Davis, 2012). In order to do so, they wanted to gain an understanding of mental distress among residents of a community that already struggled with economic distress. They tried using a standardized tool—the Hospital Anxiety and Depression Scale (HADS)—but community members found it too intrusive. Other standardized tools to measure individual mental health status were also rejected by community members, who responded with statements such as "You have to be mad to access these services!" The use of standardized assessment tools risked increasing the stigma around mental illness and mental health care that the planners were working to combat.

In a second example, John Gonzalez and Edison Trickett (2014) describe a community-based research project on suicide and alcohol use prevention with two Alaska Native communities. (The concept and practice of community-based research will be addressed in chapter 8.) The participants were particularly concerned about young people and their levels of risk. An outside consultant strongly encouraged use of the Suicide Ideation Questionnaire (Reynolds, 1988) to measure youth risk. Community leaders, however, found the questionnaire too intrusive and culturally inappropriate. Over a multiyear process the research team collaborated with tribal members on the development of culturally relevant measures in order to ask the right questions and ask them the right way.

A third example comes from Kristin Smith's critical analysis of the Patient Health Questionnaire (PHQ-9), a nine-question self-administered tool to assess for symptoms of depression. Smith (2011) describes how the PHQ-9 became a standard component of mental health assessment in primary health clinics in Canada where she was employed in 2008. Government-funded mental health services had experienced significant funding cuts in the preceding few years, leaving mental health workers overworked and overwhelmed. The PHQ-9 was introduced in required professional training as a tool to streamline the process of assessment and diagnosis, with the expectation that staff would incorporate it into their practice. Smith critically deconstructed the tool and its use, showing how it serves to direct attention away from the structural inequities and socio-political context of a client's life experience and focus attention on only those few factors that could lead to a diagnosis of depression and a prescription from a staff physician for antidepression medication.

Further, Smith points out that Pfizer, a major pharmaceutical company, owns the copyright on the PHQ-9 and is the producer of Zoloft, the most heavily prescribed antidepression medication. Pzifer reported earnings of $46 billion in 2005, with Zoloft, one of its best-selling drugs, accounting for $3.3 billion in sales (Smith, 2011, p. 206). Smith's careful "unmapping" of the corporate-government nexus in the marketing of mental health diagnoses and treatment raises critical ethical, political, and economic questions. These examples illustrate the importance of *problematizing* the use of assessment tools and questioning the assumptions, beliefs, and generalizations that become embedded in them, which may render them inappropriate and potentially harmful to particular individuals or groups.

Class Learning Activity: Assessing the Assessment Tools

This exercise offers an opportunity to learn about the ways practitioners in your community assess problems and strengths. As a class, identify five or six areas of social work practice that you want to learn more about (e.g., child welfare, aging, mental health, school social work, or housing). Break into groups, each focused on one practice area. In the small group, identify several local agencies or organizations that address this area and divide the list among group members. Each member will take responsibility for contacting an agency or organization; arranging a time to discuss the assessment process with an organizational representative; and requesting copies of tools, forms, or guidelines used in making an assessment. Reconvene in small groups to assess the assessment tools. The following questions serve as a guide; however, new questions may arise from the group discussions.

- What values are reflected in the tool?
- What assumptions are made about the cause of problems and directions for intervention?
- What assumptions are made about the person or group being assessed (e.g., assumptions about age, gender, or ability)?

- What aspects of a person's life are addressed? What aspects are not addressed? Where does the tool direct your attention?
- Does the tool take a problem-focused approach?
- How are strengths addressed?
- What is the norm against which "deviance" is assessed?
- What sort of language does the tool use?
- Does the tool promote participation in the assessment process?
- How would you assess the cultural relevance of the tool? For whom?
- What do you see as the possible strengths of this tool? The possible limitations?

SHIFTING OUR APPROACH: FROM ASSESSMENT TO TEACHING-LEARNING

Developing Critical Consciousness

We conceptualize teaching-learning as a dialogical process of developing critical consciousness about the relationship between individual struggles and social issues (Hardina, 2014). It is a participatory process in which all parties are both learners and teachers with potential for transformative learning (Mezirow, 2009). It entails relationship building, question posing, systematic inquiry, and ongoing critical reflection. Iverson and colleagues (2005) speak of "a collaborative inquiry into transformative possibilities" and an "appreciation of the not-yet-seen, the yet-to-be-storied" (p. 704). Teaching-learning goes beyond discovery, fact finding, and diagnosis. It includes *learning to learn from others* through which we recognize multiple ways of knowing, challenge dichotomous thinking, and question underlying assumptions. It entails systematic inquiry into questions of meaning, context, power, and history in which both problems and possibilities are embedded.

According to Valerie Miller and Lisa VeneKlasen (2012) critical consciousness "involves learning to question and challenge the explanations for why things are the way they are and what is 'normal,' perpetually seeking a deeper understanding of power and inequality from the intimate and personal to the more public realms of decision making" (p. 3). VeneKlasen and Miller (2007; cited in Hardina, 2013, p. 119) describe the key components of critical consciousness as:

- Knowledge about how political and economic systems function
- Sense of history and current events
- Lens for analyzing why and how imbalances of power operate
- Concern about how these things destroy human potential and dignity
- Sense of rights, responsibilities, and solidarity with excluded groups

Each party to the process brings knowledge grounded in personal experience and cultural history. Together we begin to map out what we know, consider what we need to learn more about, seek out knowledge, consider underlying forces and patterns that shape experiences, and bring our collective wisdom to bear in translating data into a meaningful guide for action.

Through the teaching-learning process we pose questions to inform critical awareness, disrupt assumptions, and invite dialogue (Gil, 2013). As social justice workers we act as animators to spark consciousness and dialogue and as facilitators and researchers who recognize the limits of our own experience and the partiality of our knowledge. We work to create a climate that promotes co-learning. We support and encourage the process of critical reflection about people's concerns and what we need to know through posing questions. That may require processes of *unlearning* as we come to question deeply held certainties about problems, causes, and possibilities for change. We help people systematically examine the information at hand, theorize about problems and possibilities, and strategize courses of action. We are learning in the context of partnership with those who possess the wisdom of lived experience. And we are teachers, helping others develop knowledge and skills needed to carry out their own assessments and develop action plans in the future.

Embracing the Role of Learner

When we position ourselves as learners, we open ourselves to alternative explanations of another's actions or circumstances (Solomon, 1976). For example, Charles Waldegrave (2000, 2009; Waldegrave & Tamasese, 1994) describes how dominant theoretical approaches to addressing family dysfunction focus on intrafamilial patterns of interaction and communication. However, when Waldegrave and his colleagues truly listened to the so-called multi-problem families with whom they worked they found that families located their problems in events and circumstances external to the family. The pain and dysfunction they experienced were symptoms of external problems, not the root problem. When we truly listen to and learn from another's perspective, Waldegrave argues, we may move our practice beyond symptom management to *just therapy* that responds meaningfully to the complex circumstances of people's lives.

As learners we seek critical awareness, which entails not only understanding why something exists but also how people are affected by it and who benefits from it (McPhail, 2004; Nybell & Gray, 2004). We seek to understand how others see their circumstances, define their needs and capabilities, give meaning to the process of seeking help, and regard the agencies and organizations for whom we work (Jani & Reisch, 2011). This entails learning about the broader contexts of people's lives and the forces that may constrain or enable their capabilities. It involves posing critical questions and learning from the perspectives of those with whom we are working. For example VeneKlasen and Miller (2007) encourage us to ask, what is happening here? Why is it happening? To whom is it happening? Who is affected and how? What led to this situation? What might be the causes? What further problems might this situation lead to? What else do we need to consider? Larry Ortiz and Jayshree Jani (2010, p. 184) draw on critical race theory, addressed in chapter 4, in posing critical questions about practice: Do the guiding theories and assumptions of our agencies fit with understandings and assumptions of service users? Are the services that our agencies offer relevant to the clients served and respectful of their culture and social location? Will they make a meaningful difference in their lives? Do our theories and services reflect the client's view of his concerns and needs? What questions are not being asked?

As we probe these questions, we open the spaces for developing a broader and deeper understanding of the situation and possible courses of action informed by those directly affected. We may start to notice patterns that connect struggles across individuals and point to common factors affecting groups and communities that call for further investigation to inform action. The process calls for well-honed listening, question posing, and investigation skills. It requires the combined skills of cultural humility and critical structural thinking (Reisch, 2011, p. 20). Further, it requires the exercise of "anticipatory imagination" (Elkjaer, 2009, p. 75) through which we conspire with others to imagine how things could be otherwise (Mezirow, 2009).

Case Example: Learning from Rural Families Creating Change in Schools

Lisa Blitz and colleagues (Blitz, Kida, Gresham, & Bronstein, 2013) provide an insightful example of these facets of teaching-learning. They describe a collaborative project to engage poor rural families in upstate New York in a change process to make schools more responsive to their concerns and the needs of their children. When the team first began conversations with parents, they learned about distrust and the silencing parents had experienced over the years. Many parents rebuffed the team's initial overtures, stating, "you don't really want to hear what I have to say." The team persisted over months, coming to learn about the very real barriers parents faced by listening carefully to their stories.

The team also began a series of conversations with school personnel to learn how they perceived the parents and their apparent resistance to involvement with the school. Where school staff perceived parental disinterest, parents spoke to lack of basic resources for communication, such as cell phones or e-mail. Over time, the social work team came to a deeper understanding of the environmental and social stressors of poverty and the ways in which "ongoing toxic stress and intermittent traumatic events" shaped the contours of family life (Blitz et al., 2013, p. 158). At the same time, they gained a deeper appreciation for the parents' capabilities and their commitment to their children. They invited parents to participate in an ongoing group to identify and address their concerns for their children's well-being.

The parents participated in a nominal needs assessment in which they wrote lists of what they saw as barriers to their children's success, using their own definitions of success. They shared their lists and looked for common ground as well as differences in experiences. They continued the needs assessment process over a twelve-week period, defining and clarifying core issues. A core group of parents involved in the process decided to develop a leadership team to prepare themselves to interact more effectively with the school on behalf of their children. Others participated in focus group discussions in which they identified challenges to communication with the school, experiences of stigmatization and discrimination by school personnel as a result of their poverty, and a desire for systems change.

Careful attention to respectful listening and speaking, relationship building, mutual support, and group facilitation—hallmarks of teaching-learning—moved the group toward transformative collective action. As members of the social work team learned from the parents they were also teachers. They facilitated the leadership training classes through didactic and experiential learning activities. They brought theoretical lenses to bear, teaching the participants about pathways to productive engagement based on a conceptual framework that recognized parents' strengths, considered the cumulative and ongoing impacts of trauma, and offered a systems-informed approach to creating change within schools. This project illustrates the power and possibilities of collaboration between the social work team and the parents as both teachers and learners. Storytelling was central to the process. Take a moment to reflect on this case study. What specific elements and examples of teaching-learning can you identify?

Stories and Voices

In chapter 4 we addressed the importance of stories as the means through which people give meaning to their experiences and construct their reality. As we bear witness to others' stories we learn about their experiences, emotions, beliefs, hopes, and fears. We also learn about the powerful meta-narratives in which their stories are inscribed. The teaching-learning process provides an opportunity to gain a deeper understanding of the social and environmental conditions, power relations, and cultural dynamics shaping individual, group, or community experience (Marsiglia & Kulis, 2015). The questions we pose can foster a shared critical awareness, open spaces to consider alternative explanations, and generate further inquiry to guide action.

For example, there has been growing attention in recent years to trauma— the cumulative effects of trauma wrought by both structural and interpersonal forces and the need for trauma-informed social work practice (Blitz et al., 2013; Pearlman & Caringi, 2009; van der Kolk, 2014). As Blitz and colleagues (2013) describe, a basic principle of trauma-informed work is to start from the assumption that trouble is related to "what happened to you" rather than "what's wrong with you." Starting from a place of genuine curiosity about what happened invites another to tell his story and have it honored. Stories may reveal sources of toxic stress to be addressed as well as sources of strength and resilience. Stories also speak to the workings of power in everyday experience.

Recent social work research speaks to the importance of tuning in to the stories and voices of those affected by helping systems and services that too often go unheard. For example, Lynn Nybell's (2013) careful consideration of "voice" among youth in foster care illuminates ways in which the specific contexts and practices related to foster placement affect what young people in care feel they can and cannot say and how they can and cannot speak, particularly to social workers. Through interviews with former foster youth, Nybell explored ways in which "very specific contexts of power shaped the utterances of young people in the foster care system and distorted, muted, or amplified their efforts to express their needs, concerns, and interests" (Finn, Shook, et al., 2013, p. 1163).

Nybell began by asking former foster youth, "If you were telling the story of how you got where you are today . . . where would you start? What is chapter one?" (Nybell, 2013, p. 1229). Her respondents shared powerful accounts of the ways in which their voices were variably silenced, amplified, and distorted by parents, foster parents, court personnel, and social workers as they navigated the complex and shifting contexts of foster care. Youth spoke of losing voice and reclaiming voice. On occasion they spoke of being genuinely heard in the context of relationships with social workers who not only believed in them but also loved them. Nybell's analysis sparks critical thinking about possibilities for challenging and changing relations and contexts of power in foster care in order to strengthen the capacity of young people in care to voice their concerns and aspirations.

Keith Anderson demonstrated the power of listening to voices that often go unheard in his research with certified nursing assistants (CNAs) in nursing homes and their experiences with "disenfranchised," or cumulative, unacknowledged grief related to deaths of patients in their care (Anderson, 2008; Anderson & Ewen, 2011). Certified nursing assistants experience close, intimate, everyday contact with nursing home residents, and yet there is little recognition at the organizational level of the grief and loss that is an integral part of their work. Anderson found that experiences of unacknowledged disenfranchised grief may have consequences across multiple domains and affect the emotional and physical well-being of CNAs, their sense of job satisfaction, and ultimately the quality of patient care because emotional exhaustion contributes to a depersonalization of nursing home residents. Anderson also learned about possibilities of enfranchised grief in promoting coping skills and quality of care. He addressed basic positive interventions to acknowledge the importance of relationships between CNAs and nursing home residents and the significance of their losses. For example, brief rituals, such as a moment of silence to recognize the death of a resident or periodic memorials to remember residents who have passed away, can enhance healing aspects of grief. Workplace-supported education on end-of-life issues and periodic bereavement training can also serve to enfranchise staff members who bear the everyday burdens of grief and loss. Both Nybell and Anderson positioned themselves as learners, listening to and respecting the experiences and expertise of those whose voices are seldom heard in order to inform and transform practice.

POWER AND THE TEACHING-LEARNING PROCESS

Awareness of Power

In chapter 5, we addressed the need for social workers to be clear about the extent and limits of professional power and authority in the engagement process. This holds true for the teaching-learning process as well. By virtue of our positions, we may have the power to attach labels to others, access resources, impose sanctions, and make recommendations with significant legal and social consequences. We need to be critically self-aware regarding the sources, forms, and limits of our power and to be able to communicate that honestly to others. Likewise, we need to be critically conscious of the various forms of informal power we may assume or that others might attribute to us, such as the power of credentials, titles, or access to information.

People and groups who have been excluded from arenas and processes of decision making may be very wary of both the formal and the informal power of the social worker. People socialized to respect the power of the expert may defer to the authority of the social worker as advice giver and decision maker. Therefore, for social workers, an integral part of the teaching-learning process is learning to acknowledge the power and expertise we have; learning and teaching the skills of participation so that our power and expertise is brought to bear honestly, effectively, and justly; learning and teaching modes of leadership that challenge top-down models of authority and promote participation; and welcoming feedback from service users regarding how they experience the helping relationship, the organizational context and climate, and the services provided.

Power, Privilege, and Oppression

Authentic teaching-learning requires ongoing attention to the interplay of privilege and oppression and the ways in which they may work in tandem to silence or devalue individuals and groups of people based on perceived differences in terms of race, class, gender identity and expression, sexual orientation, ability, age, and other facets of social identity. It calls for ongoing critical reflection and dialogue in our organizations and among social workers and service users to identify and disrupt oppressive patterns of practice that become embedded in policies, routines, and everyday interactions. Oppression creeps into social work organizations through the unacknowledged practices and effects of privilege and the decontextualization and denial of racism, sexism, heterosexism, ableism, and classism embedded in interpersonal and institutional practices. It creeps in through so-called color-blind policies and practices that ignore structured inequalities (Dominelli, 2008). It creeps in through everyday micro-aggressions and micro-inequities, those "brief and commonplace daily verbal, behavioral, or environmental indignities, whether intentional or unintentional, that communicate hostile, derogatory, or negative slights and insults to the target person or group" (Sue et al., 2007, p. 273). It becomes embedded when dominant groups fail to see privilege as a problem and when they deny or minimize oppression, blame the victim, support the status quo, claim good intentions, or say that they are tired of hearing about oppression (Mullaly, 2010, pp. 292–310). These practices and messages affect not only service users but staff as well, with racial and sexual minorities bearing the disproportionate burden.

Eli Clare warns that "our oppressions are easier to claim than our privileges" (2003, "Digging Deep," para. 4):

> How do we make the space to talk honestly and wrenchingly about all the multi-layered systems of injustice that target some of us and privilege others for who we are? The layers are so tangled: gender folds into disability, disability wraps around class, class strains against race, race snarls into sexuality, sexuality hangs onto gender, all of it finally piling into our bodies. I dare say everyone in this room has stories of both oppression and privilege. How do we dig down to find, not uncrackable, unmovable rhetoric, but the concrete daily material, emotional, and spiritual realities of privilege and oppression on this planet rife with injustice? ("Digging deep," para. 1)

Clare challenges us to "dig down deep" into the naming and owning of privilege in our practice of learning and unlearning.

Sticks and Stones and Words

Social work educator and researcher Michael Spencer (2015) addresses the prevalence of microaggressions among children and youth and our responsibilities as social workers to address these interactions:

> We can begin by educating youth and those who work with them about microaggressions in order to foster an understanding of why they are hurtful. There should be accountability for these transgressions; however, we must understand that this is not just an issue of individual attitudes—our institutions and our societal norms and values maintain and perpetuate microaggressions. We need to commit to creating an environment that is bias-free by making these unconscious hidden messages conscious and known. We can do this by providing opportunities and space for individuals to raise concerns without dismissal. We must examine policies and procedures within our settings for inclusion and potential exclusion. . . . We need to free ourselves of the interchange between guilt and denial in which we often find ourselves trapped. As social workers, we hope for reconciliation—across communities of

different identities. In order for reconciliation to occur, we first need truth: truth within ourselves, within our work settings, and within our communities. We must admit that we are imperfect and that transgressions are likely to occur because we live in a society that supports structural oppression. Be open to confrontation and challenge as a learning process. Learning involves reading, listening, engaging in dialogue, reflecting on our words, interactions and our actions. Apologize when we make mistakes and let each other know that we are works in progress. (p. 3)

Engaging in a Power Analysis

Fundamental to the teaching-learning process is an analysis of power. A power analysis informs understanding of our own sources of power; the forms of power working for and against us; and the potential power of individuals, families, groups, and communities we work with to effect change. In their development of an empowerment approach to practice with women of color, Lorraine Gutiérrez and Edith Lewis (Gutiérrez, 1990; Gutiérrez & Lewis, 1999) describe power analyses as essential components of empowerment. We summarize the steps and strategies they find useful in analyzing people's power bases to inform empowering practice (Gutiérrez & Lewis,1999, p. 19):

- Analyze how conditions of powerlessness are affecting the client's situation.
- Identify sources of potential power in the client's situation.
- Dialogue with the client about the social structural origins of the current situation.
- Focus the client's analysis on a specific situation.
- Think creatively about sources of potential power, such as forgotten skills, personal qualities that could increase social influence, members of past social support networks, and organizations in the community.
- Make connections between the immediate situation and the distribution of power in society as a whole.
- Engage in consciousness-raising exercises to look beyond the specific situation to problems shared by other clients in similar situations.
- Beware of adopting feelings of powerlessness from clients.
- Learn to see the potential for power and influence in every situation.

Gutiérrez and Lewis (1999, pp. 38–51) describe how individual practice can be transformed into an empowering process by honoring the other person's social reality, walking with rather than directing a person through the helping process, and providing mechanisms for acknowledging and responding to experiences of oppression and discrimination.

We can facilitate a power analysis by teaching participants about concepts of power over, power within, power with, and power to act (see chapter 1, p. 36) and learning how they claim and confront power in their everyday lives. We also see the need to expand the power analysis by making the power and authority of the social worker a talkable theme in the process. How do the participants in the process variably perceive the social worker's power? How comfortable is the social worker with the power, authority, and responsibility of his position? How does his power factor into the larger power dynamics of the presenting situation? These are key questions of the teaching-learning process.

Iceberg Model

As shown in figure 6.1, the iceberg model offers another possibility for power analysis, drawing from principles of popular education that engage participants in critical question posing regarding the issues they face. The iceberg metaphor provides a visual image for critical thinking about what we perceive on the surface at the *event* level and what patterns, structures, and mental models lie beneath that contribute to the event. The visual image can be presented on paper or poster board, and participants can be invited to probe deeper into what lies beneath. The iceberg model can be used to examine concrete events, such as the planned location of a toxic waste site near a low-income neighborhood, or observed phenomena, such as the disproportionate numbers of children of color in out-of-home care. First, participants consider the event or phenomenon: What has happened? What do we see? What are we reacting to? Second, they look for patterns. Are there trends over time? Third, they look for underlying structures. What has influenced these patterns? What may be causing what we are observing? Are there physical, organizational, political, or cultural factors at work here? What are the relations among these structures? Finally, participants consider the mental models. What assumptions and beliefs are at work here? How do they keep the overall system in place? The iceberg model provides a tool for critical thinking in concrete ways about the forces and relations of power at work beneath a particular phenomenon or event. It can also provide a starting point for dialogue and an entry point for change.

Figure 6.1
Iceberg model

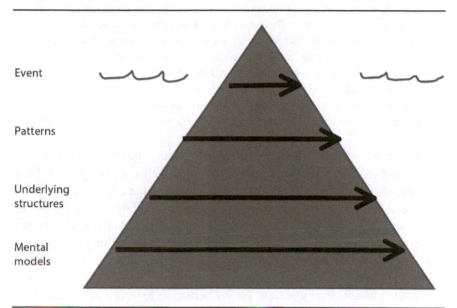

Event

Patterns

Underlying
structures

Mental
models

(Northwest Earth Institute, 2015)

Take a minute to think about how and where you might use the iceberg model. How might it serve as a starting point for critical dialogue with an individual or group? In organizational or community contexts? How might it serve as a catalyst for analyzing power? How might you make use of it in your social justice work?

TEACHING-LEARNING AND HUMAN RIGHTS

We have addressed the centrality of human rights to social justice work. We have also discussed the limited knowledge of social workers, particularly those working in a U.S. context, regarding human rights. The teaching-learning process can foster critical awareness of human rights and their relevance to the grounded struggles in people's everyday lives. For example, Teresa McDowell, Kathryn Libal, and Andrae Brown (2012) demonstrate the power of a human rights framework in assessing family issues in the context of domestic violence:

A human rights framework adds clarity and centrality to social justice in the practice of family therapy. The widespread agreement that ensuring human rights is essential for the well-being of individuals, families, communities, and societies lends credence to the stance that social justice advocacy should be central to family work. Therapists can use human rights discourse to inform and anchor what is often considered relative, in other words, social justice perspectives that are challenged or dismissed as worldview choices and/or biases. Human rights frameworks add to our contextual understanding of how societal structures, including systems that marginalize and oppress some for the benefit of others, contribute to mental health and relational problems. (p. 9)

McDowell and colleagues show how a human rights framework illuminates the particular vulnerabilities of women and children in families. They have pioneered work in addressing domestic violence as a human rights violation and in helping survivors of domestic violence situate their experiences within a broader discourse of human rights. A human rights frame challenges the notion of domestic violence as a private matter. The framing of domestic violence as a human rights violation sparks critical consciousness of women's rights and human rights and provides pathways for action and accountability beyond the level of the individual. We invite readers to return to the plain language version of the Universal Declaration on Human Rights on p. 131 and to consider the potential human rights violation resulting from domestic violence. These may include violation of rights to security, bodily integrity, freedom of movement, freedom of opinion, freedom to work, and freedom from torture. Naming domestic violence and examining it from a human rights perspective is a powerful way to recognize that terror and torture occur in the context of family.

A human rights framework provides a powerful means for consciousness raising regarding rights of domestic violence survivors and what it means to have those rights denied and violated. McDowell and colleagues argue that situating their work with domestic violence survivors within a public discourse on human rights helps break the silence and shame that hovers around individual experience as connections are made to collective rights claims. Further, they contend that a human rights framework can be a powerful consciousness raising tool for confronting perpetrators with the gravity of their actions. As social workers bear witness to human right violations and develop a critical consciousness of human rights as part of their practice, there is both opportunity and responsibility to take action. McDowell and colleagues conclude that, "through our skills in emotional, intellectual, relational, and cultural work, we can draw on the humanity central to human rights to encourage social change" (p. 19). How might you bring a human rights framework to bear as part of your everyday practice of social work? How might it critically inform practice in child welfare, juvenile justice, health and mental health, housing advocacy, addictions, aging services, or school-based social work? Where do you see possibilities for *practicing* human rights?

ON REFLECTION

Teaching and Learning on the U.S.-Mexico Border: Reflection on Human Rights

Scott Nicholson, MSW, August 2015

The Hogar de Esperanza y Paz (Home of Hope and Peace) community center where I live and work is located just three miles south of the border wall that separates Nogales, Sonora, from Nogales, Arizona. The minimum wage on this side of that wall is $4.70 per day and there are more than ninety *maquiladoras* (assembly plants) in the city.

The U.S. government recently spent $187 million to modernize the port-of-entry in Nogales so that garage door openers and tomatoes can travel north more rapidly and efficiently. The government also spent tens of millions of dollars to install a stronger wall to prevent the workers that make those openers and pick those tomatoes from crossing into Arizona—where the minimum wage is $8.05 per hour.

"We celebrate unity," said Bill Clinton at the site of the former wall that separated West Berlin from East Berlin in July 1994. "We stand where crude walls of concrete separated mother from child and we meet as one family. We stand where those who sought a new life instead found death. . . . Berliners, you have proved that no wall can forever contain the mighty power of freedom." Three months later, his administration built the Nogales wall.

Clinton had worked very hard the previous year to push the North American Free Trade Agreement (NAFTA) through Congress. That agreement enabled U.S. corporations to sell subsidized corn in Mexico at prices so low that Mexican farmers couldn't compete. Between 1.5 million and 2 million farmers lost their land during the first ten years of NAFTA. Some of those farmers decided that the only way to provide for their families was to cross into the United States in search of work.

The response of the Clinton administration was to implement a border enforcement policy based on *deterrence*. Border walls were built and more agents were deployed to prevent people from crossing the border in urban areas—where it was easier and safer. The goal was to "Raise the risk . . . to the point that many will consider it futile to attempt illegal entry. . . . Illegal traffic will be deterred or forced over more hostile terrain less suited for crossing."

According to the German government, 138 people were killed while trying to cross the Berlin wall during the twenty-eight years that it existed. More than six thousand people have died while attempting to cross into the United States since deterrence became the policy.

What does Just Practice look like in the midst of so much injustice? I believe that freedom of movement is a human right, and I think that one of the most powerful tools for changing policies is sharing the *testimonios* (lived experiences) of people who are affected by those policies.

The Home of Hope and Peace organizes educational immersion experiences for people who want to learn from our migrant sisters and brothers and from organizations that are providing humanitarian aid and working for justice. Janet Finn and I are co-professors of the class Social Work and Social Justice on the U.S.-Mexico Border that focuses on learning from people who are affected by U.S. economic and immigration policies.

My friend and teacher, Toño, sells newspapers as he walks back and forth in the lanes of cars that are waiting to cross the border into Nogales, Arizona. He's from Honduras where his father died when Toño was ten years old. He journeyed to the United States when he was thirteen and lived near Stillwater, Oklahoma, where he worked in construction. Toño has a wife and two children who are nine and eleven years old. He was separated from them when he was cited for driving without a license and deported to Honduras.

Toño told me, "I've been deported back to Honduras five times (for trying to return to the United States). I haven't seen my children in six years. My son asks me 'When are you coming back?' I'm going to try and cross again—I don't know how or when."

He walked to the front of the line of cars to shake my hand as I was waiting my turn to cross a few days ago. We let go of each other's hand and I drove up to the booth of the border agent while Toño went back to selling papers—close enough to touch and yet our lives are worlds apart.

THE SKILLS AND PRACTICE OF TEACHING-LEARNING

In this section we elaborate on the skills and practice of teaching-learning. We start with a consideration of teaching-learning as a process of systematic inquiry. We then look at teaching-learning in community, group, organizational, familial, and interpersonal contexts and provide examples of practice possibilities. We highlight their strengths, pose questions about their limitations, and consider their fit with the teaching-learning process of social justice work.

Systematization

Teaching-learning involves the systematization of experiences. This is not a common word in the English vocabulary. We borrow it from the Spanish word *sistematización*. Popular educators in Latin America, influenced by the work of Paulo Freire, describe *sistematización* as a rigorous, ordered process of taking concrete, lived experience into account; looking for generative themes; and sharing with others what we have learned from it. The concept of *generative themes* refers to those points of contradiction in people's lives where personal experience intersects with larger social forces, resulting in what Bertha Capen Reynolds termed "problems in social living." They are often laden with meaning and emotion, and they become starting points for dialogue. Systematization is a participatory process in which people critically examine their experience and social reality in order to arrive at a more profound understanding. The process involves detailed deconstruction, examination, and reconstruction of the elements, contexts, and forces shaping the experience (Jara, 1998). It may involve posing questions about the ways in which problems have been framed and creating opportunities for reframing, perhaps through lenses of capabilities and rights and perhaps through a reframing of blame and responsibility.

The key themes of Just Practice provide a foundation for systematization or systematic inquiry into experiences, conditions, and possibilities for change: How do the participants in the process variably describe and give *meaning* to their experiences, interests, and concerns? What constitutes a problem and for whom? What is the *history* of the problem and how does it intersect with the histories of the participants? What is the *context* in which participants are coming together? How is it connected to the larger contexts of their lives? What can we learn from a *power* analysis of the situation that addresses questions of power over, power with, power within, and power to do? Where and what are the *possibilities* for transformative action? What possibilities can be realized and how? What can we learn from the process that will transform our thinking and inform future practice?

Popular educator Cecilia Díaz describes a five-step process of systematization, which we summarize here (adapted from Díaz, 1995, pp. 8–11):

1. *Describe*: Invite participants to describe their social reality through interviews, dialogue, group conversations, surveys, or testimonials and gather existing data.

2. *Organize*: Consider how these descriptions of social reality might be classified into interpersonal, economic, environmental, cultural, social, spiritual, or political dimensions.

3. *Prioritize*: Identify participants' most pressing concerns. Priorities may reflect what participants see as most urgent or most serious, what affects the most people, the most deeply felt, and so on.

4. *Analyze*: Reflect on the various dimensions and look for patterns and connections. Seek to understand possible causes and consequences. How might this relate to expressed priorities?

5. *Draw conclusions*: Identify the most consistently named concerns, affirmations, and common elements across seemingly diverse problems or needs. Consider points of divergence as well. Begin to explore possible courses of action.

The process brings us to new points of arrival, which then become points of departure for further reflection and analysis. This is an example of *praxis*, the give and take of reflection and action. The language of systematization and praxis may be unfamiliar, but the process can guide our teaching-learning at multiple levels of practice from individual to group, organizational, and community work. Now let's turn to the skills and practice of teaching-learning in the context of communities.

Teaching and Learning in Communities

We addressed the importance of the community context of practice in chapter 5. Now we consider teaching-learning possibilities in the context of community. Barry Checkoway (2013) describes communities as "units of solution" where people can join together to address common concerns, confront differences, and create change. How do we learn about the communities in which we live and work and come to understand the commonalities and differences among concerns and interests of the residents? How do our ideas about what constitutes community shape the questions we ask and the strategies we use to learn about the community? And how do we teach the skills helpful to promote community change?

A number of community practitioners have created useful guides for learning about the community context of practice. We will highlight some of their work here to illustrate possible approaches to build from and to adapt to other situations.

Homan's Guide

Social worker and community organizer Mark Homan (2016, pp. 137–144) offers a helpful guide for getting to know the community by exploring its basic characteristics (e.g., demographics, physical features, social features, landmarks, and points of interaction) and how it functions to meet the needs and requirements of its members across nine domains:

- *Environmental*: What are the environmental conditions and resources? How do they affect human interaction?
- *Physical*: What is available in terms of housing, transportation, infrastructure, medical care, for example?
- *Economic*: What are the economic opportunities? How do people get goods and services?
- *Human development*: What skills and talents do members have? How can they develop them?
- *Political*: What is the governance and decision-making structure? Who participates?
- *Information and communication*: How do people learn about what is happening in the world? What are systems of formal and informal education?
- *Cultural*: How is culture acknowledged and expressed? What are the cultural influences in community life?
- *Spiritual*: How is spirituality valued in the community? In what forms is spirituality expressed? How do members attend to spiritual needs?
- *Social and emotional*: Is there a sense of well-being, belonging, and trust among community members? Do members feel part of a community?

These categories provide a useful starting point for collective inquiry into and development of basic knowledge of a social or geographic community. What might be missing from this framework? What might you add to this preliminary framework to begin your teaching-learning process in the context of community?

Listening Surveys

Another approach to getting to know the community is by meeting with members and exploring generative themes that emerge through *listening surveys*. Community members have issues that resonate for them based on the shared, contextual nature of their experience (Freire, 1974). These may include concern over economic well-being related to the start-up of new industry or the closure of a historically viable industry. They may include concern over environmental degradation and health risks to community members. There may be divisive themes around fundamental social justice issues differentially affecting community members. We introduced the concept of *generative themes* on page 257. Generative themes are issues that bring strong feelings to bear on the possibilities for sustained action. Tapping into these themes and eliciting their emotional content can be a way of sparking consciousness, stirring collective energy, and strengthening a base for action (Hope & Timmel, 1984/1999, vol. 1).

Listening surveys provide opportunities for people to share their concerns, hopes, and aspirations. They seek to discover what people care about, feel strongly about, and are willing to act upon (Hope & Timmel, 1984/1999, vol. I, p. 53). Listening surveys may be carried out through door-to-door interviews, in open neighborhood or community meetings, and through online surveys. They may also occur in strategic sites such as grocery stores, recreational events, barber shops, or places where people have to wait (e.g., doctors' offices, grocery store lines, or movie theater lines). They may include basic open-ended questions: What do you like best about your community? What are your biggest concerns for your community? What three things would you like to see changed to improve your community? How might you like to be involved in the process?

Data from the listening survey can then be systematically examined through the five-step process outlined above. How have participants described their social reality? What dimensions of social experience are reflected in their responses? What issues surface as priorities? For whom? What patterns and connection might we discover? Where do we find common ground and important differences? How does our analysis inform next steps?

Do you see possibilities for a listening survey to open space for dialogue and action in a community you care about? What might be its strengths and challenges?

Reflection Moment:
City of Seattle Race and Social Justice Initiative (RSJI)

For more than a decade, the City of Seattle has been engaged in a comprehensive initiative to eliminate racial disparities and achieve racial equality in the community by directly addressing institutional racism and its effects. In November, 2013, the RSJI launched its first biennial online listening survey to learn how people who live, work, or go to school in Seattle think the city is doing regarding racial equity in jobs, housing, health, education, transportation, and other key areas. Throughout 2014 RSJI staff conducted thirty-seven listening sessions with city employees and community members to learn about their most pressing racial equity concerns. Lessons learned have shaped next action steps and the 2016 survey. Learn more about RSJI at the city's website (http://www.seattle.gov/rsji/community/survey). How might the work of RSJI inspire thinking about teaching-learning possibilities in your community?

Culturally Based Capacity Building

Teaching-learning in the context of community calls for ongoing critical learning about power, privilege, and difference (Checkoway, 2007). It calls for consideration of how communities are affected by dimensions of diversity and their intersections and by the power of historical, political, and institutional forces, as well as how community work is affected by one's own values, lenses, and social identities (Harrell & Bond, 2006).

The National Community Development Institute's (NCDI's) work on culturally based capacity building illustrates this practice. The institute's community capacity building approach is grounded in values of engagement, openness, diversity, inclusivity, access, equity, opportunity, and accountability (Satterwhite & Teng, 2007, p. 1). The NCDI defines culturally based capacity building as "providing transformational technical support and training services for individuals, organizations, and communities in their unique cultural contexts based on knowledge, experience, and sensitivity to the issues of race/ethnicity, language, gender, sexual identity, socioeconomic status, age, disability, and religion" (p. 2). It works with community members on project teams and seeks to build capacity through listening to community voices; learning from community wisdom; building trust with community members; and collectively building a deeper understanding of social conditions, power relationships, cultural dynamics, and complex issues.

The NCDI defines the role of *capacity builder* as that of documenting and disseminating information on what is being learned in the capacity building process so that the community can use that knowledge to create change. In addition to the role of capacity builder, NCDI members see their roles as facilitators, enablers, resources, translators, and coaches as they help communities identify and articulate their own cultural context and create a supportive environment in which people can do the work of community building informed through the lenses of their own context (St. Onge, Cole, & Petty, 2003). Part of NCDI's work involves ongoing critical reflection on the cultural lenses through which it engages the world and the assumptions it brings to the process. The NCDI begins with a *listening project*, learns about the community's cultural and political history, and engages a community planning team in a process of systematic inquiry. Its technical assistance approach reflects the spirit of teaching-learning: "We identify, document, synthesize, and transfer knowledge about lessons learned and return it to the community, because it belongs to them; and we incorporate the lessons learned into our own institutional practices so that we continue to grow" (St. Onge et al., 2003, p. 6).

We have provided some frameworks to help you get to know a community. What do they have in common? How do they differ? How might they be used in the teaching-learning process? What steps would you take to facilitate a participatory process of community assessment? How would you decide what data to gather? Where would you look for information? What steps would you take to facilitate interpretation of the data?

Individual Learning Activity: Illustrating the Community Impact of an Individual Event

Human Impact Partners is an Oakland, California-based research, advocacy, and capacity building organization that works in partnership with low-income communities and communities of color to challenge inequities that harm community health. In 2013 the organization issued a report entitled *Family Unity, Family Health* (Human Impact Partners, 2013), which makes the case for family-focused immigration reform to improve the health of children, families, and communities. The report includes an illustrated story showing how one event—the detention of Jorge Garcia, an undocumented U.S. resident—can have far-reaching community consequences. Visit the Family Unity, Family Health website at http://www.familyunity familyhealth.org and find out what happens in Jorge's story. Then view the findings of the report. Take a few minutes to reflect on this report. Do the use of storytelling and images help spark critical consciousness of immigration issues? How might you incorporate this report and Jorge's story into a teaching-learning opportunity about immigration and the individual and community effects of deportation? How might you incorporate the use of simple images and storytelling to spark consciousness and dialogue regarding other social justice issues?

Community Mapping

Although it is not a framework per se, we introduce community mapping as a useful tool for getting to know the community. The practice of systematic community mapping has an important place in social work history. In 1895, the Hull

House Association of Chicago published *Hull House Maps and Papers*, which was a compilation of essays on social conditions written by Hull House residents. It included detailed maps of the social demography of the immigrant neighborhood surrounding Hull House. (View the maps at the University of Illinois-Chicago Urban Experience website, http://www.uic.edu/jaddams/hull/urbanexp/geography/nationalitymaps.htm). Mapping became a valuable tool in the sociological study of neighborhoods and communities.

More recently, John L. McKnight and John Kretzmann (1990) have adopted the practice of community mapping to inform what they term "assets-based community development." In their work on mapping community capacity they challenge *needs-oriented* approaches and focus instead on strategies for recognizing and promoting the capacities, skills, and assets of low-income people and their neighborhoods (p. 2). They frame assessment as a process of mapping the building blocks for community regeneration. Asset mapping is a participatory process in which community members actively identify the primary assets or *building blocks* that they control directly, the secondary assets controlled by sources outside the community that can be tapped for community use, and the tertiary assets, which are also outside the community and can be potentially tapped, such as grant funds (Hardina, 2013, p. 138).

Asset Mapping Resources

The Asset-Based Community Development (ABCD) Institute located at Northwestern University in Chicago offers a great range of resources, including training videos on mobilizing community assets and toolkits to get you started in developing plans for asset mapping in your community. To learn more, check out the ABCD website (http://www.abcdinstitute.org/resources). The Advancement Project, a California-based multiracial civil rights organization, launched the Healthy City Project to address health inequities by building grassroots knowledge and power for change. You can access its Participatory Asset Mapping Toolkit online (http://community science.com/knowledge4equity/AssetMappingToolkit.pdf).

Community mapping has been used to address a range of issues from child safety to health equity (Amsden & VanWynsberghe, 2005; Nelson & Baldwin, 2004). For example, Nelson and Baldwin used comprehensive neighborhood mapping (CNM) to address issues of children's safety in Edinburgh, Scotland, in a marginalized neighborhood where a high proportion of children and single mothers live. The philosophy of CNM is rooted in the belief that local knowledge can illuminate the connections between different forms of harm to children and the development of effective strategies to address their protection. Nelson and Baldwin describe CNM as "a technique for imaginatively gathering and inter-preting information relevant to young people's safety within a given geographic area which involves agencies and communities in partnership in identifying problems and seeking solutions" (2004, p. 415).

The CNM process sought to augment the work of the child protection system by building in additional safeguards informed by neighborhood residents. Besides enumerating the risks of sexual abuse, the mapping also identified dangerous physical environments, including unsafe buildings. Additionally, the process focused on neighborhood strengths such as informal networks of communication and support, a history of involvement in the arts and drama, and a tradition of community activism and campaigning. Project results revealed common concerns among agency stakeholders and community residents and a commitment to co-learning. As a whole the process and results were easily understood by all residents, easier to apply than survey methods, and reflected the priorities of residents more accurately than other approaches to understanding the community. What uses could you make of a community mapping approach to teaching and learning about the community? What might be some of the strengths of this approach? What challenges might you have to confront?

Children's Rights and Child-Friendly Cities

A human rights perspective can also inform the process of teaching-learning in the community context. For example, Jorge Garcia's story, presented in the *Family Unity, Family Health* report addressed above, set the stage for critical dialogue regarding immigrants' rights, children's rights, and the rights to family. It provided the base for developing critical awareness about the criminalization of immigrants and the practices and consequences of human rights violations affecting undocumented residents and their citizen and noncitizen children in the United States.

Communities can also be powerful contexts for teaching-learning, action, and advocacy regarding the rights of children. The UN Convention on the Rights of the Child specifically acknowledges children's right to have rights. The Child-Friendly Cities Initiative (UNICEF, 2014), spearheaded by UNICEF in 1996, seeks to bring children's rights to bear in concrete, pragmatic ways at the local level in communities across the globe. The initiative promotes children's participation in the issues that affect their lives. A child-friendly city is defined as a local system of good governance committed to fulfilling child rights for all its young citizens. The initiative provides a wide range of tools for community members to use in teaching and learning about children's rights and using those rights as building blocks for community change. The initiative has developed a variety of assessment tools geared for young children, adolescents, and parents to use in community-level data collection to both document the child friendliness of the community and raise consciousness about children's rights. The assessment tools are nested in a broader framework for action to promote children's participation in the building of child-friendly cities. The initiative provides an important opportunity and challenge for social justice workers in the United States, given its failure to ratify the Convention on the Rights of the Child as of 2016. (Visit http://childfriendlycities.org to learn more about child-friendly cities.)

What is the vision of a Child-Friendly City?

A child friendly city (UNICEF, 2014; http://childfriendlycities.org/overview/what-is-a-child-friendly-city) guarantees the right of every young citizen to:

- Influence decisions about their city
- Express their opinion on the city they want
- Participate in family, community, and social life
- Receive basic services such as health care, education, and shelter
- Drink safe water and have access to proper sanitation
- Be protected from exploitation, violence, and abuse
- Walk safely in the streets on their own
- Meet friends and play
- Have green spaces for plants and animals
- Live in an unpolluted environment
- Participate in cultural and social events
- Be an equal citizen of their city with access to every service, regardless of ethnic origin, religion, income, gender, or disability

Teaching-Learning in Groups

Groups and group work play a key role in social justice work. Even when working in direct practice with individuals, social workers are often involved in group work, whether it is in the context of families, mental health teams, school-based interdisciplinary teams, or agency-based work and supervision teams. We encourage you to think about the ways in which groups and group processes are part of everyday social work practice, ways in which group processes can be utilized in teaching-learning, and ways to continually bring group work skills to bear as part of social justice work. Much of the social work literature divides discussion of group work into broad categories of therapeutic/support (e.g., therapy, support, psychoeducational, and self-help groups) and task groups (e.g., community and social action, interdisciplinary teams, coalitions, and steering committees) (Garvin, Gutiérrez, & Galinsky, 2004; Seabury, Seabury, & Garvin, 2011, pp. 402–403). We argue that social justice work calls for an integrated approach to group work that brings the dynamics and skills of mutual aid, analysis of power, and a commitment to the equality of participants to bear as part of the teaching-learning process.

Teaching and learning happen in dialogue with others. Groups provide a space for teaching and learning where people can take risks, experiment with new ideas, and build a powerful base for change with the support of others. Groups form a base and a place for learning about effective membership and for building leadership capacity. Social justice workers need strong facilitation skills; they need to be able to bring others into the process of dialogue and to structure that process so participants have opportunities to listen as well as to speak. They serve as teachers in preparing group members to listen to, question, validate, challenge, and respect one another. And they are learners bearing witness to the stories of individual members and the experiences of the group as a whole. A well-facilitated group process ensures that decisions are made collectively. Power is distributed among members and not solely concentrated in the hands of one group leader. To work effectively with and in groups, it is important to understand about group work and group dynamics.

Processes of Mutual Aid

In chapter 5, we introduced William Schwartz's concept of mutual aid as a basis for collective support and action. Let's return to the processes of mutual aid and the implications for social justice work. By conceptualizing the group as a mutual aid system, we locate all participants, including the social worker, as learners, teachers, facilitators, and animators. We also recognize the dialectical relationship between the individual members and the group as a whole in the process (Shulman, 2012, p. 345). As participants learn and practice the skills of mutual aid, they contribute to a climate of trust and intimacy in the group that supports them in assuming the risks and opportunities of teaching-learning. Let's take a closer look at these processes and the elements of teaching-learning at work in implementing them. Lawrence Shulman (2012, pp. 342–355) has formulated ten processes that comprise what he terms the "dynamics of mutual aid" (p. 344). We will briefly summarize each of the processes. As you read about the processes, reflect on the questions how can we as social workers facilitate the process? and how does the process promote co-learning?

1. *Sharing data*: Groups provide a context for members to serve as resources for one another by sharing ideas, data, and strategies for survival and change. This process allows each member opportunities to teach from personal experience and learn from the experience of others.

2. *The dialectical process*: Members engage in debate by putting forth a thesis and antithesis and finally arriving at some form of synthesis. This process can help members explore contradictory forces that shape their everyday life experiences. It can help members grapple with ambivalent feelings and recognize internalized contradictions.

3. *Discussing a taboo area*: Groups can be powerful places to address difficult topics that are often avoided in other contexts. For example, sexuality, racism, and terminal illness are often considered taboo in dominant social discourse. Groups may experience the power of trust and intimacy as members find the courage to "speak the unspeakable."

4. *The "all in the same boat" phenomenon*: Realizing that one is not alone and that others share similar concerns and struggles is a powerful dimension of group work. As facilitators, we help members make connections and encourage others to reflect critically on the patterns that connect and the forces that shape both individual and group experience.

5. *Developing a universal perspective*: The group process helps members challenge beliefs that frame their troubles in terms of personal shortcomings. When members recognize their shared experiences of oppression, they may come to a new critical consciousness of the external sources of their problems. They are able to universalize their perspectives, let go of feelings of blame and shame, and direct energies toward personal and social change.

6. *Mutual support*: The group process creates a space where people can openly share feelings, identify common concerns, and express empathy to one another. Further, as members recognize and express their feelings toward and support of others, they grow

more self-accepting. The group as a whole develops a context of support that is greater than the sum of the parts.

7. *Mutual demand*: As members build a context of support and a base of trust, they are able to make demands on one another and hold one another accountable for responsible participation and follow-through on work. Working in a context of trust and intimacy, participants are able to help one another see contradictions between their words and actions.

8. *Individual problem solving*: Groups can move back and forth between general concerns of the group as a whole and specific concerns of individual members. Members can assist one another in concrete problem solving. Successes of individual problem solving can become resources for the group as a whole.

9. *Rehearsal*: The group setting provides members with an arena for practicing alternative responses, difficult interactions, and challenging tasks. Members provide both support and critical feedback and bolster one another's confidence in the process.

10. *Strength in numbers*: The group experience not only breaks down isolation, but it also helps members overcome feelings of powerlessness and see possibilities of collective action. As Shulman (2012) describes, "An individual's fears and ambivalence can be overcome by participation in a group effort as his or her own courage is strengthened by the course of others" (p. 354).

As members engage in these processes over time, they develop their knowledge of group work, skills of teaching-learning, and both individual and collective capacity for critical reflection and action.

Learning about Organizations

Social work happens in and with organizations. Organizations develop their unique culture, climate, and patterns of practice based on history, community context, purpose, and the pressures and dynamics of both internal and external forces. These elements affect our work with people. Formal organizational policies, implicit routines, discourses, and ways of interacting—the organizational *habitus*—and the physical arrangements, from location to use of space and setting of hours of operation, communicate meanings to services users, staff, and the broader community.

Effective engagement and teaching-learning require a welcoming and safe environment (Jennings, Medina, Messia, & McLoughlin, 2006). Organizational context, culture, and climate profoundly affect that environment. If organizations are under-resourced, understaffed, and overburdened, service users and staff alike bear the consequences. We addressed the importance of organizational awareness in chapter 5. Critical organizational awareness needs to go beyond an understanding of organizational mission, vision, goals, funding, leadership, policies, and services. It also demands consideration of how dimensions of diversity and their intersections are addressed; how historical, political, economic, and institutional forces shape organizational policies and practices; and how the varied values, lenses, and social identities of participants shape and are shaped by organizational culture, climate, and context (Harrell & Bond, 2006).

Approaches to Organizational Assessment

We will describe a few approaches to learning about social work organizations and assessing the possibilities of organizational change. Think about the types of information each approach would provide. How might they inform your organizational practice? What do you see as their strengths? Limitations? What aspects of organizational dynamics go unaddressed?

Systems Approach

Miley, O'Melia, and DuBois (2013, p. 277) present a basic systems framework for organizational assessment across three dimensions:

1. *Organizational goals and structures* include the mission, goals, and history of the organization; governance and decision making; leadership principles; and the makeup of organizational staff, memberships, and constituencies.

2. *Organization-environment relations* include the broader social, political, economic, and technological context in which the organization operates; the goodness of fit between organizational purpose and needs and available resources; environmental opportunities and threats; and the broader policy climate that affects the organization.

3. *Organizational competence* addresses how the organization evaluates and uses feedback to improve its effectiveness, its capacity for change, its ability to plan for the future, and its overall strengths and weaknesses.

This model provides a descriptive approach to understanding one's organization and constructs organizations as objective, knowable entities. What do you see as the strengths of this approach? Limitations? How might assessment across these dimensions vary depending upon one's social location in relation to the organization, for example, as service user, staff member, administrator, community member, or funder?

Getting to Know Your Organization

We have developed a basic guide to getting to know your organization (see table 6.1 below). It speaks to issues of meaning, power, history, and possibility that shape and are shaped by the organizational context of practice. How does the guide help you with learning certain aspects of your organization? What do you see as its strengths? Limitations?

Table 6.1
Getting to know your organization

Mission	What is the mission of the organization? How does it define its meaning and purpose? Has the mission changed over time?
History	What is the organization's history? Where does it fit in a larger political, social, and economic context?
Structure	How is the organization structured? What is the system of governance? How are decisions made?
Power	How is power defined and distributed? What are sources of formal and informal power? Does the organization have the power of legal authority or sanction? Does it have the material power to provide or deny resources?
Participants	Who are the people likely to be involved with the organization? As employees? As clients, members, or recipients, for example? What distinctions are made among different participants?
Capabilities	Does the organization recognize and build on the strengths and capabilities of organizational participants? Does a focus on strengths take precedence over a problem-oriented perspective?
Rights	Are human rights explicitly addressed? If so, how? How would a human rights framework inform the organization? How might it challenge organizational policies and practice?

Context	How does the organization fit into a broader community or societal context of services? Does it stand alone? Is it seen as part of a system of care? What is the nature of its physical context and location?
Communication	What are the formal channels of communication in the organization? How does information flow? What are the informal channels and sources?
Activities	What kinds of activities are associated with the organization's work? Are they broad based or specialized? In what context do they occur? How do they relate to the mission?
Funding	How is the organization funded? How does funding influence organizational activities? Does it compete for funding with other local, state, or regional organizations?
Diversity	How is social and cultural diversity represented and addressed within the organization? How does it relate to issues of power in the organization?
Resources	What resources are available to the organizational participants? What resources are lacking? What counts as a resource and for whom?
Perceptions	What are the public perceptions of the organization? How is it seen by outsiders? How is it seen by employees? By its clientele? What does it mean to be associated with the organization as a worker, patient, inmate, member, volunteer, or client, for example?
Your position	Where are you located within the organization? What is your role and the scope of your responsibilities? What is the purpose of your position? How does it relate to fulfillment of the organizational mission?
Supports	Where are your sources of formal organizational support? Of informal support? Where might you find support beyond the organization?
Barriers	Where have you encountered barriers in the organization? What activities or opportunities have they blocked? How have you attempted to address them? Have you been successful?
Values	What values are officially expressed by the organization? What values are demonstrated in everyday practice? Where have you encountered value tensions?
Effectiveness	How does your organization evaluate effectiveness? What counts as success? Who participates in the process? How is evaluative information shared and used?
Possibilities	Where do you see possibilities for social justice work in this organizational context? Who might join with you in pursuit of social justice work?

Appreciative Inquiry

Now let's take a look at a strengths-oriented approach to organizational assessment. Sarah Michael's (2005) field research using appreciative inquiry (AI) opens up new possibilities for learning about organizations. Appreciative inquiry is a teaching-learning tool that can help an organization renew a commitment to reflect upon itself, create ideas about its future, and inspire a group of people to move in that direction. Michael explains that AI is founded on the *heliotropic principle* borrowed from biology, which notes that plants grow toward their source of light. It is believed that, in the same way, people and organizations move toward that which is positive and affirming.

Appreciative Inquiry Interview Questions for Organizations (Michael, 2005, p. 225)

1. What's your favorite memory of working here?
2. What makes this [organization] a good place to work?
3. What do you like best about your job?
4. Can you tell me about the history of your organization?
5. What first attracted you to work here?
6. Can you describe the work that your organization does?
7. What part of your work are you most proud of?
8. What part of your work do you think your clients value most?
9. Which of your skills are you called on to use most often at your job?
10. How do you know when you've done a good job?
11. Can you tell me your favorite story about one of your clients?
12. What do you think attracts your clients to your organization?
13. What makes your organization special or different from other [organizations] that you know?
14. What do you think is at the heart of your organization's success?
15. Can you tell me about the groups or people who support your [organization] and its work?
16. What makes your relationship with them work?
17. Can you tell me about the donor organizations that you find to be the most supportive of your [organization]?
18. What makes your relationship with them special?
19. Can you tell me about situations in which your [organization] and the government have worked well together?.

20. If I came back to visit you in five years, what do you think your organization would look like?

21. What strengths and resources will best help you to achieve these goals?

22. If the director of an [organization] that was just starting out wanted to learn from your experience, what's the best piece of advice that you could give him or her?

Michael notes that staff and administrators are often eager to share their stories about their organizational experience. We invite you to conduct an appreciative inquiry interview with a classmate about his practicum organization or with a coworker or supervisor within your practicum agency. How does he respond to the AI approach? What new or different learning might come from this approach as compared to a more conventional organizational assessment? What might you learn about an organization following an AI approach? Might you still be able to gather information about the organization that provided you with an impression of its strengths as well as its challenges? What does an AI approach teach you about teaching-learning?

Force Field Analysis

Earlier in this chapter we addressed the importance of power analyses in the teaching-learning process. A classic approach to power analysis in organizational contexts is a *force field analysis*, through which participants map the forces for or against a planned change effort. It is based on the work of Kurt Lewin (1943), a pioneer of social and organizational psychology. Participants in an organizational change process are asked to identify whom and what they see as primary forces of support or opposition to a possible change effort. The proposed changes and the supporting and opposing forces are listed on a flip chart or newsprint as participants name them. Each of these factors is then scored (often using a one to five scale) in terms of its perceived level of influence. Forces seen as uncertain or neutral can also be considered. The numerical scoring provides a rough measure of the driving and restraining forces and feasibility of the change effort. It also provides a starting point for considering where further support might be garnered, how opposition might be countered, and whether an alternative plan for change might be needed. The process can be used in diverse interpersonal, small group, organizational, and community building contexts as a readily adaptable tool for power analysis. (For a more detailed description of how to conduct a force field analysis, see Cohen & Hyde, 2013, pp. 36–38.)

Assessing Your Organization for Racial and LGBTQ Equality

As we have described, social work organizations are also sites where racism and other forms of systemic oppression play out (Barnoff, 2011). As social workers we do not tend to perceive ourselves as agents of oppression. However, in both subtle and overt ways myriad forms and mechanisms of oppression filter into our organizations through our organizational histories, values, policies, practice frameworks, and everyday routines that go without saying. For example, racial disproportionality in child welfare, the public welfare system, and access to mental health care often goes undiscussed in social work organizations (Kolivoski et al., 2014). Color-blind policies and practices serve to both mask and reinforce institutional racism. Kolivoski and colleagues argue that critical race theory (addressed in chapter 4) can serve as a tool for analysis in examining the agency's role in perpetuating racism. Harjeet Badwall (2014) describes ways in which racism plays out in social work organizations, not only affecting clients but also affecting staff, with particular implications for workers of color. Badwall raises the concern that professional emphasis on empathy and client-centered practice may lead social workers to tolerate rather than interrupt racism on the part of clients. Workers of color are placed in a contradictory position of being targets of racism and at the same time seen as "unempathetic" if they confront or disrupt racism. Badwall argues that it is the responsibility of social work organizations to resist and disrupt racism, to intervene and show support of colleagues, and to make both racism and a positive diversity stance talkable themes in the organizational context.

The Western States Center, a capacity-building organization for progressive leadership and organizing for social, racial, gender, economic, and environmental justice based in Portland, Oregon, has developed practical tools for assessing racial and LGBTQ equity in organizations. Its framework for assessing organizational racism is part of a broader Dismantling Racism project (Western States Center, 2001, 2003). It is premised on the belief that racism is everyone's problem, whether or not there are people of color involved in the organization. The assessment is framed around a series of questions to spark dialogue among organizational participants. The following is a sampling of questions; readers are referred to "Assessing Organizational Racism" (Western States Center, 2001, pp. 14–15) for the complete assessment tool.

- *Who makes decisions in your organization?* Does your organization have a goal to dismantle racism? Is this goal reflected in your decision-making process?

- *Who has control and influence over financial resources?* When the budget or fundraising plan reflects work to be done in support of people of color communities, do these communities have input on where the money comes from or how it is spent?
- *What kind of education about racism and oppression is provided through the organization?* Are people of color supported in seeking information around issues of internalized racist oppression and self-empowerment, either within the organization or from outside the organization?
- *What is the culture of your organization?* What are the values and norms, stated or unstated?
- *How does your organization work in alliance with people of color organizations?* Does your organization provide support and resources for members, staff, and board members of color to develop leadership through working with organizations or campaigns led by people of color?

The Western States Center has also developed an assessment tool to identify gaps and opportunities to strengthen LGBTQ equality within organizations (Western States Center, 2011). The assessment process creates a starting point for organizational dialogue related to support of LGBTQ rights and issues, provides a process for assessing organizational strengths and weaknesses, and sets the stage for identifying ways to strengthen organizational capacity and leadership related to LBGTQ issues. The assessment examines five organizational dimensions: program, policies, power, culture, and people. The assessment process includes questions such as the following (excerpted from "Assessing Our Organizations," Western States Center, 2011, pp. 4–5):

- Does your organization talk about LGBTQ issues in general?
- Is your organization accountable to and does it seek leadership from LGBTQ individuals and/or organizations within your own community?
- Does your organization have antidiscrimination policies that explicitly prohibit harassment of LGBTQ members of the organization?
- Is gender identity and sexual orientation part of the diversity your organization seeks among its staff, leadership, and members?
- Do people in leadership positions participate in and support discussion of power and oppression issues, especially around LGBTQ issues?

The complete assessment and facilitation guide are available through the Western States Center website (http://www.westernstatescenter.org). These practical tools are geared to spark organizational consciousness, make oppression visible and talkable, and guide critical practice for organizational transformation.

Teaching-Learning with Individuals and Families

We now turn to approaches to learning about individual and family experience. Most social work texts start with the individual and move outward to consider organizational and community contexts of practice. We take a reverse approach. We argue that practice with individuals takes place in broader community and organizational contexts and that effective social justice work demands ongoing critical awareness of those contexts as we engage with individuals and families. In this section, we introduce some conventional approaches to assessment, reflect on their strengths and limitations, and consider further possibilities for teaching-learning.

Biopsychosocial Assessments

Traditional social work assessments generally follow a specific format. The social worker seeks a detailed description of the problem, presenting symptoms, and history from the client (Graybeal, 2001, p. 235):

- The problem's history (e.g., onset, duration, and previous treatment)
- The client's personal history (e.g., medical history, developmental milestones, and any history of abuse)
- Substance use (e.g., patterns of use, substances of choice, and consequences of use)
- Family history (e.g., description of relationships, family-related stresses, and cultural influences and history of physical or mental illness)
- Employment history (e.g., educational history, past and current employment, and employment-related stresses)
- Summary and treatment recommendations (e.g., *DSM* diagnosis, summary of concerns, and recommended treatment plan)

Biopsychosocial assessments expand on this framework, offering a more holistic perspective through exploration of the biological, psychological, sociocultural, and spiritual domains of a person's experience. The biological domain attends both to physical health and well-being and to basic needs and impact of the client's physical environment. The psychological domain explores questions of personality, identity, intelligence, and psychological history. The sociocultural domain considers family, social networks, ethnic, and social environment. The spiritual domain attends to a person's values, sense of meaning and purpose, and religious or spiritual life (Graybeal, 2001, p. 236). In the context of agency practice, the biopsychosocial assessment process is often structured and formulaic with primary attention given to the traditional assessment categories and less attention paid to the environmental and structural arrangements that shape individual experience. Take a moment to think about this traditional assessment process. What does it capture? What does it leave out?

> **Individual Learning Activity:**
> **Biopsychosocial Assessment Formats**
>
> Gather samples of biopsychosocial assessment formats from a variety of social work agencies in your community, including child and family service agencies, hospitals, youth treatment centers, and nursing homes. What are the similarities and differences among them? What do you notice about them? What do they focus on? What do they leave out?

Strengths Assessment

Clay Graybeal (2001) argues that most biopsychsocial assessments fail to attend to an individual's strengths. He has expanded and reframed the assessment process to incorporate strengths. Graybeal suggests that each of the content areas of traditional assessments can be areas for exploring strengths as well. He offers the ROPES (resources, options, possibilities, exceptions, and solutions) model as one tool for bringing strengths to bear. Each of these components provides a venue for exploring strengths (Graybeal, 2001, p. 237). What personal, family, or community resources may be available? What are other possible options that have not yet been tried? What are the possibilities for the future? When is the problem not happening? What is different then? What's working now? What are your successes?

Graybeal argues that it is possible to transform the assessment process by attending to strengths. He notes, however, that professional training that focuses on pathology and funding mechanisms that require diagnoses work against a strength-oriented approach. He challenges social workers to be part of a transformational practice by re-visioning assessment from a strengths perspective.

Assessing Individual Strengths in Older Adults

Social workers are recognizing the importance of identifying abilities, values and interests, cultural beliefs/practices, life contributions, and protections and supports as potential sources of information that provide a balanced approach to assessment with older adults. In reaction to assessment tools heavily influenced by the medical model, Helen Kivnick and Shirley Murray (2001) proposed a framework for gerontological assessment that balances problems and assets to help with intervention planning. By recognizing strengths, they challenge concepts of aging as synonymous with asset loss. They report that, although older people are teaching the practitioner about their strengths and limitations, they are also learning that their strengths are not confined to the past and can be reactivated in the present. Following is Kivnick and Murray's guide for conducting an assessment with older clients.

Strengths Assessment Interview Guide
(Kivnick & Murray, 2001, p. 32)

1. What makes a day a *good* day for you? What do you hope for at the start of a new day?
2. What are the things you do, each day or each week, because you really want to, not because you have to? When you get totally absorbed, forget about everything else, and time seems to fly?
3. What are you good at? What kinds of things did you used to be good at? What about yourself has always given you confidence or made you proud?
4. What kinds of exercise do you do regularly? What kinds could you do to help you feel better?
5. What kinds of help, service, or assistance do you give? To whom? What help or service would you like to give?
6. When you get out, what do you like to do? Where do you like to go? What would you like to do? Where would you like to go?
7. What lessons have you learned about how to cope with life from day to day? Are there ways you wish you could cope better?
8. Who are the people who are especially important to you these days? Talk about these relationships.
9. What physical things or objects do you have that are most precious to you? What things do you save? Or take special care of? If you had to relocate, what things would you take with you?

What other questions might you ask to learn about an older adult? Are there some listed you might omit or modify? If so, why? In what other ways could you apply the guide? How could you modify it for other areas of practice?

Ecomaps and Genograms

Considerable attention has been focused on an ecosystems approach to individuals in the context of family, with assessment directed toward two broad dimensions: family history and relationship to other systems in the environment. We introduce and describe two commonly used tools here—the ecomap and the genogram. The *ecomap* provides an opportunity for identifying, illustrating, and examining key aspects of a person's social context, sources of support, and stress; flows of energy and resources; and patterns among them (Hartman & Laird, 1983; Seabury, Seabury, & Garvin, 2011, pp. 356–357). Generally, the tool is used in a context of dialogue between social worker and client. With the help of prompts and questions posed by the social worker, the client maps out her current situation.

Ecomaps and Some Adaptations

In the ecomap, the client identifies people and social systems that are part of or that affect his current life situation. He links the systems to himself and possibly to and from others with lines that mark the direction of energy and resource flow in the relationship and the nature of the relationship. For example: a solid, bold line (——) indicates a strong relationship, a dotted line (- - - - -) indicates a tenuous relationship, and a slashed line (-/-/-/-/) indicates a stressful or conflicted relationship. Arrows are used to indicate the directions of energy and resource flow (toward the client, away from him, or a two-way flow). The ecomap provides a visual window into the person's current life circumstances. The client directs the process of creating the ecomap and thus presents his own perspective on his circumstances. The ecomap can serve as a basis for further questions regarding both stressors and sources of support. It can also serve as a guide for action planning.

A basic family ecomap may look something like figure 6.2. In the original formulation of ecomaps, circles represented women and squares men. The Multicultural Family Institute has since expanded on this symbolic representation using combinations of circles, squares, and triangles to represent gay, lesbian, bisexual, and transgender identities (see http://multiculturalfamily.org for examples). Here we present the example of a thirty-five-year-old heterosexual woman who is widowed (indicated by X) and has two children, an eleven-year-old boy and a seven-year-old girl. The map shows that she has stressful relations with her work and her landlord. Her daughter has a tenuous relationship with school due to absences, and her son is experiencing school-related struggles. Her church and extended family are possible sources of support, but that support is currently tenuous.

Figure 6.2
Ecomap

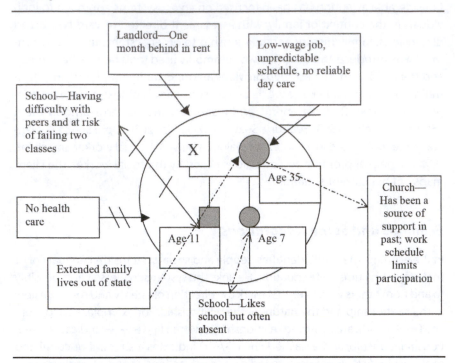

Nancy Vosler (1996) has drawn attention to poverty and food insecurity as central sources of everyday struggle and stress in the lives of social service users. She has used the ecomap to identify family issues related to economic stress. Whereas some families may have developed ingenious methods for coping with financial distress such as tapping into the resources of extended family networks, others may not have access to or developed these resources. Vosler's (1990) theoretical framework rests on understanding the effects of the larger political, social, and economic environment on families and "the link between symptoms and chronic stress from lack of basic economic resources" (p. 434).

Figure 6.3 shows the same household ecomap with a focus on the multiple facets of economic stress that the family faces. Vosler (1990) indicates "how symptomatic families are easily blamed for their inability to provide for the basic needs of family members" (p. 435). How might this particular focus of an ecomap on financial issues and connections to social service resources (or lack thereof) help in the teaching-learning process? How might it challenge us to

Figure 6.3
Household ecomap: Family unconnected to resources and stressed

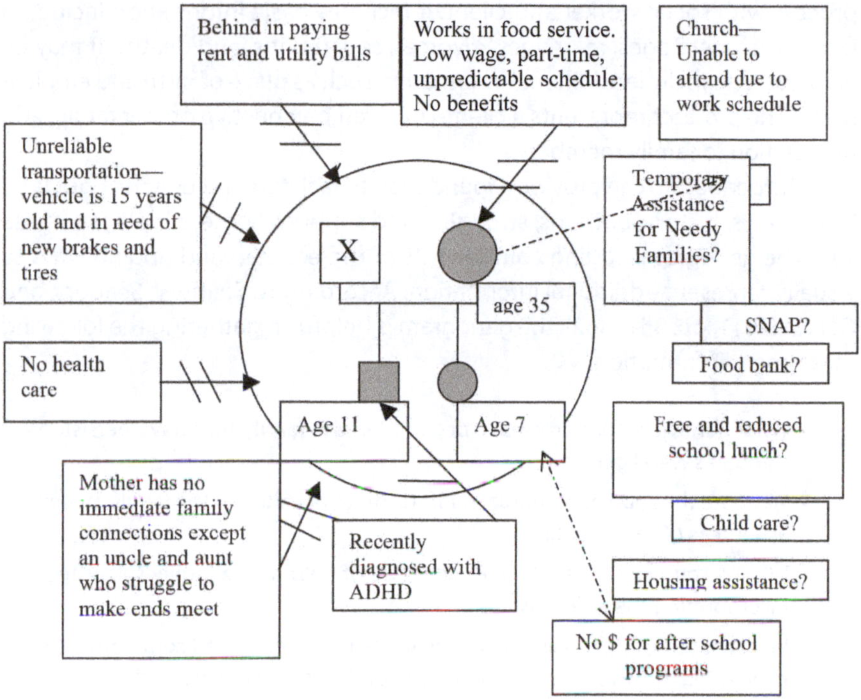

Behind in paying rent and utility bills

Works in food service. Low wage, part-time, unpredictable schedule. No benefits

Church— Unable to attend due to work schedule

Unreliable transportation— vehicle is 15 years old and in need of new brakes and tires

Temporary Assistance for Needy Families?

X

age 35

SNAP?

No health care

Food bank?

Age 11

Age 7

Free and reduced school lunch?

Mother has no immediate family connections except an uncle and aunt who struggle to make ends meet

Child care?

Recently diagnosed with ADHD

Housing assistance?

No $ for after school programs

look to events and experiences external to the family as causes of family struggles? What else would you want to consider here in terms of stresses and sources of support? How might attention to economic factors shape the direction of social work involvement with the family?

Genograms and Some Adaptations

Another commonly cited social work tool for learning about individuals in the context of family is the genogram. The genogram borrows from anthropological kinship studies and focuses on the mapping of intergenerational family relationships (Hartman, 1978). Proponents of the genogram see it as an important complement to the ecomap. The genogram contributes a historical perspective lacking in the ecomap. It can also serve as the base for exploration and discussion of family relations, cultural practices, and traditions. The genogram focuses on the intergenerational extended family, and it is represented visually as a family tree. The genogram is created in a collaborative teaching-learning process with social worker and client. It includes basic information including family members' ages, marriages, divorces, separations, and deaths. It may be elaborated to include additional information such as place of birth and employment. The product represents a client-centered perspective on her family and her relation to family members.

The genogram can provide a foundation to facilitate discussion about family relations, history, patterns, struggles, and support. Some people improvise with the genogram, adding components of the ecomap and finding ways to visually represent additional information. According to Seabury, Seabury, and Garvin (2011, pp. 361–362), the genogram is helpful in gathering the following assessment information:

- What behavioral patterns have occurred in the family that have persisted through several generations?
- What are the sources of mutual reinforcement of values in the family as well as sources of value conflict?
- What resources exist that are or could be of help to the family subsystem incorporating the client system?
- What are the kinds of issues related to the family's beliefs and common experiences that function to limit the family's problem solving and decision making or to enhance it?

Numerous scholars and practitioners have experimented with the genogram's potential as an assessment tool, created new formats and procedures, and highlighted different foci for its use. Sandy Magnuson and Holly Shaw (2003) have mapped the historical evolution of the genogram. They describe the genogram's use with couples to explore family-of-origin issues concerning sexuality, intimacy, and gender dynamics and how these influence decision making, communication patterns, and rules established to address them. For example, in the process of creating a genogram, a couple might be asked questions such as what were you taught about sexuality as a child and what did your father/mother teach you about being male/female? Magnuson and Shaw also discuss how genograms have been used to help stepfamilies understand the complexities of family structure and relationships, to address issues of grief and loss, to document the multiple foster care or residential placements of children, to identify family strengths, and to increase trainees' awareness of and sensitivity to cultural diversity. In what ways might you apply the genogram or modify this tool for relevance in another area of practice other than those suggested above? What seems to be missing in these discussions of the genogram?

Individual Learning Activity: Mapping Your Family Story

To learn more about the genogram, check out Natalie Pope and Jacquelyn Lee's (2015) guide to creating a genogram in the *New Social Worker* (2015). You can also access the guide online (http://www.mediafire.com/view/z89h9er9cpa2ue7/spring2015.pdf). Take time outside of class to prepare your own genogram. Feel free to make it as simple or elaborate as you wish, according to what best represents your concept and experience of family. After you have completed the genogram, take time to reflect on the feelings this exercise evoked for you. Are there gaps in your knowledge of family history? Do you have questions about who counts as family and where to draw the boundaries? Does the exercise bring back memories of loss or connection? What have you learned from your own experience in completing the genogram that may heighten your critical awareness about using this tool with others?

We have highlighted some of the dominant approaches to assessment with individuals and families. We invite you to reflect on your practice with individuals and families, perhaps in the context of your practicum or work experience. How might your critical understanding of the teaching-learning process change your practice? What new questions might you pose? What new learning might you encounter? How might you teach others in your social work organizations to think in critical and creative ways about the possibilities of teaching-learning?

Challenges of Teaching-Learning

As we stated at the beginning of this chapter, teaching-learning is an ongoing process that requires openness to multiple ways of knowing and critical awareness of the partiality of our knowledge and experience. Remaining open to co-learning is no small task in a Western context replete with messages about the need to make rapid-fire decisions and to move on and get it done for the sake of efficiency and expediency. The teaching-learning process is ripe with rewards for increased awareness of self and others. However, it is a humbling, time-consuming process that requires considerable attention to sustain the effort, contribute our knowledge without taking over the process, and admit we may be wrong when our ideas are challenged. Teaching-learning demands that we grapple with meanings of power on both personal and professional levels and come to understand how it works in our own lives.

SUMMARY

In this chapter we have developed the concept of teaching-learning—a collaborative process through which we give meaning to experience; learn about concerns; and systematically develop, share, and reflect on knowledge of those concerns. We have examined questions of power and power relations in the teaching-learning process and have pointed to the importance of making power a talkable theme. We have addressed human rights and the importance of a human rights framework to inform and transform the teaching-learning process. And we have spoken to the power of naming and addressing racism and other forms of oppression in practice with individuals and families as well as in organizational and community contexts. We have introduced a number of approaches for systematic inquiry into individual, family, group, organizational, and community contexts of social work practice.

In chapter 7 we will consider the possibilities for translating the process and outcomes of teaching-learning into concrete action plans. We close with a brief account of the work of the National Native Child Trauma Center, which brings processes of engagement, teaching-learning, action, accompaniment, and evidence-based research to bear in promoting the well-being of Native children and youth.

ON REFLECTION

Promoting Social Justice in Indian Country: The National Native Child Trauma Center

Marilyn Bruguier Zimmerman, MSW, Director, NNCTC

Since the sixteenth century, generations of America's indigenous people have survived an appalling history of wars, pandemics, starvation, and destructive federal policies meant to assimilate tribes into western European ways of life. Federal policies included forced relocation, forced removal of children to be educated in boarding schools, and prohibition of spiritual and cultural practices. The consequences of these catastrophic events were the erosion of the tribes' robust culture and well-established social norms. These events contributed to and intensified today's contemporary traumatic experiences of interpersonal violence, child abuse and neglect, substance abuse and addiction, suicide, and poor health outcomes (Braveheart & DeBruyn, 1998; Campbell & Evans-Campbell, 2011; Gone, 2004).

The U.S. attorney general's report on American Indian and Alaska Native (AIAN) children exposed to violence found that, for many tribal communities, 100 percent of the children had been exposed to violence (U.S. Attorney General's Advisory Committee, 2014). These levels of exposure to violence are taking a toll on the psychological well-being of AIAN children. When exposure to traumatic events occurs frequently or when traumatic stress is left unaddressed, children are susceptible to relationship problems, substance abuse, depression, suicidal thoughts and behaviors, anxiety, and traumatic stress disorders.

It is within this reality that the National Native Children's Trauma Center (NNCTC) at the University of Montana advances evidence-based trauma interventions and trauma-informed services systems that are also culturally appropriate to improve the standard of care for AIAN children and families. The U.S. Substance Abuse and Mental Health Services Administration (SAMHSA), under the National Child Traumatic Stress Initiative, funded the NNCTC in 2007.

The cultural adaptation of evidence-based interventions requires the integration of the tribal values and respect for the tribe's spiritual and cultural ways while maintaining the fidelity of the intervention. This is complicated work. It is work that must be done in relationship with local cultural practitioners willing to wrestle with concepts from both indigenous and Western worldviews in order to create healing for the children and their families. It is critical that NNCTC acknowledge the beliefs, practices, and traditions of tribes that have brought healing to their people for centuries.

The NNCTC promotes the understanding that culturally responsive childhood traumatic stress interventions are a vital component of comprehensive, community-based behavioral health programs for AIAN children and youth at risk. The NNCTC considers that, for mental health interventions to be effective, they must be locally appropriate and culturally relevant, respectful of tribal wisdom, based on the tribal communities' awareness of the impacts and prevalence of trauma (historic, intergenerational, and contemporary), and practical for use by community providers, clinicians, and family members.

Finally, the training and technical assistance provided to tribal communities by the NNCTC must respect tribal sovereignty through all phases of intervention and system implementation, relying on the guidance of tribes in establishing a collaborative process to implement, adapt, and evaluate trauma interventions. To learn more, visit the NNCTC website (http://iers.umt.edu/National_Native_Childrens_Trauma_Center/default.php).

QUESTIONS FOR DISCUSSION

1. What does it mean to *problematize* conventional thinking about assessment? What might be an example of a problematic assessment process or tool?

2. What are some of the concerns raised about a *medicalized* approach to assessment? How might it affect approaches to action and outcomes?

3. How might you use a power analysis in your current social work practice? What possibilities for co-learning and action might it offer?

4. How might you bring human rights to bear in the teaching-learning process? How might a human rights perspective inform action?

5. How might you use a listening survey in your current social work practice? What possibilities for co-learning and action might it offer?

SUGGESTED READINGS

Blitz, L.V., Kida, L., Gresham, M., & Bronstein, L. (2013). Prevention through collaboration: Family engagement with rural schools and families living in poverty. *Families in Society*, *94*, 157–165.

Graybeal, C. (2001). Strengths-based social work assessment: Transforming the dominant paradigm. *Families in Society*, *82*, 233–242.

McDowell, T., Libal, K., & Brown, A. (2012). Human right in the practice of family therapy. Domestic violence as a case in point. *Journal of Feminist Family Therapy*, *24*, 1–23.

Mezirow, J. (2009). Transformative learning theory. In J. Mezirow & E.W. Taylor (Eds.), *Transformative learning in practice: Insights from community, workplace, and higher education* (pp. 18–32). San Francisco: Jossey-Bass.

Chapter 7

Action and Accompaniment

It was so important. It was really a beautiful thing, women coming together to work together. We started small and we learned everything. We learned we were capable, we could do this. We talked and laughed and it was so special. It was a road to a new life of learning. It was a beautiful experience working and learning together, block by block, helping each other.

Ana, Villa Paula Jaraquemada, Chile (Finn, 2001)

OVERVIEW

In this chapter we explore the interwoven processes of action and accompaniment. Action entails the diverse activities of planning, supporting, decision making, mobilizing resources, motivating participants, challenging barriers, and following through in creating change. Action occurs in the company of others. A challenge of social justice work is the integration of being in a relationship with others, doing the work, and becoming more critically aware and capable in the process. It is in this spirit of being, doing, and becoming that we pair action and accompaniment. We want to challenge the view of action as the technical implementation of a series of interventions and consider it instead as an endeavor that is always carried out in the context of social relationships. We emphasize accompaniment as part of the change process as a reminder that social work is a collaborative endeavor. The relational aspect of social justice work demands ongoing attention and respect. We address the concepts, processes, and contexts of action and accompaniment and consider roles of social justice workers. We draw examples from social workers across diverse arenas of practice. We explore challenges and questions of power and difference involved in action and accompaniment. We present skills and practices of action and accompaniment and the possibilities for their integration on multiple fronts in pursuit of social justice.

CONCEPT AND PROCESS OF ACTION

We are very intentional in the use of the word *action* here. As Kelly and Sewell (1988) remind us, social work entails actual work—the *doing* that puts ideas to

287

practice. Action is inseparable from thought and feeling, but thought and feeling devoid of meaningful action are at best insincere and at worst one more form of violation. We have also chosen the word action as a way of distinguishing the process from what most social work texts refer to as *intervention*. We do this for two reasons. First, intervention connotes an expert acting on a passive subject (Deegan, 1996; Deepak, 2011; Larson, 2008). In keeping with the model of mutuality and dialogue that we have developed thus far, we contrast the Just Practice approach with this sort of top-down model. By speaking of action we honor the human agency of all participants in the process. Second, unlike intervention, which suggests the application of technologies and techniques, action is a more fluid concept, suggestive of the emergent and dynamic nature of personal and social transformation. Action simultaneously encompasses the personal and the political, doing and becoming—the grounded work and the transformational potential.

Action may take many forms, from direct service to meet immediate needs to participation in labor solidarity work, human rights campaigns, and peace and justice movements. It may be manifest in caring, protection, support, and nurturance. It may be realized through teaching of skills and political education; through exercises in consciousness raising; in confrontation and demands for work; in brainstorming, planning, and decision-making activities; through mediation, negotiation, and conflict resolution; in advocacy, organization building, and direct action campaigns; and through collaborations, coalitions, and legislative initiatives.

Action in the present contains within it reverberations of the past. Our claims and actions regarding issues such as *best interests*, *at risk*, and *in need of protection* are not chaste. They are embedded in historical, cultural, and political contexts. We cannot assume a common understanding of these concepts or the correctness of our beliefs. Instead, part of our responsibility in taking action is to bring these loaded issues forward and to create the space to listen and learn, to address them transparently and candidly, and to be willing to challenge and change our practice in ways that honor others' experience, rights, and dignity. Our action is always political in the sense that it is conceived and carried out in the context of dynamic relations of power. It is interpreted and often contested by the various meaning makers involved. And it carries with it the weight of history.

Action and critical reflection are intertwined, mutually informing processes. Resistance and refusal may also constitute powerful forms of action as we work toward elimination of oppression and promotion of social justice both within and beyond the bounds of human service organizations. Action includes a vision of a future and of an alternative reality (Reisch, 2011). Whatever forms our actions take, a distinguishing feature of Just Practice is that we do not guard our actions and skills as professional secrets. Rather, we share them with others, thereby expanding the capacities and skill repertoire of all participants. Later in the chapter we will explore forms and skills of action, illustrating how they cut across arenas and contexts of practice.

CONCEPT AND PROCESS OF ACCOMPANIMENT

Understanding Accompaniment

Accompaniment refers to the actual people-to-people partnerships through which action is realized. It represents another facet of practice in which we are once again reminded of the commitment to collaboration and dialogue over the long haul and to the interplay of power and possibility that shapes practice. Traditional approaches to the change process in social work often refer to the *monitoring* of intervention. The notion of monitoring positions the social worker outside the process and in the role of overseer. It places the burden for action on others and suggests that the worker retains the power of scrutiny. The language of monitoring disconnects the worker from her relationship to the participants in the process. We find the notion of accompaniment more conducive to the values and assumptions of social justice work.

In its simplest terms, accompaniment means "to go with another, to support and enhance the process." We develop our notion of accompaniment from the work of Canadian social workers and educators Elizabeth Whitmore and Maureen Wilson (1997, pp. 57–58), whose understanding emerged through work with colleagues in Nicaragua. Whitmore and Wilson describe the relationship of social justice workers to the communities, groups, and individuals with whom they are engaged as one of *acompañamiento*, a Spanish term that best translates as accompanying the process. They write, "We are attracted to this way of expressing such a relationship precisely because of its inherent clarity about who owns and controls the process: our partners do; it is *we* who accompany *their* process" (p. 58). They have identified a set of principles of accompaniment, which have applicability to a variety of settings (Wilson & Whitmore, 1995, 2000). These include

- Nonintrusive collaboration
- Mutual trust and respect
- Common analysis of what the problem is
- Commitment to solidarity

- Equality in the relationship
- Explicit focus on process
- Importance of language

Wilson and Whitmore (1995) contend that true partnership calls for the democratization of information flow, collaborative knowledge development and dissemination, and action networking. It demands attention to power relations, time and timing, language and meaning, and access to resources. Accompaniment is a process of "participatory alignment" that attends to the ways in which marginalized people become critical agents of transformation, going beyond personal troubles to public issues (p. 61). They describe how their own thinking was challenged through the process of accompaniment. For example, many of the conceptual frameworks that shaped their assumptions were developed in English and reflected a "long ideological history and way of life" that were not readily translatable to the Nicaraguan context (Whitmore & Wilson, 1997, pp. 66–67). Based on their experiences they conclude that "sympathetic listening, engaged questioning, nondirective suggesting, and solidarity in the face of setback are the stuff of accompaniment" (p. 68). Accompaniment is a process of joining across diverse borders to build mutual trust; explore possibilities for cooperative work and division of labor; and create a two-way movement of people, knowledge, and power (see also Whitmore & Wilson, 2005).

Wilson and Whitmore's understanding of accompaniment resonates with a number of other conceptualizations of the relational component of action. Physician and anthropologist Paul Farmer describes accompaniment as the centerpiece of lessons he has learned over his years of work in Haiti. Farmer describes the commitment over time that characterizes accompaniment:

> To accompany someone is to go somewhere with him or her, to break bread together, to be present on a journey with a beginning and an end. . . . There's an element of mystery, of openness, in accompaniment: I'll go with you and support you on your journey wherever it leads. I'll keep you company and share your fate for a while. And by "a while," I don't mean a little while. Accompaniment is much more often about sticking with a task until it's deemed completed by the person or people being accompanied, rather than by the [one accompanying]. (2011, p. 1)

Accompaniment is also central to the practice of hospice care, in which volunteers join with the person who is dying and share in the journey. Alan Wolfelt (2004) describes the process of companioning in hospice care:

- Companioning is about walking alongside; it is less about leading or being led.
- Companioning is more about curiosity; it is less about expertise.
- Companioning the dying is often more about being still; it is not always about urgent movement forward.
- Companioning is about being present to another's emotional and spiritual pain; it is not taking away or fixing it.
- Companioning is about going into the wilderness of the soul with another human being; it is not about thinking you are responsible for finding a way out.

A notion of accompaniment is also present in Bonnie Benard's (2006) discussion of the significance of caring relationships in the stories of resilient survivors of child sexual abuse. According to Benard, survivors talk about relationships characterized by "quiet availability," "fundamental positive regard," and "simple sustained kindness." Caring people who conveyed compassion and demonstrated "active genuine interest" played important roles in nurturing and sustaining the resilience of survivors (p. 200). In this sense, we can imagine accompaniment as the ongoing melding of relationship and action. Catherine Faver, in turn, provides further food for thought on the process of accompaniment. In writing about women's relational spirituality and social caregiving, Faver describes ways in which women of faith talk about the fundamental connectedness of spirituality and social justice in their lives and work: "Many described a sense of sacred companionship that pervaded their lives" (2004, p. 244). Thus, for some, social workers and participants alike, accompaniment may have a spiritual as well as a social and political dimension.

Accompaniment and Alliance

Effective accompaniment demands reflection on what it means to be an ally and how we build alliances. Effective allies are engaged in ongoing critical reflection on the balance of power and the importance of autonomy as well as connection. Gloria Anzaldúa (2000) speaks powerfully about allies from her perspective as a Chicana lesbian feminist:

> Becoming allies means helping each other heal. It can be hard to expose yourself and your wounds to a stranger who could be an ally or an enemy. But if you and I were to do good alliance work together, be good allies to each other, I

would have to expose my wounds to you and you would have to expose your wounds to me and then we could start from a place of openness. During our alliance work, doors will close and we'll have to open them again. People who engage in alliances and are working toward certain goals want to keep their personal feelings out of it, but you can't. You have to work out your personal problems while you are working out the problems of this particular community or the particular culture. (p. 495)

Anzaldúa asks those in positions of relative privilege to reflect critically on their motives for building alliances. Are they looking to assimilate the *other* voice? Are they trying to avoid charges of elitism and racism? She warns that the biggest risk in forming alliances is betrayal:

When you are betrayed you feel shitty. . . . And betrayal makes you feel like less of a person—you feel shame, it reduces your self-esteem. It is politically deadening and dangerous; it's disempowering. (p. 496)

Margaret Ledwith and Paula Asgill (2000) propose the concept of *critical alliance*, which they argue is vital to the future of community work and collective action for social justice. They draw from their identities and collaborative work experiences as an African Caribbean woman and a white British woman in attempting to articulate the crafting of alliance across difference. They begin with acknowledgment of their differences and critical reflection on the sociopolitical context in which they are coming together. They take seriously questions regarding the unspoken privileges of whiteness and questions of "'black rage,' which is silenced within this whiteness" (hooks, 1995, p. 11; as cited in Ledwith & Asgill, 2000, p. 291). They argue that effective alliances need to address the complexity of identities as "emergent histories which are located at the critical intersection of our lived experience within the social, cultural, and economic relations of our time, shifting, not fixed" (Ledwith & Asgill, 2000, p. 293). They contend that effective community work calls for honest engagement with these knotty issues.

They speak to the challenge of dialogue across difference and the need to explore the anger, the silences, and the misunderstandings between themselves through ongoing honest conversation. They echo Anzaldúa's contention that developing alliances is a painful process, but that naming and exposing pain is essential to transformative action.

ACTION AND ACCOMPANIMENT IN CONTEXT

We have developed the concept of *context* and explored ideas about diverse contexts of social work practice in earlier chapters. We ask readers to keep questions of context in mind as we explore action and accompaniment. Our actions and relations are always embedded in contexts, which shape the nature of the interpersonal encounter, the power relations among participants, the goals and pathways of action, the available resources, and the outcomes. Social justice work calls for the recognition of context, as opposed to the context stripping that has characterized too much of traditional problem-focused social work. Social justice work challenges us to engage in action that is both "context relevant and context changing" as it opens spaces for possibility and transformation (van Wormer & McKenney, 2003). Action and accompaniment may have diverse starting points: with individuals, families, organizations, governmental bodies, or community groups. By practicing contextually we are constantly mindful of the connective tissue linking people's lives to larger histories and systems. We will address context more specifically through a variety of examples presented in the rest of the chapter.

Challenging Oppression and Creating Contexts of Support

Questions of trust, power, and authority and courses of action may look very different in the context of child protective services than in the context of housing rights advocacy or hospice care. We argue, however, that a social justice approach to action calls on us to first and foremost honor human rights and dignity, *especially* in those contexts where we are working with those whose rights have been violated and with those who have violated the rights of others (Ife, 2012; Skegg, 2005). Furthermore, it is our responsibility to contribute to the creation of supportive contexts—caring communities, engaged families, welcoming schools, and learning organizations. In so doing, we need to be constantly mindful of the ways in which oppression plays out in diverse institutional, organizational, and community settings as well as the ways interpersonal relationships and family or group dynamics may be shaped by practices of power and oppression among members.

In chapter 3 we addressed the prevalence of heterosexism in schools, which produces a "toxic environment for gender-nonconforming girls and boys" (van Wormer & McKinney, 2003, p. 410). Katherine van Wormer and

Robin McKinney cite examples, from the heteronormative view of sexuality embedded in abstinence-only sex education to the prevalence of antigay epithets and verbal and physical harassment that too often goes unchecked. Unsafe school environments for lesbian, gay, bisexual, transgender, and queer (LGBTQ) youth persist when teachers and administrators are reluctant to disrupt harassment and respond as allies (Kosciw, Greytak, Palmer, & Boesen, 2014; Palmer, Kosciw, & Bartkiewicz, 2012). Van Wormer and McKinney argue that action on behalf of LGBTQ youth must be both context relevant and context changing. It is not enough to attend to the individual pain of an adolescent client trying to survive in this context. Rather, van Wormer and McKinney call for a harm-reduction approach that encompasses preventive measures aimed at helping all youth with issues of sexual identity and gender expression; public consciousness raising about sexuality, sexual identity, gender expression, and nondiscrimination; group work with young people to build support through gay/straight alliances; teacher training in crisis intervention; acquisition of library materials that speak to diverse experiences of sexual identity; program development to create school-wide anti-bullying programs; community organizing with parent-teacher associations to promote a culture of support; and advocacy work to redress discriminatory school policies. In short, they support *integrated* action that addresses the intersections of multiple forces of power and oppression that shape young people's lives in the everyday context of schooling and recognize the rights of youth to safe learning environments and to expression of gender and sexual identity. Social justice work entails concerted action on multiple fronts to respond to individual suffering and to develop welcoming school climates for all students. It also creates opportunities for accompanying those most affected by oppressive contexts through processes of environmental as well as personal transformation.

It Gets Better Project

For an inspiring example of the use of social media as a context for support and empowerment of LGBTQ young people, check out the It Gets Better Project (http://www.itgetsbetter.org). The project's mission is to communicate to LGBTQ youth around the world that life gets better and to inspire changes in attitudes, actions, and institutions. Launched in 2010 by Seattle author Dan Savage and his partner Terry Miller as a forum for sharing user-made videos, It Gets Better has grown to a global movement to promote positive change for LGBTQ youth.

Risk, Rights, and Responsibilities

Right to Take Risks

Social justice work must critically address the context of everyday life through both mindfulness of rights and challenge to discriminatory approaches to risk that jeopardize rights. As Patricia Deegan has argued, people diagnosed with mental illness have the right to take risks and the right to try and possibly fail (or succeed), whether at work, in relationships, or in community living, just as do people who do not bear a diagnostic label. Likewise, Liz Sayce calls for social workers to challenge the stereotypes that underpin unfair risk thinking in mental health, to interrupt the discourse of *us* and *them* that sustains the stigmatizing of labeled persons, and to champion the rights of labeled persons to participate as equals in the decisions that affect their lives (2005, pp. 176–177).

Much of social work practice plays out amid contexts and discourses of risk and notions of who is deemed to be a risk or at risk. Risk assessments are routinely conducted in child protection cases, mental health crisis interventions, and adult protective services. Practice in these contexts of risk often involves involuntary participants. Our social work practice may also call on us to engage with people who have acted violently toward others. We do not check social justice at the door when facing these challenges.

Risk and Protection

Viviene Cree and Susan Wallace (2005) argue that social work in relation to risk and protection needs to be grounded by four cornerstones of practice: legislation, policy, procedure, and rights. Social workers need firm knowledge of the relevant legislation regarding their area of practice, such as child and adult protection, criminal justice, domestic violence, or mental health. Furthermore, social workers need to be aware of "procedural legislation as it applies to specific work activities" (Cree & Wallace, 2005, p. 117). For example, what is the procedure for investigation and action in cases of child sexual abuse? What is the procedure for making an assessment of imminent harm to self or others? Social workers need to be aware of government policy directives that affect practice. Additionally, social workers need to continually update their knowledge regarding internal organizational policies and procedures through which larger mandates are enacted and monitored. What is the agency protocol for assessing risk in determining a child's removal to out-of-home care? What is the procedure for responding to a report of suicide risk regarding a client of a mental health facility or resident of a group home?

Too often, the authors argue, while workers are attending to these three corners of responsibility, attention to rights falls by the wayside. When we lose sight of rights, we lose cognizance of another's full humanity and of our responsibilities to honor one another's dignity. Further, attention to dignity and rights may provide grounds for questioning the assumptions informing legislation and the ways in which it is translated into policies and procedures. Concern for rights can provide the basis for grassroots advocacy for social justice. Can you think of an example from your own practice experience where policies and procedures have taken priority over client rights? How might you advocate for client rights in the context of your practice? Where might you encounter resistance and support?

Mental Health, Rights, and Anti-oppressive Practice

The preceding discussion suggests the power of risk discourse to overwhelm that of rights. Decisions may be made regarding the "best interests" of people deemed to be vulnerable without their participation in the process. Social justice work challenges us to consider risk within a broader context of rights and responsibilities. Let's take a closer look at questions of risks, rights, and responsibilities and the possibilities for challenging oppression and creating contexts of support through consideration of contemporary social justice work in mental health. Grant Larson (2008) has articulated seven principles of anti-oppressive practice to inform and transform social work in mental health settings:

1. Invite services users to be full participants in all aspects of service (including staff meetings, case conference, and other facets of organizational operation). Treat them as experts, and take what they say about their mental distress seriously.

2. Use language that is respectful and empowering. Challenge and go beyond a medicalized focus.

3. Actively deconstruct the medical model. Consciously bring a more holistic, strengths-focused perspective to bear.

4. Establish working relationships based on trust, power sharing, and collaboration.

5. Take responsibility to promote education, including anti-stigma education for professionals and a larger public along with ongoing education on anti-oppressive practice.

6. Embrace cultural diversity. Draw on the services user's cultural strengths and challenge ethnocentrism of assessment tools and diagnostic labels.

7. Promote principles of social justice by partnering with service users to ensure their rights are respected.

Consumers as Experts

Melissa Floyd (2013) has explored the possibilities for justice-oriented practice regarding involuntary mental health treatment. Starting from the principle of consumers as experts, Floyd conducted a qualitative research project to learn about experiences of involuntary treatment and offer consumer-developed recommendations. She asked consumers who had experienced involuntary treatment the following questions:

> Tell me about a time you received mental health treatment when you didn't want it. How did you feel about these events then? How do you feel now? If you could go back in time, would you change anything? What? If someone needs treatment, in that they are becoming unable to function and/or dangerous, what should happen? What shouldn't happen? Do you have anything else you would like to tell me about involuntary treatment? (2013, p. 189)

Consumers shared their feelings of humiliation, powerlessness, and anger that endured over time. They spoke of the trauma of physical restraint and involvement of law enforcement. They argued for the need to limit involuntary hospitalization and to negotiate viable alternatives such as home care, consumer-run care, and medication cards with advanced directives regarding care.

Floyd's work resonates with that of others advocating for social workers to engage in development of empowering alliances with mental health system survivors (Furlong, Helm, Otto, & Raimondo, 2013; Joseph, 2013). For example, Mark Furlong and colleagues sought to learn what consumers/survivors found most helpful in reclaiming their lives after mental health diagnosis and intervention. Survivors spoke to the importance of having a life distinct from diagnosis; being able to meet basic material needs; having power over the decisions that affect one's life; being in an environment where empowerment is possible; learning how to manage troubling thoughts and behaviors; having a sense of belonging in a supportive community; having a sense of hope that things will get better; developing a sense of optimism and gratitude; having peers to engage with who understand what one is going through; and focusing on mind, body, and spiritual wellness (Furlong et al., 2013, p. 291). They offered straightforward advice to professionals:

> Please follow my lead. Be open-minded. Relate to me as a person. . . . Don't be a closed box. Realize that I have reasons for feeling what I'm feeling. If I tell you something is not helpful, believe me. Don't drift away from what we've been doing. Stay the course. I'm proof that your work helps. (p. 296)

The above examples provide direction for social-justice-oriented action at the individual, organizational, and community levels regarding mental health. They locate questions of risk and vulnerability in a broader context of rights and social as well as personal responsibility. The Like Minds Campaign, launched by the New Zealand Ministry of Health in 1997, addresses discrimination and stigma reduction regarding mental illness at the national level through a unique public education program that includes TV campaigns; a media watch to identify and address biased, inaccurate media coverage; a website where people living with mental illness share their stories; and resources for creating supportive workplaces and communities. It is an inspiring example of the possibilities of context-relevant and context-changing action directed at the societal level. (Visit http://www.likeminds.org.nz to learn more about Like Minds.) In what other contexts of practice might concern for risk eclipse concern for rights? Child and adult protection? Criminal justice? Have you experienced this in your own practice? How might you bring consideration of rights to bear in your work to provide a counterbalance to a focus on risks? How might you expand the conversation about responsibility from the individual level to a view that is inclusive of community and societal responsibilities?

RETHINKING SOCIAL WORK ROLES

We turn now to a consideration of the different parts social justice workers may play in taking action for change. Social workers are generally prepared to play a variety of professional roles, shaped by both organizational mission and the worker's position and responsibilities therein. Roles are also shaped by the definition of the problem and proposed course of action. Most likely, you have been introduced to a number of social work roles such as enabler, broker, counselor, case manager, planner, and teacher (see, for example, Miley, O'Melia, & DuBois, 2013, pp. 12–18). We want to first reflect critically on the concept of roles and then outline what we see as approaches for enacting social justice work.

Discussion of roles generally addresses the workplace-related position a social worker assumes and the related expectations and activities. The role is thus viewed as separate from the particular person who fills it and carries out its functions. It defines and delimits the activities in which the worker engages. Questions of power and meaning seldom enter into the discussion of social work roles. We contend that social work roles are not neutral. They are infused with meaning and power and embedded in context and history.

The approaches social workers take to enact their responsibilities are shaped in part by organizational expectations and job descriptions. They are also powerfully shaped by the social worker's positionality, values, and critical understanding of societal arrangements, problems, and possibilities for intervention. A role is realized only through its practice, and in that practice social workers bring their own histories, interpretations, power, and sense of possibility to bear.

Ten roles for social justice work are outlined below. We think of roles as ways of enacting our responsibilities and commitments. We argue that these roles are relevant for all contexts of social work practice. By rethinking our roles in light of the demands of social justice work, we can better address questions of power, promote meaningful participation, and expand the possibilities for transformative action. As you consider these roles, think of specific examples of how you might carry out these roles in the context of your practicum.

1. *Learner*: Our most fundamental and constant role is that of learner, approaching situations and relationships with openness, humility, and critical curiosity. As learners we are committed to the ongoing search for our own competence (Moch, 2009).

2. *Teacher*: We not only bring our knowledge and skills to bear in the change process, but we also share them with others so that individuals, groups, and communities are better equipped to confront new challenges in the future. To do so we need to be effective teachers, able to engage learners and impart ideas clearly and effectively to diverse audiences.

3. *Collaborator*: As collaborators, we engage in genuine partnerships over the long haul. We participate as team members, joining in the give and take of dialogue and action and accepting responsibilities and risks. We bring our specific knowledge and skills to bear to carry out shared tasks and responsibilities in coordination and cooperation with others.

4. *Facilitator*: Facilitators support group processes of communication, decision making, planning, and action and encourage participants in the task-oriented and socio-emotional dimensions of their work together. Whether the group in question is a family, a mutual aid group, an interdisciplinary team, or a board of directors, skilled facilitation is key to building trust, addressing power, promoting participation, and engaging in change-oriented action.

5. *Animator*: The animator is one who brings life to the change process and sparks consciousness to motivate and mobilize for change. The animator helps sustain action for change by helping individuals and groups recognize and realize their power and develop their capacities. In a sense, an animator serves as a coach to encourage, nurture, and validate people as they take risks, try out new skills, and plan their own journeys (Finn, Jacobson, & Campana, 2004, p. 338).

6. *Mediator*: Participants in change processes come with differing understandings, interests, and expectations. Mediators help people engage in dialogue, explore and reconcile differences, reach compromise, come to mutually satisfactory resolutions, and build critical alliances (Zastrow, 2009, p. 71).

7. *Advocate*: Social justice workers speak for the rights of those who have been historically excluded from decision-making arenas. We speak against policies, practices, and social arrangements that produce and perpetuate social injustice and inequality. This does not mean that we speak *in the place of* those living the daily realities of discrimination and oppression. Rather we stand and speak in solidarity with others.

8. *Negotiator*: Critical awareness of power implies the capacity to confront conflict. As positioned actors embracing a political and ethical stance, social justice workers will face the question "Which side are you on?" We will be called on to act as negotiators seeking the best possible outcomes for those we represent. We need to be clear about our positioning and what is at stake in these contexts.

9. *Researcher*: Social justice work is an integrated approach that demands ongoing critical reflection on and evaluation of our practice. The role of researcher is not something we turn over to those in the university or something we append as an afterthought. Rather, systematic investigation and evaluation are part of our everyday practice.

10. *Bricoleur*: French anthropologist Claude Levi-Strauss (1966) envisioned cultural meaning making as a *bricolage*, the creative process of crafting new meanings and purpose from the cultural materials at hand. The concept of the *bricoleur* is an apt one for social justice work. As bricoleurs we are constantly challenged to engage with the circumstances and resources at hand with a sense of discovery, to be inventive, and to adapt and transform resources in response to new challenges.

Reflection Moment:
Social Work Roles: Expanding the Possibilities

The ten social worker roles described above stem from practice and dialogue with others engaged in social justice work. The naming and describing of social work roles is a work in progress. As we encounter new perspectives and learn from the experiences of others, we find our repertoire of roles expanding. For example, Paul Farmer's work speaks to the importance of the role of witness in social justice work. The National Community Development Institute frames its role as that of capacity builder. As you put your own vision of social justice work to practice, pay attention to the roles you are learning and enacting along the way. What additional roles come to mind? How would you name these roles? Describe and teach them to others? What do these roles allow you to accomplish? How might you apply these roles in your work with colleagues, community members, and policy makers?

SKILLS AND PRACTICE OF ACTION AND ACCOMPANIMENT

In the following sections we address skills and practice of action and accompaniment, with examples for practice with individuals, groups, and families; in organizations and communities; and in diverse arenas of decision making. Some of these examples illustrate the integration of direct practice skills with those of advocacy, education, policy work, and community building. Others point to the possibilities for cross-fertilization of knowledge and skills. These become part of our repertoire as bricoleurs creating possibility from the resources at hand. We begin with examples for justice-oriented action in the context of practice with individuals and families. We return to the centrality of groups in social justice work and offer further thoughts on effective group process. We then present approaches to planning, decision making, supervision, policy practice, advocacy, and conflict transformation that inform the skills and practice of justice-oriented action. We offer practice examples and activities along the way to illustrate some of these approaches.

Transforming Direct Practice

In talking with social workers about social justice, we have found that many practitioners have an image of social justice work as a form of *macro practice*, seeking to effect change at the level of larger systems through mass mobilization and social action. Although that may be one form social justice work takes, we have argued throughout that social justice and human rights need to be the centerpiece of all practice—from the most intimate spaces of one-to-one relationships to participation in large-scale social movements. However, as we truly embrace social justice work at the interpersonal level we cannot ignore its implications for the transformation of organizational practice, social policies, and dominant belief systems. In short, social justice work is based on an *integrated* approach to practice that does not divide personal struggles and public issues into micro and macro concerns, but looks instead to how these concerns are deeply entangled and thus require careful attention to their complex interplay. In this section we explore practice with individuals and families, develop examples of social justice work in action, and illustrate relevant practices and skills.

Just Therapy

Charles Waldegrave and colleagues at the Family Centre in Wellington, New Zealand, have developed a model for Just Therapy that makes social justice the heart of direct practice (Waldegrave, 2000). The approach is characterized by three main concepts: belonging, sacredness, and liberation. Waldegrave describes the emergence of Just Therapy in a "reflective environment" in which diverse stakeholders came together and critically examined the ways in which helping systems and demands of help seeking served to reproduce inequalities and experiences of marginalization. Participants in the process included women and men, family therapists and community workers, Maori, Samoan, and white. They began to question the dominant systems of knowledge that had informed health and welfare structures and their practice therein. The practitioners started with a process of consciousness raising regarding their place in systems that valued particular ways of knowing while relegating other "forms of meaning creation, such as gender, cultural or class knowledge" to an "inferior anecdotal status" (2000, p. 153).

Just Therapy is a form of practice developed to address these repeated failings of dominant models and systems. It is centered around values of equity and justice, and it recognizes that many mental health and relationship problems are consequences of power differences and injustice (p. 154). Waldegrave describes Just Therapy as a demystifying approach that involved a wide range of practitioners in addressing the deep social pain experienced by people who have been systematically marginalized. In crafting the approach, participants in the process questioned professionally imposed meanings of problems that failed to engage sociopolitical analysis or honor the perspectives of those seeking help. They asked how it was that spirituality was largely missing from professional discourse and practice while it was central to the lives of Centre participants. They examined the ways in which a "colonial mentality" played out in the details of organizational practice. Together they articulated a coherent theory that "provides tools for reflection, analysis, and action" and involves a shift in power and meaning (p. 158). As they reconceived their practice they found that the process led to a reconceptualization of their organization.

The Family Centre has not sacrificed direct practice for bigger issues. Rather it has developed a "congruence between casework and the rest of the work" (p. 161). Waldegrave argues that social workers are more effective at helping families with their immediate needs when the workers have direct knowledge of and involvement in the issues beyond the office. Just Therapy staff members reject the stigmatizing label of "multi-problem family" and try to honor poor people's stories of survival. One of the tasks of the social worker is to help people examine the "problem-centered webs of meaning" they bring with them to the Centre and to "weave new threads of meaning and possibility" together. As Waldegrave describes:

> For us the therapeutic conversation is a sacred encounter, because people come in great pain and share their story. The story is like a gift, a very personal offering given in great vulnerability. It has a spiritual quality. It is not a scientific pathology that requires removal, nor is it an ill-informed understanding of the story that requires correction. It is rather a person's articulation of events, and the meaning given to those events, which have become problematic. The therapist honors and respects the story, and then in return gives a reflection that offers alternative liberating meanings that inspire resolution and hope. (p. 162)

The Family Centre is an innovator in social justice work. To learn more about its projects, including a living wage campaign, post-disaster trauma counseling, and indigenous housing models as a solution to climate change visit the Centre's website (http://www.familycentre.org.nz).

Empowerment and Strengths in Action

Just Therapy has much in common with empowerment and strengths-based approaches that reframe practice in terms of liberation and transformation. All have emerged from critical dialogue among participants—both users and providers of services—who have directly experienced or witnessed unjust practices and their effects. For example, Lorraine Gutiérrez and Edith Lewis (1999) have put forth an empowerment approach to practice with women of color. They start from the assumption that the experience of being a member of a group with little social or political power has personal as well as social costs. The goal of practice is to increase personal, interpersonal, or political power. The process may take place on the individual, interpersonal, and community levels. They identify four subprocesses that comprise empowerment practice: (1) developing critical consciousness; (2) reducing self-blame; (3) assuming responsibility to participate in the change process; and (4) enhancing self-efficacy, which entails both the capacities and confidence to take effective action (Gutiérrez, 1990). Action strategies for change include:

- Building a helping relationship based on collaboration, trust, and shared power
- Accepting the client's definition of concern
- Identifying and building on strengths
- Raising consciousness around issues of gender, class, race, and power
- Actively engaging participants in the change process
- Teaching specific skills (e.g., communication skills, self-advocacy skills, and organizing skills)
- Using mutual aid groups
- Sharing power within the helping relationship
- Mobilizing resources and advocating for change (Gutiérrez, 1990; Gutierrez & Lewis, 1999)

Strengths-based practitioners also remind us to look both to and beyond families for resources and sources of strength. Bonnie Benard (2006, p. 214) calls for practice that recognizes and taps into family resilience. She offers the following steps for strengths-based practice with families:

1. Listen to their story
2. Acknowledge the pain
3. Look for strengths
4. Ask questions about survival, supports, positive times, interests, dreams, and goals
5. Point out strengths
6. Link strengths to family members' goals and dreams
7. Link family to resources to achieve goals and dreams
8. Find opportunities for family members to be teachers and supporters of others

Benard discusses the family support movement in the United States from school-based family resource programs to free-standing family centers. These strengths-based efforts share common ground. According to Benard, they are all based on caring relationships between staff and family, faith in the family's resilience and capacity to grow and change, and commitment to strengths-enhancing practice (p. 215).

The Power of Group Process

Whatever our starting point for action, much of our work is carried out in a group context. Work with individuals generally entails involvement with families or with important systems immediately affecting their lives, such as schools, hospitals, mental health centers, social welfare organizations, and housing administrations. We continually put knowledge and skills of group process to work through participation in interdisciplinary teams, in workplace staff meetings, in action planning, and in community organizing. Sometimes we may be officially charged with the task of group facilitation. At other times we may be able to draw from our facilitation skills as a member of the group to promote meaningful participation and ensure that those with less power in the setting have their rights honored and voices heard. The National Network for Immigrant and Refugee Rights (Cho et al., 2004) offers a number of tips for effective group facilitation to promote a positive and respectful collaborative environment in diverse group settings. We summarize them in the box below.

**Suggestions for Effective Group Facilitation
(adapted from Cho et al. [2004], pp. 13–14)**

- Listen to your group, pay attention to verbal and nonverbal cues, and flow with how the group is feeling.

- Develop ground rules as a group to set an atmosphere for trust and respect.

- Seek to equalize participation, giving everyone a chance to be heard as well as to listen. With larger groups, consider use of small group discussions and opportunities to report back.

- Watch for and address power imbalances between individuals or groups of participants.

- Be flexible with the agenda—be prepared to make adjustments in the moment.

- Do everything possible to ensure that logistics are addressed in advance.

- Challenge discrimination when it happens without attacking the person.

- Take breaks when needed and incorporate energizing activities to engage the group.

- Use open-ended questions to encourage participants to actively engage in exercises and discussion and allow space for participation.

- Summarize the process and key points along the way, highlighting points of connection or agreement, as well as divergence, and invite feedback.

- Create opportunities for the group to brainstorm. Avoid leading the group to a particular answer or solution.

- Create lists of participant responses and record ideas and plans. Include everyone's ideas.

- Give participants the opportunity to pass on a particular activity and respect their ability to choose their level of involvement.

- Expose yourself as a learner. Don't be afraid to say "I don't know" and to seek input from the group.

- Take care of yourself and be willing to acknowledge mistakes.

- Expect frustration and expect joy.

- Remember that good things happen when people come together.

Making Plans, Making Decisions

Action for change entails planning and decision making. Social justice work calls for the participation of all of the stakeholders in the planning process. In this section we present participatory approaches to planning and decision making that can be used in a broad range of practice contexts. We summarize Cecilia Diaz's (1997) approach to participatory planning, highlight insights from Sam Kaner and colleagues on participatory decision making, and introduce a theory of change model developed by the Aspen Institute (Anderson, n.d.) for participatory decision making and action planning for community change.

Participatory Planning

Díaz (1997, pp. 15–23) describes the process of participatory planning in terms of eight *moments*:

1. *Situation* (see discussion of systematization in chapter 6): What is our reality? What are our needs and problems? What are the causes? What can we resolve ourselves? What can't we resolve ourselves? What resources and capacities do we have to confront the situation?

2. *Participants*: Who are the people involved? What are their concerns and interests? Where might be the common ground and important differences? Are there others who should be part of the process?

3. *Vision of change*: What is our desired outcome? This is directly related to our hopes and values. Knowing where we want to arrive brings direction and clarity to the process of setting goals and objectives.

4. *Goals and objectives*: What are our general goals for more fundamental, structural change? What do we want to accomplish in the long run? What specific objectives do we have to meet in order to get there? What is our time frame for meeting these objectives? What will be the specific measures of our objectives? How will we know when we have met our objectives?

5. *Pathway*: What path should we take? What is our vision of the overall journey, and what are the possible routes that we can take to get there? What route will we select and why? Who will be part of the journey? We need a vision of the parts, of the whole, and of the final goal. This involves action, tasks, responsibilities, people, and resources.

6. *Action plan*: What is our action plan? What results do we want to achieve? What resources do we have or need? How will we get them? What specific steps must we take? Who is responsible for what?

7. *Taking action*: Get to work! In order to carry out the plans we have to engage organizational capacity and decide on a division of labor. We need to make decisions about how the implementation will be organized and overseen. Who coordinates the overall effort? How do we maintain momentum and commitment? The action is also accompanied by ongoing analysis—are we getting the work done? What is at stake in terms of risks and opportunities? Do we need to rethink our route?

8. Evaluation: As we undertake the journey, we need to stop along the way to reflect on and learn from the experience: What gains have we made? How successfully have we fulfilled our roles and assignments? How are we confronting difficulties and conflicts? Are we meeting the goals and objectives? Díaz poses three *permanent questions* for reflection along the way: (1) How are we doing? (2) Are we heading where we want to go? (3) What do we need to change? These questions may lead us back to step 1.

This model for participatory planning has broad applicability. It can be used in making plans with individuals and families, agency committees, advocacy groups, and community organizations. The eight moments follow the logic and sequencing of top-down approaches to planning. However, the test of a participatory model is in the practice. Is the process truly inclusive such that diverse stakeholders have a meaningful voice? Each step of the process is also a place for dialogue and teaching-learning. What does the step entail? Does it make sense to the participants? How might it be illustrated with examples and images? Diaz pays close attention to these issues. She encourages use of diverse approaches from discussion groups to drawings, newsprint murals, and socio-drama to ensure that participants are meaningfully engaged in every step (Díaz, 1995, 1997).

Theory of Change

The Aspen Institute, an educational and policy studies organization based in Washington, DC, has developed a community-builders' guide to a theory of change as an approach to participatory planning and action (Anderson, n.d.). A theory of change explains how accomplishment of early and intermediate objectives sets the stage for achieving long-term goals. Stakeholders join together in an in-depth process in which they make precise statements about the change they want to create and identify in detail the specific objectives and preconditions that have to be met in order to achieve the ultimate long-term change. The process is structured to enable participants to get to the big picture quickly and then engage in a process of careful *backward mapping*. Through the backward mapping, participants start from the end goal, delineate the pathways for action needed to address each precondition, identify specific indicators of successful achievement of early and intermediate outcomes, and describe the specific actions that will be taken to bring about the preconditions and meet the objectives. The process sets the stage for probing critical questions about the viability of the envisioned change and the pathways to achieving it. The Aspen Institute has developed a detailed, user-friendly guide entitled *The Community Builder's Approach to Theory of Change* (Anderson, n.d.), which is available from its website (http://www.aspeninstitute.org).

Participatory Decision Making

The change process is full of decision-making moments. Frequently, we make decisions by default as we move in a direction that goes without saying and fail to question our underlying assumptions. One of the most basic skills of decision making is learning to recognize *when* and *how* we are making decisions. Group decision making can be especially challenging. Sam Kaner (2014) offers a participatory approach to group decision making:

> Group decision making remains the best hope for solving difficult problems. There is no substitute for the wisdom that results from a successful integration of divergent points of view. Successful group decision making requires a group to take advantage of the full range of experience and skills that reside in its membership. This means encouraging people to speak up. It means *inviting* difference, not fearing it. It means struggling to understand one another, especially in the face of pressures and contradictions that typically drive group members to shut down. In short, it means operating from *participatory* values. (p. xxi)

Participatory groups will not consider a problem solved until each person present (and each person who will be affected by the decision) understands the process and the logic and has systematic opportunity to weigh in with his or her point of view. Kaner contends that full participation in the decision-making process strengthens individuals, develops groups, and fosters sustainable agreement. He sees participatory decision making as grounded in four core values: (1) full participation, (2) mutual understanding, (3) inclusive solutions, and (4) shared responsibility (2014, p. 24). He describes participatory decision making as a diamond in which groups move from the narrow space of business as usual into the wide, uncomfortable *divergent zone*, where diverse perspectives disrupt familiarity, and then into the struggle of the *groan zone*, where members grapple with a broad range of differing or opposing ideas and often find themselves frustrated and defensive. Passing through the turbulent waters of the groan zone with the help of skilled facilitation, members find a wellspring of possibilities around which new convergent thinking can coalesce in reaching a collective decision point.

> **Great Resource!**
> Check out the *Facilitator's Guide to Participatory Decision-Making* by Sam Kaner with Lenny Lind, Catherine Toldi, Sarah Fisk, and Duane Berger (San Francisco: Jossey Bass, 2014). It's a must have resource for social justice work!

Addressing Conflict—Challenges and Possibilities

Social justice work calls on us to engage with conflict as part of the work. Conflict can be a source of both constraint and possibility. The issue of conflict comes down to how we deal with it. Do we flee from controversial topics or conflictual issues? Do we see conflict as a battle to be won? Somewhere in the middle of these two polarities is the notion of conflict as opportunity. Conflict opens a space for learning and helps us see different sides of an issue. It reminds us that there are different ways of defining problems and it provides the opportunity to seek alternative solutions. Conflict makes for better decision making in the end, but in the short run it can cause discomfort. Conflict is about learning to navigate and value difference.

The National Network for Immigrant and Refugee Rights (NNIRR) acknowledges that conflict is a common outcome in efforts to build social and racial justice in communities (Cho et al, 2004). In creating its popular education resource, *BRIDGE—Building a Race and Immigration Dialogue in the Global Economy*—Cho and colleagues have developed a model for conflict transformation that begins by reframing conflict itself. They argue that conflict is an inevitable part of our lives and so we need concrete strategies to integrate conflict transformation as part of our practice repertoire. They suggest that conflict transformation can be a tool to establish a relationship based on equality and mutual respect (p. 266):

While conflict often stirs up unpleasant emotions and reactions for everyone involved, moments of conflict can also become important learning opportunities. As social justice activists, we need to practice what we preach within our own organizations, so when conflict happens within our organizations or movements, we need to develop ways to address it in a constructive way. Conflict transformation can become an important tool to increase our own capacity as organizations, communities, and individuals to fight for justice. . . . Without an intentional approach to conflict resolution, we can reproduce the methods and values of dominant cultures, focusing on only "winning" or "losing," or overpowering and destroying our opponents. In many cases, conflict occurs within our own organizations, communities, and movements, and when handled badly, results in a collective loss.

Steps for Transforming Conflict between Community Members

The NNIRR offers the following steps as a guide for transforming conflict between community members (Cho et al., 2004, p. 275):

1. Allow people to name the problem and express how it has impacted them personally and as a community.

2. Explore the historical or larger context of the conflict.

3. Listen to how the problem has affected the other side and recognize the humanity and rights of the other side.

4. Acknowledge your own role in the conflict.

5. Search for shared experiences that you have with the other side, such as shared hurts and suffering, cultural or spiritual sources of understanding and support, and common humanity.

6. Recognize the connections and interdependence between communities.

7. Determine what's appropriate for your situation. Is it building a short-term, task-oriented solution to defuse a dangerous conflict or a more long-term alliance to address deeper levels of interests?

8. Work together to elaborate win/win solutions that are mutually beneficial to all parties.

9. If necessary, develop a formal agreement to capture the spirit of the unity people reach.

10. Identify mechanisms and parties who will be responsible for convening another dialogue or problem-solving process to resolve any conflicts that may arise in the future in a mutually positive way.

11. Figure out ways to publicize and mobilize people in the broader community in order to implement the agreement or new understanding.

Skills and Practices to Support Socially Just Organizations

The preceding examples demonstrate that social justice work holds implications for the organizational context of practice. Social justice practice will be constrained within organizational contexts in which business as usual entails top-down practices that separate the worker from the client, reproduce relations of power, and value limiting concepts of expertise that exclude the grounded knowledge of service users. The ideal organizational context is the learning organization—in which there is an ongoing search for organizational competence. The learning organization "adopts a climate of openness and trust; people are unafraid to share their ideas and speak their minds. Barriers between managers and employees are eliminated and, ideally, everybody works together to support the collective well-being" (Bennett & O'Brien, 1994, p. 44). However, the reality of human service work is increasingly pushed toward privatization and a market ethic (Ferguson, Lavalette, & Whitmore, 2005; Healy, 2005). As Karen Healy notes, "In this new environment social workers face increasingly stringent expectations from funding agencies and service managers to demonstrate cost-effectiveness and evidence of service outputs and outcomes" (2005, p. 222). Thus, a serious challenge for social justice work is to critically engage with and resist these market-based imperatives on human service organizations. This is no easy task. Workers face tremendous pressure for efficiency, productivity, and standardization of practice that is often at cross-purposes with meaningful engagement, relationship building, and integrated action that resists an individual pathology frame. The costs can be high for failure to comply with business as usual. Social justice work calls for action on multiple fronts, including building alliances of solidarity among workers and other program participants that cross and bridge organizational boundaries, supporting a social work of resistance and linking direct support to advocacy and action.

Linking Direct Support to Advocacy and Action

Grant Larson's (2008) seven principles for anti-oppressive practice, described on p. 296, provide a foundation for building social-justice-oriented human service organizations. The Settlement House model, at the core of social work's history, also offers a model for building socially just organizations that attends simultaneously to direct material needs and advocacy and action for community and policy change.

Alice Gates (2014) provides an example of this integrated approach in her case study of a midwestern workers' center. The center focuses on both addressing the immediate needs of the undocumented immigrants it serves and challenging societal arrangements that compromise immigrants' rights, health, and well-being. Although the center set its primary goal as "altering the balance of power between workers and employers in favor of the workers" (Gates, 2014, p. 110), it needed first to organize around access to basic services, such as English as a Second Language (ESL) classes for immigrant workers. Describing itself as an "organizing organization," the center has effectively engaged participants in direct service provision, legal advocacy, and worker rights campaigns. Providing an ESL curriculum around worker rights served as both a recruitment and an empowerment tool to bring participants into broader campaigns for social change. Where do you see other examples of organizations that effectively integrate direct service and social change in your community? Where do you see possibilities to effectively integrate direct service with advocacy and action in the context of your practicum? How might those possibilities be expanded?

Social Work as Resistance

Social justice work often challenges us to practice "against the grain" in our organizational contexts. Reisch, Wenocur, and Sherman (1981) used the term *functional noncapitulation* to describe an approach to conflict management in which workers position themselves as active decision makers with both a right and responsibility to influence the organization and work to reverse downward organizational pressure that contributes to powerlessness. They note that social workers and clients alike may feel powerless in the face of organizational pressures, mandates, and resource limitations. The authors argue that workers need to understand power and empowerment both conceptually and experientially, use the power available to them effectively, and communicate their grasp of power dynamics to clients. They argue that a stance of functional noncapitulation

> requires workers to maintain a willingness and capacity to negotiate continually the conditions of their work. In this position, workers will have to take calculated risks to achieve their goals. The worker's posture of functional noncapitulation encourages the same stance among clients, rather than shared dependency and powerlessness. (p. 112)

In order to establish this stance the worker must become aware of and comfortable with the many sources of available power, including legal power, the power of information, situational power, expert power, coalitional power, and even negative power—the power to make the agency look bad (Reisch et al., 1981, p. 112). Thus, the analysis of power is not limited to the power dynamics of the client's situation or of the particular context of the worker-client relationship. Rather, it is part of the social justice worker's critical positionality in the organizational context.

We also find insight and inspiration in the concept of *constructive noncooperation*. Mark Mattaini and Karen Atkinson (2011; see also Atkinson & Mattaini, 2013) draw from the work of Gandhi and Vaclav Havel on nonviolent action as they explore the concept of constructive noncooperation: "At its heart constructive noncooperation involves the construction and sustainment of a new, self-reliant, and self-determining culture within the shell of—and in resistance to—structural oppression" (Mattaini & Atkinson, 2011, p. 9). Havel described this as "living in truth," which is at once a form of resistance to oppression and an affirmation of an alternative, of the possibility to think, speak, and act in ways that speak truth to power. What might constructive noncooperation look like within a human service agency? What spaces of possibility might we open within our organizations, communities, and social institutions by embracing a practice of living in truth? What are the risks of engaging in a social work of resistance?

Supervision for Social Justice

Many of you will find yourselves assuming supervisory roles in social work organizations. The skills and practice of supervision can be powerful tools in promoting social justice. We offer some concrete examples to illustrate the possibilities. Freda Brashears (1995) conceptualizes supervision as a mutual aid process. She suggests that an understanding of supervision as mutual aid

- Challenges the false dichotomy that separates supervision from practice
- Envisions the workplace as an environment in which worker potential is realized
- Reframes supervisors as change agents working on behalf of staff to promote Just Practice
- Reframes the work unit as a mutual aid group with common interests and tasks

- Counters agency hierarchy
- Creates a form of supervisory practice that is consistent with social work values
- Realizes the values of advocacy, empowerment, and self-determination in the workplace
- Provides a framework for team work, participatory decision making, and group problem solving
- Harnesses the creative energy of the group members
- Provides the base for creating organizational change

Edil Torres Rivera and colleagues (Rivera, Maldonado, & Alcaron, 2013) describe the possibilities of supervision as a form of liberatory practice. Drawing from Freirian principles, they argue that supervision can be practiced as a problematizing process to spark critical consciousness and movement toward transformative change. They describe ten principles, including the following, to guide supervision as a process of problematization and liberation:

1. Listening to grasp both the supervisee's and the client's reality
2. Ability to engage supervisee(s) in meaningful dialogue
3. Use of a language of equals
4. Opening of communicative space to allow for curiosity, creativity, emotion, humor, and dissent
5. Honoring of silence as consciousness emerges from reflection
6. Ability to concretely probe real-life, everyday experiences
7. Reflexivity in examining situations and underlying assumptions
8. Capacity to move from critical consciousness to the opening of new possibilities for understanding and action

Thus, supervision provides the opportunity for a process that parallels critical practice with clients. Supervision for social justice holds potential for linking direct practice to transformative organizational practice.

Bradley, Engelbrecht, and Hojer (2010) argue that, in order for supervision to be a force for change, supervisors need to help practitioners reflect on their work in the broader structural, political, and global context of contemporary social work. They speak to the possibilities of peer and cross-disciplinary supervision as well as the co-working of complex cases as ways to strengthen supervision as a force for change. Further, they call for the creation of new professional language and logic that may empower supervisors to be more vocal in address-ing structural inequities and in advocating for and with workers to improve both work environment and services. Think about your own experiences as a super-visor or supervisee. What have been some of the positive aspects of that expe-rience? Negative aspects? Have your experiences encouraged you and others to engage in social justice work? If so, how? Have your experiences fit with Bras-hears's concept of supervision as mutual aid? With the concept of liberatory supervision proposed by Rivera and colleagues? With Bradley's notion of super-vision as a force for change? If so, how? Do you see possibilities for incorporat-ing these approaches to supervision in your workplace? What would you add in order to promote a model of supervision as social justice work?

Building and Sustaining a Social Justice Organization: *La Fuerza Unida's Story*

On January 17, 1990, the Levi Strauss plant in San Antonio, Texas, closed with no warning. Managers announced that in order to stay competitive they were moving the factory to Costa Rica. More than one thousand peo-ple, most of them Mexican American women, lost their jobs overnight. For Viola Casares and Petra Mata, both long-time workers at the plant, the clo-sure opened their eyes to injustice. For too long, Levi Strauss had viewed women as simply part of the machine, paid them low piece-rate wages, and considered them expendable when labor could be purchased cheaper else-where. The women decided to take a stand and say "enough is enough."

Viola, Petra, and several coworkers began to talk with one another and compare their experiences of work-related injuries, bonuses promised and never received, and day-to-day struggles for family and community sur-vival. They began to organize to demand just severance pay and pensions. They formed *Fuerza Unida* (United Force) to fight for their rights as work-ers and women and launched a boycott against Levi Strauss.

Over the past twenty-five years the women have built Fuerza Unida into a formidable organization addressing intersecting issues of social, eco-nomic, and environmental justice. They have worked in solidarity with women in the *maquiladoras* (factories making products for export) on issues of wages, benefits, and health care. Fuerza Unida takes an intergen-erational approach to community-based service and empowerment through its women's sewing cooperative, community food bank, and youth leadership programs. Fuerza Unida currently works with women in Mayan communities of Mexico and Central America to empower one another in their work as seamstresses, weavers, and business owners. It has worked in solidarity with other groups to advocate for immigrants' rights. It has launched its own clothing line—Fuerza Jeans with Justice. And it continues to boycott Levi Strauss and share its story. Fuerza Unida claims that "justice is for us to create." Its twenty-five-year history of direct service, advocacy, and community action is rich in lessons for social justice work. It teaches us of the fundamental importance of commitment for the long haul and the possibilities of change from below (Finn, 2002). To learn more about Fuerza Unida, visit its website (http://www.lafuerzaunida.org).

Policy Practice and Advocacy for Social Justice

Policy Practice

There has been growing attention in recent years to naming *policy practice* as a core practice area for social work. Policy practice can be defined as "using social work skills to propose and change policies in order to achieve the goal of social and economic justice" (Cummins, Byers, & Pedrick, 2011, p. 8). Bruce Jansson, who brought the term policy practice into social work's vocabulary, describes it as "efforts to influence the development, enactment, implementation, or assessment of social policies" in organizational, community, and legislative settings (1994, p. 8). Jansson (2008) contends that effective policy practice requires strong analytical, political, interactional, and values-clarification skills.

Policy practice encompasses diverse methods and activities. Cummins, Byers, and Pedrick (2011, p. 10) describe four key policy activities:

1. Policy analysis, which involves systematic study of policy goals, knowledge-informing policy development, objectives, values, impact, and effectiveness

2. Advocating for policy change, which involves strategic interaction with stakeholders and policy makers to influence policy decisions and direction

3. Building coalitions by joining forces with other groups to coordinate a strategy and message for policy change

4. Launching campaigns to both heighten public awareness and build support for policy change

Policy practice requires skills of engagement, research, problem solving, networking, collaborating, negotiating, and building alliances. It requires time and commitment. It may entail careful, sustained research into the history, goals, and consequences of public policies. It may involve lobbying or providing testimony to influence legislators and other decision makers. It may involve reform through litigation. It may call for social action or the mobilization of people affected by the policy to join together and build an organized power base to demand change (Figueira-McDonough, 1993).

Given the inseparability of policy from the practice of social work, policy practice is an essential component of social justice work. Policy practice is seen in the work of mental health advocates calling for changes in approaches to involuntary hospitalization. It is illustrated in the advocacy work of the Family Centre of New Zealand, the Like Minds Campaign, and the immigrants' rights work of Human Impact Partners in Oakland, California. Policy practice is exemplified by the work of housing advocates that not only provide direct services through a community homeless shelter or housing access program, but also advocate for expansion of affordable housing and against statutes that criminalize homelessness. Policy practice is illustrated in van Wormer and McKinney's calls for advocacy for policy change to ensure that schools are safe and welcoming places for LGBTQ youth. Policy practice would also entail advocacy for anti-bullying legislation at the state level. Think for a moment about your social work practice. Where do you see opportunities to engage in policy practice in the context of your practicum? What do you see as challenges? Constraints? Possibilities?

Advocacy

The National Association of Social Workers describes advocacy—the championing of rights of society's most vulnerable groups—as central to the original mission of the profession (NASW, 2015a, 2016):

> Social workers continue to carry the torch for those who need help to succeed in our society. Indeed, while only a small percentage of the nation's half a million social workers count advocacy as their primary job duty, all social workers carry a philosophical charge to protect and empower the vulnerable and disadvantaged. They do so through a variety of means including writing op-ed pieces, lobbying, organizing local protests, and helping to change laws that adversely affect vulnerable and disadvantaged members of society. Today's social workers employ a full range of techniques for advocacy ranging from protests and sit-ins to harnessing the power of the Internet to network with others to affect change. (2016)

The Encyclopedia of Social Work (Edwards, 1995) defines advocacy as the "act of directly representing, defending, intervening, supporting, or recommending a course of action on behalf of one or more individuals, groups, or communities with the goal of securing or retaining social justice" (Mickelson, 1995, p. 95). Advocacy is sometimes conceived as a particular role of macro social work practice and thus the purview of those engaged in policy work and community organizing. However, the NASW describes advocacy as an essential skill and ethical responsibility for all social workers. Richard Hoefer (2012) addresses advocacy as a core part of generalist social work, and he makes the case for a unified model of advocacy that parallels the phases of generalist practice—from getting involved to understanding the issues, planning, advocating, and ongoing monitoring of actions and outcomes (p. 5). According to Hoefer, effective advocacy requires three key skills: education, negotiation, and persuasion (p. 105). Education may involve research, information sharing, and consciousness-raising activities. Negotiation involves efforts to gain support, resources, action, or acquiescence from another party (Hoefer, 2012, pp. 85–97). Persuasion entails getting another party to do what you want (p. 115). Successful advocacy efforts call for effective presentation of information. Hoefer makes the case for blending substantive information with individual stories; critical awareness of context; and careful attention to accuracy, timing, message, style, content, and clarity.

Hoefer speaks to the importance of *framing* in advocacy. Frames are "organizing principles that are socially shared and persistent over time, that work symbolically to meaningfully structure the social world" (O'Neil, Kendall-Taylor, & Bales, 2014, p. 2). Frames powerfully shape both public perceptions of people, problems, and issues and the direction of public policy. According to the FrameWorks Institute (Bales, 2002, p. 1) advocates need to carefully consider three key questions in framing issues: (1) How do we get people to think about the issue? (2) How do we get people to think about the issue in such a way that they will look beyond individual action to address it? (3) How do we get people to think about issues in such a way that they will want to solve them through public policies?

What further questions might you pose in thinking about the framing of issues for social justice advocacy? How might skills of framing be used in advocating at the individual as well as policy level?

Framing Public Issues

To learn more about framing, check out *Framing Public Issues*, a toolkit for public policy advocacy, available online through the FrameWorks Institute (http://www.frameworksinstitute.org/assets/files/PDF/FramingPublic Issuesfinal.pdf).

Possibilities of Social Justice Action:
Transforming Criminal Justice

Incarceration in the United States

Let's consider possibilities for social justice action in the context of criminal justice. Social justice principles and practices grounded in dignity, respect, and rights offer direction for working in the most constrained spaces. Prisons in the United States provide perhaps the most glaring example of a context of top-down power and control. According to the Sentencing Project (2015), a prison reform research and advocacy organization, the United States is the world's leader in incarceration with 2.2 million people in prisons or jails, a 500-percent increase over the past thirty years. The United States has an incarceration rate of 716 people per 100,000, the highest in the world (Sentencing Project, 2014). Black men between the ages of twenty-five and twenty-nine are seven times more likely than their white counterparts to be in prison or jail (Human Rights Watch, 2004). The Sentencing Project advocates social interventions that work, such as investment in early childhood education, juvenile justice programs that focus on strengthening families, and investment in communities to support neighborhood and community participation and capacity development as alternatives to a bloated prison system that takes an enormous human and economic toll. Let's take a look at some possibilities of social justice work in the context of criminal justice.

Bringing Social Work Back in

Josefina Figueira-McDonough and Rosemary Sarri (2002) have critiqued the social work profession for neglecting criminal justice in general and prison work in particular even as issues of basic human rights and social justice have increasingly come to public attention. There are, however, inspirational examples of healing, support, and advocacy in the prison context that demonstrate possibilities for social justice work. For example, social worker Jack Sternbach (2000) shares the powerful personal lessons for action and accompaniment he learned through work in a men's prison. In his prison memoir he writes,

> I want to focus on what I learned about men together with other men under conditions so oppressive and brutal you would expect to find the worst kinds of male aggression, dominance, and exploitation. There was that, in abundance. What is more important is how much I learned of the positive and affirming ways so many men found to be with each other even under such conditions. (p. 414)

Sternbach describes how prison transformed his practice of social work as he learned to nurture humanity under conditions of oppression; to accept others, where they were, in the moment; to practice from a stance of mutuality; to use self-revelation in order to facilitate honest open interaction; and to ask for help. He reminds us of the power of empathy, humility, and respect for human dignity to create moments and spaces of social justice within even the most challenging contexts.

Youth Action

Another example of the possibilities of social justice work comes from young people who have been imprisoned and have joined together in action to challenge policies and practices of youth incarceration in the adult prison system. The Philadelphia-based Youth Arts and Self-empowerment Project (YASP) is a youth-led, youth-staffed movement seeking to end the practice of youth being tried and incarcerated as adults in Pennsylvania. Beginning in 2009 as a series of workshops blending arts and empowerment training for young people who were incarcerated in Philadelphia's adult jails, it has grown into a youth-led movement advocating for prison reform, drawing attention to structural violence in the lives of young people and demanding an end to the school-to-prison pipeline that defines the trajectory of far too many young people of color (Ford et al., 2013). Youth leaders of YASP describe their process:

> Soon after forming, YASP began training and informing young people about the school-to-prison pipeline and structural violence in our society. When YASP talks about the school-to-prison pipeline, we are talking about the many ways young people, particularly young people of color and youth in poor communities, are pushed out of the school system and down a path that often leads to incarceration. In Philadelphia, the school-to-prison pipeline includes factors such as excessively harsh suspension and expulsion policies, a lack of sufficient counseling and support for students who need extra help, a state funding system that creates a deep disparity between resources available in suburban schools and city schools, and laws like Act 33 [an amendment to the Pennsylvania Juvenile Act that allows youth under eighteen to be tried as adults for certain crimes] that accelerate a young person's path into the adult prison system. We believe all of these factors are forms of structural violence, which consists of any type of violence through which an institution or a social structure harms people by keeping them from meeting their basic needs. . . . When YASP went out into the community, we noticed that it was not just the youth in our communities who didn't know about the school-to

prison-pipeline and structural violence, but many of the adults we met didn't know about it either. YASP decided to build awareness about each of these issues. (Ford et al., 2013, p. 1270)

We are deeply connected to the larger struggle against mass incarceration in Pennsylvania, particularly through our work with the recently formed coalition Decarcerate PA. The YASP organization brings a crucial component to this movement because, unfortunately, it is often one of the only youth-led groups at the table. As an organization built from the ground up by young people who were incarcerated as adults, YASP can serve as a model for building a national movement of young people to challenge policies of youth incarceration around the country. We hope other young people will read our stories and be inspired to follow our example. (Ford et al., p. 1275)

The work of YASP offers a compelling example of policy practice and of the participation of those most affected by oppressive policies and practices in creating change. To learn more about YASP, visit the website (http://www.yasproject.com).

Restorative Justice

Advocates for restorative justice are seeking fundamental changes in the philosophy and practice of criminal justice. Pamela Blume Leonard (2011, p. 31) describes restorative justice as a theory, process, and movement to promote healing for victims, offenders, and communities after a crime has occurred. A restorative justice perspective sees crime as "primarily an offense against human relationships and secondarily a violation of law" (Claassen, 1996). From a restorative justice perspective, there are three key questions to be addressed: Who has been hurt? What are their needs? Whose obligations are these needs? (Leonard, 2011, p. 32). Advocates argue for a practical approach that involves the community, focuses on the victim, and promotes inclusive processes toward justice, healing, and reconciliation. Restorative justice focuses on the harms of the crime rather than the rules that have been broken, it involves both the victims and offenders in the process, it seeks meaningful involvement of the community, it encourages collaboration and reintegration for both victims and offenders, and it is grounded in respect for all parties (Leonard, 2011, pp. 42–43).

The restorative justice process emphasizes acknowledgment, apology, and forgiveness. The main forms of practice include victim-offender dialogue, family group conferencing, peacemaking circles, and truth commissions. Victim-offender dialogues have been gaining ground as an alternative or supplemental approach within the criminal justice system. The voluntary process brings victims and offenders together with a trained facilitator to discuss the crime, its impact on their lives, and possibilities for repairing harm (Leonard, 2011). The process allows for the victims to speak directly to the offenders regarding their thoughts and feelings about the crime and its effect on their lives. The offenders have an opportunity to respond and to accept responsibility for the crime. The parties then consider possible actions to address the harm and losses resulting from the crime. As it is powerfully described by Cynthia Tobias, who recounts her personal experience, the process has transformative potential.

ON REFLECTION

Restorative Justice as a Way of Life and a Means for Social Change
Cynthia Tobias

My family had a heartbreaking and life changing experience when my sixteen-year-old daughter, who has a cognitive disability, was raped by a man living in our neighborhood. As one can imagine, the event affected me and my family in a multitude of ways. When the assault occurred, all my attention went toward my daughter, and all the blame for what happened I turned toward myself. Thoughts ran through my head like "if only I had been more loving," "if I had never let her out of my sight," "if I had paid closer attention to the people in my neighborhood," "if I had only_____," this horrible thing would not have happened to her.

Some of the ways in which our culture teaches us about human relationships is by using fear, the illusion of scarcity, division, blame, punishment, and violence in many forms. "I" becomes more important than "we"; privacy rather than transparency becomes the norm. My cultural training came up quickly when my daughter was raped. I wanted to blame myself as her mother and then blame the man who raped her. While he was responsible for what happened to her neither of those perspectives helps with healing hurts nor do they move our society toward a place of love, inclusion, community, responsibility, consideration of our "collective oppression," or justice.

Our current criminal justice system is set up to blame and punish. That is pretty much all it does, with no room for real sustainable healing of any of the parties involved in a crime. Blame and punishment is the logic that supports our ever-more-present for-profit prison system. This logic also distracts us from the creative work necessary to build a different system where the focus is on recovery, prevention, and civic inclusion rather than punishment. Restorative justice asks the questions, what harm was done, who was harmed, and what would the people harmed want to see done to restore justice? Our family looked at not just the harm done to our daughter, but to our extended community.

I believe that people are inherently good, doing their best under a very oppressive society that intentionally keeps us afraid and separated. We learn to want power over another person—violence, separation, and greed. We also learn not to care about each other too much or to care only about certain people, thinking we are separate from those with a different experience than our own. None of that is innate human behavior. Our family chose to use the restorative justice model to bring healing to our family and community and ultimately to begin undermining the system under which we live.

Using the restorative justice model helped me look at the places where I hold hatred in my heart, where I need to take responsibility not just for what happens to me or what I have done right or wrong, but for what my part is in what happens to others in my immediate and extended circles. I was forced to look at the fact that I am interdependent. This requires giving up blame. It requires forgiveness and at the same time it requires accountability. Restorative justice requires that we stay connected to a person who has hurt us, and at the same time, expect them to take full responsibility for the pain, trauma, and tragedy they have caused. In turn, this requires us as a human community to provide enough and appropriate resources to all parties involved in a crime. It requires creativity and the decision over and over again to be fully inclusive of all people. It means choosing human relationships over the accumulation of material possessions, privilege, and power over other people. This is no small task under the training and thumb of capitalism.

Using the restorative justice process forced me to look at how I am like my daughter's perpetrator. Where do I have and sometimes use "power over" another person? Where do I try to get away with not taking responsibility for my actions or inactions? How do my decisions affect others and the planet? What had to happen to me for me to behave this way? What had to happen to him for him to rape my daughter? Where had he been assaulted? Where had his "power" as a poor man of color, immigrant, and person with a disability been taken away from him systematically and intentionally? Where has he been left out? Where do I distance myself from people like him? I can ask these same questions of the police officers involved in her case, my neighbors, and the young men who beat the perpetrator so badly he spent two days in the hospital. I could ask it of the employees at the nonprofit agency who were supposed to be providing the perpetrator with counseling and housing support, but who had not followed up when he missed multiple appointments. I could ask these questions about the perpetrator's family, who was terrified to talk with anyone for fear of retribution. Where was the resource for them to truly assist not just in his rehabilitation, but so he could have a full meaningful life surrounded by many so as not to ever hurt himself or another person? I cry as I think about this now. None of us has escaped this kind of training that puts each of us in the position of constantly being both a target and an agent of oppression.

Another way that the restorative justice process assisted me in my healing is that it required me to open my heart to all of my feelings. Rage, grief, betrayal, disappointment. It gave me a place to fully feel them so I could keep thinking instead of running away from the knowledge that I am capable of hurting others and participate in systems that hurt people every day. The biggest difference between me and my daughter's perpetrator is our circumstances.

The man who raped my daughter received fifteen years in prison. The judge would not consider using restorative justice sentencing in conjunction with traditional sentencing. What I know to be true is that while he is in prison he will receive little to no assistance with healing or rehabilitation. What I know to be true is that it is very likely that he will be raped in prison and that when he is released he will rape again. Even so, I know the work our family and community did using the restorative justice process with multiple circles of participants has had a lasting impact on many of the people involved.

I know I will continue to hold out to others the possibility of an alternative to blame and punishment. Just think about what might happen if all of us had the resources we deserve to have to think well about how to be in communion with one another as we struggle to reclaim the humanity that continues to be stripped from us daily under a system that only works when a few have much and many have so little. I think this is the crux of true social work. (For more information about restorative justice practice, go to the websites of the International Institute of Restorative Practices [http://www.iirp.edu] and the Detroit Area Restorative Justice Center [https://detroitrjcenter.wordpress.com].)

Some describe restorative justice as a new paradigm for doing justice that starts at the grassroots with ordinary members of the community as well as victims and offenders, inclusive of all whose lives are affected by wrongdoing. The approach seeks to hold offenders directly accountable to the people and communities they have violated; restore emotional and material losses of the victims; and provide opportunities for dialogue, negotiation, and problem solving. The goal is to achieve a greater sense of community safety, social harmony, and peace for all involved (Bazemore & Schiff, 2001; Perry, 2002). Katherine van Wormer (2006) argues that restorative justice should be a central part of the knowledge and practice repertoire for social justice work. Here too we see hopeful efforts developing around the world, from community mediation centers and sentencing circles to peace and reconciliation commissions.

> ### Reflection Moment:
> ### Crime and Punishment Revisited
>
> In chapter 4 we introduced the work of Critical Resistance (CR), a grassroots organization dedicated to ending the prison industrial complex. Critical Resistance supports abolition of the prison industrial complex as both an approach and goal. Abolition is "a political vision with the goal of eliminating imprisonment, policing, and surveillance and creating lasting alternatives to punishment and imprisonment" (CR, 2015).
>
> The change CR envisions is possible. Finland offers a real-world model example of the possibilities of *decarceration*. Until the 1970s Finland had a highly punitive correctional system, modeled after that of the Soviet Union. In rethinking the system, policy makers opted for transformation rather than reformation. Policy changes have been crafted around justice, respect for human dignity, and harm prevention. Inmates live in dorms and address guards by their first names. They retain the right to vote. Innovative therapeutic techniques have been encouraged. Today, Finland reports a low crime rate and the lowest imprisonment rate (52 per 100,000) in the European Union (Ekunwe & Jones, 2012).

Action and Advocacy for Children of Incarcerated Parents

America's incarceration practices take a tremendous toll on children and families. More than two and a half million children in the United States have a parent who is incarcerated. While policies such as the Adoption and Safe Families Act of 1997 push social workers toward expedience in termination of parental rights when parents face lengthy sentences, advocates across the country have spearheaded grassroots efforts to support children of incarcerated parents.

For example, Joyce Dixson Haskett, a formerly incarcerated Michigan woman, organized SADOI (Sons and Daughters of the Incarcerated), a group-support program for children who have an incarcerated parent or close family member, in 1996. Joyce was convicted of killing her abusive partner and sentenced to prison in 1976. She became the first woman to earn a bachelor's degree from the University of Michigan while in prison. Upon her release in 1993, she pursued her MSW and advocated for educational opportunities for incarcerated women. As she came to a deeper understanding of the effects of her imprisonment on her own two children, Joyce turned her advocacy efforts toward children of incarcerated parents. The SADOI program provides a safe and nurturing environment where youth come together and talk openly about the experience of their parents' incarceration and its effect on their lives. The groups address topics such as grief and loss, stigma, emotional expression, coping skills, self-esteem, critical inquiry into the causes and effects of incarceration, and what happens when parents come home (Ascione & Dixson, 2002).

In San Francisco a group of child and parent advocates with similar concerns came together in 2000 to form San Francisco Children of Incarcerated Parents Partnership. They agreed that their work should be approached from a children's perspective, and together they crafted a bill of rights for children of incarcerated parents, which guides their advocacy practice (San Francisco Children of Incarcerated Parents Partnership, n.d.). Among these rights are "I have the rights to be heard when decisions about me are made. I have the right to speak with, see, and touch my parent. I have the right not to be judged, blamed, or labeled because my parent is incarcerated. I have the right to a lifelong relationship with my parent." (See http://www.sfcipp.org/images/brochure.pdf for full text.)

Action and Advocacy for Incarcerated Women

The number of women incarcerated in the United States has grown exponentially in the past fifteen years. Of the five hundred thousand women incarcerated around the world, nearly half are in U.S. prisons (American Civil Liberties Union, 2014c). The rights of women prisoners have been the focal point of feminist artist, activist, and professor Carol Jacobsen's life work. Jacobsen grew up in the shadow of Michigan's Jackson Prison, the world's largest prison. Her activism for peace, justice, and women's rights took her around the globe and into the world of photography and film making. Eventually her journey brought her back to the confined space of a prison cell and the stories of women's lives therein. As Carol listened to the life stories of women in prison the barriers between *us* and *them* broke down—she saw herself in their words. She turned her camera on the prisons to bear witness to women's accounts of prison experience, positioning women as both narrators of their own lives and critics of the justice system (Jacobsen, 2013). Her Women in Prison project, begun in 1990, consists of numerous documentary films and video installations.

In the early 1990s Carol joined with Susan Farr, founder of the Michigan Women's Justice and Clemency Project, and a small group of dedicated women—an attorney, a social worker, and former prisoners—to advocate for the release of battered women who had been wrongly convicted for the murder of their abusive partners. The successes of the Clemency Project were modest. In 1998–99 they were able to free two women through motions in court, and they kept going (Jacobsen, 2013).

Over the years Carol brought social work student volunteers into the project, sparking consciousness of the state of women in prison, teaching about human rights through action, and providing opportunities to practice skills of advocacy. Every Sunday afternoon a team gathered at Carol's home to work on petitions; write letters to women in prison; report on case and legal research; and arrange film screenings, talks, and other public relations events. In 2007, in anticipation of Michigan Governor Jennifer Granholm's final term in office, Carol and a group of students engaged in creative political activism and statewide advocacy on behalf of the women. Between 2008 and 2010 the Michigan Women's Justice and Clemency Project represented forty women for clemency or parole. It was successful in getting clemency or parole for six more women (Jacobsen, 2013, p. 97).The project's tireless efforts reflect commitment for the long haul that is central to social justice work.

EXPANDING THE POSSIBILITIES

Social justice workers are pushing the boundaries of creative and critical action on multiple fronts. Many have embraced interdisciplinary collaboration, creative arts, and diverse modes of expression and communication to raise consciousness and to create individual and social change. In this final section we share some examples of innovative action, including approaches such as photovoice and popular theater. We will also highlight examples of actions that tackle the complex interplay of social and environmental justice.

Photovoice

Photovoice is a participatory approach to research, advocacy, and action that involves participants in representing their social realities through photography critical reflection, and presentation of results (Wang & Burris, 1997). Photography provides people a means of accessing and depicting their worlds and providing others with windows into their worlds (Wang, Burris, & Ping, 1996). As participants take cameras into their own hands, they take up the task of visually representing their experiences and concerns and communicating them to others, with the goal of changing policies and practices. The approach, developed by Caroline Wang and Mary Ann Burris (1997), is grounded in principles of popular education. It enables people to systematically document their concerns, engage in critical dialogue about those concerns, and reach those with decision-making power. Wang and colleagues (Wang, Morrel-Samuels, Hutchinson, Bell, & Pestronik, 2004, p. 912) use the mnemonic device *SHOWeD* to describe the basic process of posing questions that participants engage in while viewing one another's photos and contemplating what to say in brief narratives to accompany the photos: What do you **S**ee here? What is really **H**appening? How does this relate to **O**ur lives? **W**hy does this problem or strength **e**xist? What can we **D**o about it? These questions set the stage for participants to identify common issues and themes that emerge from critical group reflection.

Jennifer Molloy (2007) asserts that photovoice, as a participatory approach to research and advocacy, has the potential for furthering the social justice mission of social work. Further, she describes photovoice as a form of empowering group work in which participants learn and practice the skills of mutual aid. And as participants come together in a group context they may develop a deeper awareness of their common struggles and probe possibilities for collective action. There is a burgeoning literature in social work that utilizes photovoice as a key participatory research strategy to document the experiences and perspectives of diverse groups from young women experiencing serious illness (Burles & Thomas, 2013) to youth identifying personal and community strengths (Dakin, Noyes, Arnell, & Rogers, 2015) and women engaged in sex work using images to document their agency and resistance (Desyllas, 2014). Debby Florence describes the possibilities of photovoice as a tool for consciousness raising and action based on her experience with the Work through My Lens project addressing the everyday realities of food service workers in Missoula, Montana.

ON REFLECTION

Work through My Lens

Debby Florence, MSW, Director of Organizing, Good Jobs Missoula

Good Jobs Missoula formed in response to growing concerns across the country about low-wage work. The organizers developed a research project, interviewing downtown food workers. Through these conversations, we identified themes, such as the worker's desire for benefits, living wages, fair scheduling, and paid leave. To complement these interviews, Good Jobs Missoula also decided to use photovoice as an awareness raising and organizing tool.

After making direct contact with more than sixty workers through our survey process, we assumed it would be easy to assemble a group of eight to twelve participants. However, we quickly realized that the same problems that affected the workers were barriers to our project. Many don't know their work schedules more than four days in advance, and even then, there are last minute changes. We couldn't get them in the room at the same time. Even with the promise of a $50 gift card, it took months of failed meetings to realize we needed to do something different.

In the late fall of 2014, we formed a partnership with our local food bank. Rather than focus only on the food industry, we adjusted our wording to invite everyone who is "struggling to get by" to join us to share their experiences through photography. After just two weeks of recruiting, we gathered a group of twelve people, including some food service workers. All twelve showed up to our first meeting, eagerly describing their working conditions, their struggle to put food on the table, and their desire to make a difference.

What unfolded next was nothing short of breathtaking. Our participants weren't sure how to use photography to tell their stories at first. But after we took them through some workshops using a photovoice curriculum, the group, as if by magic, produced striking, poignant images. One participant, Geri Stiffarm, shared a picture from inside her car. She works six to seven days per week. Geri writes: "Driving used to be fun for me, but now I'm the main provider for my family because my wife can't work and I have to drive her to many appointments. Life has become very difficult."

We held an open house at the food bank. Images made by people facing food insecurity were displayed next to the same loaves of bread and cans of beans the photographers depend on. After everyone had a chance to see the photos, our photographers spoke to an emotional audience about their lives.

The entire process transformed individuals from a place of frustration, unsure how to make a difference, into advocates for their own conditions. Photovoice helped people find power and pride in their own story, and it is helping to educate our community. Since then, we have brought the photos to show policy makers and economic developers, and the photos have been displayed for a full month in a local coffee shop. The partnership with our local food bank will continue, and we plan to do another photovoice project in the fall of 2015.

Popular Theater

We introduced popular education in chapter 5. Popular education uses a variety of tools to help people gain deeper understanding of cultural, economic, and political influences on their lives. Popular theater is a form of popular education that uses performance as a tool for dialogue, consciousness raising, and transformation (Bates, 1996; Boal, 1979/1985). Popular theater covers a wide range of activities including drama, dance, puppetry, and song. These theatrical techniques engage people in examination of issues that affect their lives, facilitate communication and interaction that spark awareness of collective oppression, and encourage development of strategies for action (Finn, Jacobson, & Campana, 2004). In popular theater performances the boundaries between actor and audience are challenged, and the audience is encouraged to take an active role in the process of performance and critical reflection.

Popular theater has deep roots in centuries-old political movements as a strategy for consciousness raising. However, popular theater is most closely associated with noted Brazilian director, activist, and educator Augusto Boal, who took Freirian principles of popular education and translated them into the medium of theater as a tool for creating knowledge and change among people living in conditions of poverty and oppression (Bates, 1996). Boal's *Theatre of the Oppressed* (1985) develops the philosophy and practice of popular theater and offers examples of this strategy for change in action. The use of theater and performance has come to play an important role in popular education. Boal (1998) has also written about the use of popular theater as a strategy to change social policy. Through the use of *legislative theater*, a form of popular theater, participants research social issues and use performance as a means of education and advocacy. For instance, legislative theater played a key role in the passage of progressive geriatric health care legislation in Rio de Janiero in 1995 (Boal, 1998).

Social justice workers around the world have embraced popular theater as a strategy for social change. For example, Northern California's El Teatro Campesino, founded in 1965 by Luiz Valdez to support the United Farmworkers Union, performs short skits addressing the plight of migrant farmworkers, challenging stereotypes, and supporting workers' rights (Jacobs, 2007). Stan Houston and colleagues incorporated Theatre of the Oppressed into a Donegal County, Ireland, community employment project with poor unemployed adults to uncover their common experiences of oppression, explore barriers to employment, and strengthen their capacities for realization of their social and economic potential (Houston, Magill, McCollum, & Spratt, 2001). More recently, Izumi Sakamoto and colleagues used democracy theater, a form of popular theater, as a component of a participatory research project to explore the employment challenges facing skilled immigrant workers in Canada (Chin, Sakamoto, & Bleuer, 2014; Sakamoto, Chin, & Young, 2010). An inspiring example of the possibilities of popular theater comes from Laura Wernick and colleagues, who used popular theater to empower lesbian, gay, bisexual, transgender, queer, and questioning (LGBTQQ) youth in raising the consciousness of adults about school climate and engaging adults in changing attitudes, actions, and policies (Wernick, Dessel, Kulick, & Graham, 2013; Wernick, Woodford, & Kulik, 2014). We will feature their story in chapter 8 (p. 359) as an example of action-oriented research.

Linking Social and Environmental Justice

Social workers have been challenged in recent years to actively engage in the work of environmental justice as part and parcel of social justice. The Council on Social Work Education specifically addresses advocacy for environmental justice as part of a broader commitment to human rights and global justice. A number of social work scholars have addressed the disproportionate burden of environmental damage and degradation that poor and marginalized people bear (Gray & Coates, 2012; Jarvis, 2013). Some have addressed the ethical responsibility of social workers to promote environmental as well as social justice (Kemp, 2011). The inequities are glaring. Minority and low-income groups are much more likely to live near environmental hazards that jeopardize health and well-being. Locally unwanted land uses (LULUs), such an industrial waste sites, disproportionately affect poor and minority communities (Jarvis, 2013, p. 39;

Mohai & Saha, 2006). Access to clean water and healthy, affordable food and a sustainable environment are fundamental issues of social and environmental justice and human rights (see Katherine Deuel's story, p. 135, and Bonnie Buckingham's story, p. 234). We close this chapter with an account by Ann Rall, assistant professor of Social Work at Eastern Michigan University, describing the fight for water as a human right in Detroit.

SUMMARY

Throughout this chapter we have examined ways in which the knowledge and values of social justice work are translated into concrete actions for change. We have explored the meaning and power of accompaniment in diverse contexts of practice. Drawing inspiration from critical and creative practitioners around the world, we have demonstrated ways of engaging in and promoting Just Practice across diverse social work arenas, from direct practice with children and families to prison settings and community change efforts. The practice of social justice work calls for a reconceptualization of social work roles in order to address questions of power and positionality and a commitment to critical curiosity, the challenges of collaboration, and the possibilities of creative intervention.

We recognized that the proof of social justice work is in the meaningful participation of those affected in challenging and changing the conditions of their lives. To that end we have addressed skills and strategies for participatory planning, decision making, and action. People-to-people partnerships that respect difference pose both challenges and possibilities. Conflict is part of the process. As social justice workers we need to be able to confront strong feelings, both our own and those of others, and to give time, space, and value to the recognition and expression of feelings.

We have probed the linkage of policy and practice and place of advocacy in social justice. And we have offered concrete examples to both challenge and inspire social workers to *practice* human rights and environmental justice as part of social justice work. We invite you to return to the questions regarding action and accompaniment that we outlined in the Just Practice matrix at the end of chapter 4 (pp. 179–180). How might these questions guide you in developing action plans, building critical alliances and supportive partnerships, and realizing the possibilities of social justice work? What questions would you add to the matrix? As we noted in chapter 1, action and reflection are dialectical, mutually informing processes. As we take time to evaluate and reflect on our practice and celebrate our achievements, we open up new possibilities for action. In chapter 8 we will explore the processes of evaluation, reflection, and celebration.

ON REFLECTION

Social Workers and the Struggle for Water as a Human Right

Ann Rall, MSW, PhD, assistant professor, Eastern Michigan University
School of Social Work

When I first moved to Detroit in 2005, I was working as a case manager during the day, but I also became deeply involved in community organizing as a volunteer with Michigan Welfare Rights Organization (MWRO). The MWRO is a group that has served as a sort of union for low-income people for more than forty years by working with other welfare rights organizations around the country to advocate with and on behalf of people who are trying to access public benefits (such as welfare, disability payments, or public housing assistance).

In the 1990s, in the face of severe cutbacks in public assistance, MWRO began noticing that low-income people were increasingly being confronted with the disconnection of their utilities, including water. Water shutoffs were a particular cause for alarm because of the threats to human life and public health that they represent. The MWRO began to organize to bring public attention to this situation and to call for a number of remedies. The MWRO worked with a utilities expert and some legal aid lawyers to create a Water Affordability Plan in which low-income people would be required to pay only about 3 percent of their income for water.

Members of MWRO repeatedly testified before the city councils of Detroit and Highland Park (HP) to demand that the Water Affordability Plan be approved and implemented. In Highland Park (a small city inside Detroit), the MWRO also lobbied the city council and helped organize demonstrations to oppose the privatization of the HP water department. This struggle is depicted in the film "The Water Front" by Liz Miller.

In Detroit, the city council approved the Water Affordability Plan in 2006, and the Detroit Water and Sewerage Department (DWSD) said that it would implement the plan, but never did. In both Highland Park and Detroit, unpaid water bills began to be added to people's property taxes, which increased the rates of foreclosures and evictions. It became clear that water shutoffs were being used to force low-income people out of areas that had become desirable to wealthy people.

In 2009, the MWRO was part of the formation of the People's Water Board Coalition, an organization that brings together environmental organizations, unions, and organizations concerned with economic justice and racism to advocate for the protection and conservation of water, access to water as a human right for all, and the need to hold water as a public trust.

In 2014, Detroit was accused of financial mismanagement and forced to accept Governor Rick Snyder's appointment of an emergency manager (EM).

The EM, a bankruptcy attorney, promptly announced his plans to declare bankruptcy on behalf of the city. Part of this process included massive water shutoffs. This was supposedly done to get the city's books in order in preparation for the bankruptcy settlement, but many social justice activists believed that it was aimed at pressuring low-income people out of the parts of the city that the wealthy interests were planning to "develop."

During a nine-month period in 2014, more than 30,000 households had their water shut off, denying access to life-sustaining water to more than 100,000 low-income people. The MWRO and the People's Water Board Coalition have been involved in a number of efforts to address the situation, including:

- Working with water activist Maude Barlow and her organization (the Council of Canadians) to write a report on the denial of access to affordable water for the UN Special Rapporteur on the Human Right to Safe Drinking Water and Sanitation. This report generated widespread attention from the mainstream media, and MWRO members provided countless interviews and documentation to media sources around the country and the world.
- Helping to create a water hotline for people experiencing or in danger of experiencing shutoffs.
- Helping to file a class action lawsuit against the City of Detroit by being a bridge between the legal team and the plaintiffs (i.e., the people who were experiencing shutoffs).
- Helping to organize street demonstrations to draw attention to the issue of water as a human right. One of these demonstrations, held in conjunction with the Netroots Nation conference, had more than one thousand participants.
- Meeting with representatives from the city to discuss the level of suffering that the MWRO was witnessing and to urge them to consider the Water Affordability Plan as an alternative to the inhumanity of shutoffs.
- Helping to organize a visit from two UN special rapporteurs: one for water as a human right and one for housing as a human right. This visit mobilized hundreds of Detroiters to testify about their experiences of shutoffs and foreclosures and brought increased national and international attention to the inhumane treatment of Detroiters by the city government.

Separately from the People's Water Board, MWRO helped to organize and conduct civil disobedience actions in which protestors blocked the driveway of the contractor hired to do the shutoffs.

As of 2015 the widespread harassment of low-income Detroiters through both water shutoffs and foreclosures is continuing. The MWRO is intensifying its work with the People's Water Board Coalition and other organizations to advocate for the implementation of the Water Affordability Plan and to oppose the gentrification of Detroit. One of our next steps is to form alliances with activists from other parts of the country and the world who are advocating for access to water and housing for all people.

QUESTIONS FOR DISCUSSION

1. What social work roles are you most comfortable enacting? What roles do you find challenging? Why? What additional roles, beyond those described on p. 299, might be valuable for social justice work?

2. Where do you see possibilities for accompaniment in your social work practice? For building critical alliances?

3. How would you go about assessing the climate for LGBTQ youth in your community's school system? What are some possible courses of action you might take to improve school climate?

4. How does the concept of *framing* inform your thinking about problems and the approaches we take to solve them? What frames dominate understanding of problems in your field of social work practice? What might be alternative frames? How might an alternative frame open possibilities for alternative action?

5. Where do you see possibilities for using creative actions, such as photovoice or popular theater in your social work practice?

SUGGESTED READINGS

Boal, A. (1982). *Theatre of the oppressed*. New York: Routledge.

Hoefer, R. (2012). *Advocacy practice for social justice* (2nd ed.). Chicago: Lyceum Books.

Pyles, L. (2009). *Progressive community organizing: Reflective practice in a globalizing world*. New York: Routledge.

Wilson, M., & Whitmore, E. (2000). *Seeds of fire: Social development in an era of globalization*. Halifax, Nova Scotia: Fernwood.

Chapter 8

Evaluating, Reflecting On, and Celebrating Our Efforts

Every choice we make can be a celebration of the world we want.
Frances Moore Lappé (1971)

OVERVIEW

In chapter 8 we elaborate on the Just Practice core processes of evaluation, critical reflection, and celebration. We begin by defining evaluation and considering its importance for social justice work. We look at different approaches to evaluation and highlight participatory approaches that involve people in addressing the concerns that affect their lives. We show how participatory evaluation can contribute to personal, organizational, community, and sociopolitical empowerment and how the processes and outcomes contribute to critical theory and practice knowledge. We link evaluation to the ongoing process of teaching-learning. We address the relevance of social work values, capabilities, and human rights to social-justice-oriented evaluation.

In this chapter we also identify characteristics of the reflective thinker and explore ways to build capacity for critical reflection. We conceptualize critical reflection as both a tool of inquiry and a constant companion of evaluation practice. We consider the kinds of questions the Just Practice framework asks us to reflect upon in order to make meaningful connections between personal struggles and larger social, political, economic, cultural, and environmental forces. We discuss the importance of critical reflection in guiding us to question the structures and relations of power embedded in the definitions of personal and societal concerns.

We address the core process of celebration and argue the importance of recognizing successes, appreciating contributions, and relishing in the learning that happens along the way. We highlight ways to embrace celebration in the practice of social justice work. We draw attention to the aesthetics of practice and the importance of finding joy and beauty in the work we do. We close this chapter with a summary of key principles of social justice work.

EVALUATION

Evaluation is essential to ethical, accountable, and just social work practice. The Council on Social Work Education requires that social workers be prepared to engage in practice-informed research and research-informed practice (CSWE; 2015a). Further, the Council expects that "social workers understand quantitative and qualitative research methods and their respective roles in advancing a science of social work and in evaluating their practice" (CSWE, 2015a, p. 5). We anticipate that you will develop a practical understanding of social work research methods in the context of research courses. We focus here on evaluation of our change efforts, and we start by defining evaluation and considering its purpose.

Defining Evaluation

Evaluation is traditionally defined as "the systematic application of scientific research procedures to inform evaluative judgments" that entails "collection of empirical information about the activities, characteristics, and outcomes of programs," interventions, and policies to make judgments about their worth, improve their effectiveness, and inform future decision making and action (Patton, 2007, p. 360). We can think of evaluation as the act of taking stock and determining the significance, effectiveness, or quality of a change effort. It is also about asking questions to assess whether actions were consistent with the values of social justice work. One can think of evaluation in a number of ways:

1. *Evaluation as research.* Evaluation is a form of research that follows a systematic process of planning, implementation, data collection, interpretation, and dissemination of the results. Evaluation may focus on assessing both the process and outcomes of a change and the strengths, skills, and challenges of those involved in the effort.

2. *Evaluation as a benchmark.* Evaluation needs to be an ongoing process with checkpoints along the way. Benchmarks are stopping-off places at which participants reflect on the change effort up to that point, make comparisons to other checkpoints, and appreciate the distance covered in understanding and altering attitudes and events. It is a point at which we ask are we moving in the direction that we want to go?

3. *Evaluation as an individual and group memory process.* Evaluation is the act of recording lessons learned and creating a history to inform

ongoing learning. Frances Moore Lappé and Paul Martin DuBois (1994) describe this as a process of creating individual and group memory. As participants in the change process share their experiences, they contribute to critical consciousness and collective memory of histories, struggles, hopes, and actions that inform the process and motivate the participants.

4. *Evaluation as a statement of assumptions and values.* Behind every evaluation method or strategy is a set of assumptions about people, power, and the nature of reality. It is important to think about these assumptions and how they influence and shape evaluation practice. Just as we spoke of valuing as an ethical and political practice in chapter 3, we can think of evaluation as the systematization of valuing.

5. *Evaluation as private and participatory processes.* Evaluation is a private, personal, reflective act. Paulo Freire (Moch, 2009) describes the progressive social worker as someone who is on a lifelong search for competence. Self-evaluation is key to this search. Evaluation is also a participatory process done *with* rather than *to* others. Thinking of evaluation as a collaborative project is a way to value the contributions of others and open up possibilities for new solutions to old problems.

6. *Evaluation as accountability.* Evaluation is a process of demonstrating accountability to participants in the change process, to those affected by the change process, to our organizations, and to funding sources. Participatory approaches to evaluation of change efforts are time consuming. They require commitment from all parties involved. Has time been well spent? Has the process enhanced participants' skills and capacities? Made the most of available resources? Strengthened organizational capacity?

7. *Evaluation as an opportunity to reflect on and promote social justice.* Evaluation provides the opportunity to assess our efforts from a social justice perspective. Were those most affected part of the process of deciding what questions to be asked and what counted as measures of success? Did the change effort create enduring shifts in power for those most disadvantaged? Did the change effort result in a more equitable distribution of resources? Did the effort further recognition, protection, or promotion of human rights?

Why Evaluate?

Evaluation allows time for rethinking and reorganizing change efforts and strategies based on reflection, interpretation, and analysis. Evaluation calls on participants to see gains, growth, and successes in organized efforts and to use these as a springboard into subsequent action. Evaluation also calls attention to the challenges of our change efforts and provides a process to address these challenges and build new knowledge to forge subsequent efforts. There is also subsidiary knowledge gained from a participatory evaluation process that has little to do with programs or policy but everything to do with people. Involving people in a partnership to investigate social reality can be an empowering and transformative process for all.

Social work programs, services, and projects are expected to be accountable to service users, funders, the profession, and a broader public. Governmental, community, and private funders require results to show that their money is well spent. Social workers are often accountable to diverse entities with differing interests at stake and differing views of what counts as success. Accountability to external funders and policy makers may be in tension with accountability to service users, and social workers need the knowledge and skills to navigate that tension and engage in meaningful evaluation of practice that addresses client rights, dignity, and needs. We, as social workers, also need to recognize the importance of evaluation in our ongoing "search for competence" (Moch, 2009). Evaluation opens us to scrutiny and leaves us vulnerable. At the same time it opens us to possibility, innovation, and renewed commitment.

Evaluation and Evidence-Based Practice

More and more, social workers are called upon to engage in *evidence-based practice*. Evidence-based practice is defined as the "conscientious, explicit, and judicious use of current best evidence in making decisions about the care of individual [clients]" (Sackett, Rosenberg, Gray, Haynes, & Richardson, 1996, p. 71). As described by the CSWE (2015b), "this definition requires a process that is comprised of several steps for finding and employing appropriate interventions for every client, and also requires that the client's preferences and actions, as well as their clinical state and circumstances, must be part of the decision-making." Specifically, the steps involve formulation of a client-, community-, or policy-related question; review and appraisal of relevant literature; application of findings to practice; and evaluation of results. Evidence-based practice calls for the integration of relevant research on social work interventions and outcomes and research on the reliability and validity of assessment measures with social worker's expertise and client values in making practice decisions (McNeese & Thyer, 2004, p. 9). As evidence-based practitioners, social workers are expected to be informed systematic *evaluators* of research and practice. They are also expected to be mindful, drawing from cumulative professional knowledge and experience in making diagnoses, considering intervention options, and implementing and evaluating selected intervention plans. At the same time, social workers are expected to be mindful of the unique needs, values, and preferences of the client in the moment (Cournoyer, 2004, p. 4).

Let's take a moment to consider these expectations. On the one hand, the language of evidence-based practice emphasizes the role of social worker as "expert." Its definitional language implicitly incorporates a medical model approach to diagnosis and intervention. It privileges particular kinds of data and research in determining what counts as evidence. As Barbara Klugman (2010) observes,

> Contemporary beliefs about what constitutes valid evidence tend to be shaped by particular paradigms, most notably from the West. Confidence exists in findings produced only by certain research designs, but does not exist for findings based on alternative approaches, even when the context or the research questions require them. (p. 6)

Thus, dominant notions of evidence may be informed by very narrow definitions of what data, research, and knowledge count in determining problem definition, evaluating possible courses of action, and measuring outcomes.

On the other hand, evidence-based practice calls on social workers to use the best available knowledge to guide ethical practice. Therefore, despite our criticisms, we are not arguing that social justice workers should resist the call for evidence-based practice. We agree that systematic ethical use of available evidence is essential for research-informed practice and practice-informed research. Rather, we argue that social justice workers have a responsibility to critique and expand narrow understandings of "evidence." Further, social justice workers have the opportunity and responsibility to learn from and engage service users and program participants in gathering and evaluating evidence that may provide richer and more nuanced context-relevant understandings of the nature of the problem or issue, possibilities for action, and meanings and measures of success. Now that we have addressed the why of evaluation, let's consider what needs to be evaluated.

What Needs to Be Evaluated?

Think for a moment of the varied work situations social workers find themselves in and the multiple functions of social work within particular settings. What should we evaluate and why? What would be important for the child protection services worker to evaluate, for example? Or what might be an important question for a school social worker to pose regarding a school program that seeks to facilitate parents' increased involvement with their children's education? Anne Hope and Sally Timmel (1984/1999, vol. 2, p. 124) suggest a number of areas to consider in the evaluation process. We add social justice and human rights to their list and pose questions for you to think about as they relate to each area. We invite you to add to the list.

- *Aims.* Given the original mission and purpose of the organization or the goals laid out by participants, where are we now? Are we far adrift from these aims or right on the mark?

- *Ethics.* Are practices and procedures ethical and by whose standards? Who is included, who is left out, and why? Are we adhering to the principles of social justice work? Do practices and procedures reflect a commitment to social justice?

- *Participation.* Who is involved in the organization's decision making? Are the voices of those the program was meant to benefit valued? Who participates and how?

- *Methods.* Are methods used consistent with the values of social justice work? Do procedures, policies, and practices allow for the contributions of those most directly concerned with the issues we wish to address? How do these address the issue of difference?

- *Content.* Does the program or project address participants' expectations? Does it address the root causes of concerns?

- *Animators and administrators.* What are the leadership skills of the project animators or program administrators? What are their strengths and challenges?

- *Follow-up.* How is the program or the project assessed when the work is completed? At checkpoints down the road? Is there a mechanism in place to conduct follow-up?

- *Time and money.* How much time and money goes into this program or project? Has the time and money produced visible, sustainable results? Is sufficient time and money put toward the effort? Would a different allocation of time and money produce better results?

- *Planning, coordination, and administration*. What is the quality of program or project planning? How would you rate the level of coordination among participants, projects, programs, and other community groups and organizations? How are programs and projects administered? What are the strengths and challenges of planning, coordination, and administration?

- *Decision making*. How are decisions made? Are these top-down, bottom-up, or a little bit of both? What process is used to make decisions? Is this process collaborative? Whose voices contribute to the decision-making process?

- *Social justice and human rights*. How does the project or program address issues of social justice and human rights? Does it contribute to protection or promotion of human rights? Does it result in a shift in the balance of power in favor of marginalized or disadvantaged individuals or groups? Does it make connections between personal struggles and structural arrangements?

Social Worker as Participatory Researcher

In order to effectively evaluate our practice, we need to embrace the role of researcher. As discussed in chapter 7, researcher is not a role apart from that of practitioner; it is one of the central social work roles. Research guides and informs our practice, provides means of determining the success of our efforts, and contributes to the overall knowledge base of the profession. Unfortunately, many social workers would prefer to distance themselves from the researcher role. Perhaps that is because the research process itself has largely been presented as something that takes place at a distance from hands-on practice.

Much of traditional research is informed by *positivist* assumptions. As we addressed in chapter 4, positivism is rooted in the idea that there is a single, stable, and ultimately knowable reality outside ourselves that we can subject to study. In traditional positivist research, the researcher is seen as an objective outsider who is separated from the subject being researched—the object of inquiry (Maguire, 1987). If the researcher's methods are thought to be objective, then it follows that these methods control for the personal values and assumptions of the researcher. Inquiry based on a positivist perspective is thus considered to be value free.

Participatory Assumptions

Participatory approaches to knowledge development question positivist assumptions. They challenge notions of objectivity and value-free inquiry and practices that separate the researcher from the researched. Participatory researchers see themselves not as neutral observers but as positioned actors engaged in relationship and dialogue with coresearchers and community members (Barbera, 2008). They recognize that all inquiry is value laden, strive to clarify values and assumptions, and openly address how values and assumptions may affect the research process and outcome. They strive for critical awareness of their own subjectivity in the research process (Finn, 1994; Lather, 1986, 1991; Maguire, 1987).

Participatory research supports the meaningful involvement of people in addressing the concerns that affect their lives, recognizes knowledge as a form of power, and sees research as a catalyst for action (Barbera, 2008; Finn, 1994; Israel, Eng, Schulz, & Parker, 2005; Maguire, 1987). Participatory research is characterized by consciousness raising, collaboration, capacity building, recognition of diverse voices, explicit attention to values, and commitment to promoting strengths of participants in the pursuit of justice-oriented change (Becker, Israel, & Allen, 2005; Branom, 2012; Finn, 1994). Evaluation is viewed as a social process and the participants have a role and an effect in the process. It is, nonetheless, a systematic and rigorous practice that attempts to account for the ways in which values, positioning, and perspective may shape the research process.

We contend that participatory approaches to evaluation research are well suited to social justice work. Participatory approaches provide opportunities to learn directly from those involved and affected by a program, policy, or course of action. This co-learning helps us ask the right questions in the right way (Gonzalez & Trickett, 2014). Participatory approaches provide participants with ownership and voice in a democratic process of knowledge development, recognize the value of contextually grounded knowledge, put social justice values of inclusion and empowerment to practice, and create opportunities for capacity building (Checkoway & Richards-Schuster, 2001, 2003; Klugman, 2010; Weaver & Cousins, 2004).

Participatory approaches to evaluation incorporate both qualitative and quantitative methods of inquiry. Most simply put, qualitative research is interested in how people construct meaning and make sense of their world. It is a situated activity, interpretive in nature (Denzin & Lincoln, 2005, p. 3). Quantitative research seeks to explain the relationship between variables through use of numerical data that can be measured in terms of amount, frequency, or intensity and subjected to mathematical analysis. Although there is debate over which approach is better or more rigorous, the two approaches can be complementary. Each approach brings its own strengths to the process, and they can be effectively combined. In fact, part of a participatory process may involve decisions to gather very specific quantitative information or use existing quantitative measures in order to evaluate ways in which particular programs, policies, or practices affect certain groups. These data can be combined with qualitative inquiry, through means such as interviews, case studies, and small group conversations, to capture a more holistic understanding of the process and outcomes of a change effort.

Validity and Reliability

Some critics have argued that participatory modes of inquiry are too subjective to count as real research and have raised questions regarding the *validity* and *reliability* of data produced, collected, and interpreted by those with a stake in the process. These terms may be familiar to you if you have already taken a research methods course. Reliability and validity relate to the trustworthiness of the research knowledge and its results (Lincoln & Guba, 1985). The test of reliability is whether an evaluation tool produces stable, consistent results when the measure is repeated over time. The concept of validity relates to

> the ways in which the research design ensures that the introduction of the independent variable (if any) can be identified as the sole cause of change in the dependent variable . . . and the extent to which the research design allows for generalization of the findings of the study to other groups and other situations. (Grinnell & Unrau, 2005, p. 194)

For example, in a study to determine whether drug abuse causes domestic violence, the independent variable is drug abuse and the dependent variable is domestic violence. Internal validity asks how we know that changes in domestic violence (dependent variable) are a result of drug abuse (independent variable) and not a result of other factors. External validity asks how we can be sure that the information we have gathered reflects only respondents' information and not the researcher's biases or judgments (Marlow, 2005). Can we generalize our information to other circumstances and situations? The ideal study is thought to be one whose research design attempts to control both internal and external threats to validity (Rubin & Babbie, 2013).

Particia Lather (1986, 1991) specifically addresses the subjects of reliability and validity in research with a participatory approach and a social justice aim. She contends that participatory inquiry can stand up to the test of rigor and relevance in research and must do so to promote the emancipatory possibilities of participatory research and evaluation. Further, she argues that researchers who blend theory and justice-oriented action (praxis) may want to consider the less well-known notion of *catalytic validity* as a guiding principle. Lather defines catalytic validity as "the degree to which the research process re-orients, focuses, and energizes participants toward knowing reality in order to transform it" (1991, p. 68). She ties this in with the Freirean concept of *conscientiza-tion*, meaning that all involved in the knowledge generation process (research) and changed through this process, "gain self-understanding and, ultimately, self-determination through research participation" (p. 68).

PARTICIPATORY APPROACHES TO EVALUATION

Participatory evaluation is a process whereby all participants are afforded opportunities to reflect on programs, projects, and policies; the mission and aims of the organization; and their own and others' involvement in change efforts. Stakeholders determine what to evaluate and how (Cousins & Whitmore, 1998). Evaluation is something done *with* people, not *to* people. According to the University of Kansas Work Group for Community Health and Development (2016),

> Participatory evaluation . . . isn't simply a matter of asking stakeholders to take part. Involving everyone affected changes the whole nature of a project from something done for a group of people or a community to a partnership between the beneficiaries and the project implementers. Rather than power-less people who are acted on, beneficiaries become the copilots of a project, making sure that their real needs and those of the community are recognized and addressed. Professional evaluators, project staff, project beneficiaries or participants, and other community members all become colleagues in an effort to improve the community's quality of life. (University of Kansas, 2016)

Positive outcomes of conducting evaluations *with* people include a greater likelihood that the results will be accepted by program personnel and incorporated into practice, increased sensitivity to the social and political context of the organization (Cherin & Meezan, 1998), and much higher rates of effect on organizational decision making (Rossi & Freeman, 1993). In this section we elaborate on participatory approaches to evaluation and present background information on their history, objectives, principles, and methods. We further delineate the benefits of participatory evaluation. Case examples of evaluations guided by participatory assumptions are presented to provide you with possibilities for your own evaluation practice.

Origins and Objectives

Scholars of participatory approaches to research describe their emergence in the 1960s in countries such as Latin America, India, and Africa, where understandings of power and domination forged resistance to knowledge development and research methods based on the positivist paradigm (Park, 1993). For example, traditional survey research questions designed by an outside researcher may reflect the biases and assumptions of the researcher and fail to capture the experiences and understandings of the respondents. In contrast, participatory researchers have developed alternative strategies for information gathering and analysis that value and include people's lived experience in every stage of the research process (Hall, 1993). Research by the people and for the people is a powerful tool for addressing power imbalances and other forms of inequality that shape people's lives. Attention to issues of power in knowledge generation and to the exploitive history of research on the lives of Native Americans and other groups of indigenous people has forged new approaches to research that attend to issues of culture and history and highlight assets and strengths (Christopher, 2005; Smith, 1999).

In social work's own history, attention to issues concerning people's everyday lives and the glaring need to address growing social inequalities has shaped approaches to research. As described in chapter 2, early settlement house workers around the turn of the twentieth century engaged in participatory research methods by enlisting neighborhood residents as research team members (Addams, 1910). They gathered data on neighborhood health and sanitation, working conditions in factories, and maternal and infant mortality. They designed and implemented survey research to assess community needs and conditions (Kellogg, 1914; Zimbalist, 1977). Their methodology was shaped by the historical, political, and economic context at the time.

Principles of Participatory Evaluation

Participatory evaluation calls for meaningful engagement of those affected in all phases of the evaluation, from the naming and framing of the problem, to identifying questions about the project and the best ways to ask, implementation of the evaluation, and interpretation and dissemination of results (University of Kansas Work Group, 2016). As discussed earlier in the chapter, participatory evaluation has a number of assumptions that differ from those underlying traditional forms of evaluation. Based on these assumptions, participatory evaluation is guided by the following principles.

A Dialogical Process

Dialogue is a distinguishing feature of participatory evaluation. As we have seen in the preceding chapters, *dialogue* is the conduit of knowledge. Participatory evaluation brings individuals most affected by an issue together with administrators and researchers to pose questions and arrive at solutions. People learn from each other through collective interaction. For example, in participatory evaluation, questionnaires are seen as a "vehicle of dialogue" (Park, 1993, p. 12). Through dialogue, we come to know our communities and ourselves. Park comments on dialogue as a tool of research:

> Dialogue produces not just factual knowledge but also interpersonal and critical knowledge, which defines humans as autonomous social beings. This is an essential reason for the people's participation in research. It is not just so they can reveal private facts that are hidden from others but really so they may know themselves better as individuals and as a community. (pp. 12–13)

Attention to Issues of Power

Participatory approaches challenge the lack of attention to *power* in traditional evaluation research. They assume that everything we do is embedded within a political context, and this context shapes the questions we ask and the kinds of research we conduct. Participatory evaluation disrupts the idea of expert knowledge and research as a tool solely of the "educated." It holds that all people have the capacity to better understand their lives and shape their own reality.

Control of Decision Making

Closely linked to issues of power is control of decision making (Weaver & Cousins, 2004). Participatory evaluation seeks to democratize decision-making power at every step of the research process, from determining what needs to be evaluated to defining the research questions, deciding on modes of data collection, clarifying what counts as success, determining roles and responsibilities for the evaluation process, implementing the evaluation plan, interpreting and presenting outcomes, and proposing changes in response to evaluation results (Foster & Louie, 2010). Social workers facilitate this process by gathering people together, conducting small and large group discussions, and helping to formulate the problem in such a way that it can be researched.

An Empowering, Capacity-Building Process

Program or project participants also learn the transferable skills of collecting, analyzing, and disseminating evaluation knowledge. Participatory evaluation is thus a form of capacity building at multiple levels. Theoretically, participatory evaluation shares common ground with social work's empowerment perspective. Both seek to promote social justice and equality through full participation in society.

Some scholars have described *empowerment evaluation* as a form of participatory evaluation that pays particular attention to stakeholder ownership of the research process and product and to the transfer of research and evaluation knowledge to stakeholders to foster self-determination (Cox, Keener, Woodward, & Wandersman, 2009; Fetterman, 1996). Empowerment evaluation is based on principles of community ownership, inclusion, democratic participation, community knowledge, evidence-based strategies, accountability, continuous improvement, organizational learning, social justice, and individual and organizational capacity building. Although these principles reflect those of participatory evaluation more broadly, those who embrace the concept of empowerment evaluation have specifically grounded this approach in empowerment theory (Secret, Jordan, & Ford, 1999). The Centers for Disease Control and Prevention (Cox et al., 2009) has published a seven-step approach to empowerment evaluation that provides a detailed user-friendly overview of the concept and process. The Community Toolbox, compiled by the University of Kansas Work Group for Community Health and Development (2016), is a great hands-on resource for participatory evaluation.

Diverse Methods Used to Conduct Participatory Evaluation

Participatory evaluation can take many different shapes and forms. It borrows its methods from a variety of social science tools used to conduct other types of research. However, some methods are modified to allow increased interaction between those administering the methods and those providing information. Below we outline some evaluation methods. Can you think of specific situations when different methods might be helpful or when they might be counterproductive?

- *Written questionnaires.* Questionnaires are a common method used for participatory evaluation because of their versatility. They can be used when evaluating efforts with individuals, groups, neighborhoods, and entire communities. Through a collaborative process, participants tailor questionnaires to the investigation at hand by prioritizing questions and ensuring that the wording is clear and easy to understand. Question- naires may include both closed-ended questions, which can be answered with a yes/no response or with a specific piece of information, and open- ended questions, which provide opportunity for elaboration. Each type of question has its advantages and disadvantages. Questionnaires can be used as a tool to stimulate dialogue. Questionnaires administered face-to-face generally have higher response rates than those sent by mail or administered online. They also provide opportunities for gathering richer data (Neuman, 2005; Rubin & Babbie, 2013).

- *Informal interviews.* Conducting informal interviews is another useful way to gather information. Informal interviews are especially useful at the beginning of an evaluation project when there is a need to gather pre- liminary information. Perhaps the research team is not sure what they need to evaluate, what strategies may be best, or what questions to ask. Conducting informal interviews can be a good way to begin (Neuman, 2005; Rubin & Babbie, 2013). Informal interviews provide a format in which people can discuss their experiences in their own words and high- light the issues of most importance to them.

- *Structured and semi-structured interviews.* As the group becomes more familiar with the issues and concerns, more focused interviewing can take place. With structured and semi-structured interviews, the interviewer asks questions beginning with the general and moving to the specific and from the least personal to the more personal. The research team plans the questions beforehand. Structured and semi-structured inter- views are appropriate for repeat interviews once rapport and trust have been developed and the focus of the evaluation narrowed down (Neu- man, 2005; Rubin & Babbie, 2013). The interview process itself may be a catalyst for change (Brown & Tandon, 1978).

- *Small and large group discussion.* Group discussions allows for maximum participation. Groups can also be sources of support as well as venues for addressing differences and conflict. Focus groups are a good example of small group discussion as an evaluation research method (Krueger, 1994; Krueger & King, 1998). Krueger defines the focus group as a special kind of group that values participants' experiences, attitudes, and opinions. The open, semi-directed format allows participants a voice in the issues that concern their lives and creates a space where responses to questions can be open rather than constrained by a yes or no reply. Moreover, when people are gathered in a group context, they learn from and can be further stimulated in their thinking by the responses of other participants. This allows the discussion to reach greater depth than would be possible in a structured or semi-structured one-on-one interview. Typically, focus groups consist of approximately six to ten people. They can be conducted in a series to allow for richer discussion and a more thorough purview of the issue at hand. Community members familiar with the focus group participants can be trained to facilitate the meeting, thereby maximizing the potential for trust to develop more rapidly (Krueger & King, 1998).

- *Surveys.* Although surveys typically conjure up images of telephone interviews, survey methods can be rethought to include participatory components. For example, Roy Carr-Hill (1984) argues that survey research can be "radicalized" and transformed into a process in which the inquiry creates a catalyst for participation and change. For example, we described the use of a listening survey (Hope & Timmel, 1984/1999, vol. 1, p. 24) as a tool for teaching-learning in chapter 6. It is also useful as an approach to evaluation. The listening survey is quite different from the typical survey in which questions are decided beforehand by a group of "experts." Rather, it provides an opportunity for understanding what people are concerned about and what they feel strongly about.

- *Case studies.* Case studies are becoming more common in evaluation research (Yin, 2008). They best address the how and why research questions, making them well suited to evaluation: How does the program or project deal with difference? Why does the program or project work so well? Cases can be programs, projects, processes, neighborhoods, whole organizations, and communities. Although case studies zero in on a specific entity, such as a program or project, they view this entity within its historical, political, and social context (Stake, 1995; Yin, 2008). Case study methodology considers the multiple systems in play that affect organizations and projects, thereby enriching evaluation information and making it contextually relevant. Case studies use multiple methods such as interviewing, participant observation, focus groups, and questionnaires to achieve these ends.

- *Illustrated presentations.* Slides, photos, or drawings help to catalogue the history of a program, a project, or an individual change effort. They can evoke a historical perspective, aid in the recall of significant memories, signify points of comparison, and serve as a jumping-off place for critical reflection. The photovoice process (see chapter 7), in which participants use photos to document aspects of their reality, has been applied with increasing regularity as a participatory evaluation method with a strong action component (Wang & Burris, 1997). Photos can be used to capture powerful before and after images that may speak to the outcomes of change efforts.

- *Skits, dramatizations, and other visual representations.* Enacting the change effort using prepared scripts or impromptu dramatizations is an exciting and energizing way to get body and spirit into the evaluation process. Visual representations of efforts create pictures or images of the work accomplished, its surprises, successes, and challenges. The Gayrilla Theater's use of popular theater as a vehicle to communicate results of a study of school climate provides a powerful example of the use of dramatization in evaluation (Wernick et al., 2014). The practice of *strategic illustration* is another innovative example of the use of visual imagery as part of a participatory evaluation process. Strategic illustration is a process whereby artists capture a real-time visual record of a group's activities, such as an organization's strategic planning session, a community brainstorming or problem-solving meeting, or an interactive conference. The illustrations, often drawn on mural-size (4- × 6-ft) paper, provide a unique record of themes, discussions, and questions that participants can revisit and respond to. The visual record can serve as a catalyst for evaluating both process and outcome (see, for example, Alchemy, 2015).

- *Testimonials.* Individual and/or group testimonials are yet another way to bring the voices of those involved in the process to bear on analyzing efforts, appreciating the work, and creating a memorable moment for all participants. Testimonials are a way to put a human face and voice on the message. We referred to the practice of bearing witness in chapter 5. Testimonials are first person accounts of lived experience. When diverse audiences bear witness to the testimonials of those affected by a particular policy, program, or practice, they gain new insight to inform evaluation. For example, the documentary film "From Place to Place" depicted the struggles faced by young people aging out of the foster care system (Anderson & Williams, 2011). Congressional testimony presented by two young people resulted in a reevaluation of foster care policy. The film itself serves as a testimonial regarding youth aging out of care and has prompted critical reflection and evaluation of foster care policies and practices on multiple fronts. The film earned the NASW Media Award for best documentary in 2012.

Benefits and Challenges of Participatory Evaluation

We have already provided a rationale for the use of participatory evaluation and described its alignment with social justice work. Highlighted here are some of the benefits of participatory evaluation as articulated by the University of Kansas Work Group for Community and Health Development (2016):

- It offers a better perspective than traditional approaches on both the initial needs of those affected by the problem or issue and the ultimate effects of an intervention effort.
- It provides information you might not otherwise get.
- It tells you what works or does not work from the perspectives of those most directly involved and provides insights into why.
- It can inform effective change.
- It provides a voice to stakeholders who have often not been heard.
- It builds confidence, skills, knowledge, and capacities among participants.
- It encourages ownership of the evaluation process.
- It provides a model for ongoing collaboration.

Participatory approaches to evaluation also pose challenges. Participatory evaluation demands responsibility and commitment to the process. The three major aims of participatory research—to investigate, to educate, and to take action—require versatile, risk-taking participants who are comfortable playing the roles of researcher, educator, and activist. They are time-intensive processes. To be done well, participatory approaches require time to identify stakeholders and bring a group together. It takes time to build trust among participants, commitment to the process, and the skill base to carry out research. Participatory evaluations are, by definition, group efforts, and they face the challenges, conflicts, and logistics issues inherent to group work. Participatory evaluations challenge traditional thinking, and some funders or administrators may be resistant to the process. Time and effort may be needed to convince these stakeholders of the value of participatory evaluation. Genuine participation requires ongoing attention to questions of power to ensure that everyone is meaningfully involved and that those with more institutional power and authority do not take over the process (University of Kansas Work Group, 2016). Despite these challenges, we contend that participatory evaluation is worth the effort.

Participatory evaluation methods must be tailored to the particular context and include consideration of available resources and the assets participants bring with them to the effort. It is important to assess each method for its strengths and limitations. We encourage you to consider the five key concepts of meaning, context, power, history, and possibility as you undertake this assessment. For example:

- Does this method allow for the expression of multiple meanings of experiences, events, and situations? And does it fit with the experiences and capacities of the group?
- Does this method help connect personal problems and their larger political, economic, and sociocultural contexts?
- Does this method consider power as it affects relationships among participants? Is this method empowering?
- Does this method allow for points of comparison so that history can be a source of learning?
- What are some creative uses for this method and what possible approaches to evaluation does it bring to mind?

As this discussion suggests, there are multiple ways in which to engage in the development of knowledge. Each strategy for collecting information has its strengths and limitations. Consideration must be given to how a certain strategy will fit in a particular context, as well as the resources in terms of time, money, and expertise that will be needed to carry it out. It is also important to consider that each strategy by itself gathers a partial picture of the phenomenon under study. We suggest that you think of ways in which you can incorporate different strategies to enrich and deepen the quality of information you collect. Recall from our earlier discussion that a mixed-methods approach also provides an opportunity to triangulate data, thereby increasing its reliability or trustworthiness. We present these strategies as possibilities for further exploration and ask you to add to this list and think of ways to combine approaches with ideas of your own.

Class Learning Activity: Making it Participatory

Interview an administrator or supervisor of a local service, advocacy, or social action organization. Your task is to find out what evaluation means to the organization and what methods the organization uses to evaluate its programs, projects, and personnel. To prepare for this process, the class will divide into small groups and draw up a tentative list of interview questions to ask an administrator or supervisor of the organization. What questions might you ask and why? After you have conducted your interview, bring the results with you to class for discussion. What methods does the organization use to evaluate itself? What does it evaluate? People? Policies? Practices? How often? Who conducts the evaluation? How are the results used? What is the degree of participation in the process?

Try applying the five key concepts of Just Practice—meaning, context, power, history, and possibility—as a framework for critique. What *meaning* does evaluation have for the organization? In what *context(s)* does it occur? Who has the *power* to make decisions regarding what to evaluate and which methods to choose? How has *history* affected these decisions and methods? What other evaluation *possibilities* exist?

Now think about how you might transform this organization's evaluation strategy to be empowering and participatory. What would you do differently? How would you do it? How does your transformation incorporate the key concepts and what role do they play in building your evaluation process? How do the values of Just Practice translate into a working model of evaluation when you bring the concept of collaboration to bear on your reflections? What might be some of the challenges and constraints of implementing your model in an organization? What might be some of its successes?

PARTICIPATORY EVALUATION IN ACTION

More and more, social work scholars and social justice advocates are embracing participatory approaches to evaluation and demonstrating their benefits. In this section we share some models, examples, and lessons from practice.

Evaluating Social Justice Advocacy Efforts

Barbara Klugman is a consultant based in South Africa and the United States who has worked with advocacy groups and governmental and nongovernmental organizations to strengthen their capacity to strategically address and evaluate social justice objectives in their work. First she puts forth a clear definition of social justice advocacy as work for enduring structural change that addresses the concerns of those who are most disadvantaged, tackles root causes of historic and persistent inequities, and promotes human rights (2010, 2011). Klugman frames social justice advocacy around the three core values of equitable resource distribution, recognition of human diversity and rights, and representation or the right to participation. The value and practice of *participation* guide the process of evaluating social justice advocacy. Klugman writes that effective social justice advocacy evaluation looks first for the three core values listed above in the goals of advocacy. How were the goals determined? Whose interests do they represent? Who will benefit if the goals are achieved? To what extent did those with the least power participate in setting the goals?

Second, effective social justice evaluation looks for the values in the theory of change (see chapter 7) that informed the advocacy effort. What dynamics shaped the formation of the problem statement? What was the process for proposing possible solutions to the problem? Whose voices and views were represented and how?

Third, Klugman states that the interim outcomes in the theory of change process need to be evaluated. Was organizational capacity strengthened in terms of social justice? That might mean a more equitable distribution of organizational resources among staff or between paid staff and volunteers. Did the effort strengthen the base of organizational support? Did those most affected have a meaningful say in terms of perspectives on the problem and proposed actions or were they only represented by experts who spoke "for" them? Are social justice goals maintained as coalition and alliances are forged? How are research questions framed in analyzing the outcomes of social justice advocacy efforts? What are the short- and long-term impacts of the advocacy effort? Klugman's questions provide a guide to evaluating the validity of social justice claims in advocacy efforts.

Participatory Action Research Design Teams in Child Welfare

What might organizational innovation and workforce reconfiguration look like in the child welfare system if envisioned and designed by child welfare workers themselves? Hal Lawson and James Caringi (2015) describe an innovative process of participatory evaluation and action research in which public child welfare workers come together in design teams to identify workplace problems, propose organizational change to optimize conditions for protection and support of vulnerable children and families, and create team-generated improvements. The authors address the challenges of public child welfare systems characterized by high caseloads, top-down and at times punitive leadership, competing demands for investigation and support, and high staff turnover, which combine to have negative effects on the outcomes for children and families. They describe design teams as "workforce, organizational, and policy interventions" (p. 40). Made up of eight to twenty-five members, design teams represent the various official roles, informal groups, and networks within the agency. With the help of a skilled facilitator, the team investigates causes of workforce problems and develops plans for improvement.

Caringi describes his role in facilitating design teams as they learn to use a *logic model* to develop a theory of the problem that serves as a guide for action. He translates the complexity of theory into three clear questions (Lawson & Caringi, 2015, p. 50):

1. What's wrong that needs fixing and what are the causes?
2. What's good and strong that needs to be kept as part of the solution?
3. How can we be sure that the solution(s) we identify will fix the problem (i.e., to what extent does the solution address the causes)?

In effect, the design team members are engaged in a process of participatory evaluation of their organizational context. Caringi describes his roles as those of "teacher, group process clinician, and capacity builder" (p. 50). Design teams evaluate workplace structures, conditions, and practices from the inside out. They systematically explore problems, causes, and effects; brainstorm ideal situations; reflect on the history of what has been tried and perhaps worked in the past; and consider solutions needed to optimize workplace condition such that children and families receive just treatment.

Youth as Evaluators

Barry Checkoway and Katie Richards-Schuster (2001, 2003) describe the capacities and possibilities of young people's participation in evaluation processes of organizational and community change efforts. Based on their long-term engagement with a number of youth-driven community change efforts through the Lifting New Voices Project, they have learned firsthand about young people's ability to create change and evaluate their efforts. For example, they describe the participatory evaluation process employed by People United for a Better Oakland (PUEBLO), which has a young person on staff as a community-based evaluator and a youth-adult evaluation team that meets regularly. The team uses a range of approaches including interviews, written journals, surveys, participant observation, and video documentation.

Youth are actively engaged in evaluation of actions related to issues directly affecting their lives, such as the increasing rates of suspensions and expulsions of students of color (Checkoway & Richards-Schuster, 2003, pp. 28–29). The authors challenge adultist attitudes and practices that too often limit youth participation in designing, running, and evaluating community change initiatives, and they point to the benefits of youth participation in community evaluation. Participation in building knowledge and capacity for social action provides youth an opportunity to exercise their political rights and to share in democratization of knowledge, and it contributes to youth empowerment (p. 30).

Social Work Students as Program Evaluators

Over the past several years, BSW and MSW students at the University of Montana School of Social Work have played an active research role in the program evaluation process. Students have developed surveys to assess the program's effectiveness and administered them to fellow students, faculty, and alumni. They have conducted individual interviews with faculty and focus groups with social work majors and practicum supervisors. They have utilized both qualitative and quantitative data collection methods and analyses, which allow them to translate abstract research concepts into practice. They have also made the connection between research and practice and have applied the skills they learned in previous practice courses to their work as program evaluators (i.e., observation, individual interviewing, small group facilitation, and establishing the reliability of evidence). They have presented their results and recommendations for change at faculty meetings and research forums. Their recommendations have informed curricular changes with positive results. One student summarized her sentiments toward the project: "When you participate and are able to see the results you have a sense of ownership and involvement." Another student commented that she now realized "how much research and evaluation can be used to create change."

We hope that these brief examples will offer an emerging picture of the possibilities of participatory evaluation as a component of Just Practice. The following case example by Alex Kulick and Laura Wernick describes the participatory action research initiated by Riot Youth, Ann Arbor, Michigan, to assess school climate and create institutional change for lesbian, gay, bisexual, transgender, queer, questioning, intersex, and agender/asexual (LGBTQQIA) young people.

ON REFLECTION

Participatory Action Research to Change School Climate

Alex Kulick, PhD student, University of California, Santa Barbara,
and Laura Wernick, MSW, PhD, assistant professor, Fordham University
School of Social Work

Riot Youth is an organization of LGBTQQIA young people, based in the Neutral Zone—a youth-driven, youth-led teen center in Ann Arbor, Michigan. The program provides a safe space for young people to come together, socialize, build community, develop leadership skills, and organize to create change. Riot Youth is a vital resource for the many LGBTQQIA teens throughout the county who face persistent violence, discrimination, harassment, micro-aggressions, and erasure in their schools and communities. For many who participate in Riot Youth programs, it is the only space in which they are able to interact with friends and peers who share a similar sexual and/or gender identity.

To work against the isolation, silence, and erasure they experienced in schools, Riot Youth leaders engaged in participatory action research, including developing, distributing, and analyzing a climate survey in local public high schools. This project was also embedded in Riot Youth's model of programming and community organizing, which centers youth leadership and development throughout the process. For instance, through the development of the climate survey questions, young people engaged in difficult conversations with one another about their experiences of harassment and bullying; feeling excluded by heteronormative assumptions in the school curriculum; and the complex relationships between issues related to race, sexuality, gender, and other social norms in their high school settings. As they distributed the survey in four local public high schools, Riot Youth leaders worked with gay-straight alliances in these schools to invite a larger portion of their community to reflect on these issues. Survey questions were accompanied by definitions of terms such as gay, coming out, heterosexual privilege, and gender queer. Questions on the survey also ask students to reflect on how issues of sexuality, gender, and race influence school curricula, harassment, and everyday language. Further, through the process of analyzing the survey results and writing up a report of findings, youth leaders continued to work together to discover the stories of their peers and connect these stories to a larger agenda for creating change.

In addition to presenting the report of findings, Riot Youth leaders worked with an adult scriptwriter to develop, write, and stage a theater performance called "Gayrilla." This performance includes a number of different scenes and activities that can be adapted and combined to suit various audiences as well as different groups of performers. Performances are followed by an interactive session between the performers and the audience, allowing audience members to engage directly, ask clarifying questions, and develop ideas for potential action steps.

Riot Youth teens also worked with adult advisors to develop a pre-test/post-test evaluation of the Gayrilla performances, which they used to develop new scenes based on the feedback provided by audience members. The evaluations themselves have helped Riot Youth to expand the reach of their efforts and to sustain the organizing work they do. Teen leaders have used the affirmative findings of the Gayrilla evaluations to persuade administrators in additional schools to allow performances in their schools. Further, these evaluations have been crucial in securing and maintaining funding for the program and its continued existence and growth. Among the results of the combined survey and performances, there was an increase in individual awareness and action. Two local school districts changed their nondiscrimination policies to include sexual orientation, gender identity, and gender expression; the superintendent supported inclusion of LGBTQQ curricular content; gender neutral bathrooms were built; and the experience transformed Riot Youth participants' lives.

RESOURCES AND POSSIBILITIES

In this section we offer a starter tool kit for evaluators. It contains ideas and examples helpful for conceptualizing and conducting practice and program evaluations. As you read through these, consider how they translate into social-justice-oriented practice. How might you make use of these in your current practice? How might you alter the tools so that they better reflect the values of social justice work?

Getting Started

In their description of evaluation and its applicability to participatory democracy, Hope and Timmel (1984/1999, vol. 2, pp. 121–133) suggest how workers might enlist people's participation in reflecting critically on people's own projects, programs, aims, and leadership. They start by conducting a workshop with potential participants in which they define evaluation; discuss potential pitfalls;

and learn when to conduct evaluations, why these should be conducted, and how to use various evaluation methods and strategies. Then a group plan is developed to implement the participatory evaluation process. Hope and Tim-mel use the following questions to initiate this process:

1. What aspects of your program do you aim to evaluate?
2. What methods will you use for each of the aims you have men-tioned? What indicators and what questions are important to include?
3. Who will do what, when, and where? Make out a time, place, and person chart to indicate your plan.

The final step is sharing all plans with the whole group (p. 130).

Simply Simple

Lappé and DuBois (1994, p. 281) outline some simple questions that they believe are powerful tools for change when applied to small and large group evaluation processes:

- How do you feel about what happened? (Answers can be one-word descriptions of emotions: upset, happy, relieved, angry, energized. No intellectualizing allowed.)
- What worked?
- What didn't work?
- What could we do better?

Elegant in their simplicity, these questions provide a framework for group discussion. Responses can be tape recorded or written out on flip chart paper. This will preserve the discussion for later reflection so that history can become a basis for continued learning.

Class Learning Activity:
The Universal Declaration of Human Rights in Your Community

In chapter 4 we suggested using the Universal Declaration of Human Rights (UDHR) as a foundation for ethical practice. In this exercise, you will be using the UDHR as an evaluation tool. Use the plain language version of the UDHR (p. 131 of this book) as your guide. Break into small groups and divide the thirty articles of the UDHR among the groups. You will be evaluating the human rights climate in your community. Each group will complete three tasks:

1. Review the articles, discuss their meaning, and be prepared to explain their meaning to the main group when you report on your discussion.
2. Decide to what extent people in your community enjoy these human rights: everyone, most people, some people, a few people, or no one?
3. If everyone does not enjoy a particular right, write down who is excluded.

Share your small group evaluations with the larger group and discuss how you might go about developing an evaluation instrument to assess the human rights climate in your community. How might your evaluation steer social-justice-oriented practice? How could you use your results to stimulate action in your community? How would you disseminate your findings?

Now turn to the UN Convention on the Rights of the Child. Repeat the process outlined above with a focus on children in your community. Across the world, citizens are coming together to pledge a commitment to human rights at the community level. Learn more about the possibilities of Human Rights Cities (http://www.pdhre.org/projects/hrcommun.html) and check out how Eugene, Oregon, is becoming a Human Rights City (http://www.humanrightscity.com).

CRITICAL REFLECTION

What Is Critical Reflection?

Evaluation goes hand in hand with reflection. We begin this section by looking at the meaning of reflection and then comparing the differences when we add the word *critical*. Mezirow (1998, pp. 185–186) defines reflection as a "turning back" on experience, but he contends that it can mean many things. It can include simple awareness of objects or events or states of being. It can also mean the act of considering something, letting our thoughts wander and contemplating alternatives. Reflection, however, does not imply *assessing* the object of contemplation and herein lies the crucial difference between reflection and critical reflection. Critical reflection includes questioning implicit beliefs that relate to different aspects of our experiences. It is the process of asking why. These beliefs may be about how the world works economically, politically, philosophically, psychologically, and culturally. Think for a minute of a belief that you once held firm but no longer believe in. Think of the reasons you used to bolster your faith in this belief. Now recall the process or event that made you question this long-held assumption.

Critical reflection is a structured, analytic, and emotional process that helps us examine the ways in which we make meaning of circumstances, events, and situations. Critical reflection pushes us to interpret experience, question our taken-for-granted assumptions of how things ought to work, and reframe our inquiry to open up new possibilities for thought and action. Posing critical questions is key to critical reflection.

Critical Reflection and Social Justice Work

There are a number of reasons why we include critical reflection as a core process of justice-oriented social work practice. Our list below is far from inclusive; what are other reasons you might add?

- *Critical reflection promotes continuous self-assessment.* Posing questions about our own performance is key to social work practice that takes social justice seriously. Assessing personal, emotional, and intellectual challenges and successes and addressing them through augmenting or changing the ways in which we work increases personal and professional competence and integrity (Moch, 2009).

- *Critical reflection fosters connections and linkages between personal and social concerns.* The dominant mode of thought in U.S. culture is based on individualism. The tendency is to look only within ourselves for causes of our concerns. Critical reflection demands that we look at the linkages between personal issues and the ways these are influenced and shaped by systems much larger than ourselves.

- *Critical reflection invites questioning of dominant explanations and observations.* Engaging with issues in a critical way means questioning the power structures and the structuring of power embedded in the definitions attributed to social problems and concerns. Think of some unquestioned myths you adhered to, later discovering that you simply lacked sufficient information for an informed opinion. How were these myths perpetuated?

- *Critical reflection opens up and strengthens spaces of possibility.* As discussed earlier, binary logic or the logic of *either/or* is the dominant social logic in U.S. culture (Kelly & Sewell, 1988). The primary limitation of this particular mode of thinking is that it narrows choices. For example, something is either right or wrong—there are no shades of gray. Kelly and Sewell remind us that *trialectic logic* or the logic of wholeness provides a space to "grasp the wholeness which emerges" (p. 22–23) when we consider relationship among factors in terms of threes instead of twos.

- *Critical reflection links to problematizing.* At the heart of critical reflection is posing problems. Certain types of questions promote critical inquiry. Posing the subject matter as a problem or what Freire called "problematizing the ordinary" connects us to the work of evaluation and systematization. We are engaged in an ongoing process of examining the conditions of our lives, identifying concerns, asking the why questions, and looking for themes and patterns that connect. These become the foundations for developing action plans.

The Critically Reflective Thinker

John Dewey (1910, 1933), early twentieth century educator and philosopher, emphasized the importance of reflection and understood it as both an intellectual and an emotional endeavor:

> Given a genuine difficulty and a reasonable amount of analogous experience to draw upon, the difference, *par excellence*, between good and bad thinking is found at this point. The easiest way is to accept any suggestion that seems plausible and thereby bring to an end the condition of mental uneasiness. Reflective thinking is always more or less troublesome because it involves overcoming the inertia that inclines one to accept suggestions at their face value; it involves willingness to endure a condition of mental unrest and disturbance. Reflective thinking, in short, means judgment suspended during further inquiry; and suspense is likely to be somewhat painful. . . . To maintain the state of doubt and to carry on systematic and protracted inquiry—these are the essentials of thinking. (Dewey, 1910, p. 13)

The goal then of critical reflection is to promote tension and uncertainty. As Dewey suggests above, we must be prepared to deal with the discomfort that comes from having our long-held assumptions open for question. Dewey

(1933) identified three characteristics of the reflective thinker that negotiate the "mental unrest and disturbance" resulting from the contradictions between old and new ways of thinking: open-mindedness, responsibility, and whole-heartedness. Open-mindedness is the desire to hear more than one side of an issue, to listen to alternative perspectives, and to recognize that even the most engrained beliefs are open to question. Responsibility connotes the desire to seek out the truth and apply new information learned to troublesome situations. Wholeheartedness encompasses the emotional aspect of reflective thinking. It implies that, through commitment, one can overcome fear and uncertainty to make meaningful change and marshal the capacity to critically evaluate self, others, and society.

Building Critical Reflection Capacity

Dewey's characteristics of the reflective thinker are not innate, inborn attributes bestowed on some of us and not on others. In fact, these characteristics and the skills of critical reflection can be developed. Here are some suggestions for fine tuning your critical reflection skills:

- *Dialogue*. As we discussed earlier, engaging in participatory learning is the primary way we develop critical reflection capacity. Discussing our ideas, thoughts, and feelings with others externalizes our thinking and helps us engage with others and work on open mindedness. It is also one of the most viable ways we learn. True dialogue occurs when we open ourselves to new learning and challenge ourselves and change in the process.

- *Critical friend dyads*. Hatton and Smith (1995) describe the use of critical friend dyads and how these critical relationships help to develop higher levels of thinking. A critical friend is someone who is not afraid to disagree, who will challenge your viewpoint and question your assumptions about reality. Think for a moment what it might be like if the expectation of the critical friend were part of your work in a community organization. How might the notion of critical friend change the ways in which we think about our work and how might this notion of continual critique provide permission for altering structures toward more just and equitable arrangements?

- *Research*. As we have noted earlier in this chapter, research nurtures reflective practice and critical reflection skills. The research process itself mirrors the critical reflection process. First, a hypothesis is formulated or a topic of inquiry to investigate is decided. Then literature addressing the topic area is searched. Next, decisions are made regarding how to collect and analyze the information. Finally, conclusions are drawn and decisions are made concerning how to disseminate the results of the research.

- *Writing experiences*. Journaling and other forms of reflective writing are ways to keep a record of personal growth and changing perceptions. There are a number of approaches to journal writing that range from unstructured narrative to focused writing on specific topics with specific intent. Journals can be used to catalogue and reflect upon critical perplexing incidents or to examine particular case studies in depth. Journals can also provide the means for linking theory and practice.

- *Artistic reflection*. Photos, artwork, and theater can be used to stimulate critical thinking in their production and presentation. We have discussed the power of photovoice and strategic illustration previously. A great example of the power of art to stimulate critical thinking can be seen in the work of the Beehive Design Collective. Beehive Design is a grassroots activist arts group that uses images and stories to raise consciousness and support action around key environmental and social justice issues. The collective creates graphics, shares stories, tours with its work, and connects with local to global efforts for social transformation. To learn more visit the website (http://beehive collective.org).

CELEBRATION

Why Celebration as a Core Process?

Scour the social work literature and you will find hardly a mention of celebration as a core process of social work practice. Yet on the other hand, conduct a literature search on burnout and be prepared to find an abundance of articles written on the subject. How do you make sense of this—is it a mere oversight or is celebration a concept incongruent with the practice of social work? Although our inclusion of celebration as a core process in the Just Practice framework may make us appear too idealistic or out of touch with the real world of practice, we believe it fits well in a model of social-justice-oriented practice. We hope to challenge traditional meanings and practices of social work and nurture idealism in others and ourselves. We see celebration as a key component of practice that allows us to look beyond the present and keep our sights on a vision of a just world. Typically, traditional meanings of social work highlight the drudgery of practice and emphasize burnout, compassion fatigue, or secondary traumatic stress. We pay attention to questions of self-care to mitigate the impact of emotionally challenging work. Most self-care focuses on the individual worker and strategies for wellness and stress reduction. Seldom do we speak of collective well-being and the place of celebration therein.

Celebration as an Integral Part of Practice

What would it mean to bring the notion of celebration into our work as social justice workers? How might celebration reconfigure the ways in which we envision practice? Lappé and DuBois (1994) remind us that the most effective organizations see celebration and appreciation as integral to their work. Celebration and appreciation breathe new life into the work and recharge the batteries; at the same time they build loyalty and strengthen relationships. Lappé and DuBois provide a list of suggestions or how-to's to brush up on our celebration and appreciation skills. We share some of their wisdom below (Lappé & DuBois, 1994, pp. 278–279):

- *Celebrate the learning, not just the winning.* We don't always get what we want, but out of every effort comes learning to be appreciated. After one citizen group's legislative campaign failed, we noticed that its newsletter celebrated how much members had learned about both the issue and the citizen lobbying process. So by *celebration* we don't necessarily mean throwing a party. We also mean acknowledging and expressing satisfaction in what has been accomplished, even when an intended target is not met. (p. 278)

- *Create a celebratory spirit.* Colored balloons. Noisemakers. Streamers. Amusing Props. Live music. All these features create a mood of celebration, even in a public gathering dealing with deadly serious problems. Each time we've attended public meetings held by the Sonoma County Faith-Based Organizing Project, for example, our moods are lifted as soon as we enter the auditorium. These techniques infuse their meetings with a spirit of celebration despite the fact that this group faces such difficult issues as affordable housing and school reform. (pp. 278–279).

- *Show appreciation of your adversaries as well as your allies.* The most successful groups that we know acknowledge their volunteers at events in which the particular contribution of each individual is described. As members hear what others do, appreciation becomes a means of building a sense of interdependence within the group . . . letters and calls of thanks (even when you disagree with the person) do not signal weakness. You'll establish your credibility as a person or group with strength, who knows you'll be around for the long haul.(p. 279)

Now we'll add a few of our own:

- *Animation.* Think of the animator role (discussed in chapter 7) in part as one that sparks the celebratory spirit and brings joy to life. It may be through gestures such as remembering participants' birthdays, celebrating organizational anniversaries and milestones, and recognizing successes along the way—the first time a participant speaks in public about an issue he cares about or a child's first month in a new school. It may be taking time to recognize events and transitions that shape personal and collective history and memory, such as the naming of a group or a move to a new home.

- *Celebration as resistance.* Celebrating rights is a way of claiming voices and time and space or resisting forces trying to silence and threaten. Celebration of social holidays and religious feast days marks the right to practice and to honor histories. For example, during the 1980s the people of La Victoria, a poor *poblacion* (community) in Santiago, Chile, publicly celebrated International Women's Day as a form of resistance to the military dictatorship. The celebration was a way of enabling residents to move beyond the fear and into the streets. It was both a celebration and a strategy for community mobilization (Finn, 2005).

- *Celebration also means finding joy in the work.* Townsend and colleagues (1999), in writing about women and power in Mexico, acknowledge the importance of enjoyment in women's discovery of power from within. Women take and express pleasure in their achievements, in getting out of the house and coming together with others. Likewise, the women of Villa Paula Jaraquemada, another Santiago *poblacion*, joined together to build community from the ground up through a housing-construction project in which women learned technical skills and built or remodeled their own homes. They expressed a sense of joy in both the process and products of their work: "I love it, that's why I do it. As you learn something new you get more enthused about learning. I love it. I love the learning. I love seeing results. That's what keeps me coming back" (Finn, 2001, p. 191). They speak often of the beauty of the experience of participation, and they celebrate the beauty of their successes large and small. They talk of the positive outlook they now have and their faith in their own capacity to create change.

Class Learning Activity: Celebrating Small Steps

With your class, brainstorm what the word *celebration* means to the members of your group. How do you celebrate birthdays, holidays, and rites of passage such as moving from adolescence to adulthood or the end of a long week in school? Brainstorm another list of successes and challenges you have experienced individually and as a group that spring from your involvement in class this term. Decide as a group how you might celebrate your work together.

COMING FULL CIRCLE: SUMMARIZING PRINCIPLES OF SOCIAL JUSTICE WORK

Throughout this book, we have been bridging social work and social justice and seeking ways to translate our visions of social justice work into concrete principles and practices. As we have critically reflected on the development of the Just Practice concepts and processes, we have identified several *generative themes*. In this section we summarize these generative themes as principles for social justice work. These sixteen principles are interrelated and mutually informing. We see them as a work in progress that will be shaped over time through dialogue about our diverse efforts to engage in social justice work. We invite readers to add to the list.

1. *Take a global perspective.* Social justice work challenges us to look both to and beyond the immediate context of our work and consider the larger structures and forces that bear on the situation. By taking a global perspective, we challenge our assumptions about borders and boundaries in their many forms. In taking a global perspective, we are challenged to continually address questions of human rights and capabilities. Further, we have both the opportunity and responsibility to join in solidarity with global movements for social, economic, and environmental justice. A global perspective also serves as a reminder of the partiality of our knowledge and of the many ways of seeing and knowing refracted through

the lenses of cultural and historical experience. Even in our most micro or local practice of social work it is possible to think and act from a global perspective.

2. *Link poverty and inequality*. Poverty is a pervasive form of injustice that compromises human rights, capabilities, and the potential for full citizenship. Social justice work calls on us to go beyond provision of aid to tackle the connection between poverty and inequality. Understanding how some maintain social and economic privilege at the expense of others is fundamental to social justice work. We need to question explanations of poverty as a moral, personal, or cultural problem and consider poverty within structured systems of wealth and inequality. As Oxfam (2013) contends, extreme wealth and inequality are economically inefficient, politically corrosive, socially divisive, and environmentally destructive. But they are not inevitable. Understanding the dynamics of poverty and inequality is critical for social justice work.

3. *Appreciate interconnectedness*. Social justice work challenges us to explore the patterns that connect, often across seemingly disparate contexts and experiences. In order to meet the complex challenges of twenty-first century social work, we cannot limit our efforts to the safety of narrow specialization. We need to grapple with the relationships among individual, family, and community struggles and broader political, social, and economic arrangements. Likewise, we need to maintain the connectedness of head, heart, and hand in our work such that our actions are guided by both grounded knowledge and by a felt connection and commitment to human dignity and relationships. As we explore and appreciate the patterns that connect, we may discover opportunities for new partnerships and networks to support social justice work.

4. *Take history seriously*. People, problems, and ideas have histories. Throughout the book, we have stressed the importance of a historical perspective both in understanding contemporary concerns and in appreciating a sense of the possible. People are historical beings, conscious of time, and at once makers and products of history. It is through attention to the histories of people, problems, and ideas that we come to question certainties of the moments and inevitabilities of the future. Too often, our engagement with history in social work is limited to a class on the history of social

welfare. Social justice work calls for critical reflection on our own histories and the history of our policies, practices, and certainties as part of the work.

5. *Challenge our certainties.* Social justice work demands that we be willing to constantly question our assumptions, especially those that we hold most dear. We cannot effectively open ourselves to new ways of hearing, seeing, and thinking without ongoing reflection on what and how we know. Moreover, social justice work calls on us to let go of our certainties and be willing to embrace ambiguities and engage with contradictions. In so doing, we open ourselves to learning about the ways in which others attempt to negotiate the conflicting and often contradictory expectations of everyday life and make sense of their experiences in the process. It is often in the slippery spaces of ambiguity and contradiction that the possibilities for transformational change emerge.

6. *Listen and learn through dialogue.* In contrast to approaches that value the "expert" role, social justice work asks us to begin from a place of not knowing. We begin by opening ourselves to hearing and receiving another's story. We enter into each new relationship and change process as learners, with humility and openness, cognizant of the limits of our worldview. It is through listening and dialogue that we come to appreciate new meanings and interpretations and alternative ways of seeing, being, and acting in the world. We do not necessarily come to accept or adopt others' interpretations of social reality as our own. Rather, it is through respectful dialogue that we question and disagree as well. Social justice work involves the art of diplomacy, in which we help bring to light diverse views and interests, identify differences as well as common ground, examine the power relations at stake, and seek courses of action that value human dignity and rights.

7. *Confront questions of power.* Social justice work recognizes the importance of thinking and talking about power in its many forms. Possibilities for meaningful change emerge when people come to recognize and analyze the forms and relations of power that constrain their lives and realize personal and collective forms of power—power to be, to act, and to join together. We have pointed to the power of discourse in the construction of both problems and interventions. We have examined the power of labels to define and,

in effect, stand for the person and the power of the expert to diagnose and treat. We have also demonstrated the power of people to create change as they join together, question their life circumstances, develop critical awareness, build personal and group capacity, and utilize collective knowledge and capacity to challenge and change the conditions of their lives. Social justice workers exert their own power to question, resist, and act in ways that open spaces of hope and possibility.

8. *Recognize and embrace the political nature of social work.* As Paulo Freire (Moch, 2009) reminds us, social justice workers are not neutral agents. As social justice workers we are positioned and acting in contexts of power and inequality. In so doing we must not only acknowledge but also embrace the political nature of the work and prepare ourselves to carry out our work with integrity. The commitment to social justice work is both an ethical and a political commitment. Exercising this commitment demands knowledge of the power relations in which our practice is situated, an understanding of strategies and tactics that enable us to effectively engage as players, and the will and skills to enable others to participate in the work of justice-oriented change.

9. *Value difference and address the production of difference.* A critical understanding of difference is central to social justice work. The production of difference—different ways of interpreting, organizing, and acting in the world—is part of our capacities as meaning-making cultural beings. Encounters with difference can challenge our most deeply held truths about the world; our place in it; and our abilities to remain open to alternative ways of thinking, feeling, being, and acting. Moreover, social justice work challenges us to grapple with the politics of difference. By this we mean the processes, mechanisms, and relations of power through which particular forms of difference and inequality are produced, maintained, and justified. We need to both value the meaning and power of difference and question the construction and representation of differences and the multiple meanings and values attached to them. Social justice work calls on us to ask, what differences make a difference here and to whom?

10. *Be cognizant of positionality.* The social work profession has always recognized the significance of self-awareness for social workers.

Self-awareness most often takes on the meaning of reflecting on the "baggage" the worker brings to the work, that is, thinking about personal attitudes and beliefs and how these might get in the way of working with particular clients or specific situations. Positionality, however, encapsulates this notion of knowledge of the self and expands it to include awareness of the powerful shaping influences of gender and gender expression, race, class, sexual identity and orientation, and ability status—how these shape attitudes and beliefs, and how these locate the worker differently in reference to differently positioned clients. Fully comprehending this idea of positionality is a humbling endeavor. It serves as a constant reminder of one's social/political location, the challenges and strengths inherent in one's location, and the partiality of one's worldview.

11. *Promote participation*. There is no such thing as empowerment without participation. We must be vigilant in our search for ways to encourage the participation of people in the full range of change endeavors, from the interpersonal to the social. When in doubt, we must ask ourselves who is included, who is excluded, and why. We must also begin the process of evaluating programs and projects based on the criteria of participation, and for social justice work, this means giving people a voice in the issues that most directly concern their lives and their well-being.

12. *Keep the* social *in social work*. As we have tried to illustrate throughout the book, social justice work is a collective endeavor. We cannot readily go it alone. We have pointed to the importance of raising critical consciousness through dialogue and building team work and coalitions for change-oriented action as central components of social justice work. This holds true not only for our actions with individuals, families, and communities, but also for building support, solidarity, and quite literally a movement of social justice workers. It can be risky to pose critical questions in the context of our everyday practice. If we are attempting to engage in a social work of resistance in isolation from others, we can become frustrated and overwhelmed. As social justice workers, we need to build relationships with one another, through intraorganizational and interorganizational networks, with local, national, and international social justice organizations, with service users, and with activists and

advocates in our own communities. Together we can nurture our relationships and ourselves and fuel our sense of possibility and commitment to praxis.

13. *Build and share leadership.* Social justice work is about building capacity and sharing leadership. Starting with the participatory democracy exemplified in the work of Jane Addams and other social reformers at the turn of the twentieth century, a pattern emerges and weaves its way through social work history. This pattern is one of having faith in the capacity of humans, even under the most severe conditions, to challenge the conditions of their lives and participate in transformation. Thinking of our practice at least partly as a way to create opportunities for participation and leadership development provides us with a clear goal upon which to set our sights. It forces us to pose the following questions: How do I do my work in such a way that I build and support new forms of leadership? What forms might leadership take? How might my organization expand leadership capacities and opportunities for their development?

14. *Take "bold and courageous action" (Roby, 1998).* Social justice workers need to act courageously to confront the multiple barriers, both real and imagined, that maintain conditions that need to be changed. Confronting barriers means confronting unfair policies and practices in welfare agencies that prevent some people from moving out of poverty through postsecondary education and training. It means organizing a rally for laborers overlooked in recent legislation passed by Congress that provides funding and tax relief for corporations hurt by economic recession but ignores the plight of common laborers who have far fewer resources at their disposal. It means getting angry and sustaining anger as a motivating force, choosing your battles well, and taking bold moves with others as a base of power and support. Pamela Roby (1998, p. 13) contends that "moment to moment we have complete freedom to decide our actions."

15. *Create a spirit of hope and spaces of possibility.* A major theme of social justice work is creating spaces of hope and possibility through visions of a more just tomorrow. Throughout history, others have shared and acted on similar visions and sought to carve out the possible from seemingly impossible situations and cir-

cumstances. These individuals and groups understood that without hope there is no purpose and in some cases loss of hope meant loss of life itself. Although for some this notion of the possible spurred on dreams of a better world, for others it meant contemplating and acting upon alternative ways of being and doing in the world at that very moment. We must continually challenge ourselves to ask how we can infuse our work with this same sense of purpose and recognize the dialectical relationship of hope and possibility—hope brings possibility and possibility brings hope.

16. *Find and create joy in the work.* It is incumbent upon us to celebrate the joy and recognize the beauty of our work. We continue to question why the concept of celebration is foreign to our work on U.S. soil and probe the possibility of reconfiguring programs, policies, practices, and projects and our relationships with others and ourselves if we take celebration seriously. We learn from our students who teach us that the core process of celebration is one they embrace to combat societal stereotypes of social work. They appreciate the permission that celebration gives to carve out space for patting themselves on the back, supporting each other in the hard work that they do, and giving new meaning to social work that elicits pride and renewed commitment.

SUMMARY

In this chapter we have developed the Just Practice core processes of evaluation, critical reflection, and celebration. We have defined evaluation and explored different approaches to it, and we have highlighted participatory approaches for their congruence with social-justice-oriented social work practice. We have provided examples of participatory evaluation and explored participatory processes, and we have asked readers to examine these examples and processes for the key principles that underlie social-justice-oriented practice. We have outlined what we need to evaluate and provided some basic tools for evaluation. We have defined critical reflection and its importance to social justice work and addressed methods for developing our critical reflection capacity. Finally, we have introduced and defined celebration as a core process and we have presented strategies that draw attention to the need to see the beauty in our work and help us sustain the momentum necessary for Just Practice. We concluded by summarizing key principles we have discussed throughout this book.

QUESTIONS FOR DISCUSSION

1. In the design of an evaluation for your social work practicum organization or workplace, what are three key aspects that you would evaluate and why? How might you design the evaluation?

2. What might be some of the challenges of constructing a participatory evaluation process in the context of your practicum or work place? Opportunities?

3. What initial steps would you take in developing a participatory evaluation process for your practicum or workplace? What methods of evaluation might be most appropriate for the context? Why?

4. Are there other suggestions you might have for building critical reflection skills beyond those discussed in this chapter?

5. What skills and habits can you build into your professional practice in order to ensure that you are a critical reflective thinker? What is your plan for maintaining a stance of "permanent critical curiosity" in relation to your practice?

6. What suggestions or how-tos would you add to celebrate and find joy in your work?

SUGGESTED READINGS

Branom, C. (2012) Community-based participatory research as a social work research and intervention approach. *Journal of Community Practice, 20,* 260–273.

Klugman, B. (2010). *Evaluating social justice advocacy.* Center for Evaluation Innovation. Retrieved from http://www.evaluationinnovation.org

Lappé, F., & Lappé, A. (2003). *Hope's edge: The next diet for a small planet.* New York: Tarcher/Putnam.

Lawson, H., Caringi, J., Pyles, L., Jurowski, J., & Bozlak, C. (2015). *Participatory action research.* New York: Oxford University Press.

Stoecker, R. (2013). *Research methods for community change: A project-based approach.* Thousand Oaks, CA: SAGE.

Epilogue: Just Futures

> While we can't guess what will become of the world, we can imagine what we would like it to become. The right to dream wasn't in the 30 rights of humans that the United Nations proclaimed at the end of 1948. But without it, without the right to dream and the waters that it gives to drink, the other rights would die of thirst.
>
> **Eduardo Galeano, "The Right to Dream" (1995)**

What if we were to envision social justice work as advocacy for the right to dream? How might it enrich and expand our imagination about the possibilities of practice? Throughout this text we have posed challenges to conventional thinking about social work thought and practice and argued for a critical, transformational approach with social justice as its guiding value and goal. We have attempted to speak to the concerns and challenges of twenty-first century social work. We have recognized that our knowledge of the world is partial and shaped by our perspectives and positionalities. We have presented a vision of social work as an emergent, dialogue-based process gained through engagement with changing contexts and the forces that shape them.

We have offered a framework for multilevel social work practice that integrates historical consciousness, political and ethical commitment, and practical skills. We have tried to craft a flexible frame that helps us structure inquiry and action and remain open to challenge and possibility. This question-posing approach serves to disrupt our certainties and keep us engaged as open, curious learners. It is our hope that the Just Practice framework offers social workers both breadth and depth of sight and insight regarding what we see, how we see it, and what we do in each unique moment and context of practice. The framework is meant to be tested, critiqued, challenged, and changed through individual and collective engagement in social justice work. Most fundamentally, we hope that the framework guides us as we nurture and accompany others in naming and claiming their right to dream.

We have not provided a cookbook approach to social work in which we attempt to pair specific problem definitions with corresponding clinical diagnoses and interventions. We have offered little in the way of answers. There are no easy answers for the complex challenges people confront each day. Rather, we have encouraged social workers to identify and grapple with tensions and contradictions, to struggle with personal and professional discomfort and uncertainty, and to approach the work with deep humility and brash courage. It is humility that keeps the seduction of expertise in check, and it is courage that allows us to take risks, question assumed truths, and join in conspiracies of hope.

Some readers may argue that, in the face of overwhelming demands and increasingly scarce resources, our vision of social justice work is simply too idealistic. Some may argue that the idea of social justice is all well and good, but the realities of everyday practice demand attention to more immediate and pragmatic concerns, such as responding to crises, getting clients access to benefits, and keeping our jobs in the era of downsizing. We do not underestimate the daily stresses and struggles of social work practice in a context of increasing complexity of problems and scarcity of resources. We take them quite seriously. In fact, given these pressures, we contend that the need for social justice work is all the more urgent and that possibilities await us in every practice setting. The Just Practice framework presents an alternative way of thinking about our practice settings, relationships, possible courses of actions, and fundamentally ourselves. Many social workers in hospitals, prisons, schools, women's shelters, child welfare offices, and other settings are realizing their own possibilities for social justice work in ways large and small every day. We have offered a framework with which to embrace that energy and creativity; build on the possibilities; and hopefully bring together knowledge, power, and commitment for a new collective vision and practice of social work that is grounded in the best of our history and up to the task of twenty-first century challenges.

The opening quote for this epilogue is taken from Eduardo Galeano's prose poem "The Right to Dream." It speaks to our fierce human capacity to imagine that another world is possible and then to act *as if* it were our world and in so doing to spark the power and possibility of transformation. Galeano was a noted Uruguayan writer, poet, and radical journalist whose political acumen and provocative words gave voice to Latin American people's struggles throughout the late twentieth and early twenty-first centuries. He wrote against the violence of military regimes and the dangers of historical amnesia. He described himself as a writer obsessed with remembering. He wrote to recover the beauty and memory of the great "human rainbow." When Uruguay was taken over by military rule in 1973, Galeano was imprisoned and then forced into exile. First from Argentina and later from Spain, he documented the chilling realities of state violence under military rule in Argentina, Bolivia, Brazil,

Chile, and Uruguay in the 1970s and 1980s (Galeano, 1983, 1992). Returning to Uruguay in 1985, he became a powerful spokesman for people's struggles to reclaim democracy. Galeano died on April 13, 2015; his words, however, are immortal.

In July 1988, Galeano addressed an international gathering of activists in the arts and sciences supporting the "No" campaign in Chile, in which the Chilean people said "no" to more years of military rule and demanded return of democracy. Galeano's speech was entitled "We Say No" (1992). Hopefully, these brief excerpts convey his capacity to give voice to the collective pain of injustice and promise of hope:

> We say no to the praise of money and death. We say no to a system that assigns prices to people and things, within which he who has the most is hence he who is most worthy . . . and we say no to a world that spends millions each minute on arms for war while each minute kills 30 children with hunger or curable illness. . . . We say no to the lie. . . . The powerful opinion-makers treat us as though we do not exist, or as though we are silly shadows. . . . They reward our obedience, punish our intelligence, and discourage our creative energy. We are opinionated, yet we cannot offer our opinions. We have a right to the echo, not to the voice. . . . We say no: we refuse to accept this mediocrity as our destiny. . . . We say no to fear. No to the fear of speaking, of doing, of being. We say no to the divorce of beauty and justice, because we say yes to the powerful and fertile embrace they share. . . . By saying no we are saying yes. By saying no to dictatorships, and no to dictatorships disguised as democracies, we are saying yes to the struggle for true democracy, one that will deny no one bread or the power of speech, and one that will be as beautiful and dangerous as a poem by Neruda or a song by Violeta [Parra]. . . . By saying no to the freedom of money we are saying yes to the freedom of people. [By] saying no to the sad charm of disenchantment we are saying yes to hope . . . famished and crazy and loving and . . . obstinate hope. (pp. 240–244)

We find inspiration for the future of social work in Galeano's words. Our commitment to social justice calls for an integrated approach in which social work is both an act of resistance and an act of hope. It is a practice of saying no and of saying yes. As social justice workers, we say no to historical amnesia that dooms us to reproduce old failings and miss opportunities for new learning. We say no to a social work practice that uncritically reflects and reproduces embedded inequalities. We say no to reductionist thinking that collapses the lived consequences of social injustice into facile assumptions about individual pathology. We say no to the forms and mechanisms of oppression that produce notions of *us* and *them* and conflate difference with deviance. We say no to the charm of certainty that assures us we know what is in another's best interest. We say no to context stripping that robs people of meaning, power, and history. We say no to interventions that render vulnerable people silent and invisible. We say no to measures of outcomes and success driven by particular political and economic interests rather than by those directly affected by social work policies, programs, and practices.

By saying no we are saying yes. We are saying yes to the complex richness of human experience. We are saying yes to the embrace of human dignity and rights. We are saying yes to others' voices, visions, and right to reality. We are saying yes to a critical practice of social work in which we continually question received truths. We are saying yes to our role as agents of change. We are saying yes to the creation of spaces for dialogue, places for healing, and bases for action. We are saying yes to uncertainty and the exhilaration of new learning. We are saying yes to the right to risk and the opportunity to experiment. We are saying yes to the potential yet to be tapped and dreams yet to be fulfilled. We are saying yes to the powerful and fertile embrace of justice and beauty as we nurture relationships, accompany one another, build solidarity, and find joy in our work. We are saying yes to the right to dream.

Saying yes to the right to dream challenges us to bring our best selves to the daily practice of social justice work. As Paulo Freire suggests, "the social worker uncovers and makes explicit a certain dream about social relations, which is a political dream" (Moch, 2009, p. 94). Further, as Freire reminds us, social justice work demands that we nurture certain virtues, such as convergence between what we say and what we do; permanent critical curiosity and search for competence; true tolerance; the quality of "living in impatient patience"; and an understanding of what is historically possible (Moch, 2009, p. 96). Freire believed that we nurture these virtues through dialogue and that honest, genuine dialogue is founded on love. We suggest that a language and practice of love has enriched and informed the best of social work. We invite readers to think about references to love throughout *Just Practice*. Sadye Logan asked us if we could imagine a world based on love. Paulo Freire claimed that genuine dialogue must be founded upon love. Dennis Saleebey embraced humble and loving dialogue as a foundation from which to recognize and build on strengths. Lynn Nybell described how foster youth felt that they were heard in the context of relationships with social workers who not only believed in them but loved them. The presence of love is perhaps muted in our current practice of social justice work, but it is there. We can and must reclaim the language and practice of love as we conspire in the creation of just futures (see Finn [2010] for a discussion of love and justice).

Looking back, we see that both faith-based traditions and strong loving bonds among residents and toward community members guided the work of Jane Addams and the women of Hull House (Addams, 1910; Stebner, 1997). As Eleanor Stebner described, long-term loving friendships among Hull House residents "helped them form the meaning of their lives and became central to their vocation at Hull House" (1997, p. 166). These loving bonds of friendship enlarged each woman's world and provided a location from which to act in the world. The bonds were forged in a dialectics of love and justice among the women themselves and in their relations to the larger community of which they were a part. As Stebner concluded, "These relationships were based not only on loving, supporting, and critiquing one another but also on making the world more just and loving" (p. 186, cited in Finn, 2010, p. 183).

The language of love filtered through the work of Helen Harris Perlman as well. Perlman (1979) described the relationship that gives social work its uniqueness as one characterized by a special kind of love rooted in warmth; concern; and, most fundamentally, acceptance. According to Perlman, a good relationship is characterized by warmth, love, caring, acceptance, responsiveness, empathy, genuineness, attentiveness, concern, support, and understanding. It was her belief that we grow in humanness through the nurture of the emotional experience of relationship. She saw the social work relationship as one of caring, and she described caring as "love in its giving, protective, nurturing aspects" (1979, p. 59).

According to feminist theologian Rosetta Ross (2003), a discourse of love reverberates through African American women leaders' accounts of the struggle for civil rights. Ross addressed the interlocking power of religion and activism in the individual and collective efforts of antebellum activist Sojourner Truth, turn-of-the-century leader Nannie Helen Burroughs, early civil rights activists Ella Baker and Septima Poinsette Clark, and grassroots leaders Fannie Lou Hamer and Victoria Way DeLee, among others. In summarizing the power of faith and love as motive forces in their lives, Ross (2003) writes:

> The religious language of love may more appropriately express the values enacted in these women's practices. Love may be identified with recognizing, valuing and respecting persons by seeking their flourishing as human beings, including attending to material well-being, affirming human mutuality through increasing opportunities for all to participate, empowering people to fully realize their potential, and affirming as beneficial the gifts that each

individual brings to human society. This emphasis on love as a means of attending to human flourishing through practices of organizing, teaching, protesting, advocating, and agitating pervaded these religious Black women's civic participation. (p. 235)

For example, the intimate bonds of love and justice were central to Diane Nash's civil rights activism (Ross, 2003). Nash, a founding member and leader of the Student Nonviolent Coordinating Committee (SNCC) and coordinator of the Freedom Rides, spoke of the oppressive force of racism and segregation to deny human dignity and mutuality. Nash firmly believed that a "situation that denies mutuality of persons living in social relationship is a circumstance of radical moral evil, or sin" and that the response to radical evil was the "militant practice of radical love" (Ross, 2003, p. 187). Nash argued that the nonviolent movement was based on and motivated by love. She claimed,

We used nonviolence as an expression of love and respect of the opposition, while noting that a person is never the enemy. The enemy is always attitudes, such as racism or sexism, political systems that are unjust; economic systems that are unjust—some kind of system or attitude that oppresses. (2003, p. 188)

Connections of love and justice are also woven deeply into the history of social welfare practices and rights claims of women of color in the United States. Some women invoke a faith-based love of humanity as an expression of God's love. Others invoke loving bonds of friendship or the maternal love for family and children. For example, sociologist Nancy Naples (1998), in her study of grassroots women activists in the war on poverty, explored the history of women's activism and put forth the concept of "activist mothering," wherein maternal love serves as an ethical base and motive force for political action. Activist mothering combines women's practices of nurturing their own and others' children with political activism. Their activism is motivated by love and concern for the well-being of their children, families, and communities (Naples, 1998).

The intimate connections between love and justice resonate for many scholars and practitioners whose thinking informs social work. For example, social psychologist and philosopher Erich Fromm defined genuine love as "the productive form of relatedness to others and to oneself. It implies responsibility, care, respect, and knowledge, and the wish for the other person to grow and develop" (Fromm, 1947, p. 116). Fromm saw love as a pathway to knowledge and meaning connected to one's sense of belonging in the world. Fromm (1956) described love as "the active power in man: a power which breaks through the walls which separate man from his fellow men, which unites him with others; love makes him overcome a sense of isolation and separateness, yet it permits him to be himself, to retain his integrity" (p. 24). Fromm's grasp of love bridges the individual and the sociopolitical realms: "Love requires us to re-explore the nature of self and other; it requires us to re-examine the nature of social realities; and it demands that we re-formulate society" (DuBois, 1983).

Sociologist Mordechai Rimor (2003) suggests that "both love and justice have deep and similar roots in the religious, social, and philosophical heritage of our culture. Thus their interdependence." His main thesis, however, is that love is the prerequisite of justice on both the micro and macro levels (pp. 167–168). According to Rimor,

> we argue that at the social level, acts of individual compassion, trust, or tenderness find their weak echo in the just norms and laws we impose and to which we adhere. It is as if justice is a pale imitation of the idea of love we all have in us from the start. It seems that humanity uses justice as an 'in-the-meantime' device in order to keep society running. (p. 169)

Rimor contends that love rather than justice can heal the ills of society. He asserts that it is only through compassion, tenderness, and empathy toward others that we can change our national priorities and address our global problems. The principal route to justice, Rimor suggests, is a bottom-up approach built through "warm and open relationships among people, relationships of understanding, compassion, empathy, tenderness, and love" (2003, p. 175). By giving priority to the way of love, justice will be an outcome.

Judith Jordan, one of the founding scholars of the Jean Baker Miller Training Institute in the Stone Center at Wellesley College, has revisited the place, power, and silencing of love in interpersonal practice (Jordan, 2003). Jordan writes of the centrality of mutual empathy, mutual vulnerability, and therapeutic authenticity as core aspects of interpersonal transformation, and she claims these acts as expressions of love. She poses a challenge to dominant concepts of *boundaries* that render such talk of love taboo. Jordan calls for a reframing of the concept of boundaries in line with a shift from a separate-self paradigm to a relational-cultural paradigm of practice (pp. 7–8). Jordan asks, "Why is love, as part of the therapeutic relationship, part of the healing, spoken of so little in therapeutic literature, or in therapy itself?" (p. 11). She contends that the dominant culture's emphasis on power and control has eclipsed an appreciation for love in the healing process. She invites us to act courageously and to (re)embrace the healing, transformative force of love.

The power and possibility of love as a motive force in personal and social transformation are always and everywhere at hand. The molders and shapers of social justice work have intuitively grasped and explicitly engaged the dialectics of love and justice. They have found inspiration in their spirituality, communities, friendships, and families and in the lives and struggles of strangers. Dominant discourses regarding expertise and professionalism have muted but not silenced a language and practice of love in the pursuit of justice. Perhaps it is in our capacity for love and our daily decisions to act lovingly in the world that we find hope for the future. In order to claim our place in the struggles for social justice and to advocate for the right to dream, we must first (re)claim love as a basis for social work.

BIBLIOGRAPHY

Abramovitz, M. (1996). *Regulating the lives of women: Social welfare policy from colonial times to the present*. Boston: South End Press.

Abramovitz, M. (1998). Social work and social reform: An arena of struggle. *Social Work, 43*, 512–526.

Abramovitz, M. (2012). Theorizing the neoliberal welfare state for social work. In M. Gray, J. Midgely, & S. Webb (Eds.), *The SAGE handbook of social work* (pp. 33–51). London: SAGE.

Abramson, M. (1996). Reflections on knowing oneself ethically: Toward a working framework for social work practice. *Families in Society, 77*, 195–201.

Adams, D. W. (1995). *Education for extinction: American Indians and the boarding school experience, 1875–1928*. Lawrence, KS: University Press of Kansas.

Adams, M., Blumenfeld, W., Castañeda, R., Hackman, H., Peters, M., & Zuñiga, X. (2000). *Readings for diversity and social justice*. New York: Routledge.

Adams, R., Dominelli, L., & Payne, M. (Eds.). (2005). *Social work futures: Crossing boundaries and transforming practice*. New York: Palgrave Macmillan.

Adams, R., Dominelli, L., & Payne, M. (Eds.). (2009). *Social work: Themes, issues and critical debates* (3rd ed.). New York: Macmillan.

Addams, J. (1899). The subtle problems of charity. *The Atlantic Monthly 83* (496). Retrieved from http://www.theatlantic.com/magazine/archive/1899/02/the-subtle-problems-of-charity/306217

Addams, J. (1910). *Twenty years at Hull House*. New York: Crowell/Macmillan.

Advancement Project. (2012). *Participatory asset mapping*. Los Angeles: Author. Retrieved from www.healthycity.org

Agger, B. (2006). *Critical social theories: An introduction*. Boulder, CO: Westview Press.

Agnew, E. (2004). *From charity to social work: Mary E. Richmond and the creation of an American profession*. Chicago: University of Illinois Press.

Albee, G. (1986). Toward a just society: Lessons on observation of primary prevention of psychopathology. *American Psychologist, 41*, 891–898.

Alchemy. (2015). *Alchemy: The art of transforming business*. Retrieved from http://link2alchemy.com

Allan, J., Pease, B., & Briskman, L. (Eds.). (2009). *Critical social work: An intro-duction to theories and practices*. (2nd ed.). Crows Nest NSW, Australia: Allen & Unwin.

Altman, J. C. (2008). A study of engagement in neighborhood based child welfare services. *Research on Social Work Practice, 18*, 555–564.

Alvarez, A. (2003). The Lane Report: Defining the field of community organiz-ing in 1939. *Journal of Community Practice, 11*, 101–103.

American Civil Liberties Union. (2009). *Human rights at home: Mental illness in U.S. prisons and jails*. Washington, DC: Author.

American Civil Liberties Union. (2014a). *Alone and afraid. Children held in solitary confinement and isolation in juvenile detention and correctional facilities*. Retrieved from https://www.aclu.org/files/assets/Alone%20and%20Afraid%20COMPLETE%20FINAL.pdf

American Civil Liberties Union. (2014b). *The dangerous overuse of solitary confinement in the United States* [Briefing paper]. New York: Author.

American Civil Liberties Union. (2014c). *Worse than second-class: Solitary confinement of women in the U.S.* Retrieved from https://www.aclu.org/sites/default/files/assets/worse_than_second-class.pdf

American Civil Liberties Union. (2015, November 20). There's only one country that hasn't ratified the Convention on Children's Rights: US [Blog post]. *Speak Freely*. Retrieved from https://www.aclu.org/blog/speak-freely/theres-only-one-country-hasnt-ratified-convention-childrens-rights-us

American Heritage Dictionary of the English Language (4th ed.). (2000). New York: Houghton Mifflin.

Amnesty International. (2015). *Convention on the rights of the child. Frequently asked questions*. Retrieved from http://www.amnestyusa.org/our-work/issues/children-s-rights/convention-on-the-rights-of-the-child-0

Amsden, J., & VanWynsberghe, R. (2005). Community mapping as a research tool with youth. *Action Research, 3*, 357–381.

Anastas, J. (2012, February). Eugenics: What we can learn from history. *NASW News, 57*(2). Retrieved from http://www.socialworkers.org/pubs/news/2012/02/eugenics.asp

Anderson, A. (n.d.) *Community-builder's approach to a theory of change*. New York: The Aspen Institute. Retrieved from https://www.aspeninstitute.org/sites/default/files/content/docs/rcc/rcccommbuildersapproach.pdf

Anderson, K. (2008). Grief experiences of CNAs. *Journal of Gerontological Nursing, 34*, 42–49.

Anderson, K., & Ewen, H. (2011). Death in the nursing home: An examination of grief and well-being in nursing assistants. *Research in Gerontological Nursing, 4,* 87–94.

Anderson, M., & Collins, P. H. (2015). *Race, class, gender: An anthology* (9th ed.). Boston: Cengage.

Anderson, M. (producer), & Williams, P. (director). (2011). *From place to place* [Film]. Fayetteville, GA: Porch Productions.

Anderson, R., & Carter, I. (1990). *Human behavior in the social environment: A social systems approach* (4th ed.). New York: Aldine de Gruyter.

Andrews, J., & Reisch, M. (1997). Social work and anti-communism: A historical analysis of the McCarthy era. *Journal of Progressive Human Services, 8*(2), 29–49.

Angier, N. (2013, November 26). The changing American family. *New York Times.* Retrieved from http://www.nytimes.com/2013/11/26/health/families.html?pagewanted=all&_r=0

Anzaldúa, G. (2000). Allies. In M. Adams, W. Blumfeld, R. Castañeda, H. Hackman, M. Peters, & X. Zuñiga (Eds.), *Readings for diversity and social justice* (pp. 475–477). New York: Routledge. (Reprinted from *Sinister Wisdom, 52,* Spring/Summer 1994, pp. 47–52.)

Aotearoa New Zealand Association of Social Workers. (2015). Codes of Ethics. Retrieved from http://anzasw.nz/wp-content/uploads/COE-for-website-chapter-3.pdf

Apple, M. (2011). *Education and power* (3rd ed.). New York: Routledge.

Arendt, H. (1973). *The origins of totalitarianism.* New York: Harcourt Brace Jovanovich.

Argyris, C. (1970). *Intervention theory and method.* Reading, PA: Addison-Wesley.

Ascione, W., & Dixson, J. (2002). Children and their incarcerated mothers. In J. Figueira-McDonough & R. Sarri (Eds.), *Women at the margins: Neglect, punishment, and resistance* (pp. 271–294). New York: Haworth Press.

Asociación Latinoamericana de Enseñanza e Investigación en Trabajo Social. (2013). *Algunas consideraciones y aportes en torno a la definicion international de trabajo social* [Some considerations and contributions around the international definition of social work]. Cordoba, Argentina: Author.

Atkinson, K., & Mattaini, M. (2013) Constructive noncooperation as political resistance. *Journal of Progressive Human Services, 24,* 99–116.

Atkinson, D., Morten, G., & Sue, D. (1989). *Counseling American minorities: A cross-cultural perspective* (3rd ed.). Dubuque, IA: W. C. Brown.

Baber, K., & Allen, K. (1992). *Women and families: Feminist reconstructions*. New York: Guilford Press.

Badwall, H. (2014). Colonial encounters: Racialized social workers negotiating professional scripts of whiteness. *Intersectionalities, 3*, 1–23.

Bailey, R., & Brake, M. (1975). *Radical social work*. London: Edward Arnold.

Baines, D. (2011). *Doing anti-oppressive practice: Social justice social work* (2nd ed.). Black Point, Nova Scotia: Fernwood Publishing.

Bales, S. (2002). *Framing public issues*. Washington, DC: FrameWorks Institute.

Bandura, A. (2006). Toward a psychology of human agency. *Perspectives on Psychological Science, 1*, 164–180.

Banerjee, M. (2005). Applying Rawlsian social justice to welfare reform: An unexpected finding for social work. *Journal of Sociology and Social Work, 32*(2), 35–57.

Barbera, R. (2008). Relationships and the research process: Participatory action research and social work. *Journal of Progressive Human Services, 19*, 140–159.

Barker, R. (2003). *The social work dictionary* (5th ed.). Washington, DC: National Association of Social Workers Press.

Barker, R. (2014). *The social work dictionary* (6th ed.). Washington, DC: National Association of Social Workers Press.

Barnoff, L. (2011). Business as usual: Doing anti-oppressive organizational change. In D. Baines (Ed.), *Doing anti-oppressive practice: Critical social justice social work* (2nd ed., Chapt.11, pp. 176–194). Halifax, Nova Scotia: Fernwood Publishing.

Bartlett, H. (1970). *The common base of social work practice*. New York: National Association of Social Workers Press.

Bartley, A. (2006). Charity Organization Society. In M. Odekon (Ed.), *Encyclopedia of world poverty*. Thousand Oaks: SAGE. Retrieved from http://dx.doi.org/10.4135/9781412939607.n105

Bates, R. (1996). Popular theatre: A useful process for adult educators. *Adult Education Quarterly, 46*, 224–236.

Baum, G. (1971). *Man becoming* (pp. 41–42). New York: Herder and Herder.

Bazemore, G., & Schiff, M. (2001). *Restorative community justice: Repairing harm and transforming communities*. Cincinnati, OH: Anderson.

Becker, A., Israel, B., & Allen, A. (2005). Strategies and techniques for effective group process in CBPR partnerships. In B. Isreal, E. Eng, A. Schulz, & E. Parker (Eds.), *Methods in community-based participatory research for health* (Chapt. 3, 52–72). San Francisco: Wiley.

Beckett, C. (2006). *Essential theory for social work practice.* London: SAGE.

Beers, C. (1904). *A mind that found itself.* New York: Longman.

Bell, B. (2001) *Walking on fire: Haitian women's stories of survival and resistance.* Ithaca, NY: Cornell University Press.

Bell, J. (2014). *The Black power movement and American social work.* New York: Columbia University Press.

Belle, D., & Doucet, J. (2003). Poverty, inequality, and discrimination as source of depression among U.S. women. *Psychology of Women Quarterly, 27,* 101–113.

Benard, B. (2006). Using strengths-based practice to tap the resilience of families. In D. Saleebey (Ed.), *The strengths perspective in social work practice* (4th ed., pp. 197–215). Boston: Pearson Education.

Bennett, J., & O'Brien, M. (1994). The building blocks of the learning organization. *Training, 31*(6), 41–49.

Berger, P., & Luckman, T. (1966). *The social construction of knowledge: A treatise in the sociology of knowledge.* New York: Anchor Books.

Berlin, S. (2005). The value of acceptance in social work direct practice. A historical and contemporary view. *Social Service Review 79,* 482–510.

Bevel, H. (2013). *The Nonviolent Right to Vote Movement almanac.* Chicago, IL: The Peace Institute.

Biestek, F. (1957). *The casework relationship.* Chicago: Loyola University Press.

Birkenmaier, J., Berg-Weger, M., & Dewees, M. (2014). *The generalist practice of social work* (3rd ed.). New York: Routledge.

Blackburn, S. (2001). *Being good: A short introduction to ethics.* Oxford, UK: Oxford University Press.

Blau, J., & Abramovitz, M. (2010). *The dynamics of social welfare policy* (3rd ed.). New York: Oxford University Press.

Blitz, L. V., Kida, L., Gresham, M., & Bronstein, L. (2013). Prevention through collaboration: Family engagement with rural schools and families living in poverty. *Families in Society: The Journal of Contemporary Social Services, 94,* 157–165.

Boal, A. (1985). *Theatre of the oppressed*. New York: Routledge. (Original work published 1979)

Boal, A. (1998). *Legislative theatre*. New York: Routledge.

Boris, E. (1995). The radicalized gender state: Constructions of citizenship in the United States. *Social Politics, 2*, 160–180.

Bosk, E. (2013). Between badness and sickness: Reconsidering medicalization for high risk children and youth. *Children and Youth Services Review, 35*, 1212–1218.

Bourdieu, P. (1984). *Distinction: A social critique of the judgment of taste* (R. Nice, Trans.). Cambridge, MA: Harvard University Press. (Original work published 1979)

Bourdieu, P. (1986). The forms of capital. In J. Richardson (Ed.), *Handbook of theory and research for the sociology of capital*. New York: Greenwood.

Bourdieu, P. (1990). Structures, habitus, practices. In *The logic of practice*. Cambridge, UK: Polity Press.

Brace, C. L. (1872). *The dangerous classes of New York and my twenty years' work among them*. New York: Wynkoop & Hallenbeck.

Bradley, G., Engelbrecht, L., & Hojer, S. (2010). Supervision: A force for change? Three stories told. *International Social Work, 53*, 773–790.

Branom, C. (2012) Community-based participatory research as a social work research and intervention approach. *Journal of Community Practice, 20*, 260–273.

Brashears, F. (1995). Supervision as social work practice. *Social Work, 40*, 692–699.

Brave NoiseCat, J. (2015, June 5). Canada just confronted its 'cultural genocide' of Native people. Why can't U.S. do the same? *Huffington Post*. Retrieved from http://www.huffingtonpost.com/2015/06/05/native-american-boarding -schools_n_7513310.html

Braveheart, M. Y. H., & DeBruyn, L. M. (1998). The American Indian holocaust: Healing historical unresolved grief. *American Indian and Alaska Native Mental Health Research, 8*, 56–78.

Bread for the World. (2013). *The state of poverty in the U.S. for 2012* [Fact sheet]. Washington, DC: Author.

Briggs, L. (2012) *Somebody's children: The politics of transnational and trans-racial adoption*. Durham, NC: Duke University Press.

Brill, N., & Levine, J. (2002). *Working with people: The helping process* (7th ed.). Boston: Allyn & Bacon.

Briskman, L. (2008). Decolonizing social work in Australia. In M. Gray, J. Coates, & M. Yellow Bird (Eds.), *Indigenous social work around the world: Towards culturally relevant education and practice* (Chapt. 6, pp. 83–96). Burlington, VT: Ashgate.

Brown, L. D., & Tandon, R. (1978). Interviews as catalysts. *Journal of Applied Psychology, 63*, 197–205.

Brown, T. (1998). *Dorothea Dix: New England reformer*. Cambridge, MA: Harvard University Press.

Browning, D., & Cooper, T. (2004). *Religious thought and the modern psychologies* (2nd ed.). Minneapolis, MN: Fortress.

Bruno, F. (1948). *Trends in social work, as reflected in the Proceedings of the National Conference of Social Welfare, 1874–1946*. New York: Columbia University Press.

Bryant, J. (2002). Ku Klux Klan in the Reconstruction era. *New Georgia Encyclopedia*. Athens, GA: University of Georgia Press. Retrieved from http://www.georgiaencyclopedia.org/articles/history-archaeology/ku-klux-klan-reconstruction-era

Bryant-Davis, T., & Ocampo, C. (2005). The trauma of racism: Implications for counseling, research, and education. *The Counseling Psychologist 33*, 574–578.

Bubeck, D. (1995). *Care, gender, and justice*. Oxford, UK: Clarendon Press.

Bulhan, H. (1985). *Frantz Fanon and the psychology of oppression*. New York: Plenum Press.

Buber, M. (1937). *I and Thou* (R. G. Smith, Trans.). Edinburgh: T. & T. Clark.

Burdge, B. (2007). Bending gender, ending gender: Theoretical foundations for social work practice with the transgender community. *Social Work 52*, 243–250.

Burkett, I., & McDonald, C. (2005). Working in a different space: Linking social work and social development. In I. Ferguson, M. Lavalette, & E. Whitmore (Eds.), *Globalisation, global justice and social work* (pp. 173–188). New York: Routledge.

Burles, M., & Thomas, R. (2013). 'But they're happening to you at the wrong time:' Exploring young adult women's reflection on serious illness through photovoice. *Qualitative Social Work, 12*, 671–678.

Cabezas, A., Reese, E., & Waller, M. (2007). *The wages of empire: Neoliberal policies, repression, and women's poverty*. Boulder, CO: Paradigm.

Campbell, C. (2011). Competency-based social work. A unitary understanding of our profession. *Canadian Social Work Review, 28*, 311–315.

Campbell, D., & Evans-Campbell, T. (2011). Historical trauma and Native American child development and mental health: An overview. In M. C. Sarche, P. Spicer, P. Farrell, & H. E. Fitzgerald (Eds.), *American Indian and Alaska Native children and mental health: Development, context, prevention, and treatment* (pp. 4–26). Santa Barbara, CA: Praeger.

Canadian Association of Social Work. (2005). *Code of ethics*. Ottawa, Canada: Author. Retrieved from http://www.casw-acts.ca/en/what-social-work/casw -code-ethics

Caputo, R. (2002). Social justice, the ethics of care, and market economies. *Families in Society, 83*, 355–364.

Caringi, J., & Hardiman, E. (2011). Secondary traumatic stress among child welfare in the United States. *International Journal of Child and Family Welfare 14*(2), 50–63.

Carlton-LaNey, I. (1996). George and Birdye Haynes legacy to community practice. *Journal of Community Practice, 2*(4), 27–48.

Carlton-LaNey, I. (2001). *African American leadership: An empowerment tradition in social welfare history*. Washington, DC: National Association of Social Workers Press.

Carniol, B. (1990). *Case critical: Challenging social work in Canada* (2nd ed.). Toronto: Between the Lines.

Carr, E. S. (2010). *Scripting addiction: The politics of therapeutic talk and American sobriety*. Princeton, NJ: Princeton University Press.

Carr-Hill, R. (1984). Radicalizing survey methodology. *Quality and Quantity, 18*, 275–292.

Chamberlin, J. (1998). Confessions of a non-compliant patient. *Journal of Psychosocial Nursing and Mental Health Services, 36*(4), 49–52.

Chambers, C. (1963). *Seedtime of reform: American social service and social action—1918–1933*. Minneapolis: University of Minnesota.

Chambon, A. (1999). Foucault's approach: Making the familiar visible. In A. Chambon, A. Irving, & L. Epstein (Eds.), *Reading Foucault for social work* (pp. 51–82). New York: Columbia University Press.

Chambon, A., Irving, A., & Epstein, L. (Eds.). (1999). *Reading Foucault for social work* (pp. 51–82). New York: Columbia University Press.

Chavez-Garcia, M. (2007). Intelligence testing at Whittier School, 1890–1920. *Pacific Historical Review, 76*, 193–228.

Checkoway, B. (1995). Six strategies of community change. *Community Development Journal, 30*, 2–20.

Checkoway, B. (2007). Community change for diverse democracy. *Community Development Journal, 42*, 1–12.

Checkoway, B. (2013). Social justice approach to community development. *Journal of Community Practice, 21*, 472–486.

Checkoway, B., & Richards-Schuster, K. (2001). Lifting new voices for socially just communities. *Community Youth Development, 2*, 32–37.

Checkoway, B., & Richards-Schuster, K. (2003). Youth participation in community evaluation research. *American Journal of Evaluation, 24*, 21–33.

Chepaitis, J. (1972). Federal social welfare progressivism in the 1920s. *Social Service Review, 46*, 213–229.

Cherin, D., & Meezan, W. (1998). Evaluation as a means of organizational learning. *Administration in Social Work, 22*(2), 1–21.

Chin, M., Sakamoto, I., & Bleuer, J. (2014). The dynamics of show-and-tell: Arts-based methods and language ideologies in community-based research. *Journal of Community Practice, 22*(1/2), 256–273.

Cho, E., Chin, D., & Shin, S. (2010, July). Supporting transnational families. *Young Children*, 30–37. Retrieved from https://www.naeyc.org/files/yc/file/201007/ChoOnline.pdf

Cho, E., Paz y Puente, F., Louie, M., & Khokha, S. (2004). *Bridges: Building a race and immigration dialogue in a global economy*. Oakland, CA: National Network for Immigrant and Refugee Rights.

Christens, B. (2012). Toward relational empowerment. *American Journal of Community Psychology, 50*, 114–128.

Christopher, S. (2005). Recommendations for conducting successful research with Native Americans. *Journal of Cancer Education, 20*, 47–51.

City and County of Denver. (2013). *Sun Valley neighborhood Decatur-Federal Station area plan*. Retrieved from https://www.denvergov.org/Portals/193/documents/DLP/Decatur-Federal/Decatur_Federal_Adopted42213.pdf

Claassen, R. (1996). *Restorative justice: Fundamental principles*. Center for Peacemaking and Conflict Studies. Fresno, CA: Fresno Pacific University. Retrieved from http://www.fresno.edu/pacs/docs/restj1.html

Clare, E. (in press). *Brilliant imperfection: Grapple with cure*. Durham, NC: Duke University Press.

Clare, E. (2003) *Excerpt from "Digging deep: Thinking about privilege."* Retrieved from http://eliclare.com/what-eli-offers/lectures/privilege

Clare, E. (2015a). *Eli Clare: About Eli*. Retrieved from http://eliclare.com/background/bio

Clare, E. (2015b). *Excerpt from "Defective, deficient, and burdensome: Thinking about bad bodies*. Retrieved from http://eliclare.com/what-eli-offers/lectures/bad-bodies

Clark, R. (1988). Social justice and issues of human rights in the international context. In D. Sanders & J. Fisher (Eds.), *Vision for the future: Social work and the Pacific-Asian perspective* (pp. 3–10). Honolulu: University of Hawaii Press.

Clarke, J. (2012). Beyond child protection: Afro-Caribbean service users of child welfare. *Journal of Progressive Human Services, 23*, 223–257.

Clarke, J., Gewirtz, S., & McLaughlin, E. (2000). *New managerialism, new welfare?* London: SAGE.

Clifford, J. (1986). Introduction: Partial truths. In J. Clifford & G. Marcus (Eds.), *Writing culture: The poetics and politics of ethnography* (pp. 1–26). Berkeley: University of California Press.

Coates, J. (1992). Ideology and education for social work practice. *Journal of Progressive Human Services, 3*(2), 15–30.

Coates, J., & McKay, M. (1995). Toward a new pedagogy for social transformation. *Journal of Progressive Human Services, 6*, 27–43.

Coates, T. (2015a). *Between the World and Me*. New York: Spiegel & Grau.

Coates, T. (2015b). Letter to my son. *The Atlantic,* July, 2015. Retrieved from http://www.theatlantic.com/politics/archive/2015/07/tanehisi-coates -between-the-world-and-me/397619

Coates, T. (2015c, October). The Black family in the age of incarceration. *The Atlantic*. Retrieved from http://www.theatlantic.com/magazine/archive/2015/10/the-black-family-in-the-age-of-mass-incarceration/403246

Cohen, M., & Hyde, C. (2014). *Empowering workers and clients for organizational change*. Chicago: Lyceum Books.

Collins, P. H. (2000). *Black feminist thought: Knowledge, consciousness, and the politics of empowerment* (2nd ed.). New York: Unwin Hyman.

Congress, E. (2000). What social workers should know about ethics. Understanding and resolving practice dilemmas. *Advances in Social Work, 1*, 1–25.

Corbin, J., & Strauss, A. (1990). Grounded theory research: Procedures, canons, and evaluative criteria. *Qualitative Sociology, 13*, 3–21.

Cormier, S., Nurius, P., & Osborn, C. (2013). *Interviewing and change strategies for helpers* (3rd ed.). Belmont, CA: Brooks/Cole.

Council on Social Work Education. (2015a). *Educational policy and accreditation standards*. Alexandria, VA: Author. Retrieved from http://www.cswe.org/File.aspx?id=81660

Council on Social Work Education. (2015b). *Teaching evidence-based practice*. Retrieved from http://www.cswe.org/CentersInitiatives/CurriculumResources/TeachingEvidence-BasedPractice.aspx

Cournoyer, B. (2004). *The evidence-based social work skills book*. Boston, MA: Allyn & Bacon.

Cousins, J., & Whitmore, E. (1998). Framing participatory evaluation. In E. Whitmore (Ed.), *Understanding and practicing participatory evaluation*. San Francisco: Jossey Bass.

Cousins, L. (2015). Culture. In E. Hutchison (Ed.), *Dimensions of human behavior: Person and environment* (5th ed., pp. 257–290). Los Angeles: SAGE.

Cowger, C. (1994). Assessing client strengths: Clinical assessment for client empowerment. *Social Work, 39*, 262–268.

Cox, P., Keener, D., Woodward, T., & Wandersman, A. (2009). Evaluation for improvement: A seven-step empowerment evaluation approach for violence prevention organizations. Atlanta: Centers for Disease Control and Prevention.

Cree, V., & Wallace, S. (2005). Risk and protection. In R. Adams, L. Dominelli, & M. Payne (Eds.), *Social work futures: Crossing boundaries, transforming practice* (pp. 115–127). New York: Palgrave Macmillan.

Crenshaw, K., Gotanda, N., Peller, G., & Thomas, K. (Eds.). (1995). *Critical race theory: An introduction*. New York: New York University Press.

Critical Resistance. (2015). *Mission*. Retrieved from http://criticalresistance.org/about

Cummins, L., Byers, L., & Pedrick, L. (2011). *Policy practice for social workers: New strategies for a new era*. Upper Saddle River, NJ: Pearson Education.

Dakin, E., Noyes, S., Arnell, J., & Rogers, B. (2015). Seeing with our own eyes: Youth in Mathare, Kenya, use photovoice to examine individual and community strengths. *Qualitative Social Work, 14*, 170–192.

Davies, C. A. (1999). *Reflexive ethnography: A guide to researching selves and others*. London: Routledge.

Davis, A. (1967*). Spearheads for reform: The social settlements and the progressive movement 1890–1914*. New York: Columbia University Press.

Davis, I. (1997). *The disabilities studies reader*. New York: Routledge.

Day, P., & Scheile, J. (2012). *A new history of social welfare* (7th ed). Boston: Pearson.

Dean, R. (2001). The myth of cross-cultural competence. *Families in Society, 82*, 623–630.

Deegan, M. (1988). *Jane Addams and the men of the Chicago School*. New Brunswick, NJ: Transaction Press.

Deegan, P. (1990). Spiritbreaking: When the helping professions hurt. *The Humanistic Psychologist, 18*, 301–313.

Deegan, P. (1996). *Recovery and the conspiracy of hope*. Presentation at the 6th Annual Mental Health Services Conference of Australia and New Zealand, Brisbane, Australia.

Deepak, A. (2011). Globalization, power, and resistance: Colonial and transnational feminist perspectives for social work practice. *International Social Work, 55*, 779–793.

Delgado, R., & Stefancic, J. (2012). *Critical race theory: An introduction* (2nd ed.). New York: New York University Press.

Denzin, N., & Lincoln, Y. (Eds.). (2005). *Handbook of qualitative research* (3rd ed.). Thousand Oaks, CA: SAGE.

Desai, A. (1987). Development of social work education. In *Encyclopedia of social work of India*. New Delhi: Government of India, Ministry of Social Welfare.

Desjarlais, R. (1997). *Shelter blues: Sanity and selfhood among the homeless*. Philadelphia: University of Pennsylvania Press.

Dessel, A. (2011). Dialogue and social change: An interdisciplinary and transformative history. *Smith College Studies in Social Work, 81*, 167–183.

Desyllas, M. (2014) Using photovoice with sex workers: The power of art, agency, and resistance. *Qualitative Social Work, 13*, 477–501.

Devine, E. (1919*). Misery and its causes.* New York: Macmillan.

Dewees, M. (2006). *Contemporary social work practice.* Boston: McGraw Hill.

Dewey, J. (1910). *How we think.* Boston: Heath.

Dewey, J. (1933). *How we think: A restatement of the relations of reflective thinking to the educative process.* Boston: Heath.

DeWitt, J. L. (1942, November 26). Letter to Richard M. Neustadt, regional director, Federal Security Agency. CSDSW War Services Bureau Records, WCCA Control Stations, July 1942–January 1943, folder no. F3729:37. California State Archives, Sacramento.

Díaz, C. (1995). *El diagnóstico para la participación.*[Diagnosis for participation]. San Jose, Costa Rica: Alforja.

Díaz, C. (1997). *Planificación participativa* [Participatory planning]. San Jose, Costa Rica: Alforja.

Dirks, N., Eley, G., & Ortner, S. (1994). Introduction. In N. Dirks, G. Eley, & S. Ortner (Eds.), *Culture/power/history: A reader in contemporary social theory* (pp. 3–45). Princeton, NJ: Princeton University Press.

Dlamini, T., & Sewpaul, V. (2015). Rhetoric versus reality in social work practice. Political, neoliberal, and new managerial influences. *Social Work* (Stellenbosch. Online), *51*(4). Retrieved from http://www.scielo.org.za/scielo.php?pid=S0037-80542015000400003&script=sci_arttext&tlng=en

Dobelstein, A. (1999). *Moral authority, ideology and the future of American social welfare.* Boulder: Westview Press.

Dominelli, L. (1996). Deprofessionalizing social work: Anti-oppressive practice, competencies and post-modernism. *British Journal of Social Work, 26*, 153–175.

Dominelli, L. (2002). *Anti-oppressive social work theory and practice.* London: Macmillan.

Dominelli, L. (2008). *Anti-racist social work* (3rd ed.). New York: Palgrave Macmillan.

Dominelli, L., & McLeod, E. (1989). *Feminist social work.* London: Macmillan.

Donaldson, T. (1996). Values in tension: Ethics away from home. *Harvard Business Review, 74*(5), 48–62.

Donovan, J. (2012). *Feminist theory: Intellectual traditions* (4th ed.). London: Continuum International Publishing.

Douglass, F. (1848a, July 28). The rights of women. *The North Star,* Rochester, NY.

Douglass, F. (1848b, January 21). The war with Mexico. *The North Star,* Rochester, NY.

Downey, K. (2009). *The woman behind the New Deal: The life and legacy of Frances Perkins, social security, unemployment insurance.* New York: Anchor.

Drolet, J. (2010). Feminist perspectives in development: Implications for women and microcredit. *Affilia: Journal of Women and Social Work, 25,* 212–225.

DuBois, W. D. (1983). *Love, synergy, and the magical: The foundations of a humanistic sociology* (Unpublished doctoral dissertation). Oklahoma State University. Retrieved from http://hdl.handle.net/11244/19324

DuBois, W. E. B. (1903). *The souls of Black folk.* New York: Bantam.

Duffus, R. (1939). *Lillian Wald: Neighbor and crusader.* New York: The Macmillan Company.

Dujon, D., & Withorn, A. (Eds.). (1996). *For crying out loud: Women's poverty in the United States.* Boston: South End Press.

Dunlap, K. (2011). Functional theory and social work practice. In F. Turner (Ed.), *Social work treatment: Interlocking theoretical approaches* (5th ed., Chapt. 14, pp. 225–241). New York: Oxford University Press.

Eagleton, T. (1990). *The significance of theory.* Cambridge, MA: Blackwell.

Eckholm, E. (2010, September 16). Recession raises poverty rate to a 15-year high. *New York Times.* Retrieved from http://www.nytimes.com/2010/09/17/us/17poverty.html?pagewanted=all&_r=0

Edelman, M. W. (2001, October). *A prayer for the children in the 21st century.* Paper presented at The Call to Service: Renewing the University's Social Justice Mission. Georgetown University, Washington, DC.

Edwards, E. (2015). *The DOJ Ferguson Report isn't just an indictment of Ferguson police, but of American policing writ large* [Blog post]. ACLU Criminal Law Reform Project. Retrieved from https://www.aclu.org/blog/speakeasy/doj-ferguson-report-isnt-just-indictment-ferguson-police-american-policing-writ-large

Edwards, R. L. (Ed.). (1995). *Encyclopedia of social work* (19th ed., Vol. 1, pp. 95–100). Washington, DC: National Association of Social Workers Press.

Edwards, W., & Gifford, C. (Eds.). (2003). *Gender and the social gospel.* Urbana, IL: University of Illinois Press.

Ehrenreich, B., & English, D. (2005). *For her own good: Two centuries of experts' advice to women.* New York: Anchor Books.

Ehrenreich, J. H. (1985). *The altruistic imagination: A history of social work and social policy in the United States.* Ithaca, NY: Cornell University Press.

Ekunwe, I., & Jones, R. (2012). Finnish criminal policy: From hard time to gentle justice. *The Journal of Prisoners on Prisons, 21*(1-2), 173–189.

Elkjaer, B. (2009). Pragmatism: A learning theory for the future. In K. Illeris (Ed.), *Contemporary theories of learning* (pp. 74–89). New York: Routledge.

Enloe, C. (2000). *Bananas, beaches, and bases: Making feminist sense of international politics.* Berkeley: University of California Press.

Enloe, C. (2004). *The curious feminist: Searching for women in the new age of empire.* Berkeley: University of California Press.

Erickson, M. (1954). Special techniques of brief hypnotherapy. *Journal of Clinical and Experimental Hypnosis, 2,* 109–129.

Escuela de Trabajo Social, Universidad de Costa Rica. (2000). *Principios éticos y políticos para las Organizaciones Profesionales de Trabajo Social del Mercosur* [Ethical and political principles for the professional social work organizations of the Mercosur countries]. Retrieved from http://www.ts.ucr.ac.cr/decla-002 .htm

Farmer, P. (2003). *Pathologies of power: Health, human rights, and the new war on the poor.* Berkeley: University of California Press.

Farmer, P. (2011, May 25). *Accompaniment as policy.* Speech at Kennedy School of Government, Harvard University. Retrieved from http://www.lessonsfrom haiti.org/press-and-media/transcripts/accompaniment-as-policy

Faver, C. (2004) Relational spirituality and social caregiving. *Social Work, 49,* 241–249.

Ferguson, I., Lavalette, M., & Whitmore, E. (2005). *Globalisation, global justice, and social work.* New York: Routledge.

Ferguson, K. (1984). *The feminist case against bureaucracy.* Philadelphia: Temple University Press.

Ferré, F. (2001). *Living and value: Toward a constructive postmodern ethics.* Albany: State University of New York Press.

Fetterman, D. (1996). Empowerment evaluation: Introduction to theory and practice. In D. Fetterman, S. Kaftarian, & A. Wandersman (Eds.), *Empowerment evaluation: Knowledge and tools for self-assessment and accountability* (pp. 3–27). Thousand Oaks, CA: SAGE.

Figueira-McDonough, J. (1993). Policy practice: The neglected side of social work intervention. *Social Work, 38,* 179–188.

Figueira-McDonough, J. (2007). *The welfare state and social work.* Thousand Oaks, CA: SAGE.

Figueira-McDonough, J., Netting, F. E., & Nichols-Casebolt, A. (Eds.). (1998). *The role of gender in practice knowledge: Claiming half the human experience.* New York: Garland.

Figueira-McDonough, J., & Sarri, R. (Eds.). (2002). *Women at the margins: Neglect, punishment, and resistance.* New York: Haworth Press.

Fine, M., & Asch, A. (1988). Disability beyond stigma: Social interaction discrimination and activism. *Journal of Social Issues, 44,* 3–21.

Fine, M., Weis, L., Powell, L., & Wong, L. M. (Eds.). (1997). *Off white: Readings on race, power and society.* New York: Routledge.

Finn, J. (1994). The promise of participatory research. *Journal of Progressive Human Services, 5,* 25–42.

Finn, J. (1998a). Gender and families. In J. Figuiera-McDonough, F. Netting, & A. Nichols-Casebolt (Eds.), *The role of gender in practice knowledge* (pp. 205–239). New York: Garland.

Finn, J. (1998b). *Tracing the veins: Of copper, culture, and community from Butte to Chuquicamata.* Berkeley: University of California Press.

Finn, J. (2001).The women of Villa Paula Jaraquemada: Building community in Chile's transition to democracy. *Community Development Journal, 36*(3), 183–197.

Finn, J. (2002). Fuerza Unida. *Affilia, 17,* 497–500.

Finn, J. (2005). La Victoria: Claiming memory, history, and justice in a Santiago *población. Journal of Community Practice, 13*(3), 9–31.

Finn, J. (2010). Love and justice: A silenced language of integrated practice? In W. Borden (Ed.), *Reshaping theory in contemporary social work* (Chapt. 7, pp. 179–209). New York: Columbia University Press.

Finn, J. (2012). *Mining childhood: Growing up in Butte, Montana, 1900–1960.* Helena: Montana Historical Society Press.

Finn, J., & Jacobson, M. (2003). Just practice: Steps toward a new social work paradigm. *Journal of Social Work Education, 39,* 57–78.

Finn, J., Jacobson, M., & Campana, J. (2004). Participatory research, popular education, and popular theatre. In C. Garvin, L. Gutiérrez, & M. Galinsky (Eds.), *Handbook of social work with groups* (pp. 326–343). New York: Guilford Press.

Finn, J., Nybell, L., & Shook, J. (2010). The meaning and making of childhood in the context of globalization. *Children and Youth Services Review, 32,* 246–254.

Finn, J., Perry, T., & Karandikar, S. (Eds.). (2013). *Gender oppression and globalization: Challenges for social work.* Alexandria. VA: Council of Social Work Education.

Finn, J., Shook, J., & Nybell, L. (2013). Place, power and possibility: Remaking social work with children and youth. Introduction. *Children and Youth Services Review, 35,* 1159–1165.

Fitzsimons, P. (1999). Managerialism and education. *Encyclopaedia of Philosophy of Education.* Retrieved from http://eepat.net/doku.php?id= managerialism_and_education

Five College Archives and Manuscript Collections. (n.d.). Biographical note. In *Mary Van Kleeck Papers, 1849–1998.* Retrieved from http://asteria.fivecolleges .edu/findaids/sophiasmith/mnsss150_bioghist.html

Flexner, A. (1915). Is social work a profession? *Proceedings of the National Conference of Charities and Corrections at the Forty-second Annual Session.* Chicago: Hildmann.

Floyd, M. (2013). Involuntary mental health treatment: The mental health consumer as expert. *Journal of Progressive Human Services, 24,* 187–198.

Fook, J. (2012). *Social work: A critical approach to practice* (2nd ed.). Los Angeles: SAGE.

Fook, J., & Gardner, F. (2007). *Practising critical reflection: A resource handbook.* Maidenhead, UK: Open University Press.

Ford, R., Hershberger, S., Glenn, J., Morris, S., Saez, V., Togba, F., . . . Williams, R. (2013). Building a youth-led movement to keep young people out of the criminal justice system. *Children and Youth Services Review, 35,* 1268–1275.

Forgacs, D. (Ed.). (1988). *An Antonio Gramsci reader: Selected writings, 1919–1935.* New York: Schocken Books.

Fossen, C., Anderson-Meager, J., & Zellmer, D. (2014). Infusing a new ethical decision making model throughout a BSW curriculum. *Journal of Social Work Values and Ethics*, *11*, 66–81.

Foster, C., & Louie, J. (2010). *Grassroots action and learning for social change: Evaluating community organizing*. Center for Evaluation Innovation. Retrieved from www.innonet.org/client_docs/File/center_pubs/evaluating_community _organizing.pdf

Foucault, M. (1972). *The archaeology of knowledge* (A. Sheridan, Trans.). New York: Harper & Row. (Original work published 1969)

Foucault, M. (1979). Truth and power. In M. Morris & P. Patton (Eds.), *Michel Foucault: Power, truth, and strategy* (pp. 29–48). Sydney: Feral Publications.

Foucault, M. (1980). *Power/knowledge: Selected interviews and other writings, 1972–77* (C. Gordon, Ed. & Trans.). New York: Pantheon.

Fraser, N., & Gordon, L. (1994). A genealogy of dependency: Tracing a keyword of the U.S. welfare state. *Signs, 19*, 309–336.

Freire, P. (1974). *Pedagogy of the oppressed*. New York: Seabury/Continuum.

Friedman, T. (1999). *The lexus and the olive tree*. New York: Farrar, Straus, & Giroux.

Fritz, N. (2015, March 31). Economic inequality: It's far worse that you think. *Scientific American*, Retrieved from http://www.scientificamerican.com/ article/economic-inequality-it-s-far-worse-than-you-think

Fromm, E. (1947). *Man for himself: An inquiry into the psychology of ethics*. New York: Holt.

Fromm. E. (1956). *The art of loving*. New York: Harper.

Fuller, T., & Pacely, M. (2011). "They treated me like a real person": Family perspectives on effective engagement strategies. Presented at the American Humane Association Conference on Differential Response in Child Welfare, Chicago. Retrieved from http://www.americanhumane.org/assets/pdfs/ children/differential-response/they-treated-me-like-a-real.pdf

Furlong, M., Helm, S., Otto, R., & Raimondo, L. (2013). Reclaiming life: Six consumers of mental health services talk about what helped and what did not help them get their lives back. *Journal of Progressive Human Services, 24*, 290–297

Galeano, E. (1983). *Days and nights of love and war*. New York: Monthly Review Press.

Galeano, E. (1992). *We say no: Chronicles 1963–1991*. New York: Norton.

Galeano, E. (1995, July 5). The right to dream. *The New Internationalist Magazine, 1995*(269). Retrieved from https://newint.org/features/1995/07/05/right

Galper, J. (1975). *The politics of social services.* Englewood Cliffs, NJ: Prentice-Hall.

Gambrill, E. (2014). The *Diagnostic and Statistical Manual of Mental Disorders* as a major form of dehumanization in the modern world. *Research on Social Work Practice, 24,* 13–36.

Gardner, F. (2012). The care, the rain, and meaningful conversation. In S. Witkin (Ed.), *Social construction and social work practice* (Chapt. 5, pp. 103–126). New York: Columbia University Press.

Garvin, C., Gutiérrez, L., & Galinsky, M. (Eds.). (2004). *Handbook of social work with groups.* New York: Guilford Press.

Gasker, J., & Fischer, A. (2014). Toward a context specific definition of social justice work social work. *Journal of Social Work Values and Ethics, 11,* 42–53.

Gates, A. (2014). Integrating social services and social change: Lessons from an immigrant worker center. *Journal of Community Practice, 22*(1/2), 102–129.

Gergen, K. (1999). *An invitation to social construction.* London: Sage Publications.

Germain, C. (1994). Emerging conceptions of family development over the life course. *Families in Society, 75,* 259–268.

Gharbi, M. (2014). Social media and the Arab Spring: "Tunisnews" as a model. In S. Hessle (Ed.), *Global social transformation and social action: The role of social workers* (pp. 25–30). Burlington, VT: Ashgate.

Giddens, A. (1979). *Central problems in social theory: Action, structure and contradiction in social analysis.* Berkeley: University of California Press.

Gil, D. (1994). Confronting social injustice and oppression. In F. Reamer (Ed.), *The foundations of social work knowledge* (pp. 231–263). New York: Columbia University Press.

Gil, D. (2013). *Confronting injustice and oppression: Concepts and strategies for social workers.* New York: Columbia University Press.

Gilligan, C. (1982). *In a different voice.* Cambridge: Harvard University Press.

Gilson, S., Bricou, J., & Baskind. F. (1998). Listening to the voices of individuals with disabilities. *Families in Society: The Journal of Contemporary Human Services, 79,* 188.

Gitterman, A., & Germaine, C. (2008). *The life model of social work practice* (3rd ed.). New York: Columbia University Press.

Glaser, B., & Strauss, A. (1967). *The discovery of grounded theory: Strategies for qualitative research*. Chicago: Aldine Publishing Company.

Gone, J. P. (2004). Mental health services for Native Americans in the 21st century United States. *Professional Psychology: Research and Practice, 35*, 10–18.

Gonzalez, J., & Trickett, E. (2014). Collaborative measurement development as a tool in CBPR: Measurement development and adaptation within the cultures of communities. *American Journal of Community Psychology, 54,* 112–124.

Goodman, B., & Maggio, J. (Directors). (2008). The lobotomist [Television series episode]. In *American experience*. Arlington, VA: PBS Productions.

Goodman, L., Bohlig, A., Witman, A., Weintraub, S., Green, A., White, L., & Ryan, N. (2007). Applying feminist theory to community practice: A case example of a multi-level empowerment intervention for low-income women with depression. In E. Aldarando (Ed.), *Promoting social justice through mental health practice* (pp. 265–290). Florence, KY: Erlbaum.

Gordon, L. (1988). *Heroes of their own lives: The politics and history of family violence*. New York: Viking Penguin.

Gordon, L. (1994) *Pitied but not entitled: Single mothers and the history of welfare*. New York: Free Press.

Gould, S. (1981). *The mismeasure of man*. New York: Norton.

Gramsci, A. (1987). *The modern prince and other stories*. New York: International Publishers. (Original work published 1957)

Gray, M., & Coates, J. (2012). Environmental ethics for social work. Social work's responsibility to the non-human world. *International Journal of Social Welfare, 21*, 239–247.

Gray, M., Coates, J., & Yellow Bird, M. (Eds.). (2008). *Indigenous social work around the world: Towards culturally relevant education and practice*. Burlington, VT: Ashgate.

Gray, M., & Webb, S. (2013). *The new politics of social work*. New York: Palgrave Macmillan.

Graybeal, C. (2001). Strengths-based social work assessment: Transforming the dominant paradigm. *Families in Society, 82*, 233–242.

Greenwood, E. (1957). Attributes of a profession. *Social Work, 2*(3), 45–55.

Gringeri, C., & Roche, S. (2010) Beyond the binary: Critical feminisms in social work. *Affilia: Journal of Women and Social Work, 25,* 337–340.

Grinnell, R., & Unrau, Y. (2005). *Social work research and evaluation: Quantitative and qualitative approaches.* New York: Oxford University Press.

Guba, E., & Lincoln, Y. (1994). Competing paradigms in qualitative research. In N. Denzin & Y. Lincoln (Eds.), *Handbook of qualitative research* (pp. 105–117). London: SAGE.

Gutiérrez, L. (1990). Working with women of color: An empowerment perspective. *Social Work, 35,* 149–153.

Gutiérrez, L., & Lewis, E. (1999). *Empowering women of color.* New York: Columbia University Press.

Guzman Bouvard, M. (1994). *Revolutionizing motherhood: The mothers of the Plaza de Mayo.* Wilmington, DE: Scholarly Resources.

Hall, B. (1993). Introduction. In P. Park, M. Brydon-Miller, B. Hall, & T. Jackson (Eds.), *Voices of change: Participatory research in the United States and Canada* (pp. xiii–xxii). Westport, CT: Bergin & Garvey.

Hamilton, G. (1940). *The theory and practice of social casework.* New York: Columbia University Press.

Hankivsky, O. (Ed.). (2012). *An intersectionality-based policy analysis framework.* Vancouver, BC: Institute of Intersectiontality Research and Policy.

Hanmer, J., & Statham, D. (1989). *Women and social work: Towards a woman-centered practice.* Chicago: Lyceum Books.

Hansan, J. E. (2011). *Poor relief in early America.* Retrieved from http://www .socialwelfarehistory.com/programs/poor-relief

Hansan, J. E. (2013). *Charity Organization Societies (1877–1893).* Retrieved from http://www.socialwelfarehistory.com/?p=8401

Hardina, D. (2013). *Interpersonal social work skills for community practice.* New York: Springer.

Hardina, D. (2014). The use of dialogue in community organizing practice. Using theory, values, and skills to guide group decision making. *Journal of Community Practice, 22,* 365–384.

Harrell, S., & Bond, M. (2006). Listening to diversity stories. *American Journal of Community Psychology, 37,* 365–376.

Harrington, M. (1962) *The other America: Poverty in the United States*. New York: Macmillan.

Harris, J. (2005). Globalisation, neo-liberal managerialism and UK social work. In I. Ferguson, M. Lavalette, & E. Whitmore (Eds.), *Globalisation, global justice and social work* (pp. 81–93). New York: Routledge.

Hartman, A. (1978). Diagrammatic assessment of family relationships. *Social Casework, 59*, 465–476.

Hartman, A., & Laird, J. (1983). *Family-centered social work practice*. New York: Free Press.

Hartmann, H. I. (1987). The family as the locus of gender, class, and political struggle: The example of housework. In S. Harding (Ed.), *Feminism and methodology: Social science issues* (pp. 109–134). Bloomington: Indiana University Press.

Harvard University Library Open Collections Program. (n.d.) *Settlement House Movement*. Retrieved from http://ocp.hul.harvard.edu/immigration/settlement.html

Harvey, D. (2007). *A brief history of neoliberalism*. Oxford, UK: Oxford University Press.

Hase, M. (1994). *W. Gertrude Brown's struggles for racial justice. Female leadership and community in Black Minneapolis, 1920–1940* (Unpublished PhD dissertation). University of Minnesota, Minneapolis.

Hatton, N., & Smith, D. (1995). Reflection in teacher education: Towards definition and implementation. *Teaching and Teacher Education, 11*, 33–39.

Hawken, P. (2007). *Blessed unrest*. New York: Viking Press.

Healy, K. (2002). Managing human services in a market environment: What role for social workers? *British Journal of Social Work, 32*, 527–540.

Healy, K. (2005). Under reconstruction: Renewing critical social work practices. In S. Hick, J. Fook, & R. Pozzuto (Eds.), *Social work: A critical turn* (pp. 219–229). Toronto: Thompson Educational Publishing.

Healy, K. (2014).*Social work theories in context: Creating frameworks for practice* (2nd ed.). New York: Palgrave Macmillan.

Healy, L. M. (2007). Universalism and cultural relativism in social work ethics. *International Social Work, 50*, 11–26.

Healy, L. M. (2008). *International social work: Professional action in an interdependent world* (2nd ed.). New York: Oxford University Press.

Hearn, G. (1969). *The general systems approach: Contributions to a holistic conception of social work.* New York: Council on Social Work Education.

Held, V. (2006). *Ethics of care: Personal, political, and global.* New York: Oxford University Press.

Hess, C. (2013, April). *Women and the care crisis: Valuing in-home care in policy and practice* [Briefing paper IWPR #C401]. Institute for Women's Policy Research. Retrieved from http://www.iwpr.org/publications/pubs/women -and-the-care-crisis-valuing-in-home-care-in-policy-and-practice

Hessle, S. (2014). *Global transformation and social action: The role of social workers.* Burlington, VT: Ashgate.

Hicks, S. (2008). Thinking through sexuality. *Journal of Social Work, 8,* 65–82.

Hill, D., & Jones, C. (Eds.). (2003). *Forms of ethical thinking in therapeutic practice.* Berkshire, England: Open University Press.

Ho, C., & Loucky, J. (2012). *Humane migration: Establishing legitimacy and rights for displaced people.* Sterling, VA: Kumarian Press.

Hobdy, D., Murray, A., & Morgan, S. (2006). *Social work ethics summit. Summary report and recommendations.* Washington, DC: National Association of Social Workers.

Hochschild, A. (2000). Global care chains and emotional surplus value. In W. Hutton & A. Giddens (Eds.), *On the edge: Living with global capitalism* (p. 13). London: Jonathon Cape.

Hochschild, A. (2012). *The outsourced self: Intimate life in market times.* New York: Metropolitan Books.

Hoefer, R. (2012). *Advocacy practice for social justice* (2nd ed.). Chicago: Lyceum Books.

Hohman, B. (2013, September 13). *Cultural humility as lifelong practice* [Blog post]. IN SITU, the Blog of San Diego State University School of Social Work. Retrieved from http://socialwork.sdsu.edu/insitu/diversity/cultural-humility -a-lifelong-practice

Holloran, P. (1989). *Boston's wayward children: Social services for homeless children, 1830–1930.* Madison, NJ: Fairleigh Dickinson University Press.

Homan, M. (2016) *Promoting community change: Making it happen in the real world* (6th ed.). Boston: Cengage.

hooks, b. (1984). *Feminist theory from margin to center.* Boston: South End Press.

hooks, b. (1994). *Teaching to transgress.* New York: Routledge.

hooks, b. (1995) *Killing rage: Ending racism.* Harmondsworth, UK: Penguin.

Hope, A., & Timmel, S. (1999). *Training for transformation: A handbook for community workers* (Books 1–4). London, England: Intermediate Technology Publications. (Original published 1984)

Hopkins, J. (1999). *Harry Hopkins: Sudden hero, brash reformer.* New York: Palgrave Macmillan.

Hopkins, J. (2011). *Harry Hopkins and work relief.* Retrieved from http://www.socialwelfarehistory.com/eras/harry-hopkins-and-work-relief-during-the-great-depression

Howard, D. (1943). American social work and World War II. *Annals of the American Academy of Political Science, 229,* 138–139.

Howe, D. (1994). Modernity, postmodernity, and social work. *British Journal of Social Work, 24,* 513–532.

Hounmenou, C. (2012). Black settlement houses and oppositional consciousness. *Journal of Black Studies, 43,* 646–666.

Houston, S., Magill, T., McCollum, M., & Spratt, T. (2001). Developing creative solutions to the problems of children and their families: Communicative reason and the use of forum theatre. *Child and Family Social Work, 6,* 285–293.

Huff, D. (2006). *Social work history station.* Retrieved from http://www.idbsu.edu/socwork/dhuff/history

Hugman, R. (2012). *Culture, value and ethics in social work.* London: Routledge.

Hull-House Residents. (1895). *Hull-House maps and papers.* New York: Crowell.

Human Impact Partners. (2013). *Family unity, Family health: How family-focused immigration reform will mean better health for children and families.* Oakland, CA: Author.

Human Rights Watch. (2004). Human rights overview: United States. Retrieved from https://www.hrw.org/legacy/english/docs/2006/01/18/usdom12292.htm

Hunter, F. (1953). *Community power structure.* Chapel Hill: University of North Carolina Press.

Hurtado, A., & Cervantez, K. (2009). A view from within and from without: The development of Latino feminist psychology. In F. Villarruel, G. Carlo, J. Grau, M. Azmita, N. Cabrera, & T. Tahin (Eds.), *Handbook of U.S. Latino psychology* (pp. 171–190).Thousand Oaks, CA: SAGE.

Husock, H. (1993). Bringing back the settlement house. *Public Welfare, 51*(4), 16–25.

Hutchison, E. (2015). *Dimensions of human behavior: Person and environment* (5th ed.). Los Angeles: SAGE.

Iannello, K. (1992). *Decisions without hierarchy: Feminist interventions in organization theory and practice.* London: Routledge.

Ife, J. (2000). Localized needs and a globalized economy: Bridging the gap with social work practice. *Canadian Social Work, 2,* 50–64.

Ife, J. (2010). *Human rights from below. Achieving rights through community development.* Melbourne: Cambridge University Press.

Ife, J. (2012). *Human rights and social work: Towards rights-based practice* (3rd ed.). Cambridge, UK: Cambridge University Press.

Ife, J., & Fiske, L. (2006). Human rights and community work. *International Social Work,* 49, 297–308.

Iglehart, A., & Becarra, R. (2000). *Social services and the ethnic community.* Prospect Heights, IL: Waveland Press.

International Federation of Social Workers. (2012). *Statement of ethical principles.* Bern, Switzerland: International Federation of Social Workers. Retrieved from http://ifsw.org/policies/statement-of-ethical-principles

International Federation of Social Workers. (2014). *Global definition of social work.* Retrieved from http://ifsw.org/get-involved/global-definition-of-social -work

International Federation of Social Workers. (2016). *What we do.* Retrieved from http://ifsw.org/what-we-do

International Federation of Social Workers, International Association of Schools of Social Work, and International Council on Social Welfare. (2012). The global agenda for social work and social development: Commitment to action. *Journal of Social Work Education, 48,* 837–843.

Irwin, K. (1992). Towards theories of Maori feminisms. In R. du Plessis (Ed.), *Feminist voices: Womens' studies texts for Aotearoal, New Zealand* (p. 5). Auckland, New Zealand: Oxford University Press.

Israel, B., Eng, E., Schulz, A., & Parker, E. (Eds.). (2005). *Methods in community-based participatory research for health.* San Francisco: Wiley.

Iverson, R., Gergen, K., & Fairbanks II, R. (2005). Assessment and social construction: Conflict or co-creation? *British Journal of Social Work, 35,* 689–708.

Jabour, A. (2012). Relationship and leadership: Sophonisba Breckinridge and women in social work. *Affilia: Journal of Women and Social Work, 27,* 22–37.

Jackson, V. (2003). In our own voice: African American stories of oppression, survival, and recovery in mental health systems. *Off Our Backs, 33*(7/8), 19–21.

Jacobs, Elizabeth. (2007). The theatrical politics of Chicano/Chicana identity: From Valdez to Moranga. *New Theatre Quarterly, 23*, 25–34.

Jacobsen, C. (2013). Breaching the fence: Claiming justice and human rights for incarcerated women. In J. Finn, T. Perry, & S. Karandikar (Eds.), *Gender oppression and globalization: Challenges for social work* (Chapt. 4, pp. 79–100). Alexandria, VA: Council of Social Work Education Press.

Jani, J., & Reisch, M. (2011). Common human needs, uncommon solutions: Applying a critical framework to perspectives on human behavior. *Families in Society, 92*, 13–20.

Jansson, B. (1994). *Social welfare policy from theory to practice.* New York: Wadsworth.

Jansson, B. (2008). *Becoming an effective policy advocate: From policy practice to social justice* (5th ed.). Pacific Grove, CA: Brooks/Cole Publishing.

Jara, O. (1998). *Para sistematizar experiencias* [Systematization of experiences]. San Jose, Costa Rica: Alforja.

Jarvis, D. (2013). Environmental justice and social work: A call to expand the profession. *Columbia Social Work Review, 4*, 36–45.

Jeansonne, G., & Luhrsson, D. (2006). *A time of paradox: America since 1870.* Oxford, UK: Rowman & Littlefield.

Jenkins, K. (1995). *On 'What is history?' From Carr and Elton to Rorty and White.* London: Routledge.

Jennings, L., Medina, D., Messia, D., & McLoughlin, K. (2006). Toward a critical theory of youth empowerment. *Journal of Community Practice, 14*(1-2), 31–55.

Jennissen, T., & Lundy, C. (2011). *One hundred years of social work: A history of the profession in English Canada, 1900–2000.* Waterloo, Ontario: Wilfrid Laurier University Press.

Jessup, P. (2009). Constructing ability and disability among preschoolers in the Crestview Headstart Program. In L. Nybell, J. Shook, & J. Finn (Eds.), *Childhood, youth, and social work in transformation* (Chapt. 11, pp. 239–260). New York: Columbia University Press.

Jimenez, M., & Aylwin, N. (1992). Social work in Chile: Support for the struggle for justice in Latin America. In M. C. Hokenstad, S. K. Khinduka, & J. Midgley (Eds.), *Profiles in international social work.* Washington, DC: National Association of Social Work.

Johnson, A. (1955). Educating professional social workers for ethical practice. *Social Service Review*, *29*, 125–136.

Johnson, A. G. (2006). *Privilege, power, and difference* (2nd ed.). Boston: McGraw Hill.

Johnson, L., & Yanca, S. (2007). *Social work practice: A generalist approach* (9th ed.). Boston: Allyn & Bacon.

Jones, C. (2005). The neo-liberal assault: Voices from the front line of British state social work. In I. Ferguson, M. Lavalette, & E. Whitmore (Eds.), *Globalisation, global justice and social work* (pp. 97–109). New York: Routledge.

Jordan, J. (2003). Valuing vulnerability: New definitions of courage [Work in Progress Paper 102]. Wellesley, MA: Stone Center, Wellesley Center for Women, Wellesley College.

Joseph, A. (2013). Empowering alliances in pursuit of social justice: Social workers supporting psychiatric-survivor movements. *Journal of Progressive Human Services*, *24*, 265–288.

Kaner, S. (2014). *Facilitator's guide to participatory decision-making*. San Francisco: Jossey Bass.

Kanter, R. M. (1977). *Men and women of the corporation*. New York: Basic Books.

Karger, H., & Lonne, B. (2010) Unionization: A necessary strategy to address professional decline? In P. A Kurzamn & R. P. Maiden (Eds.), *Union contributions to labor welfare policy and practice: Past, present, and future* (pp. 23–46). New York: Routledge.

Kellogg, P. U. (Ed.). (1914). Field work of the Pittsburgh survey. In *The Pittsburgh District Civic Frontage* (pp. 492–515). New York: Russell Sage Foundation.

Kelly, A., & Sewell, S. (1988). *With head, heart and hand: Dimensions of community building* (4th ed.). Brisbane, Queensland: Boolarong Press.

Kelly, P. (2011). Narrative theory and social work treatment. In F. Turner (Ed.), *Social work treatment: Interlocking theoretical approaches* (5th ed, pp. 315–326). New York: Oxford University Press.

Kemp, S., & Brandwein, R. (2010) Feminisms and social work in the United States: An intertwined history. *Affilia: Journal of Women and Social Work*, *25*, 341–364.

Kemp, S. P. (2011). Recentering environment in social work practice: Necessity, opportunity, challenge. *British Journal of Social Work*, *41*, 1198–1210.

Kempshall, A. (1943). *Family service during war time: A report to the Board of Directors of the Community Service Society of New York*. Retrieved from http://www.socialwelfarehistory.com/eras/family-service-war-time

Kilty, K., & Segal, E. (2006). *The promise of welfare reform*. New York: Haworth.

Kivnick, H., & Murray, S. (2001). Life strengths interview guide: Assessing elder clients' strengths. *Journal of Gerontological Social Work, 34*(4), 7–32.

Klugman, B. (2010). *Evaluating social justice advocacy: A values based approach*. Center for Evaluation Innovation. Retrieved from http://www.innonet.org/resources/files/klugman_evaluating_social_justice_advocacy.pdf

Klugman, B. (2011). Effective social justice advocacy: A theory-of-change framework for assessing progress. *Reproductive Health Matters, 19*(38), 146–162.

Kohls, L. R. (1984). *The values Americans live by*. Washington, DC: Meridian House International. Retrieved from http://www2.pacific.edu/sis/culture/File/sec1-4-2h1.htm

Kolivoski, K., Weaver, A., & Constance-Huggins, M. (2014). Critical race theory: Opportunities for application in social work practice and policy. *Families in Society, 95*, 269–276.

Kornbluh, F. (2007). *The battle for welfare rights*. Philadelphia: University of Pennsylvania Press.

Korten, D. (2001). *When corporations rule the world*. West Hartford, CT: Kumarian Press.

Kosciw, J. G., Greytak, E. A., Palmer, N. A., & Boesen, M. J. (2014). *The 2013 National School Climate Survey: The experiences of lesbian, gay, bisexual and transgender youth in our nation's schools*. New York: Gay, Lesbian & Straight Education Network.

Kotlowitz, A. (1991). *There are no children here*. New York: Doubleday.

Koven, S., & Gotske, F. (2010). *American immigration policy: Confronting the nation's challenges*. New York: Springer.

Kozol, J. (1991). *Savage inequalities: Children in America's schools*. New York: Crown.

Kozol, J. (2005). *The shame of the nation: The restoration of apartheid schooling in America*. New York: Random House.

Krueger, R. (1994). *Focus groups: A practical guide for applied research*. Thousand Oaks, CA: SAGE.

Krueger, R., & King, J. (1998). *Involving community members in focus groups*. Thousand Oaks, CA: SAGE.

Krumer-Nevo, M., Weiss-Gal, I., & Monnickendam, M. (2009) Poverty-aware social work practice: A conceptual framework for social work education. *Journal of Social Work Education*, *45*, 225–243.

Laird, J. (1993). Theorizing culture: Narrative ideas and practice principles. In M. McGoldrick (Ed.), *Revisioning family therapy* (2nd ed.). New York: Guilford Press.

Langhorne, M. (2000). The African-American community: Circumventing the compulsory education system. *Beverly Hills Bar Association Journal, 12*, 13–17.

Lappé, F. M. (1971). *Diet for a small planet.* New York: Ballantine Books.

Lappé, F. M., & DuBois, P. M. (1994). *The quickening of America: Rebuilding our nation, remaking our lives.* San Francisco, CA: Jossey-Bass.

Lappé, F., & Lappé, A. (2003). *Hope's edge: The next diet for a small planet.* New York: Tarcher/Putnam.

Larson, G. (2008). Anti-oppressive practice in mental health. *Journal of Progressive Human Services, 19*, 39–54.

Lasch-Quinn, E. (1993). *Black neighbors. Race and the limits of reform in the settlement house movement, 1890–1945.* Chapel Hill: University of North Carolina Press.

Lather, P. (1986). Research as praxis. *Harvard Educational Review, 56*, 257–277.

Lather, P. (1991). *Getting smart: Feminist research and pedagogy with/in the postmodern.* New York: Routledge.

Lawrence, J. (2000). The Indian Health Service and the sterilization of Native American women. *American Indian Quarterly, 24*, 400–419.

Lawson, H., & Caringi, J. (2015). Child welfare participatory action research design teams for workforce reconfiguration, organizational innovation, and policy change. In H. Lawson, J. Caringi, L. Pyles, J. Jurowski, & C. Bozlak (Eds.), *Participatory action research* (pp. 35–66). New York: Oxford University Press.

Ledwith, M., & Asgill, P. (2000). Critical alliance: Black and white women working together for social justice. *Community Development Journal, 35*, 290–299.

Lee, J. (2001). *The empowerment approach to social work practice* (2nd ed.). New York: Columbia University Press.

Leighninger, L., & Knickmeyer, R. (1976). The rank and file movement: The relevance of radical social work traditions to modern social work practice. *Journal of Sociology and Social Welfare, 4*, 166–177.

Lemert, C. (2004). *Social theory: Multicultural and classical readings*. Boulder, CO: Westview Press.

Lemons, S. (1969). The Sheppard Towner Act: Progressivism in the 1920s. *Journal of American History, 55*, 776–786.

Lengermann, P., & Niebrugge-Brantley, J. (1998). *The women founders: Sociology and social theory, 1830–1930*. Boston: McGraw-Hill.

Leonard, P. B. (2011). An introduction to restorative justice. In E. Beck, N. Kropf, & P. B. Leonard (Eds.), *Social work and restorative justice* (Chapt. 3, pp. 31–63). New York: Oxford University Press.

Levi-Strauss, C. (1966). *The savage mind* (2nd ed.). Chicago: University of Chicago Press.

Levy, C. S. (1973). The value base of social work. *Journal of Education for Social Work, 9*, 34–42.

Levy, C. S. (1976). *Social work ethics*. New York: Human Sciences Press.

Lewin, K. (1943). Psychological ecology. In D. Cartwright (Ed.), *Field theory in social science*. London: Social Science Paperbacks.

Lincoln, Y., & Guba, E. (1985). *Naturalistic inquiry*. Newbury Park, CA: SAGE.

Link, R. (1999). Infusing global perspectives into social work values and ethics. In C. Ramanathan & R. Link (Eds.), *All our futures: Social work practice in a global era* (pp. 69–93). Belmont, CA: Wadsworth.

Lloyd, M. F. (2008). *100 years: A centennial history of the University of Pennsylvania's School of Social Policy and Practice*. Philadelphia: University of Pennsylvania School of Social Policy & Practice.

Locke, B., Garrison, R., & Winship, J. (1998). *Generalist social work practice: Context, story, and partnerships*. Pacific Grove, CA: Brooks/Cole.

Loewenberg, F., & Dolgoff, R. (1996). *Ethical decisions for social work practice* (5th ed.). Itasca, IL: Peacock.

Loewenberg, F., Dolgoff, R., & Harrington, D. (2000). *Ethical decisions for social work practice* (6th ed.). Itasca, IL: Peacock.

Logan, S. (Ed.). (2014). *The spirit of an activist: The life and work of I. deQuincey Newman*. Columbia: University of South Carolina Press.

Lott, B. (2002). Cognitive and behavioral distancing from the poor. *American Psychologist, 57*, 100–110.

Lum, D. (1999) *Culturally competent practice: A framework for growth and action*. New York: Wadsworth.

Lum, D. (2011). *Culturally competent practice: A framework for understanding diverse groups and justice issues.* Belmont, CA: Brooks/Cole, Cengage Learning.

Lundy, C. (2011). *Social work, social justice, and human rights: A structural approach to practice* (2nd ed.). Toronto: University of Toronto Press.

Lyons, K. (1999). *International social work: Themes and perspectives.* Brookfield, VT: Ashgate.

Mabee, C. (1995). *Sojourner Truth, slave, prophet, legend.* New York: New York University Press.

Macfarlane, P. (1915, February/March). Diagnosis by dreams. *Good Housekeeping, 60,* 125–133.

MacLeod, D. (1998). *The age of the child: Children in America, 1890–1920.* New York: Twayne.

MacDonald, C. (2006). *Challenging social work: The institutional context of practice.* New York: Palgrave.

Mackelprang, R., & Salsgiver, R. (2015). *Disability: A diversity model approach in human service practice* (3rd ed.). Chicago: Lyceum Books.

Magnuson, S., & Shaw, H. (2003). Adaptations of the multifaceted genogram in counseling, training and supervision. *The Family Journal: Counseling and Therapy for Couples and Families, 11,* 45–54.

Maguire, P. (1987). *Doing participatory research: A feminist approach.* Amherst, MA: Center for International Education, University of Massachusetts.

Mahoney. M. (1995). *Cognitive and constructive psychotherapies.* New York: Springer.

Mannes, M. (1995). Factors and events leading to the passage of the Indian Child Welfare Act. *Child Welfare, 74,* 264–282.

Mapp, S. (2007). *Human rights and social justice from a global perspective.* New York: Oxford University Press.

Marchand, R. (1972). *The American peace movement and social reform, 1889–1918.* Princeton, NJ: Princeton University Press.

Margolin, L. (1997). *Under the cover of kindness: The invention of social work.* Charlottesville: University of Virginia Press.

Marlow, C. (2005). *Research methods for generalist social work* (4th ed.). Belmont, CA: Brooks/Cole.

Marsiglia, F. F., & Kulis, S. (2015). *Diversity, oppression, and change* (2nd ed.). Chicago: Lyceum Books.

Matson, F., & Montagu, A. (1967). *The human dialogue: Perspectives on communication*. New York: Free Press.

Mattaini, M., & Atkinson, K. (2011). Constructive noncooperation: Living in truth. *Peace and Conflict Studies, 18*, 1–43.

Mattaini, M., & Meyer, C. (2002). The ecosystems perspective: Implications for practice. In M. Mattaini, C. T. Lowery, & C. H. Meyer (Eds.), *Foundations of social work practice: A graduate text* (pp. 3–24). Washington, DC: NASW Press.

McCabe, A., & Davis, A. (2012). Community development as mental health promotion: Principles, practice, and outcomes. *Community Development Journal, 47*, 506–521.

McCormick, P. (2003).Whose justice? An examination of nine models of justice. *Social Thought, 22*(2/3), 7–25.

McCracken, S., & Rzepnicki, T. (2010). The role of theory in conducting evidence based clinical practice. In W. Borden (Ed.), *Reshaping theory in contemporary social work: Toward a critical pluralism in clinical practice* (pp. 210–233). New York: Columbia University Press.

McDowell, T., Libal, K., & Brown, A. (2012). Human rights in the practice of family therapy. Domestic violence as a case in point. *Journal of Feminist Family Therapy, 24*, 1–23.

McGerr, M. (2003). *A fierce discontent: The rise and fall of the Progressive Movement in America, 1870–1920*. New York: Free Press.

McGrath-Morris, P. (2002). The capaibilities perspective: A framework for social justice. *Families in Society, 83*, 365–373.

McIntosh, P. (1995). White privilege and male privilege: A personal account of coming to see correspondences through work in women's studies. In M. Anderson & P. H. Collins (Eds.), *Race, class, and gender: An anthology* (2nd ed., pp. 76–87). Belmont, CA: Wadsworth Publishing.

McKnight, J., & Kretzmann, J. (1990). *Mapping community capacity. Report of the Neighborhood Innovations Network*. Evanston, IL: Northwestern University Institute for Policy Research.

McMichael, P. (2000). *Development and social change: A global perspective*. Thousand Oaks, CA: Pine Forge Press.

McNeese, C. A., & Thyer, B. A. (2004). Evidence-based practice and social work. *Journal of Evidence-Based Social Work, 1*, 7–25.

McPhail, B. (2004). Questioning gender and sexuality binaries. *Journal of Gay and Lesbian Social Services, 17,* 3–21.

Mehrotra, G. (2010). Toward a continuum of intersectionality theorizing for feminist social work scholarship. *Affilia: Journal of Women and Social Work, 25,* 417–430.

Merriam-Webster. (2005). *Merriam Webster collegiate dictionary.* Springfield, MA: Author.

Meyer, C. (1970). *Social work practice: A response to the urban crisis.* New York: Free Press.

Meyer, C. (Ed.). (1983). *Clinical social work and the eco-system perspective.* New York: Columbia University Press.

Mezirow, J. (1998). On critical reflection. *Adult Education Quarterly, 48,* 185–198.

Mezirow, J. (2009). Transformative learning theory. In J. Mezirow, E. W. Taylor, & Associates (Eds.), *Transformative learning in practice: Insights from community, workplace, and higher education* (pp. 18–32). San Francisco: Jossey-Bass.

Michael, S. (2005). The promise of appreciative inquiry as an interview tool for field research. *Development in Practice, 15,* 222–230.

Mickelson, J. (1995). Advocacy. In R. L. Edwards (Ed.), *Encyclopedia of social work* (19th ed., Vol. 1, pp. 95–100). Washington, DC: National Association of Social Workers Press.

Miley, K., O'Melia, M., & DuBois, B. (2013). *Generalist social work practice: An empowering perspective* (7th ed.). Boston: Allyn & Bacon.

Miller, D. (1976). *Social justice.* Oxford, UK: Clarendon Press.

Miller, V., & VeneKlasen, L. (2012). *Feminist popular education and movement-building* [Draft discussion paper]. Retrieved from https://www.justassociates .org/sites/justassociates.org/files/feminist-popular-education-movement -building-miller-veneklasen.pdf

Mintz, D. (2004). *Huck's raft: A history of American childhood.* Cambridge: Harvard University Press.

Moch, M. (2009). A critical understanding of social work by Paulo Freire. *Journal of Progressive Human Services, 20,* 92–97.

Mohai, P., & Saha, R. (2006). Reassessing racial and socioeconomic disparities in environmental justice research. *Demography, 43,* 383–399.

Molloy, J. (2007). Photovoice as a tool for social justice workers. *Journal of Progressive Human Services, 18*(2), 39–55.

Moosa-Mitha, M., & Ross-Sheriff, F. (2010). Transnational social work and lessons learned from transnational feminism. *Affilia: Journal of Women and Social Work, 25,* 105–109.

Moraga, C., & Anzaldúa, G. (Eds.). (1983). *This bridge called my back. Writings by radical women of color.* New York: Kitchen Table/Women of Color Press.

Moreau, M. (1979). A structural approach to social work practice. *Canadian Journal of Social Work Education, 5,* 78–94.

Moreau, M. (1989). *Empowerment through a structural approach to social work: A report from practice.* Ottawa: Carleton University.

Morgaine, K. (2014). Conceptualizing social justice in social work: Are social workers "too bogged down in the trees?" *Journal of Social Justice, 14,* 1–18.

Morgan, J. T. (1973). Annual report of the Commissioner of Indian Affairs. In W. Washburn (Ed.), *The American Indian and the United States: A documentary history* (Vol. 1). New York: Random House (Original work published 1889)

Morrow, D. (2006). Sexual orientation and gender identity expression. In D. Morrow & L. Messinger (Eds.), *Sexual orientation and gender expression in social work practice* (Chapt. 1, pp. 3–17). New York: Columbia University Press.

Mullaly, B. (2006). *Structural social work: Ideology, theory and practice* (3rd ed.). Oxford, UK: Oxford University Press.

Mullaly, B. (2010). *Challenging oppression and confronting privilege: A critical social work approach* (2nd ed.). Oxford, UK: Oxford University Press.

Munck, R. (2005). *Globalization and social exclusion: A transformationalist perspective.* Bloomfield, CT: Kumarian Press.

Nadasen, P. (2005). *Welfare warriors: The welfare rights movement in the United States.* New York: Routledge.

Nagenast, C., & Turner, T. (1997). Introduction: Universal human rights versus cultural relativity. *Journal of Anthropological Research, 53,* 269–272.

Nagoshi, J., & Brzuzy, S. (2010). Transgender theory: Embodying research and practice. *Affilia: Journal of Women and Social Work, 25,* 431–443.

Nagoshi, J., Nagoshi, C., & Brzuzy, S. (2014) *Gender and sexual identity: Transcending feminist and queer theory.* New York: Springer.

Nakanishi, M., & Ritter, B. (1992). The inclusionary cultural model. *Journal of Social Work Education, 28,* 27–35.

Naples, N. (1998). *Grassroots warriors: Activist mothering, community work, and the war on poverty*. New York: Routledge.

National Archives. (n.d.). *The Freedmen's Bureau, 1865–1872*. Retrieved from http://www.archives.gov/research/african-americans/freedmens-bureau

National Association of Black Social Workers. (1971). *Code of ethics of the National Association of Black Social Workers*. Detroit, MI: Author. Retrieved from http://nabsw.org/?page=CodeofEthics

National Association of Black Social Workers. (1998). Position statement of the NABSW. In *Harambee—30 years of unity*, Thirtieth Annual Conference, New Orleans, LA. Retrieved from http://http://cymcdn.com/sites/nabsw.org/resource/resmgr/position_statements_papers/nabsw_30_years_of_unity_-_ou.pdf (Original work published 1968)

National Association of Black Social Workers. (2015). *Mission statement*. Retrieved from http://nabsw.org/?page=MissionStatement

National Association of Social Workers. (1960). *NASW code of ethics*. Retrieved from https://www.socialworkers.org/nasw/ethics/ethicshistory.asp

National Association of Social Workers. (1967). *NASW code of ethics*. Retrieved from https://www.socialworkers.org/nasw/ethics/pdfs/Code%20of%20Ethics%201st%20Revision%201960%20and%20amended%201967.pdf

National Association of Social Workers. (1977). *Encyclopedia of social work*. New York: Author.

National Association of Social Workers. (1979). *Code of Ethics of the National Association of Social Workers*. Silver Spring, MD: Author.

National Association of Social Workers. (1997). *Code of ethics of the National Association of Social Workers*. Retrieved from https://www.socialworkers.org/nasw/ethics/pdfs/1979-Code-of-Ethics.pdf

National Association of Social Workers. (1999). *Code of ethics of the National Association of Social Workers*. Retrieved from http://umaine.edu/socialwork/files/2013/02/NASW-Code-of-Ethics.pdf

National Association of Social Workers. (2003). *Essential steps for ethical problem-solving*. Washington, DC: Author. Retrieved from http://www.social workers.org/pubs/code/oepr/steps.asp

National Association of Social Workers. (2006). *Ethics summit report. Summary and recommendations*. Washington, DC: Author.

National Association of Social Workers. (2007). *Institutional racism and social work: A call to action*. Washington, DC: Author.

National Association of Social Workers. (2008). *Code of ethics of the National Association of Social Workers*. Washington, DC: Author.

National Association of Social Workers. (2015a). *Advocacy*. Retrieved from http://www.socialworkers.org/advocacy

National Association of Social Workers. (2015b). *Code of ethics: History*. Retrieved from https://www.socialworkers.org/nasw/ethics/ethicshistory.asp

National Association of Social Workers. (2015c). *Practice*. Retrieved from http://www.naswdc.org/practice

National Association of Social Workers. (2016). *Advocacy and organizing*. Retrieved from https://www.socialworkers.org/pressroom/features/issue/advocacy.asp

Nelson, S., & Baldwin, N. (2004). The Craigmillar Project: Neighbourhood mapping to improve children's safety from sexual crime. *Child Abuse Review, 13*, 415–425.

Netting, F. E., & O'Connor, K. (2003). *Organization practice: A social worker's guide to understanding human services*. Boston: Allyn & Bacon.

Neubeck. K., & Cazenave, N. (2001). *Welfare racism: Playing the race card against America's poor*. New York: Routledge.

Neuman, W. L. (2005). *Social research methods: Quantitative and qualitative approaches* (6th ed.). Boston: Allyn & Bacon.

Nicholson, L. (1986). *Gender and history: The limits of social theory in the age of the family*. New York: Columbia University Press.

Nicholson, M. (2006). Without their children. Rethinking motherhood among transnational migrant women. *Social Text, 24*(3), 13–33.

Northwest Earth Institute. (2015). *A systems thinking model: The iceberg*. Retrieved from http://www.nwei.org/resources/iceberg

Nozick, R. (1974). *Anarchy, state, and utopia*. New York: Basic Books.

Nussbaum, M. (2011). *Creating capabilities: The human development approach*. Cambridge, MA: Belknap Press.

Nybell, L. (2013). Locating "youth voice": Considering the context of speaking in foster care. *Children and Youth Services Review, 35*, 1227–1235.

Nybell, L., & Gray, S. (2004). Race, place, space: Meanings of cultural competence in three child welfare agencies. *Social Work, 49*, 17–26.

O'Neil, M., Kendall-Taylor, N., & Bales, S. (2014, October). *Finish the story on immigration: A Frameworks message-memo*. Washington, DC: FrameWorks Institute.

Ong, A. (1987). *Spirits of resistance and capitalist discipline: Factory women in Malaysia*. Albany: State University of New York.

Orleck, A. (2009). Rose Schneiderman. *Jewish women: A comprehensive historical encyclopedia*. Retrieved from http://jwa.org/encyclopedia/article/schneiderman-rose

Orozco, A. (2009). *Global care chains* (Working paper 2, Gender, migration, and development series). Santo Domingo, Dominican Republic: United Nations Research and Training Institute for the Advancement of Women.

Ortega, R., & Faller, K. C. (2011). Training child welfare workers from an intersectional cultural humility perspective. A paradigm shift. *Child Welfare, 90*(5), 27–49.

Ortiz, L., & Jani, J. (2010). Critical race theory: A transformational model for teaching diversity. *Journal of Social Work Education, 46*, 175–193.

Ortner, S. (1989) *High religion*. Princeton: Princeton University Press.

Ortner, S. (1994). Theory in anthropology since the sixties. In N. Dirks, G. Eley, & S. Ortner (Eds.), *A reader in contemporary social theory*. Princeton, NJ: Princeton University Press.

Oxfam. (2013, January 18). *The cost of inequality: How wealth and income extremes hurt us all* [Media briefing]. Oxford, UK: Oxfam International.

Oxfam America. (2014). *Inequality and extreme poverty* [Fact sheet]. Boston: Oxfam America. Retrieved from https://www.oxfamamerica.org/explore/research-publications/inequality-and-extreme-poverty

Palmer, N. A., Kosciw, J. G., & Bartkiewicz, M. J. (2012). *Strengths and silences: The experiences of lesbian, gay, bisexual and transgender students in rural and small town schools*. New York: Gay, Lesbian, and Straight Education Network.

Park, P. (1993). What is participatory research: A theoretical and methodological perspective. In P. Park, M. Brydon-Miller, B. Hall, & T. Jackson (Eds.), *Voices of change: Participatory research in the United States and Canada* (pp. 1–19). Westport, CT: Bergin & Garvey.

Park, Y. (2008). Facilitating injustice: Tracing the role of social workers in the World War II internment of Japanese Americans. *Social Service Review, 82*, 447–483.

Park, Y., & Kemp, S. (2006). "Little alien colonies": Representations of immigrants and their neighborhoods in social work discourse, 1875–1924. *Social Service Review, 80*, 705–734.

Patton, M. (2007). Evaluation research. In C. Bryant & D. Peck (Eds.), *21st century sociology*. Thousand Oaks, CA: SAGE.

Payne, M. (2014). *Modern social work theory* (4th ed.). Chicago: Lyceum Books.

Pearlman, L., & Caringi, J. (2009). Vicarious traumatization and complex trauma. In C. Courtois & J. Ford (Eds.), *Complex traumatic stress disorders: An evidence-based clinician's guide*. New York: Guilford Press.

Pease, B. (2010). *Undoing privilege: Unearned advantage in a divided world*. London: Zed Books.

Perlman, H. H. (1957). *Social casework: A problem solving process*. Chicago: University of Chicago Press.

Perlman, H. H. (1979). *Relationship: The heart of helping people*. Chicago: University of Chicago Press.

Perry, J. (Ed.). (2002). *Restorative justice: Repairing communities through restorative justice*. Lanham, MD: American Correctional Association.

Perry, T., & Kim, J. (2013). Pounding the yam: AIDS/HIV related knowledge and behaviors of young Accra market women and intersections of gendered livelihoods. In J. Finn, T. Perry, & S. Karandikar (Eds.), *Gender oppression and globalization: Challenges for social work* (Chapt. 6, pp. 119–148). Alexandria, VA: Council of Social Work Education.

Peterfreund, D. (1992). *Great traditions in ethics* (7th ed.). Belmont, CA: Wadsworth.

Pevar, S. (2002). *The rights of Indians and tribes*. Carbondale: Southern Illinois University Press.

Phillips, N. (1985, June). Ideology and opportunity in social work during the New Deal years. *Journal of Sociology and Social Welfare, 12*(2), 251–273.

Phillips, R., & Pittman, R. (Eds.). (2009). *An introduction to community development*. New York: Routledge.

Picht, W. (1916). *Toynbee Hall and the Settlement Movement*. London: G. Bell.

Pincus, A., & Minahan, A. (1973). *Social work practice: Model and method*. Itasca, IL: Peacock.

Pincus, F. (2000). Discrimination comes in many forms: Individual, institutional, and structural. In M. Adams, W. J. Blumenfeld, R. Castenada, H. W. Hackman, M. L. Peters, & X. Zuniga (Eds.), *Readings for diversity and social justice* (pp. 31–34). New York: Routledge.

Piott, S. (2006). *American reformers, 1870–1920. Progressives in word and deed.* Oxford, UK: Rowman & Littlefield.

Pogue, R. (2011). Theoretical frameworks for social justice education. In J. Birkenmaier, A. Cruce, E. Burkemper, J. Curley, R. J. Wilson, & J. J. Stetch (Eds). *Educating for social justice: Transformative experiential learning* (Chapt. 2, pp. 29–50). Chicago: Lyceum Books.

Polack, R. (2004). Social justice and the global economy: New challenges for social work in the 21st century. *Social Work, 49,* 281–290.

Pon, G. (2009). Cultural competency as the new racism. An ontology of forgetting. *Journal of Progressive Human Services, 20,* 59–71.

Pope, N., & Lee, J. (2015). A picture is worth a thousand words: Exploring the use of genograms in social work practice. *The New Social Worker, 22*(2), 9–12. Retrieved from http://www.mediafire.com/view/z89h9er9cpa2ue7/spring 2015.pdf

Portelli, A. (1991). *The death of Luigi Trastulli and other stories.* Albany: State University of New York Press.

Pound, J. (1986). *Poverty and vagrancy in Tudor England.* London: Routledge.

Poverty Program. (2016). *Poverty statistics: Human rights.* Retrieved from http://www.povertyprogram.com/human_rights.php

Powell, B., Blozendahl, C., Geist, C., & Carr Steelman, L. (2010). *Counted out: Same-sex relations and America's definition of family.* New York: Russell Sage Foundation.

Prilleltensky, I. (2008). The role of power in wellness, oppression, and liberation: The promise of psychopolitical validity. *Journal of Community Psychology, 36,* 116–136.

Punke, M. (2006). *Fire and brimstone: The North Butte mining disaster of 1917.* New York: Hyperion.

Pyles, L. (2009). *Progressive community organizing: Reflective practice in a globalizing world.* New York: Routledge.

Rabinow, P. (1984). *The Foucault reader.* New York: Pantheon.

Ransby, B. (2003). *Ella Baker and the Black freedom movement*. Chapel Hill: University of North Carolina Press.

Rao, A. (1995). The politics of gender and culture in international human rights discourse. In J. Peters & A. Wolper (Eds.), *Women's rights, human rights: International feminist perspectives* (pp. 176–188). New York: Routledge.

Rasmussen, F. (2001, March 17). Mary Richmond was a pioneer in social work nationally. *Baltimore Sun*. Retrieved from http://articles.baltimoresun.com/2001-03-17/features/0103170131_1_charity-organization-society-social-workers-society-of-baltimore

Rawls, J. (1995). *A theory of justice* (2nd ed.). Cambridge, MA: Harvard University Press. (Original work published 1971)

Reamer, F. (1998). *Ethical standards in social work: A critical review of the NASW code of ethics*. Washington, DC: National Association of Social Workers.

Reamer, F. (2006). *Social work values and ethics* (2nd ed.). New York: Columbia University.

Reamer, F. (2013). Social work in a digital age. Ethical and risk management challenges. *Social Work, 58*, 163–172.

Reamer, F. (2014). The evolution of social work ethics. Bearing witness. *Advances in Social Work, 15*, 163–181.

Reamer, F., & Conrad, A. (1995). *Professional choices: Ethics at work* [Video]. Washington, DC: National Association of Social Workers.

Redfield, R. (1960). *The little community and peasant society and culture*. Chicago: University of Chicago Press.

Reed, B. G., Newman, P., Suarez, Z., & Lewis, E. (1997). Interpersonal practice beyond diversity and toward social justice: The importance of critical consciousness. In C. Garvin & B. Seabury (Eds.), *Interpersonal practice in social work: Promoting competence and social justice* (2nd ed., pp. 44–78). Boston: Allyn & Bacon.

Reichert, E. (2011). *Social work and human rights: A foundation for policy and practice* (2nd ed.). New York: Columbia University Press.

Reisch, M. (1998a). *Economic globalization and the future of the welfare state. Welfare Reform and Social Justice Visiting Scholars Program*. Ann Arbor: University of Michigan School of Social Work.

Reisch, M. (1988b). The uses of history in teaching social work. *Journal of Teaching in Social Work, 2*, 3–16.

Reisch, M. (1993). Lessons from the history of social work for our time. *The Jewish Social Work Forum, 29,* 3–27.

Reisch, M. (2002). Defining social justice in a socially unjust world. *Families in Society, 83,* 343–354.

Reisch, M. (2005). American exceptionalism and critical social work: A retrospective and prospective analysis. In I. Ferguson, M. Lavalette, & E. Whitmore (Eds.), *Globalisation, global justice, and social work* (pp. 157–172). New York: Routledge.

Reisch, M. (2011). Defining social justice. In J. Birkenmaier, A. Cruce, E. Burkemper, J. Curley, R. J. Wilson, & J. J. Stetch (Eds.), *Educating for social justice: Transformative experiential learning* (Chapt. 1, pp. 11–28). Chicago: Lyceum Books.

Reisch, M. (2013). Social work education and the neoliberal challenge: The US response to increasing global inequality. *Social Work Education, 32,* 715–733.

Reisch, M. (Ed.). (2014). *The Routledge international handbook of social justice.* New York: Routledge.

Reisch, M., & Andrews, J. (2001). *The road not taken: A history of radical social work in the United States.* New York: Brunner/Routledge.

Reisch. M., & Jani, J. (2012).The new politics of social work practice: Understanding context to promote change. *British Journal of Social Work, 42,* 1132–1150.

Reisch, M., & Wenocur, S. (1986). The future of community organization in social work: Social activism and the politics of profession building. *Social Service Review, 60,* 70–91.

Reisch, M., Wenocur, S., & Sherman, W. (1981). Empowerment, conscientization, and animation as core social work skills. *Social Development Issues, 5*(2/3), 108–120.

Reynolds, B. C. (1942). *Learning and teaching in the practice of social work.* New York: Farrar & Rinehart, Inc.

Reynolds, B. C. (1951). *Social work and social living.* New York: Citadel Press.

Reynolds, B. C. (1963). *An uncharted journey.* Washington, DC: National Association of Social Workers Press.

Reynolds, B. C. (1992). Rethinking social case work. *Journal of Progressive Human Services, 3,* 73–84. (Original work published 1932)

Reynolds, W. (1988). *Suicide ideation questionnaire.* Odessa, FL: Psychological Assessment Resources.

Rhodes, M. (1986). *Ethical dilemmas in social work practice.* Boston: Routledge & Kegan Paul.

Richmond, M. (1897). Need of a training school in applied philanthropy. In I. C. Barrows (Ed.), *Proceedings of the National Conference of Charities and Corrections* (pp. 181–187). Boston: Ellis.

Richmond, M. (1917). *Social diagnosis.* New York: Russell Sage Foundation.

Riis, J. (1890). *How the other half lives.* New York: Scribner.

Rimor, M. (2003). If love then justice. *Sociological Inquiry, 73,* 167–176.

Rivera, E., Maldonado, J., & Alcaron, L. (2013). From Vygotsky to Martin Baro: Dealing with language and liberation during the supervision process. *Universal Journal of Psychology, 1*(2), 32–40.

Robbins, S. P., Chatterjee, P., & Canda, E. R. (2006). *Contemporary human behavior theory: A critical perspective for social work* (2nd ed.). Needham Heights, MA: Allyn & Bacon.

Roby, P. (1998). Creating a just world: Leadership for the twenty-first century. *Social Problems, 45,* 1–20.

Rogers, C. (1951). *Client-centered therapy: Its current practice implications and theory.* Boston: Houghton Mifflin.

Rogers, C., Gendlin, E., Kiesler, D., & Truax, C. (1967). *The therapeutic relationship and its impact: A study of psychotherapy with schizophrenics.* Madison: University of Wisconsin Press.

Rosaldo, R. (1989). *Culture and truth: The remaking of social analysis.* Boston: Beacon Press.

Rose, S. (2000). Reflections on empowerment based practice. *Social Work, 45,* 403–412.

Ross, R. (2003). *Witnessing and testifying: Black women, religion, and civil rights.* Minneapolis, MN: Fortress Press.

Ross-Sheriff, F. (2007). Globalization as a women's issue revisited. *Affilia: Journal of Women and Social Work, 22,* 133–137.

Rossi, P., & Freeman, H. (1993). *Evaluation: A systematic approach.* Newbury Park, CA: SAGE.

Rossiter, A. (1996). A perspective on critical social work. *Journal of Progressive Human Services, 7*(2), 23–41.

Rossiter, A. (2005). Where in the world are we? Notes on the need for a social work response to global power. In S. Hick, J. Fook, & R. Pozzuto (Eds.), *Social work: A critical turn* (pp. 189–202). Toronto: Thompson Educational Publishing.

Rossiter, A., de Boer, C., Narayan, J., Razack, N., Scollay, V., & Gillette, C. (1998). Toward an alternative account of feminist practice ethics in mental health. *Affilia: Journal of Women and Social Work, 13,* 9–22.

Rothman, D. (2002). *The discovery of the asylum* (revised ed.) Chicago: Aldine Transaction.

Rubin, A., & Babbie, E. (2013). *Research methods for social work* (8th ed.). Belmont, CA: Brooks/Cole Cengage Learning.

Sackett, D., Rosenberg, W., Gray, J., Haynes, R., & Richardson, W. (1996). Evidence-based medicine: What it is and what it isn't. *British Medical Journal, 312*(7023), 71–72.

Sakamoto, I. (2007). An anti-oppressive approach to cultural competence. *Canadian Social Work Review, 24,* 105–114.

Sakamoto, I., Chin, M., & Young, M. (2010). "Canadian experience," employment challenges, and skilled immigrants. *Canadian Social Work Journal 10,* 145–151.

Sakamoto, I., & Pitner, R. (2005). Use of critical consciousness in anti-oppressive social work practice: Disentangling power dynamics at personal and structural levels. *British Journal of Social Work, 35,* 435–452.

Saldanha, K., & Parenteau, D. (2013). "Well, if you can't smile you should go home!" Experiences and reflective insights on providing outreach to young sex trade workers. *Children and Youth Services Review, 35,* 1276–1283.

Saleebey, D. (1996). The strengths perspective in social work practice: Extensions and cautions. *Social Work, 41,* 296–305.

Saleebey, D. (2001). The diagnostic strengths manual? *Social Work, 46,* 183–187.

Saleebey, D. (Ed.). (2006). *The strengths perspective in social work practice* (4th ed.). Boston: Pearson Education.

Saleebey, D. (2011). Some basic ideas about the strengths perspective. In F. Turner (Ed.), *Social work treatment: Interlocking theoretical approaches* (5th ed., pp. 477–485). New York: Oxford University Press.

San Francisco Children of Incarcerated Parents Partnership. (n.d.). *A bill of rights.* Retrieved from http://http://www.sfcipp.org

Sarri, R., & Finn, J. (1992). Child welfare policy and practice: Rethinking the history of our certainties. *Children and Youth Services Review, 14*(3/4), 219–236.

Satterwhite, F., & Teng, S. (2007). *Culturally-based capacity building*. Oakland: National Community Based Development Institute.

Sayce, L. (2005). Risk, rights and anti-discrimination work in mental health: Avoiding the risks in considering risk. In R. Adams, L. Dominelli, & M. Payne (Eds.), *Social work futures: Crossing boundaries, transforming practices* (pp. 167–181). New York: Palgrave Macmillan.

Schiele, J. (2011). *Social welfare policy: Regulation and resistance among people of color*. Thousand Oaks, CA: SAGE.

Scholte, J. (2008). *Globalization: A critical introduction*. London: Macmillan.

Schreiber, J., Groenhout, R., & Brandsen, C. (2014). Introducing a virtue perspective for social work and helping. *Social Work and Christianity, 41*(2/3), 113–136.

Schriver, J. (2004). *Human behavior and the social environment: Shifting paradigms in essential knowledge for social work practice* (4th ed.). Boston: Pearson.

Schwartz, W. (1986). The group work tradition and social work practice. *Social Work with Groups, 8*(4), 7–27. (Original work published 1961)

Scott, J. (1985). *Weapons of the weak: Everyday forms of resistance*. New Haven: Yale University Press.

Seabury, B., Seabury, B., & Garvin, C. (2011). *Foundations of interpersonal practice in social work*. Thousand Oaks, CA: SAGE.

Secret, M., Jordan, A., & Ford, J. (1999). Empowerment evaluation as a social work strategy. *Health and Social Work, 24*, 120–128.

Seldes, G. (Ed.). (1985). *The great thoughts*. New York: Ballantine Books.

Sentencing Project. (2014). *Incorporating racial equity in criminal justice reform*. Retrieved from www.sentencingproject.org/detail/publication.cfm?publication_id=566&id=136

Sentencing Project. (2015), *Incarceration*. Retrieved from http://www.sentencingproject.org/template/page.cfm?id=107

Sethi, B., & Hankivsky, O. (2013). Immigration and intersectionality. In J. Finn, T. Perry, & S. Karandikar (Eds.), *Gender oppression and globalization: Challenges for social work* (Chapt. 9, pp. 207–232). Alexandria, VA: Council of Social Work Education.

Sheafor, B., & Horejsi, C. (2012). *Techniques and guidelines for social work practice* (9th ed.). Boston: Pearson Education.

Shepard, B., & Hayduk, R. (2002). *From ACT UP to the WTO: Urban protest and community building in the era of globalization*. London: Verso Press.

Shor, I. (1980). *Critical teaching and everyday life*. Boston: South End Press.

Sheedy, M. (2013). *Core themes in social work: Power, poverty, politics, and values*. New York: Open University Press.

Shulman, L. (1986). The dynamics of mutual aid. In A. Gitterman & L. Shulman (Eds.), *The legacy of William Schwartz* (pp. 51–60). Binghamton, NY: Haworth.

Shulman, L. (2012). *The skills of helping individuals, families and groups* (7th ed.). Belmont, CA: Brookes Cole/Cengage Learning.

Siegel, B. (1983). *Lillian Wald of Henry Street*. New York: Macmillan.

Silverman, E. (2015). Organizational awareness: A missing generalist social work competency. *Social Work, 60*, 93–95.

Simon, B. (1994). *The empowerment tradition in American social work: A history*. New York: Columbia University Press.

Skegg, A. (2005). Human rights and social work: Western imposition or empowerment to the people? *International Social Work, 48*, 667–672.

Sklar, K. (2004). Florence Kelley and women's activism in the Progressive Era. In L. Kerber (Ed.), *Women's America* (6th ed., pp. 327–338). New York: Oxford University Press.

Smith, D. (1990). *The conceptual practices of power: A feminist sociology of knowledge*. Boston: Northeastern University Press.

Smith, K. (2011). Occupied spaces: Unmapping standardized assessments in health and social service organizations. In D. Baines, *Doing anti-oppressive practice: Social justice social work* (2nd ed., Chapt. 12, pp. 197–212). Black Point, Nova Scotia: Fernwood Publishing.

Smith, L., Chambers, D., & Bratini, L. (2009). When oppression is the pathogen. The participatory development of socially just mental health practice. *American Journal of Orthopsychology, 79*, 159–168.

Smith, L. T. (1999). *Decolonizing methodologies: Research and indigenous people*. London: Zed.

Social Welfare History Project. (2014). *Frances Perkins (1882–1965). Secretary of labor in Franklin Roosevelt's administration*. Retrieved from http://www.social welfarehistory.com/people/perkins-frances-2

Social Welfare History Project. (n.d.). *Mary Ellen Richmond, social work pioneer, administrator, researcher, and author*. Retrieved from http://www.socialwelfare history.com/people/richmond-mary

Solomon, B. (1976). *Black empowerment*. New York: Columbia University Press.

Specht, H., & Courtney, M. (1994). *Unfaithful angels: How social work has abandoned its mission*. New York: Free Press.

Spencer, M. (2015). Sticks and stones and words can hurt: Microaggressions among children and youth. *Children, Adolescents, and Young Adults Newsletter*, Fall/Winter, 2–3. Retrieved from http://www.socialworkers.org/assets/secured/documents/sections/caya/newsletters/2015-%20CAYA%20Fall%20Issue.pdf

Staniforth, B., & Noble, C. (2014). Social work education in Aotearoa/New Zealand and Australia. In C. Noble, H. Strauss, & B. Littlechild (Eds.), *Global social work. Crossing boundaries, blurring borders* (Chapt. 13, pp. 171–184). Sydney: Sydney University Press.

St. Onge, P., Cole, B., & Petty, S. (2003). *Through the lens of culture: Building capacity for social change and sustainable communities*. Oakland: National Community Development Institute. Retrieved from http://www.seven -generations.org/resources/ThroughTheLensofCultureNCDI.pdf

Stake, R. E. (1995). *The art of case study research*. Thousand Oaks, CA: SAGE.

Stebner, E. (1997). *The women of Hull House*. Albany: State University of New York.

Stern, A. (2005). *Eugenics nation: Faults and frontiers of better breeding in modern America*. Berkeley: University of California Press.

Sternbach, J. (2000). Lessons learned about working with men: A prison memoir. *Social Work*, *45*, 413–423.

Stiglitz, J. (2002). *Globalization and its discontents*. New York: Norton.

Stoddart, M. (2007). Ideology, hegemony, discourse: A critical review of theories of knowledge and power. *Social Thought and Research*, *28*, 191–225.

Sue, D. W., Capodilupo, C. M., Torino, G. C., Bucceri, J. M., Holder, A. M., Nadal, K. L., & Esquilin, M. (2007). Racial microaggressions in everyday life: Implications for clinical practice. *American Psychologist*, *62*, 271–286.

Sullivan, M. (1993). Social work's legacy of peace: Echoes from the early 20th century. *Social Work*, *38*, 513–520.

Swigonski, M. (1994). The logic of feminist standpoint theory for social work research. *Social Work*, *39*, 387–393.

Szasz, M. C. (1974). *Education and the American Indian: The road to self-determination since 1928*. Albuquerque: University of New Mexico Press.

Taylor, D. (2014). *Toxic communities: Environmental racism, industrial pollution, and residential mobility*. New York: New York University Press.

Thompson, E. P. (1966). *The making of the English working class*. New York: Vintage.

Todd, S. (2012, October 12). *An alternative to competency-based pedagogy*. Presentation to Canadian Association of Deans and Directors of Schools of Social Work.

Toennies, F. (1957). *Community and society* (C. Loomis, Ed. & Trans.). Mineola, NY: Dover Publications.

Tough, P. (2009). *Whatever it takes: Geoffrey Canada's quest to change Harlem and America*. New York: Houghton Mifflin.

Towle, C. (1945). *Common Human Needs*. Washington, DC: US Department of Health, Education, and Welfare.

Townsend, J., Zapata, E., Rowlands, J., Alberti, P., & Mercado, M. (1999). *Women and power: Fighting patriarchies and poverty*. London: Zed Books.

Transit, R. (2004). *Disciplining the child via the discourse of the professions*. Springfield, IL: Thomas.

Trattner, W. (1989). *From poor law to welfare state* (4th ed.). New York: Free Press.

Truth and Reconciliation Commission of Canada. (2015). *Honoring the truth, reconciling for the future*. Winnipeg, Manitoba: National Centre for Truth and Reconciliation.

UN Women. (2011). *UN women annual report, 2010–2011*. New York: United Nations.

UN Women. (2012). Executive summary. In *2011-2012 Progress of the world's women: In pursuit of justice*. New York: United Nations. Retrieved from http://www2.unwomen.org/~/media/headquarters/attachments/sections/library/publications/2011/progressoftheworldswomen-2011-executive summary-en.pdf?v=1&d=20150402T222839

UNICEF. (n.d). *Convention on the rights of the child*. Retrieved from http://www.unicef.org/crc

UNICEF. (2014). *Child friendly cities*. Retrieved from http://www.childfriendly cities.org

United Nations. (1948). *Universal Declaration of Human Rights: Preamble*. Retrieved from http://www.un.org/en/universal-declaration-human-rights

United Nations. (1987). *Human rights: Questions and answers*. New York: Author.

United Nations Development Programme. (2014). *Human development report 2014: Sustaining human progress*. New York: Author.

United Nations High Commissioner for Refugees. (2014). *Children on the run.* Washington, DC: UNHCR Regional Office for the U.S. and the Caribbean.

U.S. Attorney General's Advisory Committee on American Indian and Alaska Native Youth Exposed to Violence. (2014). *Ending violence so children can thrive.* Washington, DC: Office of Juvenile Justice and Delinquency Prevention. Retrieved from https://www.justice.gov/sites/default/files/defending childhood/pages/attachments/2014/11/18/finalaianreport.pdf

U.S. Catholic Bishops. (1986). *Economic justice for all: Pastoral letter on Catholic social teaching and the U.S. economy.* Washington, DC: National Conference of Catholic Bishops.

University of Chicago School of Social Service Administration. (2008). *SSA profiles of distinction series: Charlotte Towle.* Retrieved from http://ssacentennial .uchicago.edu/features/features-towle.shtml

University of Kansas Work Group for Community Health and Development. (2016). *Community tool kit.* Retrieved from https://communityhealth.ku.edu/ services/ctb

Van der Kolk, B. (2014). *The body keeps score.* New York: Viking.

Van Kleeck, M. (1991). Our illusions regarding government. *Journal of Progressive Human Services, 2,* 75–86. (Original work published 1934)

Van Soest, D. (1994). Strange bedfellows: A call for reordering national priorities from three social justice perspectives. *Social Work, 39,* 710–717.

Van Soest, D., & Garcia, B. (2003). *Diversity education for social justice: Mastering teaching skills.* Alexandria, VA: Council on Social Work Education.

van Wormer, K. (2006). A case for restorative justice: A critical adjunct to the social work curriculum. *Journal of Teaching Social Work, 26,* 57–69.

van Wormer, K. (2007). *Human behavior in the social environment: Micro level individuals and families.* New York: Oxford University Press.

van Wormer, K., & McKinney, R. (2003). What schools can do to help gay/lesbian/ bisexual youth: A harm reduction approach. *Adolescence, 38*(151), 409–420.

Velasquez, C., Andre, T., Shanks, T., & Meyer, M. (2014). *Thinking ethically: A framework for moral decision-making.* Santa Clara, CA: Markkula Center for Applied Ethics, Santa Clara University. Retrieved from http://www.scu.edu/ ethics/publications/iie/v7n1/thinking.html

Velasquez, C., Andre, T., Shanks, T., Moberg, D., McClean, M., DeCosse, D., . . . Meyer, M. (2004). *A framework for ethical decision-making.* Santa Clara, CA:

Markkula Center for Applied Ethics, Santa Clara University. Retrieved from http://www.scu.edu/ethics/practicing/decision/framework.html

VeneKlasen, L., & Miller, V. (2007). *A new weave of power, people, and politics. The action guide for advocacy and citizen participation.* Bourton-on-Dunsmore, Warwickshire, UK: Practical Action.

Villarreal Sosa, L., & Moore, A. (2013). Chicana feminisms, intersectionality, and social work. In J. Finn, T. Perry, & S. Karandikar (Eds.), *Gender oppression and globalization: Challenges for social work* (Chapt. 7). Alexandria, VA: Council on Social Work Education.

Von Bertalanffy, L. (1968). *General systems theory.* New York: Braziller.

Voshel, E. H., & Wesala, A. (2015). Social media and social work ethics: Determining best practices in an ambiguous reality. *Journal of Social Work Values and Ethics, 12,* 67–76.

Vosler, N. (1990). Assessing family access to basic resources: An essential component of social work practice. *Social Work, 35,* 434–441.

Vosler, N. (1996). *New approaches to family practice: Confronting economic stress.* Thousand Oaks, CA: SAGE.

Wacquant, L. (2005). Habitus. *International Encyclopedia of Economic Sociology* (J. Becket & Z. Milan, Eds.). London: Routledge.

Wacquant, L. (2009). *Punishing the poor: The neoliberal government of social insecurity.* Durham, NC: Duke University Press.

Wacquant, L. (2010). Crafting the neoliberal state: Workfare, prisonfare, and social insecurity. *Sociological Forum, 25,* 197–220.

Wade, C., & Travis, C. (2007). *Invitation to psychology* (4th ed.). Upper Saddle River, NJ: Prentice Hall.

Wakefield, J. (1988). Psychotherapy, distributive justice and social work: Part I—Distributive justice as a conceptual framework for social work. *Social Service Review, 62,* 187–210.

Wald, L. (1915). *The house on Henry Street.* New York: Holt.

Waldegrave, C. (2000). Just therapy with families and communities. In G. Burford & J. Hudson (Eds.), *Family group conferencing: New directions in community-centered child and family practice* (pp. 153–163). New York: Aldine de Gruyter.

Waldegrave, C. (2005). Just therapy with low-income families. *Child Welfare, 84,* 265–276.

Waldegrave, C. (2009). Cultural, gender, and socioeconomic contexts in therapeutic and social policy work. *Family Process, 48*, 85–101.

Waldegrave, C., & Tamasese, K. (1994). Some central ideas in the "Just Therapy" approach. *The Family Journal: Counseling and Therapy for Couples and Families, 2*, 94–103.

Walker, L., & East, J. (2014). The benefits of including engaged residents and professionals in low-Income neighborhood redevelopment planning processes. *Journal of Community Practice, 22*, 342–364.

Wang, C., & Burris, M. (1997). Photovoice: Concept, methodology, and use for participatory needs assessment. *Health Education & Behavior, 24*, 369–387.

Wang, C. C., Burris, M. A., & Ping X. Y. (1996). Chinese village women as visual anthropologists: A participatory approach to reaching policymakers. *Social Science Medicine, 42*, 1391–1400.

Wang, C. C., Morrel-Samuels, S., Hutchinson, P. M., Bell, L., & Pestronik, R. M. (2004). Flint Photovoice: Community building among youths, adults, and policy makers. *American Journal of Public Health, 94*, 911–913.

Warren, R. (1963). *The community in America*. Chicago: Rand McNally.

Weaver, H. (1998). Indigenous people in a multicultural society: Unique issues for human services. *Social Work, 43*, 203–211.

Weaver, H. (2008). Indigenous social work in the United States. In M. Gray, J. Coates, & M. Yellow Bird (Eds.), *Indigenous social work around the world: Towards culturally relevant education and practice* (pp. 71–82). Burlington, VT: Ashgate.

Weaver, I., & Cousins, J. (2004). Unpacking the participatory process. *Journal of Multidisciplinary Evaluation, 1*, 19–40.

Weber, M. (1922). Bureaucracy. In H. Gerth & W. Mills (Eds.), *Max Weber: Essays on sociology*. Oxford, UK: Oxford University Press.

Weick, A. (1983). Issues in overturning a medical model of social work practice. *Social Work, 28*, 467–471.

Weick, K. (1995). *Sensemaking in organizations*. Thousand Oaks, CA: SAGE.

Weiler, K. (1988). *Women teaching for change: Gender, class and power*. New York: Bergin & Garvey.

Weinberg, M. (2008). Structural social work: A moral compass for ethics in practice. *Critical Social Work, 9*(1). Retrieved from http://www1.uwindsor.ca/criticalsocialwork/structural-social-work-a-moral-compass-for-ethics-in-practice

Weinberg, M., & Campbell, C. (2014). From codes to contextual collaborations: Shifting the thinking about ethics in social work. *Journal of Progressive Human Services, 25,* 37–49.

Wells, H. G. (1911). *The country of the blind and other stories.* New York: Nelson.

Wendt, S., & Seymour, S. (2010) Applying post-structural ideas to empowerment: Implications for social work education. *Social Work Education, 29,* 670–682.

Wenocur, S., & Reisch, M. (1989). *From charity to enterprise: The development of American social work in a market economy.* Chicago: University of Illinois Press.

Wernick, L., Dessel, A., Kulick, A., & Graham. L. (2013). LGBTQQ youth creating change: Developing allies against bullying through performance and dialogue. *Children and Youth Services Review, 35,* 1576–1586.

Wernick, L., Woodford, M., & Kulick, A. (2014) LGBTQQ youth using participatory action research and theater to effect change: Moving adult decision-makers to create youth-centered change, *Journal of Community Practice, 22*(1–2), 47–66.

Western States Center. (2001). Assessing organizational racism. *Western States Center Views.* Winter, 14–15. Retrieved from http://www.racialequitytools.org/resourcefiles/westernstates2.pdf

Western States Center. (2003). *Dismantling racism: A resource book for social change groups.* Portland, OR: Western States Center. Retrieved from http://www.westernstatescenter.org/tools-and-resources/Tools/Dismantling%20Racism

Western States Center. (2011). *Assessing our organizations.* Retrieved from http://www.westernstatescenter.org/tools-and-resources/Tools/assessing-our-organizations

Whitacre, P., Tsai, P., & Mulligan, J. (2009). *The public health effects of food deserts.* Workshop summary. Retrieved from https://www.iom.edu/Reports/2009/FoodDeserts.aspx

White, M. (2006). Unsettling reflections: The reflective practitioner as "trickster" in interprofessional work. In S. White, J. Fook, & F. Gardner (Eds.), *Critical reflection in health and social care* (pp. 21–39). Buckingham, UK: Open University Press.

White, M., & Epston, D. (1990). *Narrative means to therapeutic ends.* New York: Norton.

White, M. B., & Tyson-Rawson, K. J. (1995). Assessing the dynamics of gender in couples and families: The genogram. *Family Relations, 44,* 253–260.

Whitmore, E., & Wilson, M. (1997). Accompanying the process: Social work and international development practice. *International Social Work, 40*, 57–74.

Whitmore, E., & Wilson, M. (2005). Popular resistance to global corporate rule: The role of social work (with a little help from Gramsci and Freire). In I. Ferguson, M. Lavalette, & E. Whitmore (Eds.), *Globalisation, global justice and social work* (pp. 189–206). New York: Routledge.

Whittaker, J., Schinke, S., & Gilchrist, L. (1986). The ecological paradigm in child, youth, and family services: Implications for policy and practice. *Social Service Review, 60*, 483–503.

Williams, Jr., R. (1979). Change and stability in values and value systems: A sociological perspective. In M. Rokeach (Ed.), *Understanding human values: Individual and societal* (pp. 15–46). New York: Free Press.

Wilson, M., & Whitmore, E. (1995). Accompanying the process: Social work and international development practice. *Canadian Journal of Development Studies, 1*, 57–74.

Wilson, M., & Whitmore, E. (2000). *Seeds of fire: Social development in an era of globalization*. Halifax, Nova Scotia: Fernwood.

Withorn, A. (1984). *Serving the people: Social services and social change*. New York: Columbia University Press.

Witkin, S. (1998). Human rights and social work. *Social Work, 43*, 197–201.

Witkin, S. (Ed.). (2012). *Social construction and social work practice*. New York: Columbia University Press.

Wolfelt, A. (2004). *The understanding your grief support group guide*. Fort Collins, CO: Companion Press.

Wong, Y. (2004). Knowing through discomfort: A mindfulness-based critical social work pedagogy. *Critical Social Work, 5*(1). Retrieved from http://www1.uwindsor.ca/criticalsocialwork/knowing-through-discomfort -a-mindfulness-based-critical-social-work-pedagogy

Wrong, D. (1995). *Power: Its forms, bases and uses*. New Brunswick, NJ: Transaction.

Yan, M. C. (2004). Bridging the fragmented community: Revitalizing settlement houses in the global era. *Journal of Community Practice, 12*(1/2), 51–69.

Yellow Bird, M., & Gray, M. (2008). Indigenous people and the language of social work. In M. Gray, J. Coates, & M. Yellow Bird (Eds.), *Indigenous social work around the world: Towards culturally relevant education and practice* (pp. 59–70). Burlington, VT: Ashgate.

Yellow Bird, P. (n.d.). *Wild Indians: Indian perspective on the Hiawatha Asylum for Insane Indians*. Retrieved from https://www.power2u.org/downloads/NativePerspectivesPeminaYellowBird.pdf

Yin, R. (2008). *Case study research: Design and methods* (4th ed.). Thousand Oaks, CA: SAGE.

Young, I. M. (2011). *Justice and the politics of difference*. Princeton, NJ: Princeton University Press.

Younge, G. (2013, July 23). Eduardo Galeano: 'My greatest fear is that we are all suffering from amnesia.' *The Guardian*. Retrieved from http://www.theguardian.com/books/2013/jul/23/eduardo-galeano-children-days-interview

Zastrow, C. (2009). *Introduction to social work and social welfare* (10th ed.). Belmont, CA: Brooks/Cole.

Zayas, L. (2001). Incorporating struggles with racism and ethnic identity in therapy with adolescents. *Clinical Social Work Journal, 29*, 361–373.

Zayas, L. (2015). *Forgotten citizens: Deportation, children, and the making of American exiles and orphans*. New York: Oxford.

Zimbalist, S. (1977). *Historic themes and landmarks in social welfare research*. New York: Harper & Row.

Zinn, H. (1997). *The Zinn reader: Writings on disobedience and democracy*. New York: Seven Stories Press.

Zinn, H. (2003). *A people's history of the United States: 1492–present*. New York: HarperCollins.

PERMISSIONS AND CREDITS

Chapter 1
"Just Practice: Making Sense of the Five Key Themes" used with permission of the author, Seth Quackenbush, MSW.

Chapter 2
"Discovering Lillian Wald" used with permission of the author Robin Larrick Graham, MSW.

"I. DeQuincey Newman, Servant Leader" used with permission of the author Sadye L. M. Logan, MSW, DSW, Distinguished Professor Emerita and I. DeQuincey Newman Professor of Social Work Emerita, University of South Carolina.

Chapter 3
Code of Ethics of the National Association of Black Social Workers (NABSW) reprinted with permission of NABSW, Washington, DC.

"Practicing Social and Environmental Sustainability" used with permission of the author, Katherine Deuel, MSW.

Chapter 4
"Resident Engagement during Public Housing Redevelopment" used with permission of the author, Laurie A. Walker, MSW, PhD.

Chapter 5
Excerpt on "Popular Education," from *Building a Race and Immigration Dialogue in the Global Economy: A Popular Education Resource for Immigrant and Refugee Community Organizers*, reprinted with permission of the National Network for Immigrant and Refugee Rights.

"Promoting Social, Economic, and Environmental Justice through a Community Food System" used with permission of the author, Bonnie Rae Buckingham, MSW.

Chapter 6
Excerpt from "Digging Deep: Thinking about Privilege" used with permission of the author, Eli Clare.

"Teaching and Learning on the U.S.-Mexico Border: Reflection on Human Rights," used with permission of the author, Scott Nicholson, MSW.

"Appreciative Inquiry" questions from Sarah Michael, "The Promise of Appreciative Inquiry as an Interview Tool for Field Research," *Development in Practice*, 15 (2005), 222–230, reprinted with permission of the publisher, Taylor and Francis, Ltd.

"Promoting Social Justice in Indian Country: The National Native Child Trauma Center," used with permission of the author, Marilyn Bruguier Zimmerman, MSW.

Chapter 7
"Work through My Lens" used with permission of the author, Debby Florence, MSW. Accompanying photo and quote courtesy of Gerri L. Stiffarm.

"Restorative Justice as a Way of Life and a Means for Social Change," used with permission of the author, Cynthia Tobias.

"Social Workers and the Struggle for Water as a Human Right," reprinted with permission of the author Ann Rall, MSW, PhD.

Chapter 8
"Participatory Action Research to Change School Climate" used with permission of the authors, Alex Kulick, PhD student, and Laura Wernick, MSW, PhD.

INDEX

ABOUT THE AUTHOR

Janet L. Finn is professor of Social Work at the University of Montana and faculty member in the International Development Studies Program and the Women's, Gender, and Sexuality Studies Program. She holds an MSW from Eastern Washington University and a PhD in social work and anthropology from the University of Michigan. Her interests are in the areas of community practice, women's activism, critical childhood and youth studies, social work in a global context, and social work theory and history. She has conducted community-based research with women and grassroots organizations in Montana and Chile. She has authored and coedited numerous books and articles about social justice, community, women, childhood, youth, and transnational issues including *Gender Oppression and Globalization: Challenges for Social Work* (2013); *Mining Childhood: Growing Up in Butte, 1900–1960* (2012); *Childhood, Youth, and Social Work in Transformation* (2009); *La Victoria: Rescatando su Historia* (2007); *Motherlode: Legacies of Women's Lives and Labors in Butte, Montana* (2005); *Tracing the Veins: Of Copper, Culture, and Community from Butte to Chuquicamata* (1998); and a special issue of *Children and Youth Services Review* entitled "Place, Power, and Possibility: Rethinking Social Work with Children and Youth" (2013). Janet lives in Missoula, Montana, with her husband, Dave Ames, and their spirited Shetland Sheepdog, Aly.